Understanding Limerick
Social Exclusion and Change

Understanding Limerick

Social Exclusion and Change

Edited by

NIAMH HOURIGAN

CORK UNIVERSITY PRESS

First published in hardback in 2011 by
Cork University Press
Youngline Industrial Estate
Pouladuff Road, Togher
Cork, Ireland
This paperback edition published in 2011

British Library Cataloguing in Publication Data
A CIP catalogue record for this book is available from the British Library.

Hardback ISBN-978-185918-457-8
Paperback ISBN-978-185918-484-4

Typeset by Tower Books, Ballincollig, Co. Cork
Printed in Malta by Gutenberg Press

www.corkuniversitypress.com

Contents

Contributors   vii

Editor's Preface   ix

Introduction
Social Exclusion and Change in Limerick   xi
Niamh Hourigan

Part One: Contexts

1. Divided City: the social geography of Post-Celtic Tiger
   Limerick   3
   Des McCafferty

2. Getting a Fix on Crime in Limerick   23
   Ciarán McCullagh

Part Two: Living with Fear and Feuding in Limerick

Introduction   41
Niamh Hourigan

3. A History of Social Exclusion in Limerick   44
   Niamh Hourigan

4. Divided Communities: mapping the social structure of
   disadvantaged neighbourhoods in Limerick   60
   Niamh Hourigan

5. Organised Crime and Community Violence: understanding
   Limerick's 'regimes of fear'   74
   Niamh Hourigan

6. The Sociology of Feuding: Limerick gangland and
   Traveller feuds compared   103
   Niamh Hourigan

7. Lessons from Limerick: policing, child protection,
   regeneration   126
   Niamh Hourigan

8. Neighbourliness and Community Spirit in Moyross and
   Southill: life narratives   155
   Máire Treasa Nic Eochagáin and Frances Minahan

Part Three: Key Research Perspectives

9. Men on the Margins: masculinities in disadvantaged
   areas in Limerick city   169
   Patricia Kelleher and Pat O'Connor

10. Social Capital, Health and Inequality: what's the problem
    in the neighbourhoods?   185
    Eileen Humphreys

11. Behind the Headlines: media coverage of social exclusion
    in Limerick city – the case of Moyross   211
    Eoin Devereux, Amanda Haynes and Martin J. Power

12. City, Citizenship, Social Exclusion in Limerick   230
    Cathal O'Connell

Conclusion
 Understanding Limerick? Conclusions   245
 Niamh Hourigan

Notes and References   253
Index   291

Contributors

EDITOR
Niamh Hourigan is a lecturer and head of graduate studies in Sociology at University College Cork.

Contributors
Eoin Devereux is senior lecturer and head of department at the Department of Sociology, University of Limerick.

Amanda Haynes is a lecturer at the Department of Sociology, University of Limerick.

Eileen Humphreys works as a consultant social researcher. She is currently completing a study on children and families in Limerick for the Limerick City Children's Services Committee.

Patricia Kelleher is an adjunct senior lecturer in the Department of Sociology, University of Limerick.

Des McCafferty is professor of Geography at Mary Immaculate College Limerick.

Ciarán McCullagh is senior lecturer in Sociology at University College Cork.

Frances Minahan, a Sister of Mercy, is a family therapist who lives and works in Southill, Limerick.

Máire Treasa Nic Eochagáin is a resident engaged with the community in Moyross.

Cathal O'Connell is senior lecturer at the School of Applied Social Studies, University College Cork and director of the school's BSoc science programme.

Pat O'Connor is professor of Sociology and Social Policy at the University of Limerick.

Martin J. Power is a lecturer in Sociology with a focus on Regeneration at the University of Limerick.

Editor's Preface

As a sociologist who grew up in Limerick, I have always believed that there was much that was distinctive about the social structure and culture of the city.

When the Regeneration programmes for Limerick were launched in 2007, I approached Cork University Press with the idea of compiling an edited collection of expert research on social exclusion in the city. I quickly realised that almost all the research available focused on poverty and inequality while no scholarly research had been devoted to criminality. With this in mind, I asked my colleague Ciarán McCullagh (UCC) to examine local crime statistics and I began to conduct a three-year study on intimidation, fear and feuding in Limerick. This collection links this new strand of criminological analysis to the more established social policy tradition of research on Limerick

I wish to thank the National University of Ireland Research Publication Fund and University College Cork Research Publication Fund for supporting this volume. In addition, I would like to thank all the contributors for their endless co-operation and patience, as well as Mike Collins, Maria O'Donovan, Eibhear Walshe and all the team at Cork University Press.

Finally, I wish to dedicate my own contribution to my brother Patrick Hourigan who died in 2008 at the age of just 25. He loved Limerick very much.

N.H.

INTRODUCTION

Social Exclusion and Change in Limerick

Niamh Hourigan

> *'An ancient city well versed in the arts of war'*
> Motto of Limerick City

The city of Limerick truly earned its motto 'an ancient city well versed in the arts of war'[1] during a series of sieges by Oliver Cromwell and the Williamites in the late seventeenth century. Citizens of the city were acclaimed for their capacity to withstand attack and survive in harsh siege conditions. Today this reputation for a certain 'toughness' continues to inform the image of Limerick in popular consciousness. The successes of the Munster rugby team[2] are acclaimed because they represent the best of robust masculinity linked to physical strength, loyalty and a willingness to 'stand up and fight'.[3] Ironically, it is the darker inverted version of these same values which informs the culture of Limerick gangs: criminal organisations which have contributed to the negative image of the city in the national and international media.

Ordinary citizens of Limerick are apt to complain that the media's focus on criminality is unfair and bears no relationship to their lived experience of life in Limerick. The research presented in this volume confirms that impression, mapping the huge differentiation in the experiences of Limerick's residents linked to the deep divisions which exist in the city. For the vast majority of Limerick citizens, the city remains a good place to live with reasonably priced property, good schools, third-level institutions and excellent sports facilities. For a small minority, however, life in Limerick city can be fraught with difficulty as they struggle to provide for their families and survive in neighbourhoods which have serious problems with drugs and feud-related criminality.

Limerick would appear to embody a number of key contradictions. It is one of the Irish cities most integrated into the global economy, yet it has been torn apart by a feud reminiscent of the most ancient forms of tribal conflict. City leaders in Limerick have gone to great lengths to build the infrastructure vital for integration into the global economy, with airport, transport links, a university and technology parks; yet Limerick has the highest proportion of local authority housing of any Irish city (41 per cent),[4] the highest rate of suicide, self-harm[5] and marriage breakdown,[6] as well as extremely high rates of unemployment and single parenthood.[7] These figures suggest that there are many citizens of Limerick who remain excluded from the economic benefits of its high-tech infrastructure. Ultimately, Limerick city provides a fascinating site to explore a number of key questions:

- What happens to those who become socially excluded in a small divided city which is highly integrated into the global economy?
- How is social exclusion experienced in communities where the extended family rather than ethnicity is the critical source of identity?
- How do those who are excluded engage with the underbelly of globalisation (the global drugs trade and international criminal networks) in order to renegotiate their social exclusion?
- What are the broader consequences for disadvantaged communities and for the city itself when they have to learn to live with the violence and stigma which are the inevitable consequences of this 'dark side' of globalisation?

The depth of social exclusion and the particular problems posed by poverty-related crime in Limerick have already been recognised by the Irish state. The Limerick Regeneration project which was launched in 2007 has constituted the state's most wide-ranging response to social exclusion in the city. A plan based on the findings of the Fitzgerald Report,[8] the Regeneration project aims to entirely re-constitute the communities of Moyross, Southill, St Mary's Park and Ballinacurra Weston.[9] In addition to Regeneration, there have been a number of specific criminal justice responses to Limerick-based criminality. The most significant intervention has been the increase in the numbers of police and the move to community policing within the city.[10] An armed Emergency Response Unit has been established and electronic surveillance equipment has been installed as part of a package of measures designed to target Limerick criminal gangs.[11] It is within this context that *Understanding Limerick* has become a book about change: the need for change, the process of change and the question of whether long-term social change is sustainable. As editor of this volume, I would argue that a detailed and comprehensive understanding of the poverty and crime-related issues which continue to exist in Limerick is vital in generating long-term sustainable change.

Given this focus on change, the book has four main objectives. The first section of the book contains two chapters which aim to describe the *context* for change in Limerick. In the opening chapter, Des McCafferty provides a geographical overview of social exclusion in the city, highlighting the sharp divisions between rich and poor in the greater Limerick conurbation and the depth of social exclusion in specific neighbourhoods. Ciarán McCullagh tackles the crime statistics in Chapter Two, finding that since 2003 Limerick has been a low-crime city with some very specific and serious crime problems.

The second objective of the book is to provide a more robust *understanding* of the dynamics of organised crime, feuding and community violence, problems which were only briefly addressed within the Fitzgerald Report. The findings of a three-year community-level study on fear, feuding and intimidation in the city conducted by Niamh Hourigan are outlined in Part Two. This study opens with a detailed history of social exclusion and crime in the city from a sociological perspective. A mapping of the micro-social structure of socially excluded communities is provided in Chapter Four. The link between organised crime and community violence is explored in Chapter Five, which focuses on the following themes: (1) masculinities and status; (2) family gang criminal hierarchies; (3) fear, intimidation and community violence; (4) prison and (5) globalisation. Chapter Six presents a comparative analysis of gangland and Traveller feuding based on data gathered during the Limerick fear study and a major Traveller research project conducted by Hourigan and Campbell in 2010.[12]

The third objective of the book is to provide a *preliminary analysis* of state responses to social exclusion and poverty-related criminality in the city. As comprehensive funding for Limerick Regeneration was only granted by the Irish government in June 2010, it is too early to provide a full analysis of the impact of Regeneration on social exclusion in the city.[13] However, after three years of 'social regeneration' and a series of wide-ranging criminal justice responses, it is already possible to identify some strengths and weaknesses in the current configuration of policy responses which will be examined in Chapter Seven. Part Two concludes with two life narratives from residents in Southill and Moyross which highlight the strength of community spirit and neighbourliness which has emerged in these communities despite the difficulties experienced by local residents.

The chapters presented in Part Three of the volume contribute to the fourth key objective of the book which involves *linking* the experiences of socially excluded communities to broader Limerick society, the local and national media and the socio-economic models of the Irish state. Kelleher and O'Connor's research on 'Men on the Margins' demonstrates the difficulties experienced by men in disadvantaged neighbourhoods who reject criminality but struggle to integrate themselves into what they perceive as an alien mainstream Limerick culture. As 'bystanders in two cultures', they have few outlets for self-expression apart from sport. Eileen Humphreys' research compares health and community relationships across a number of advantaged and disadvantaged parishes in the city. She finds that although members of disadvantaged communities often have strong community relationships, these bonds are not sufficient to overcome the stress which social exclusion can place on families.

The research conducted by Eoin Devereux, Amanda Haynes and Martin J. Power focuses on the media construction of 'Moyross' and examines the news producer's role in re-producing stigma associated with the area. They highlight the significant power disparities between local residents in disadvantaged areas who seek to present positive images of their community life and the conflicting agendas of contemporary news organisations who are governed by the mantra 'if it bleeds, it leads'. Finally, Cathal O'Connell presents the most wide-ranging contribution to the discussion by examining what social exclusion in Limerick tells about the broader citizenship crisis in Irish society. The volume concludes by asking whether lessons can be learned from the case of Limerick which can improve future policy formulation and inform broader processes of socio-cultural transformation in twenty-first-century Ireland.

Social Exclusion, Globalisation and Family

The concept of social exclusion underpins all the contributions to this book and is defined by Combat Poverty as 'a process whereby certain groups are pushed to the edge of society and prevented from participating fully by virtue of their poverty, inadequate education or life-skills'.[14] The term social exclusion originated in France in the 1970s where René Lenoir sought to explain how *les exclus* (the excluded in French society) were systematically overlooked by the more prosperous majority.[15] Empirical studies of social exclusion have tended to focus on spatial exclusion, the division of urban spaces into separate neighbourhoods for the disadvantaged and the more affluent.[16] A series of studies demonstrated the existence of *neighbourhood effects*.[17] Wendy Bottero explains:

> The suggestion is that ... neighbourhood concentration reinforces
> social exclusion ... concentration of poverty affects residents through

> peer-group influences spreading anti-social behaviour and through
> lack of positive neighbourhood role models.[18]

The existence of these neighbourhood effects linked to crime and anti-social behaviour makes the experience of poverty and inequality even more difficult for the socially excluded individual.

As Chapter Three demonstrates, Limerick, like other Irish towns and cities, had a socially excluded class in the 1930s, '40s and '50s, long before the term 'social exclusion' gained currency. However, the integration of Limerick's economy into global capitalism since the 1970s has done little to narrow the pre-existing gap between rich and poor in the city or, indeed, lessen the cultural divisions between the two groups. As Peader Kirby has demonstrated, the dividends of the Celtic Tiger boom in Ireland were not distributed equally throughout the social spectrum but rather exacerbated socio-economic polarisation.[19] Thus, the same mechanisms which produce social exclusion are also those which have privileged Irish economic elites and the agenda of the transnational capitalist class.[20] Jo Beall has argued that political elites within globalised societies become complacent about social exclusion, viewing it as 'an unfortunate but inevitable side effect of global economic realignment'.[21] This official complacency is difficult to sustain, however, in the face of rising crime rates and youth delinquency which are the inevitable consequence of social exclusion.

Within international criminology, there is a long-established link between social exclusion, organised crime and juvenile justice issues. Jock Young argues that those who grow up in marginalised communities recognise their social exclusion and turn to criminality in order to subvert this process.[22] Beall argues that 'people who are marginalized from formal labour market experience a rupture of the social bond that constitutes an under-girding of both the *rights* and *responsibilities* of citizenship'.[23] It is this rupture linked to social exclusion which generates organised crime and drugs-related criminality. Viewed from these perspectives, Limerick would appear to represent a classic example of a city where deep social exclusion has generated serious criminality. However, as editor I would argue that the insights to be gleaned from the case of Limerick stretch beyond this classic framework.

In examining conflict in marginalised communities in Europe and the United States, sociologists have highlighted how interracial tensions can emerge as the focus for conflict among socially excluded groups.[24] The case of Limerick is striking as, despite having a large recent migrant population,[25] racial and ethnic tensions have been almost entirely absent from the *collective* violence spawned by social exclusion in Limerick, though individual racist assaults have occurred. Instead, it is tensions between extended family networks which constitute the most significant source of conflict in the city. Thus, the extended family rather than ethnicity has become the primary source of identity, status and meaning for those excluded from broader Limerick society.

Since the publication of Arensberg and Kimball's seminal work *Family and Community in Ireland* (1940), the centrality of family to individual and collective identity in Ireland has been a constant theme in sociological and anthropological research.[26] During the Celtic Tiger boom, Keohane and Kuhling argued that this commitment to family did not diminish but became transformed into commitments to consumption on home, children and special family celebrations.[27] Tom Inglis's most recent research on the 'meaning of life' for Irish people suggests that even while popular commitment to organised religion is declining, family remains the central organising structure and critical source of belonging and meaning for Irish people.[28] Within this context, the emergence of family-based criminal organisations and inter-family feuds among the socially excluded in Limerick suggests that family offers a culturally specific way of creating meaning, belonging and status for those who are excluded from all other forms of status in Irish society.

Ultimately, the research presented in this volume suggests that the ordinary citizens of Limerick who complain about the negative media depictions of the city are both right and wrong. Criminality and severe poverty are a relatively small part of Limerick's story, a story which also includes economic growth, sporting success, urban renewal and vibrant cultural activity.[29] Yet there is also evidence that the poverty-linked crime in the city represents a very distinct problem which must be fully understood to be resolved. It is hoped that this volume will go some way towards providing these enhanced understandings.

PART ONE

Contexts

1. Divided City

The social geography of Post-Celtic Tiger Limerick

Des McCafferty

As the country's third-largest urban centre, and the industrial and commercial capital of the Mid-West region, Limerick has grown rapidly in terms of population, labour force and economic activity in recent years. Between 1996 and 2006 the population of the urban area expanded by 14 per cent, the labour force by 32 per cent and the total number at work by 40 per cent.[1] In the six years from 2000 to 2006, disposable income per head of population in the wider City and County area grew at a rate of almost 7 per cent per annum, with the result that, by 2006, the combined area had the fourth-highest standard of living in the country.[2] However, the impressive economic performance of the urban hinterland was not matched by that of the core City, which continued to experience acute levels of poverty and deprivation. In 2000–1, the rate (or risk) of both income poverty and consistent poverty in Limerick City was 50 per cent above the national average, and the highest (on both measures) amongst the country's five cities.[3] Since 2002, the City has been ranked as the second most disadvantaged of the country's thirty-four local authority areas in socio-economic terms, and the gap between the City and the rest of the state widened substantially between 1996 and 2006.[4] In 2006, the City contained the single most disadvantaged of over 3,400 electoral districts in the Irish state.

As this data suggests, Limerick emerged from the economic boom of the Celtic Tiger period as an urban area characterised by sharp spatial contrasts in levels of socio-economic well-being. These contrasts have historical roots in a radical restructuring of the local economy which took place from the 1960s onwards, when traditional sources of employment in the food and clothing sectors were gradually replaced by new enterprises in high-technology sectors such as electronics and computers.[5] The effects of industrial restructuring have been socially and spatially uneven, imparting to the city a distinctive, and highly differentiated, social

3

geography. This geography has also been shaped by a strong and accel-erating trend towards suburbanisation of both population and economic activity. In 1971, just 9 per cent of the population in Limerick urban area resided outside the City boundary; by 1996 this proportion had increased to 38 per cent, and by 2006 it stood at 42 per cent. Between 1996 and 2006, almost the entire net gain in the population of the urban area took place in the suburbs.[6] As in other cities where it has occurred, suburbani-sation has been strongly selective in terms of attributes such as age, marital status, family status and income level. By and large, it is younger, family-based, middle-class households that have been most attracted to the suburbs, and as a result, significant socio-demographic contrasts have now developed between the new estates on the outskirts and the older residential parts of the City.

Given the strength of suburbanisation, it is not surprising that popula-tion growth in the City has been sluggish in recent years, with an increase between 1996 and 2006 of under 1 per cent, contrasting with a growth rate of over 14 per cent in the urban area as a whole. In fact, the popula-tion of the City would undoubtedly have decreased were it not for the influx of immigrants, a trend that was particularly notable following the accession to the EU of ten new member states in 2004. Between 2002 and 2006 the number of non-Irish nationals in Limerick urban area almost doubled (from 5,330 to 10,072), and by the end of the period they consti-tuted nearly 11 per cent of the population. Foreign nationals are as highly suburbanised as the indigenous population, in fact slightly more so in 2006, but within the City they have shown a much stronger concentra-tion in the city centre, as opposed to the inner suburban areas. The result is that the impact and visibility of immigration is much greater in the centre. Thus, foreign nationals constituted over one-half of the population in the area located along the quays from Sarsfield Bridge to the docks, and over one-third of the population in four other parts of the city centre. While refugees and asylum seekers represented a significant element of immigration in the earlier part of the period, more recent arrivals have been mainly labour market migrants. No less than the foreign-owned companies located on the city's industrial estates and business parks, and the international retail chains in its shopping centres, the new immigrants attest to the ongoing globalisation of the local economy.

This chapter examines the way in which these economic, social and demographic transformations have played out in terms of the social geog-raphy of the city. In particular, I focus on the extent of socio-economic disparities between areas within the city, and the influence of public policy in shaping those disparities. The chapter begins with a broad overview of some of the key dimensions of contemporary social differentiation in Limerick, and the way in which these define a number of distinct types of social area. This analysis points to a relatively high level of social segregation in the city, the nature, causes and consequences of which, in terms of spatial inequality, are examined in more detail in the next section. The penultimate section develops the discussion of outcomes further, by focusing on the problems of poverty and deprivation in City Council housing estates. The chapter then concludes with a look at some emerging trends in Limerick's social geography, and an assessment of their implications for the multi-billion-euro Regeneration programme launched in October 2008.

The Urban Mosaic: contemporary socio-spatial variation in Limerick

As a form of social organisation, cities are characterised by a high degree of diversity and heterogeneity. This social diversity tends not to be expressed in a random mixing of different types of individuals, households or groups in urban space. Instead, an array of processes, some market-related, others having their origins in the urban governance and planning systems, results in the filtering of different social types to different areas, and hence the emergence of a structured social geography in which clear patterns of social variation across space can be identified. Limerick's social geography, like that of all large urban settlements, is a complex and ever-changing mosaic formed by the cross-cutting patterns of demographic, economic and social differentiation. Areas within the city differ from each other in terms of the age profile of their populations, the sizes and types of families and households present, the educational attainment levels, occupations, and social class of residents, their income and levels of consumption, and, increasingly, their cultural and ethnic backgrounds. These myriad differences between areas have important implications for everyday activity patterns and lifestyles, for the socialisation processes of residents, their access to social and economic opportunities, and the demand for, and supply of, both private and public services (e.g. shops, personal services, childcare, health facilities, day-care facilities for the elderly).

As a first step in the exploration of the city's multifaceted social geography, the technique of factorial ecology can be applied to data from the census of population, to identify common patterns in socio-spatial variation, from which, in turn, a typology of social area types can be derived. Though less extensively applied in urban social geography nowadays as compared to its heyday in the 1970s (when it tended to be used within the theoretical framework of social area analysis), factorial ecology remains a useful descriptive tool. It is used here not as an end in itself, nor to advance a particular theory of urban social structure, but to provide a general spatial framework for the analysis to follow. In interpreting the results of the factorial ecology, a number of caveats need to be borne in mind. First, the technique is based on the measurement of socio-economic variables for discrete small areas within the city. While these variables represent the aggregate conditions for each area, it must not be assumed that all individuals or households in a given area share these aggregate characteristics.[7] It should also be clear that the output from the factorial ecology is strongly influenced by the geographical framework on which it is based, which, in the present case, is provided by the city's electoral districts (EDs). In most cases, these units are larger than neighbourhoods or 'natural communities', so the output inevitably over-generalises the spatial pattern, obscuring what in some instances might be significant local variations. Later we will see that some of the large-scale patterns of socio-economic variation in Limerick are beginning to break down, with immigration and increased mobility between areas producing a more complex and fine-grained geography. This trend has been widely reported in international studies which have characterised the social geographies of cities in the post-Fordist era as increasingly 'splintered' or 'fractured'.[8]

The application of factorial ecology to the Limerick urban area results in the identification of four key ways in which areas in the city differ from each other with regard to their social characteristics.[9] We can refer to these as the four fundamental dimensions or axes of socio-spatial differentiation in the city. The four dimensions, and the key indicator variables associated with them, are outlined in Table 1.

TABLE 1: DIMENSIONS OF SOCIAL VARIATION IN LIMERICK

AXIS OF SOCIAL DIFFERENTIATION	INDICATOR VARIABLES
Family Status/Urbanism	Percentage of family-based households; percentage of non-Irish nationals; residential mobility; housing tenure
Socio-Economic Status	Educational attainment; unemployment rate; percentage in higher/lower social classes; car ownership; Internet access
Labour Market Status	Labour force participation rate; female activity rate; part-time working
Age profile	Percentage of older persons; older housing; elderly living alone

Taking these fundamental dimensions of social variation into account simultaneously, Limerick (i.e. the City and suburbs) can be divided into six different social area types (Figure 1). These differ from each other with regard to one or more of the four dimensions of social variation, and also with regard to their geographical location in the city.[10] Social area type one is the suburbs, and takes in all of the major residential areas outside the City, including Westbury and Shannon Banks (County Clare), and Castletroy, Dooradoyle and Raheen (all in County Limerick). In addition, it includes a number of more recently developed private housing areas within the City boundary, such as Rhebogue and Singland. These areas are characterised by above-average rates of population growth and relatively high percentages of children. Family households predominate, and, compared to the average, a high proportion is at the pre-school stage of the family cycle. Housing tends to be of recent construction and owner-occupied. The social class profile is very much weighted towards the higher (professional and managerial) social classes. Unemployment is relatively low, while levels of car ownership are the highest of all six social area types. The areas in question score above average in terms of overall affluence.[11]

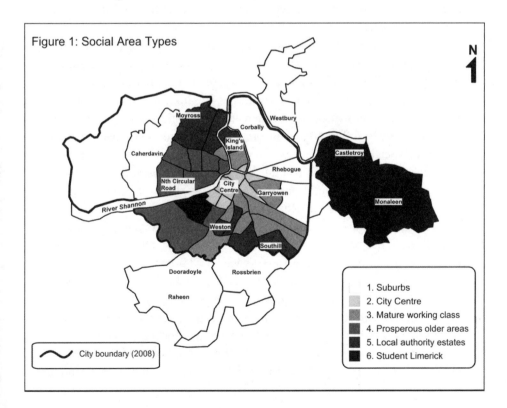

Figure 1: Social Area Types

N

1. Suburbs
2. City Centre
3. Mature working class
4. Prosperous older areas
5. Local authority estates
6. Student Limerick

City boundary (2008)

Social area type two is found at the centre of the city, in an area corre-sponding to the central business district. The defining characteristic of this area is the predominance of private rented accommodation, mainly in the form of apartments, and the high proportion of young adults. Recent population growth is the highest across the six social area types, but this is partly due to the relatively low initial population base that resulted from decades of decline. Population growth has been fuelled almost entirely by in-migration, and the result is that the area now shows the highest per-centage of foreign nationals. There is a low level of car ownership. Rather than being indicative of lower levels of affluence and consumption, this reflects the centrality of the area, and its consequentially high levels of accessibility to services and employment. This interpretation is supported by the fact that levels of educational attainment are high, as is labour force participation. These are the new urban neighbourhoods that have emerged in the last decade or so as the city centre has been extensively rebuilt. In many respects, this social area type corresponds to what might be termed 'big city' or cosmopolitan Limerick. However, the area is not solely the preserve of cosmopolites: an interesting characteristic is that the rate of lone-parent families is the second highest among the social area types, a feature that links the area to social area type five and that will be commented on again later.

Social area types three (mature working class areas) and four (pros-perous older areas) are located within the City and share a common demographic profile. They are both characterised by mature or older age profiles, with relatively high percentages of the population aged over sixty-five, and high rates of so-called 'empty-nest' families.[12] However, they are sharply differentiated in other respects, most particularly with regard to social class. Whereas the professional and managerial classes outnumber the unskilled and semi-skilled manual classes by three to one in prosperous older neighbourhoods, such as those located along the Ennis Road/North Circular Road and the South Circular Road, the ratio is reversed in mature working class areas. Levels of consumption and of overall affluence are also much lower in the latter. These areas, which include Garryowen and Janesboro, as well as Thomondgate, were origi-nally developed by Limerick City Council (formerly Limerick Corporation) and, while a large part of the housing stock has now been privatised through tenant purchase, the percentage of households renting from the local authority is still above the average for the urban area.

A relatively high proportion of rented housing is one of the common characteristics of the two remaining social area types: public-sector renting in the case of the local authority estates (social area type five) and private renting in the case of 'student Limerick' (social area type six). The emergence of the latter reflects recent 'studentification' of a number of areas. This has been brought about by the growth in the number of students in the city's third-level institutions, and the increased provision of purpose-built student accommodation which has had the effect of spatially concentrating this population more than in the past. Studentified areas are characterised by low levels of labour force participation, high levels of part-time working and, of course, high levels of educational attainment. In contrast, the local authority estates of social area type five are characterised by the lowest standards of educational attainment among all six social area types. This category, which includes the estates of Moyross, Ballynanty, Kileely and St Mary's Park on the north-side of the City, as well as Southill and Ballinacurra Weston on the south-side, is in fact exceptional in a wide range of attributes. As well as having the highest percentage of public rented housing, it has the highest unemployment rate and the highest percentages of unskilled and semi-skilled manual social classes, children under fifteen years of age and lone-parent families. Consumption levels and the affluence score are the lowest of all six social area types.

This typology of neighbourhoods in Limerick is based primarily on their social composition, which, as noted earlier, gives rise to contrasts in social activity patterns and lifestyles. Such contrasts are evident, for example, between student Limerick and the redeveloped areas on the one hand, and the more family-oriented areas on the other. Related to the social differences, there are important contrasts in respect of factors like environmental character, as exemplified, for example, by differences in the density of development between redeveloped areas and the new suburbs. These differences are important from the point of view of physical (land use) planning. From a social policy point of view, the most significant feature of the social area typology is the marked variation among areas in socio-economic well-being, as indicated, for example, by the affluence/deprivation index. Such variation is most pronounced as between the suburbs and prosperous older areas on the one hand, and the local authority estates (and, to a lesser extent, mature working class areas) on the other. This feature suggests that the social area typology is underpinned by spatial patterns not just of difference but, more problematically, of socio-economic disparity and inequality. It is to this issue that we turn next.

Social Segregation, Spatial Inequality and Marginalisation

Differences in standards of living between social groups are a feature of all urban areas, and indeed of market-oriented economies in general, though the extent of these differences varies between countries, depending on factors such as the degree of redistribution of income through the social welfare system. The mechanism that translates social inequality into disparities between areas is the spatial separation, or seg-regation, of social groups on the basis of residence. In Limerick, the pronounced spatial differences in socio-economic well-being noted above are the outcome of a comparatively high degree of residential segrega-tion. Using small area data from the 2006 census of population, levels of segregation of various social groups in the city can be compared with those in the other medium-sized Irish cities of Cork, Galway and Water-ford. Segregation is assessed here using the well-known Dissimilarity Index (also known as the Displacement Index) which measures the extent to which the distributions of two population groups differ from each other across a series of spatial units.[13] While segregation is a complex and multifaceted concept, and its measurement presents diffi-cult methodological challenges, the Dissimilarity Index (DI) is one of the most widely used and robust measures. The Index ranges from zero, when both groups have the exact same spatial distribution (hence zero segregation), to 100, when the two groups live in entirely separate areas (complete segregation). The Index value can be interpreted as the per-centage of either group that would need to move between areas (or be displaced) in order for the two distributions to match exactly. In the analysis reported here the spatial units are census enumeration areas (EAs) which are smaller in terms of both area and population than the EDs, and therefore permit a more detailed investigation.[14]

Table 2 presents the Dissimilarity Index for selected groups in the four cities. In each case, DI is measured by comparing the distribution of the group in question with a reference group, e.g. unemployed persons are compared to those at work. For each of the social classes, the reference group is all other social classes, i.e. the Index measures the spatial separa-tion of each class from the rest of the population. The results indicate that, in terms of social class, Limerick is, on average, the most segregated of the four cities, with an average DI of 22.0 compared to 17.0 for the city with the lowest level of segregation, Galway.[15] Although average levels of social class segregation are comparatively low for all four cities, there are con-siderable variations across the social classes. In general, residential segregation is highest for the groups at either end of the class spectrum, i.e. the professional social class and the unskilled social class, and it is the latter which contributes most in comparative terms to the higher average level of social class segregation in Limerick. When the geographical distributions of these two social groups are directly compared, Limerick shows a level of segregation (DI = 63.7) that is 10 per cent higher than the next most segregated city, Waterford (DI = 57.9), and almost 40 per cent higher than the city in which the two groups show the highest level of residential integration, Galway (DI = 45.8).

TABLE 2: DISSIMILARITY INDEX BY CITY FOR SELECTED GROUPS

GROUP	CORK	LIMERICK	GALWAY	WATERFORD
Professional social class	31.4	36.0	25.1	37.7
Managerial and technical social class	22.2	25.2	16.8	25.1
Non-manual social class	9.0	8.0	6.4	7.4
Manual social class	18.8	18.9	16.5	16.2
Semi-skilled social class	22.3	25.0	22.5	19.8
Unskilled manual social class	33.2	39.7	26.6	30.7
Average social class segregation	20.3	22.0	17.0	19.8
Unemployed persons	20.8	32.3	19.1	25.7
Children in lone-parent families	27.4	33.1	21.8	27.8
Persons in local authority rentals	61.5	66.4	59.6	48.6

Higher levels of segregation in Limerick as compared to the other cities are evident with respect to variables other than social class. Thus, Limerick also displays the highest segregation of children in lone-parent families (compared to children in families consisting of couples with children) and of the unemployed (vis-à-vis those at work), both of which groups are particularly significant in terms of the geography of poverty and social exclusion (see next section). For the range of social groups examined here, the highest levels of segregation in all four cities are for households renting their living accommodation from the local authority (compared to owner-occupier households), and again, it is in Limerick that this group is most segregated. The results indicate that if, say, public policy-makers were to set out to bring the geographical distribution of local authority tenant households into line with that of owner occupiers, two-thirds of households in either category would have to be relocated between areas. The corresponding figure for the city with the lowest level of segregation between local authority tenant households and owner-occupier households, Waterford, is 49 per cent.

Social segregation in Limerick is the result of a range of factors and processes that have operated over several decades. The particularly high level of segregation according to tenure suggests that one of the most crucial influences has been the city's housing system. This influence is exerted in the first instance through the filtering effect whereby those on lower incomes who cannot afford to meet their accommodation needs through the private housing market are channelled into areas of public housing. While this filtering process operates in all cities with mixed public/private housing systems, particular features of Limerick have contributed to relatively high levels of segregation. The first of these is the sheer size of the public (local authority) housing sector in the City. According to the Fitzgerald Report, Limerick is 'unique' (in the Irish context) in its high proportion of social housing, which accounts for approximately 8,000 of the 18,900 housing units in the City (i.e. 42 per cent).[16] Secondly, individual housing schemes are also relatively large, with over 1,160 houses in total in the Southill scheme which was built between 1966 and 1972, and a similar number in the Moyross development built between 1974 and 1987. In addition, both estates were located adjacent to older public housing estates (Janesboro/Kennedy Park in the case of Southill, and Ballynanty/Kileely in the case of Moyross), thereby increasing the spatial concentration of public housing. Finally, in sharp contrast with the City, the volume of public housing provided in the suburbs by Limerick and Clare County Councils has been very low. According to the 2006 census, only 3.5 per cent of the inhabited housing stock in the suburbs was rented from the local authority.[17] This means that just 15 per cent of households renting from the local authorities in Limerick urban area are located in the suburbs, as compared to 40 per cent of all households. While suburbanisation has proceeded apace over recent years, therefore, the section of the population depending on local authority housing provision has remained substantially confined to the City. Clearly, the City boundary has been a significant divide in terms of housing, and more generally in terms of the city's social geography.

The high degree of residential segregation of households according to tenure and social class has had long-term negative consequences for social cohesion in Limerick, and has contributed in recent years to the increasing marginalisation of certain areas, in particular the local authority estates. One reason for this is that segregation has meant that the negative effects of industrial restructuring have been spatially focused and uneven. The loss of jobs in both indigenous and foreign-owned industries impacted disproportionately on areas with high proportions of lower-skilled workers, for whom these sectors were traditionally among the main sources of employment. The closure of Ferenka in 1977 during the course of an economic recession had a particularly severe impact on the Southill area of the city, from which many of the workers were drawn and which was still in the early stages of its settlement. The 1998 closure of Krups, following a series of rationalisations, impacted negatively on the same area, and in particular on female employment, though the effects were somewhat mitigated by the general growth of employment opportunities during the boom years of the Celtic Tiger economy. The social–geographical effects of the recent Dell downsizing, which represents the largest ever loss of jobs in the city, have been widely felt throughout the city and region, but, given the relatively low skills profile of the jobs lost, it is likely that these effects too will be particularly focused on areas of lower socio-economic status.

Economic change, in a context where there was an already high degree of social segregation, has contributed strongly to widening the gap in standards of living between public and private estates. However, other factors have also been implicated in this process, including certain features of public housing policy and management that have changed the profile of households renting in the public sector.[18] Among these is the differential rents scheme, under which the weekly rent payable by a household renting from the City Council is based on the combined income of all persons in the household. The scheme is based on the socially equitable and progressive principle of households paying according to their means. However, it has had the unintended consequence of incentivising higher-income households to move from local authority tenancies into the private sector. This transfer has been facilitated by other housing policy measures, including the long-established tenant purchase scheme, and the more short-lived tenancy surrender scheme introduced in the mid 1980s. The latter initiative used the mechanism of a monetary grant towards the cost of house purchase to incentivise households in the public sector to move into private housing. As with tenant purchase arrangements, the scheme was most accessible to higher-income (and, typically, employed) householders, but in this instance, the result was the movement of such individuals not just between tenure categories but between areas. Rather than helping to settle local authority estates, as has been claimed to be the effect of the tenant purchase scheme,[19] the tenancy surrender scheme destabilised estates. Moreover, evidence from Dublin suggests that the scheme affected more marginalised, less desirable, and hence lower-demand, estates more than others, due to the fact that tenant purchase on these estates was seen as a less desirable option than on more popular, high-demand estates.[20] In Limerick, it appears that the already severely disadvantaged Southill and Moyross areas were among those most severely affected by the differential outflow of better-off tenant households.

The tenancy surrender initiative was introduced during an economic recession, when constraints on public capital spending, and a consequential reduction in the house-building programme, had led to growing waiting lists for public housing. This reduction in housing output has itself been adduced as a cause of growing income disparities according to tenure, in that it meant available public housing was more likely to be allocated to the very lowest-income groups. The reduction in average income in the public sector, at least in relative terms, as a result of these various aspects of housing policy is a trend that has been identified in a number of countries with mixed public/private housing systems. It has been interpreted as a process of marginalisation or 'residualisation' of public housing estates.[21] Once established, residualisation tends to be self-reinforcing in its effects, creating a downwards spiral in the socio-economic profile of the area. This arises because of the link between residualisation and so-called 'neighbourhood effects' or 'area effects', whereby the well-being of residents is impacted upon by factors, above and beyond their own personal attributes, that are related to the social composition of the area in which they live. In principle, area effects or 'externalities' can be either positive or negative. However, where the local area is characterised by an accumulation of social problems such as unemployment, elevated rates of lone parenthood, and poverty, area effects are invariably negative. Problems that have been linked to area effects include high rates of physical and mental ill-health, 'anomie' and alienation from mainstream society, deficiencies in child development, behavioural problems in children, lower levels of school attendance, increased exposure to crime and antisocial behaviour, and deficiencies in both the quality and quantity of public and private services. Evidence from Limerick suggests that neighbourhood effects contribute significantly to problems in local authority estates.[22] These problems are examined in more detail in the next section.

Poverty and Disadvantage in City Council Estates

The outcomes of segregation and marginalisation for those living in the major City Council housing estates are revealed by small area data from the most recent (2006) census of population. These data show a strong correlation between tenure and a number of variables that, evidence suggests, are closely linked to affluence or, its opposite, poverty and disadvantage. The CSO *Survey on Incomes and Living Conditions* (SILC) indicates that, nationally, two of the strongest risk factors for poverty are unemployment and membership of a lone-parent household.[23] Thus, both unemployed persons and persons in lone-parent households are 2.3 times more likely than the general population to have incomes below the poverty line.[24] These groups also show elevated rates of consistent poverty, which occurs when an individual has an income below the poverty line and suffers material deprivation.[25] The unemployed are 3.4 times, and persons in lone-parent households 3.9 times, more likely than the general population to experience consistent poverty. In the previous section, we have seen evidence that both these groups are relatively highly segregated in Limerick. The geographies of the two groups are represented in Figures 2 and 3, which reveal a strong spatial association between them, as well as between them both and the relative predominance of renting from the local authority.[26] Thus, the 2006 rate of unemployment for Limerick City and suburbs was 11.6 per cent, but rates in excess of 30 per cent occurred in the City Council estates of Moyross, St Mary's Park, Ballinacurra Weston and Southill. Similarly, while the rate of lone-parent families for Limerick urban area as a whole (i.e. City and suburbs) was 21 per cent (itself high relative to the national average), rates in excess of 50 per cent prevailed throughout Moyross and

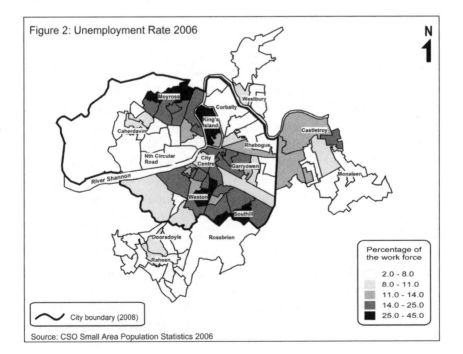

Figure 2: Unemployment Rate 2006

N
1

Percentage of the work force

2.0 - 8.0
8.0 - 11.0
11.0 - 14.0
14.0 - 25.0
25.0 - 45.0

City boundary (2008)

Source: CSO Small Area Population Statistics 2006

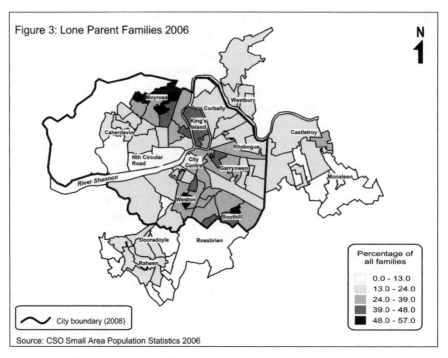

Figure 3: Lone Parent Families 2006

N

Percentage of all families

	0.0 - 13.0
	13.0 - 24.0
	24.0 - 39.0
	39.0 - 48.0
	48.0 - 57.0

City boundary (2008)

Source: CSO Small Area Population Statistics 2006

in the upper (Kilmallock Road) part of O'Malley Park, followed closely by Weston (50 per cent) and St Mary's Park (48 per cent).

This area-based data is strongly indicative of high levels of poverty and deprivation among families and individuals living in public rented housing. More direct evidence of the link between tenure and socio-economic distress are available from a recent profile of individuals living in accommodation rented from Limerick City Council.[27] The population covered by the profile overlaps with, but does not match exactly, that in social area type five, as described earlier. The information on which it is based includes the age, sex and incomes of individuals resident in tenant households as at September 2004.[28] In terms of the basic demographic attributes of sex and age, it is a highly distinctive population, with a much higher proportion of females, children and adolescents than the population as a whole. In total, 56 per cent of the renting population was female, but this rises to 62 per cent for heads of household. The youthful age profile of individuals in tenant households is reflected in the fact that 36 per cent were aged under fifteen years, with 50 per cent aged under twenty five years. The youth dependency ratio (i.e. the number of persons aged under fiteen years relative to those aged fifteen to sixty-four) was more than two-and-a-half times greater than that for Limerick urban area as a whole.[29] Household composition was also significantly different from the population at large. The most common type of tenant household consisted of a single adult (lone parent) and children, which accounted for 33 per cent of all households, and for 46 per cent of family-based households, as compared to 21 per cent in Limerick City and suburbs.

With regard to labour market engagement, the activity rate for City Council tenants aged fifteen years and over (34 per cent) was significantly below the rate for the city as a whole (59 per cent), and the unemployment rate (53 per cent) was almost five times higher. Given the low levels of employment, it is not surprising that persons aged fifteen years and over were primarily dependent on social welfare payments as a source of income. In total, welfare payments accounted for 83 per cent of all incomes. Reflecting the household composition, and in particular the high rate of lone-parent families, the single most important income source was the one-parent family payment, which was the main income source for 30 per cent of primary income recipients (i.e. those with the highest income in each household).

Social imbalances in the profile of tenant households are associated with particularly high rates of income poverty risk. Altogether, 80 per cent of individuals lived in households with incomes below the poverty line, a rate of poverty risk that was almost four times the contemporaneous (2004) national rate.[30] In general, the rate of poverty risk was somewhat greater for females than for males, with the gender gap most evident among heads of household, where the female rate was 82 per cent as opposed to 74 per cent for males. Rates of poverty risk were inversely related to age, so that the highest rate (89 per cent) was for children aged less than fifteen years. There were also differences according to household composition, the highest rate of poverty risk occurring among individuals in lone-parent households, 90 per cent of whom had incomes below the specified poverty line.

While the socio-economic attributes described above clearly differentiate local authority rented housing from other tenure categories, there is nevertheless significant variation within the tenure category, with differences evident among estates in respect of age–sex profiles, unemployment rates and income levels. In general, the pattern that emerges is of more imbalanced age, sex and family structures on estates that are located further from the city centre. Likewise, the highest rates of poverty risk tended to be in the more peripheral estates. These include the area of Moyross formerly known as Glenagross Park, in which 94 per cent of the renting population were at risk of poverty, and the Keyes Park/Carew Park area of Southill where the at-risk rate was 85 per cent. To some extent this geographical pattern corresponds with the age of the estate, less central estates generally being younger. However, the highest overall rate of poverty risk (96 per cent) was for part of the Ballinacurra Weston estate built over half a century ago, in the 1950s.

In summary, Limerick's public housing estates are characterised by a demography and pattern of household composition that is extremely imbalanced relative to that of the city as a whole and indeed the wider Irish society. These demographic and social imbalances are associated with levels of household income that place the vast majority of tenants and their families at risk of income poverty. The spatial concentration of poverty in the estates has contributed to a number of social problems. In particular, there is evidence of declining social capital and the intensification of a number of neighbourhood problems ranging from environmental degradation to antisocial behaviour, crime and intimidation of residents.[31] Given these data, it is difficult to avoid the conclusion that the City Council estates are highly marginalised in socio-economic terms within the city. It is not true to say that they have failed to participate in the economic growth of recent years, as there is some evidence that unemployment rates, for example, decreased more than in other areas during the 1996–2002 period.[32] However, such convergence tendencies have been weak at best, and the disparity between local authority estates and the rest of the city remains stark.

Remaking the Social Geography of Limerick: the challenge for Regeneration

The process of residualisation in local authority estates in Limerick is closely linked to population trends. The census suggests that there has been a general decrease in population across these estates, to an extent that has been quite exceptional in some cases, and this decrease appears to be both the outcome and the reinforcing cause of residualisation. In the period 1981 to 1991, the O'Malley Park area of Southill lost 26 per cent of its population, and analysis of the decrease has shown that there was a significantly higher level of out-migration from the area than might be expected on the basis of the net migration rates for the City as a whole.[33] This process of 'differential' out-migration has been linked to the social and economic problems experienced on the estate. In the more recent period, 1991 to 2006, against the background of a 20 per cent increase in the population of the city, the area lost a further 43 per cent of its population, which now stands at roughly two-fifths of its 1981 peak level. Perhaps more than any other single indicator, this population collapse attests to the problems experienced in the area, and the failure of the City's housing programme in recent times.

Migration from O'Malley Park and other local authority estates has been largely accommodated elsewhere in the city, and there is evidence to suggest there has been an influx to the city centre in particular. Earlier in this chapter the high rate of lone-parent families in social area type two (the redeveloped city centre) was noted. Interestingly, the 2006 census shows that, between 2002 and 2006, the number of lone-parent families in the O'Malley Park and Weston areas decreased, but there was a considerable increase in parts of the city centre.[34] A similar pattern is discernible with regard to the unskilled and semi-skilled social classes over the longer period of 1996 to 2006. The numbers in these classes declined in almost every ED containing a local authority estate, but increased in the city centre. In the Ballynanty–Moyross area the decrease was 27 per cent; in O'Malley Park–Keyes Park it stood at 47 per cent. By contrast, the two quayside EDs in the centre experienced an increase of almost 300 per cent. The data suggest, then, that there has been a dispersal of both these groups (which of course overlap to some degree) out of the local authority rented estates and into private rented housing in the centre.

Though further research is needed on these demographic changes, it would seem that dispersal has been largely facilitated by recent changes in housing policy and its mechanisms. One aspect of this is the increased activity by the City Council in acquiring private housing to let to households on the housing list. However, this activity seems to have been focused mainly on the suburbs. Of greater significance in explaining the trend towards the city centre is the rapid increase in the rent supplement scheme, which was reconfigured as the Rental Accommodation Scheme (RAS) in 2005. While there has been recognition of the potential of both these housing schemes to increase social mixing, and counter social segregation and exclusion, there have also been criticisms on a number of grounds. In particular, concerns have been expressed that vulnerable individuals and families moving into city-centre apartments may lose contact with both formal social services and informal, community-based, social support systems.[35] There is also a possibility that rent supplement/RAS could contribute to further residualisation of the local authority estates, thereby compounding the adverse consequences of past policy measures.

This is the context in which the €3.1 billion Regeneration plan for Moyross, Southill, Ballinacurra Weston and St Mary's Park was launched in 2008. Given the prevailing macro-economic climate, the plan could scarcely have been launched in more inauspicious circumstances. It is equally true that the need for large-scale intervention in the most marginalised areas of the city has probably never been greater. The plan proposes a radical solution to the problems of these areas, based on wholesale clearance and reconstruction. In rebuilding the estates, the importance of diversifying both land use and housing tenure is recognised. Thus, the Regeneration blueprint envisages the development of retail, commercial and other uses alongside residential development, and, within the latter, a variety of housing types, densities and tenures. The emphasis on land use and tenure diversification suggests that important lessons have been learned from the past, and that there is a determination not to repeat the mistake of developing over-large, single-class housing estates with poor accessibility to services.

Nevertheless, there continues to be some contention in both academic and policy discourse about the benefits of tenure-mixing policies and, more fundamentally, about the value of the area-based approach to Regeneration. Questions have been raised about the efficacy of the approach in dealing with problems that are rooted in market-based processes of economic change and in failures of national policy-making, and which, therefore, are systemic or structural in origin, rather than local.[36] There is a strong argument that the solution of these problems requires interventions at a higher level than the locality, and on a larger scale. Among the various justifications put forward in defence of area-based interventions, probably the most important in the Limerick context is the argument that the deleterious effects of systemic processes have accumulated in the Regeneration areas to such an extent that complex area effects have been created that are feeding the downward spiral of out-migration and increased residualisation. The population trends noted above lend support to this position.

If the need for an area-based approach in Limerick is accepted, the next question is whether the correct areas have been targeted. In general terms, this would appear to be the case, as the designated Regeneration areas have been shown earlier to have the highest concentrations of two of the key poverty risk factors: unemployment and lone-parent families. The 2006 data also reveal that, even before the onset of the current recession and the accompanying crisis in the public finances, there were signs of a worrying economic deterioration in these areas.[37] For example, having decreased between 1996 and 2002, the unemployment rate in both St Mary's Park and O'Malley Park increased sharply between 2002 and 2006. The economic climate and budgetary position since 2006, and the expected social fall-out from rising unemployment, welfare cuts and contracting household incomes, together point to the likelihood that the already serious problems in these areas will be exacerbated in the short to medium term. At the same time, it must be recognised that social problems are by no means confined to the Regeneration areas, in part due to the effects of the migration trends noted above in dispersing at-risk groups throughout the city and producing a more fine-grained geography of poverty and deprivation. One consequence is that there has been a decrease in the incidence of poverty in the Regeneration estates, i.e. in the percentage of the city's poor who live there, and hence a corresponding decrease in the effectiveness of area-based interventions as a means of targeting the poor. While effective or complete targeting of those in need has never been put forward as a justification of the Limerick Regeneration programme, these trends towards the de-concentration of poverty and disadvantage underscore the fact that area-based measures should be seen as a complement to, not a substitute for, the provision of mainstream social supports that are based on an individual's or a family's personal circumstances rather than their place of residence.

Closely related to the issue of whether interventions should be area-based or not is the question of the content of those measures, and in particular the mix of economic, social and environmental initiatives. The Regeneration master plan sets out a wide range of actions in all three domains, but it is the environmental or physical measures, involving the extensive construction of new housing in completely re-designed estates, that are the most detailed. They are also the only fully costed measures, presumably because they will be delivered by the Regeneration Agencies themselves as opposed to other statutory service providers. If the physical Regeneration programme is delivered on the scale that is planned, the benefits will be considerable. However, these benefits are unlikely to be sustained in the longer term if they are not supported by appropriate social measures in areas such as health, education and family support, and also by economic improvements. On the economic side, the measures proposed by the Regeneration master plan include investments in hard infrastructure and in enterprise support, as well as fiscal incentives for employers, which are designed to stimulate the demand for labour. One of the problems of localised measures designed to boost labour demand is that there can be no guarantee that the resulting jobs will go to locals. For this reason, and because the planned infrastructural investments also transcend the local scale, it is important that a wider city-region perspective be maintained. This in turn raises the issue of the linkage between the Regeneration programme and the governance of the urban area as a whole. The key element of urban governance remains the local government itself, and there is growing evidence of the importance of local government to the economic performance of urban areas. At the time of writing, the Limerick Local Government Committee has been established by the Minister for the Environment, Heritage and Local Government to review the civil administration of Limerick City and County. The committee's recommendation will have significant long-term implications not just for the provision of public services in the city but for the local and regional economy, and hence for the Regeneration areas and other disadvantaged areas of Limerick.

2. Getting a Fix on Crime in Limerick

Ciarán McCullagh

For many, the dominant framework through which Limerick is perceived is that of crime, whether this is through its incarnation as 'stab city' or its more recent re-designation as the 'murder capital of Europe', yet most forms of crime are relatively infrequent occurrences in the city. The criminal image of Limerick has come from a small but socially significant amount of criminal activity that emanates from the illegal drugs economy that has taken root in the city. Thus, Limerick is at first sight an apparent anomaly, a low-crime city with a serious crime problem.

However, crime in Limerick may not be the anomaly that it first appears. Arguably, it is simply a microcosm of how crime in many countries has developed in the last two decades. This pattern is reflected in the stabilising or lowering of rates of conventional crime, accompanied by the institutionalisation of an industry that has global reach but which thrives on local demand: the industry based on the importation, distribution and sale of illegal drugs. The illegal drugs economy takes hold most rapidly in urban areas where participation in the formal economy is weak and where involvement in the drugs economy offers alternative outlets for entrepreneurship, employment and wealth accumulation.[1] However, because the drugs trade is illegal and profits are significant and relatively recession-proof, violence and conflict around market control are endemic.

The central argument of this chapter is that while local factors are obviously important, understanding crime in Limerick requires us to look beyond local dynamics and situate the city's crime problem in a national and international framework. Hence, an unwavering focus on the individuals and criminal gangs involved is inaccurate and incomplete.[2] Ultimately, the root of this criminal activity is in the continued demand for illegal drugs and the willingness of ordinary citizens to pay high prices for them.

Figuring Out the Figures

The basis for understanding levels of crime in Limerick and throughout Ireland is the official statistics collected by An Garda Síochána and published by the Central Statistics Office.[3] Such statistics have a number of well-recognised limitations. Firstly, changes in the system of classification to accommodate new offences have made it difficult to identify precise trends in the data over time. A second and more important limitation is captured in the phrase 'crimes that became known to the Gardaí'. This classification clearly creates the possibility that crimes can, for a variety of reasons, go unreported and unknown to Gardaí.[4]

A further difficulty with official crime statistics is that they are broken down according to the six current Garda regions and further subdivided by Garda divisions which tend to follow county boundaries.[6] This means that the crime figures for Limerick are based on reported crimes in both city and county. This divisional structure creates problems in identifying and understanding the nature of serious crime in Limerick city itself. In addition, it makes it difficult to compare statistics for crime in Limerick city with other parts of the country, most notably Dublin city.

The problem of estimating the level of unreported crime in Ireland has been partially overcome through the initiation of 'victim surveys' by the Central Statistics Office since 1998. These surveys are now a recognised part of the *Household Budget Survey*. Those interviewed are asked a series of questions relating to their experiences of crime, the reporting of crime, their level of fear of crime at home and in the street, and their level of confidence in An Garda Síochána.[5] Though these surveys are not without their own problems and they are not directly comparable to Garda statistics, victim surveys nevertheless provide a useful and important complement to official crime figures.

Investigating Official Crime Statistics

Given the changes in the classification system, it was decided to restrict the analysis of crime figures in this chapter to data gathered between 2003 and 2007, in order to contextualise the launch of the Limerick Regeneration programmes.[7] During this period, Limerick had a murder rate which was consistently higher than the national average, and higher than the murder rate of all other parts of Ireland apart from Dublin North and South Central. In 2007, however, the murder rate in Limerick was higher even than Dublin North and South Central. Over this entire period, the murder rate in Limerick was significantly higher than the murder rates in Cork or Galway.

If we add 'threats to murder' to the analysis, then the profile of Limerick city in terms of violence becomes even more distinctive. Between 2003 and 2007, 37 per cent of murder threats recorded nationally occurred in Limerick, exceeding even the numbers recorded for this crime in the Dublin divisions. The rate of offences for explosives and chemical weapons in Limerick was also distinctive. The number of recorded offences for these crimes is higher in Limerick than the national average for four of the five years examined.[8]

It is in terms of firearms offences, however, that Limerick comes into its own. In 2003, the rate of these offences in Limerick city and county was twice the national average. In 2007, it was almost five times the national average. In 2003, Limerick was second only to the western Dublin Metropolitan Region (DMR) which recorded the highest rate for such offences and between 2004 and 2007, Limerick consistently had the highest rate for such offences in the country. The number of offensive weapons crimes (involving mainly knives) in Limerick was also significantly above the national average during this period, though lower than some divisions in Dublin. Limerick had the third-highest rate of this offence in 2003, 2004 and 2005, and the fourth-highest in 2006 and 2007.[9]

The notion that such violence is linked to illegal drugs is generally accepted but not quite so easily confirmed through the crime statistics. These figures, as the Central Statistics Office note, are a more reliable guide to the level of successful Garda activity against these crimes than to the actual level of criminality linked to illegal drugs.[10] Thus, there is a very high level of detection for such offences evident in the figures, 83 per cent in 2003 and 95 per cent in 2006, which may not reflect overall levels of drugs crime in the country.

The number of 'importation of drugs' offences nationally is fairly low and largely confined to urban areas.[11] The Dublin Metropolitan Region area is the main location for such offences,[12] with small numbers of offences recorded in Galway, Cork and Limerick.[13] The Limerick rate for this offence was consistently lower than the national and the Dublin rate during this period.[14] In numerical terms, the actual number of recorded importation offences in Limerick was nine in 2003, one in 2004, two in 2005, with none in 2006 and 2007. The recorded rate for 'possession of drugs for sale or supply' in Limerick was also below the national rate for 2003, 2004 and 2006 and somewhat above the national rate in 2005 and 2007. Indeed, for most of the period, the rate for such offences in Limerick city and county has been lower than in most Garda divisions in Dublin and below the rate for Cork city.[15]

In terms of the offence of 'possession of drugs for personal use', the pattern of crime between 2003 and 2007 in Limerick is not distinctive. At a national level, the number of such offences increased fairly dramatically from 3,275 in 2003 to 8,352 in 2007. This trend is reflected in Limerick by an increase from 322 offences in 2003 to 602 in 2007. But the rate of such offences in Limerick is not in any way distinctive for an urban area and, indeed, is relatively low by contrast with possession offences in Cork City, Waterford/Kilkenny, Carlow/Kildare, Laois/Offaly and many of the divisions in the Dublin Metropolitan Region.

When we look at the type of drugs that are being sold by arrested dealers and confiscated from users during this period, Limerick remains very much in line with national trends. The majority of arrests are for the possession of cannabis and cannabis resin. However, the prevalence of cannabis in terms of these crimes fell while the number of cases involving cocaine increased nationally from 11 per cent in 2003 to 16 per cent in 2007. In Limerick, the number of offences involving cocaine went up from 40 in 2003 to 135 in 2007. However, the majority of cocaine seizures during this period were still in the Dublin area and the number of drug seizure offences in Cork was higher in all five years than in Limerick.

There is little evidence of any distinctive pattern of weapon use in terms of conventional non-drug-related crime in Limerick between 2003 and 2007. In terms of 'robbery where firearms were used', the rate of such offences in Limerick was lower than the national average in four of the five years under consideration.[16] A problematic drugs culture might also become evident through a detailed examination of two specific offences: 'robberies using syringes' and 'robbery from the person', known by its more familiar and colloquial term, 'mugging'.[17] Over the five-year period, however, there was only one recorded robbery using a syringe in the Limerick division, and that was in 2004. This compares to an average of 152 per year in the Dublin Metropolitan Area.[18] Only thirty-six burglaries using syringes were recorded between 2003 and 2007, none of which were in Limerick. The number of aggravated burglaries where firearms were used in Limerick was small, two in 2003, none in 2004, five in 2005, three in 2006 and none in 2007.

The pattern in terms of 'robbery from the person' is somewhat different and the number of such offences in Limerick increased over the period, while it declined nationally. The crime rate for this offence in Limerick is higher in 2006 and 2007 than the national rates. However, the Limerick rate is still lower than most Dublin divisions and the rate in Cork city for four of the five years in question. In 2007, the average number of robberies from the person per week in the Dublin Metropolitan Region was 16, in Cork city 1.5 and in Limerick 1.38.

The crime rate for 'theft from the person' in Limerick is consistently higher than the national rate for such offences. In 2003, the national rate was 1.67, in Limerick it was 2.22. However, this rate was still significantly lower than Dublin North Central and Dublin South Central. By 2008, the rates for these crimes in Dublin and Limerick had reduced significantly, coming down to 0.68 at a national level, 5.68 in Dublin North Central, 5.83 in Dublin South Central, and 1.02 in Limerick. So while Limerick has preserved its distinctiveness as the area with the highest rate of 'muggings' outside Dublin, this rate is still significantly below that of inner-city Dublin.

This fluctuating pattern is also evident with the crime of arson. In 2003 and 2004, rates for this crime in Limerick city and county were below Dublin North but higher than anywhere else in the country. In 2005 and 2006, the highest number of recorded arson attacks in the country was in Limerick, twice the national average in 2005 and just under three times the national average in 2006 and 2007.[19] Therefore, while analysis of Garda statistics suggests that crime rates in Limerick are not notably different from the rest of the country, there are notable exceptions in terms of crimes of violence such as murder, firearms offences and arson.

What Do Victim Surveys Tell Us?

In an attempt to overcome the limitations of official crime statistics, the Central Statistics Office has added a series of questions on crime to the *Household Budget Survey*. The results have been compiled for 1998, 2003 and 2006. Because respondents are asked directly about their experiences of crime, victim surveys provide an alternative source of information on crime in Ireland. However, the degree to which these victim surveys can supplant official statistics is open to question. Firstly, it is unclear whether these experiences reported to researchers would be considered crimes if they had been reported to the Gardaí, given that many incidents can be relatively minor. One must also consider why an individual would report a crime to a researcher which they are not prepared to report to the Gardaí. Thirdly, victim surveys are based on random sampling of the national population and this sampling can miss the way in which victimisation may be concentrated in specific areas. National surveys which show low levels of fear in the country as a whole can hide the fact that such fears may be significantly higher in particular geographical areas.[20]

Finally, the geographical units of analysis used in these surveys corre-
spond to the eight regional authorities established under the Local
Government Act (1993). So, for example, the results of victim surveys are
presented for the Mid-West region, an area that includes Clare, Limerick
City, Limerick County and North Tipperary. We are obliged to use the
Mid-West figures as the closest approximation for the situation in
Limerick city, but it is quite possible that these figures underestimate the
extent of fear and victimisation in Limerick city itself.

For ease of presentation and because of some inconsistencies with the
2003 figures, we will examine figures from the 1998 and 2006 victim
surveys. In general, they confirm the image of Limerick as having a lower
level of crime victimisation, a lower level of fear of crime, and a higher
sense of safety than in Dublin. The percentage of individuals who reported that they had been victims of theft with violence, theft without
violence or physical assault increased nationally and regionally between
1998 and 2006. But the percentage of these crimes reported in the Mid-
West remained significantly below the rate in Dublin city.[21] The only
crime where trends in the Mid-West region are distinctive is 'theft with
violence', where in 1998 the region had the third-highest percentage of
victims in the country. By 2006, this figure had declined and the Mid-
West had the fourth-highest percentage of victims in the country.

There is also evidence of some slippage in term of the reporting of
offences to the Gardaí over the period, though overall the rates in the
Mid-West remained high. In 1998, over 71 per cent of thefts with violence
were reported in the Mid-West, compared to 63 per cent in the Dublin
area, 60 per cent in the South-West, 44 per cent in the North-West and
61.1 per cent nationally. In 2006, this level of reporting to Gardaí had
fallen in the Mid-West to 62.5 per cent but was still significantly higher
than the reporting rate in four of the eight areas.

The reasons given by respondents for not reporting offences to the
Gardaí are not broken down by region, but the national figures conform
to international trends, suggesting that the most significant reason for the
non-reporting of 'theft with violence' is that the incident was 'not serious
enough'. This pattern was the same for 'theft without violence'. The
other important reasons given were that the victims 'believed that the
Gardaí could do nothing' or more troublingly that they believed 'the
Gardaí would do nothing'. The victim's fear of reprisals was ranked very
low by most victims, only 2.4 per cent for theft with violence and 0.25
per cent for 'theft without violence'.

The figures for the Mid-West remain fairly consistent over the period.

The region was fourth in the country in terms of the numbers of people assaulted and second-lowest in terms of reporting to the Gardaí in both 1998 and 2006. In 1998, the Mid-West was the leading region for the percentage of assaults that involved 'use or threat of use of weapon'. In 2006, the region was ranked third for this crime. Again, the main reason offered by victims for non-reporting at a national level was that the incident was 'not serious enough or no loss'. This pattern of non-reporting rose from 22.5 per cent in 1998 to 40.5 per cent in 2006. The percentage who 'believed that the Gardaí could do nothing' declined fairly dramatically from 16.5 per cent in 1998 to 2 per cent in 2006. The percentage believing that the 'Gardaí would do nothing' declined also from 18.8 per cent in 1998 to 12.5 per cent in 2006.

The Mid-West does not differ significantly from other regions when we examine figures for 'feelings of safety'. The percentage of people who would feel unsafe 'walking alone in their neighbourhood' was above the national average but this was true of all regions with a major city in them. In 2006, the Mid-West was joint third with the South-West region in terms of the percentage who felt unsafe, fractionally below Dublin but the Midlands and the Border region recorded higher percentages of people who felt a 'lack of safety'. Indeed, the percentage who felt unsafe declined between 1998 and 2006 in the Mid-West.

The region recorded the second-highest percentage of people who would feel 'very safe alone in their home after dark'. This figure was 45.6 per cent in 2006, just slightly below the Dublin level and higher than the national average of 41 per cent. This percentage has remained largely unchanged since 1998. At the other extreme, the percentage who would feel 'very unsafe' fell from 1.5 per cent in 1998 to 0.9 per cent in 2006, just slightly above the national average of 0.7 per cent and lower than the 1.1 per cent recorded in the Midlands.

Perhaps the most significant increase recorded in the victim survey was in perceptions of the seriousness of the crime problem. In the Mid-West, 40.2 per cent saw crime as a 'very serious problem' in 1998, a rate above the national level but behind that of the Midlands and Dublin. This percentage, however, rose to 52.6 per cent in 2006, making the region the second highest in the country in terms of perceptions of the seriousness of crime problems.[22] The percentage of respondents who did not worry about becoming a victim of crime in the Mid-West region increased to 41.2 per cent in 2006 from 38.1 per cent in 1998. This figure is still significantly below the national average of 44.1 per cent in 1998 and 47.1 per cent in 2006. Those worried about becoming a victim of personal and property crime, at 42.3 per cent in 2006 was, by contrast, the highest in the country.

The Mid-West region is not particularly distinctive in terms of its rating of the 'Gardaí in local areas'. The percentage of respondents who would rate them as 'very good' fell from 14.2 per cent in 1998 to 8.9 per cent in 2006, but this decline reflects a national decrease from 18.6 per cent in 1998 to 9.6 per cent in 2006.[23] In 2006, 3.6 per cent thought that Gardaí were 'very poor' in the Mid-West region, compared to 4.1 per cent in Dublin, 4.8 per cent in the Midlands and 3.7 per cent nationally.

The final set of figures refers to whether households say they have experienced crime. Here, the Mid-West stands out. In 2006, 11.2 per cent of households experienced crime, the second-highest percentage in the country. The Dublin region, at 18 per cent, was highest. Yet the Mid-West figure is still close to the national average.[24] When we look at household burglaries, the Mid-West stands out: 61.5 per cent of such crimes were reported to the Gardaí in 1998. This figure fell to 52 per cent in 2006. In both years, this was the lowest level of reporting of this crime in the country and considerably below the national average. These figures look even more dramatic when we include 2003. Here the percentage reporting household burglaries to the Gardaí in the Mid-West rose to 72.7 per cent, a rate more consistent with the national average. Why these figures should rise and then fall in this fairly dramatic manner is unclear and may well be a product of the survey methodology. Finally, the number of people who had a vehicle stolen (including cars, vans, trucks, farm vehicles, motorcycles or mopeds) fell nationally and in the Mid-West region between 1998 and 2006.[25]

The analysis of victim surveys confirms that patterns of crime in Limerick are not distinctively different from national trends in terms of its level of victimisation, associated problems of fear and non-reporting to the Gardaí. These surveys also indicate that, on some measures at least, the Mid-West region has lower levels of crime than other urban areas, especially Dublin. In terms of the willingness to report criminal incidents to the Gardaí and in terms of the percentages who feel safe, the Mid-West performs significantly better than other regions. However, even though the figures are low for the Mid-West as a whole, there is still evidence that in certain parts of Limerick city, residents do lack a feeling of safety and experience considerable problems in relation to fear and intimidation.[26]

Given the overview presented, Limerick's key claim to criminal distinction between 2003 and 2007 is confined to high rates of specific violent crimes including murder, firearms offences and arson. These high rates for violent crimes are significant and require explanation. The illegal drugs business is the obvious place to look but it is important to add that while drugs are available in all parts of the country, their sale and distribution are not necessarily accompanied by the level of violence evident in Limerick, or indeed in Dublin. The problems evident in Limerick appear to be linked to the nature and development of the drugs business in the city and the pivotal position of local drugs gangs in national importation and distribution networks.

Murder as a Business Strategy

The intimate, intricate and cyclical nature of violence in Limerick is linked to internal splits and disputes created by the competition between criminal gangs for control over the supply of drugs in Limerick and the South-West generally, a business conservatively estimated to be worth in the region of €30 million. Thus, the murder that re-ignited the most long-standing feud between criminal gangs in the city was that of Eddie Ryan by Kieran Keane. Ryan had previously been an associate of the Keanes but decided to establish himself as an independent in the illegal drugs business. His failed attempt to murder Christy Keane in order to set himself up in the drugs business led directly to his own death.[27]

Kieran Keane was in turn murdered by Dessie Dundon. He was a member of the Dundon family that had grouped together with their cousins, the McCarthys. As a gang, the Dundons/McCarthys are allegedly responsible for a number of deaths. They have also imported significant amounts of weaponry. An idea of the scope and extent of these criminal armouries was provided as a result of Operation Anvil, a Garda operation set up in 2005 to target organised crime in Ireland. It confiscated 1,491 weapons, 857 in Dublin and 634 (42 per cent) in Limerick.

The splits within and between criminal gangs in Limerick have continued since 2000. Frank Ryan was connected to the McCarthy/Dundon gang but changed sides. He was murdered in 2006. His killer had a similar pattern of alliances, having changed sides in prison but keeping that information from his old associates. Ryan trusted the man, got into a car with him and was shot dead. It was alleged that Ryan himself had previously been involved in the murder of Aidan Kelly, and that his killing was a revenge attack. The ability of gang members to kill with what often seems like ease has been facilitated by gang control over significant parts of disadvantaged housing estates. As outlined in Hourigan's study in this volume, this control has been achieved through the intimidation of residents and manipulation of house purchases in these areas. Coupled with the financial resources that they command, Limerick's criminal gangs have been able to build up these strongholds, which function as secure bases for their operations.

A further contribution to these cycles of violence is provided by successful Garda activity. Such operations have prevented attacks on houses, intercepted weapons and explosives shipments and led to the seizure of drugs and weapons shipments. Yet their very success, especially when these operations have been 'intelligence led', has provoked a high level of suspicion among the gangs about informers and 'snitching'. These tensions have, in turn, created divisions in criminal gangs that have led to further violence. One split in the McCarthy/Dundon gang was provoked by the killing of a gang member whom they believed would give evidence in a murder case. Another split was caused by the seizure by Gardaí of 17.5 kg of commercial explosives. Constant fear of surveillance and Garda activity also exerts its own pressure on inter-gang relationships. The overall effect of this operational dynamic is to create suspicion, distrust and paranoia among gang members, which inevitably leads to violence.

The Commodity Chain of Drugs

We know little about the networks through which drugs are imported and distributed in Ireland. Lack of knowledge about the structure and operational dynamics of the global commodity chain of drugs globally,[28] nationally and in Limerick itself has considerably inhibited criminal justice responses to the issue. At a general level, we know that drugs come into Ireland through distribution networks that stretch through Holland, Spain and Morocco to Colombia. Specifically, we know little about how Limerick criminal gangs have formed links with drug brokers in Holland, for example, though research in the United States on 'middle market brokers' suggests that often 'one key individual has a pivotal role within the network'.[29]

As evident in Connolly's research in Dublin and Hourigan's research in Limerick in this volume, drugs crime is often accompanied by significant levels of fear and intimidation. Connolly comments, 'The operation of local drug markets can engender significant apprehension and reluctance among local residents to co-operate with law enforcement initiatives because of fear of reprisal from drug dealers.'[30] Therefore, while the poor and marginalised may not necessarily be the main users of many kinds of illegal drugs, particularly the more expensive ones such as cocaine, they play an inordinate price for their existence.

There has been little in terms of community response to crime in Limerick apart from a march led by the family of Roy Collins in 2009. However, the absence of community-based responses may be an indication that street markets are not as important a factor in the drugs business in Limerick as the pubs and clubs that serve as retail outlets. In this context, 'controlling the doors',[31] either through having bouncers deal the drugs or allowing drugs to be sold in their establishments, has become the focus for criminal activity in the city. It provides the context for understanding the murder of Brian Fitzgerald, head of security at Doc's nightclub, and for understanding the dangers that bouncers face in trying to limit the availability of drugs in the city.

The activities of the Limerick gangs and their feuding are similar to and possibly less dramatic than those around the gang associated with Martin Hyland in Dublin, but they illustrate the way in which suspicion, division, deceit and paranoia is an endemic feature of organised crime. Hyland's gang shot Patrick Harte in May 2006 because he was trying to set up his own business in Holland. They shot Paul Reay in November 2006 because they believed that he was a police informer. Hyland was himself murdered in December 2006 by an associate who wanted to take over the gang. This incident received widespread coverage and became the source of considerable moral outrage because Anthony Campbell was also murdered in the same attack. He was an apprentice plumber who happened to be doing some work in the house at the time. So the problems of divisions among gang members and the associated violence are not peculiar to Limerick but are inherent features of how illegal drugs economies work.

Criminological studies in the United States show that 'systemic violence over turf or as a means of punishing subordinates'[32] is endemic in the drugs business. Reuter has argued that there are two forms of violence in drugs markets, 'disciplinary' violence used against gang members and 'successional' violence used to gain control over drugs gangs and drugs markets.[33] International research has also suggested that those who operate in the middle regions of the drugs trade want stability and predictability in their business dealings. They desire co-operation rather than conflict or violence. They recognise violence as having a role in the way they do business, whether as a means of debt enforcement, market acquisition or as security against other criminals. But, as Pearson and Hobbs argue, they also see violence as something to be avoided. It is bad for business, attracts extensive police attention, drives away customers, and 'invariably leads to more violence'.[34] So co-operation is seen as more productive than turf wars and violent conflict. Those involved in this kind of serious crime would prefer it to be organised. When such co-operation does arise, there can be lulls in inter-gang violence and periods when there is some level of instrumental trust between criminals, but such periods of calm are deceptive and short-lived. Arguably the conditions that allow for successful and profitable drug supply have an inbuilt defect. The amount of profit involved, the ease with which it is made and the inability of policing to significantly disrupt drug activities allow those involved to 'develop a sense of exaggerated personal power and invulnerability'[35] and that invariably leads to them overreaching themselves.

A sense of omnipotence allows criminals to move beyond what is acceptable and necessary behaviour to protect their business and to interfere with those who might be regarded as non-combatants or innocent bystanders. Murdering outsiders is a key example, whether this be Veronica Guerin by the Gilligan gang, Anthony Campbell by the Hyland gang or Roy Collins by the McCarthy/Dundon gang. It draws the wrath of legal society down on them, disrupts their activities, subjects them to intense levels of police surveillance, and produces mutual suspicion and distrust. The ultimate contradiction in organised crime is that the very conditions that produce criminal organisations also produce the qualities that undermine them. The problem for a society is the length of time that it takes for such disorganisation and disintegration to manifest itself. Thus, as the state learns more about how to deal with drugs crime and drugs criminals, criminal gangs learn how to deal with state responses to them.

Christy Keane may have been arrested almost accidentally carrying a sack with an estimated €240,000 worth of cannabis across a field in a housing estate in Limerick in August 2001. It is unlikely that gang members are repeating this scenario. Distribution networks are in all likelihood now more sophisticated and involve more distance between senior gang members and street dealers. This development is also reflected in increased understanding of forensic technologies. When Liam Keane was arrested in May 2008 for possession of a firearm, he was wearing latex gloves. These, the judge was told in court, were to frustrate the capacity of the Gardaí to obtain forensic evidence from the weapon. Someone had obviously been watching 'CSI'[36] with some interest. There is also evidence of learning in terms of gang members' capacity to hide assets from the Criminal Assets Bureau. Indeed, they will also undoubtedly learn how to circumvent the current phone tapping and wire tap evidence legislation. Whatever initial effectiveness these measures might have, their success will be limited as gang members adapt quickly to new investigation and prosecution techniques.

Thus, the drugs business in Limerick shares features that are universal – the desire for monopoly control and the inability to obtain it, the use of violence as a business strategy, the growing sophistication of the criminals involved, and the inherent instability, paranoia and violence provoked by the level of police surveillance. However, what is most unusual about the situation in Limerick is not the degree to which it conforms to contemporary images of criminal organisation but the degree to which it is different. Research in Britain has found that the territorial basis of organised crime is disintegrating as the working-class communities that gave it shelter also disintegrate. Recent de-industrialisation 'has removed the material foundation' upon which these communities which sheltered criminal gangs were built. As the communities disintegrate and fragment, it has become 'difficult for family-based units to establish the kind of parochial dominance that they once enjoyed in the 1950s and 1960s'.[37] In the process, organised crime has become disassociated from its traditional territories and those involved have been redistributed 'over a wide, amorphous territory'.[38] The degree of embeddedness of criminal gangs in working-class communities has been broken largely because these communities have also been broken.

In Limerick, drugs gangs remain territorial in nature, although the reach of their activities extends far beyond local enclaves. While there may be a market for heroin in such disintegrating communities, the market for the more profitable drugs such as marijuana, dance drugs and cocaine extends far beyond local users. Indeed, these drugs are also commonplace in 'the newly defined leisure ghettos of the postindustrial city', areas defined by the 'whims of a predominantly youthful market'.[39] It is no longer necessary for organised drug gangs to be resident in the same areas as their clientele, but it does not reduce the need for the protections that living in a local enclave offers them. Some of their business may have left working-class areas but that does not require them to leave also.

The Elephant in the Room

The question of customers brings us to the elephant in the room. We are accustomed to think of drugs crime in Limerick, as elsewhere in the country, in terms of the malevolent personal qualities of those who deal in drugs. But this perspective ignores one crucial factor: that the illegal drugs business, like all other business, depends on customers to buy the products. The demand for drugs in Ireland appears to be significant and relatively consistent over time. It is this demand and the state's prohibition on how this demand can be satisfied that creates an illegal drugs industry. As long as this demand exists, the profits to be made from illegal drugs will be significant and criminal gangs will always emerge to serve the needs of these consumers.

Wider Irish society has tended to ignore its own role in generating the violence linked to drugs crime, with Garda and media discourse on the issue highlighting the huge gap which exists between normal law-abiding citizens and those involved in the illegal drugs industry. Central to this process is the phrase 'known to the Gardaí'. Because of this phrase, when we hear of a murder we do not release our sympathy until we know whether the person involved was 'known to the Gardaí'. If the person was 'known to the Gardaí' then that sympathy is withheld. The phrase serves two functions. It reassures us that murder is not the kind of thing that happens to people like 'us'. We may know members of the Gardaí but we are not 'known' to them. It is only disreputable people who are 'known' on these terms.

The other function performed by the phrase 'known to the Gardaí' is equally destructive. It creates the impression that people 'known to the Gardaí' who are killed either deserve it or are in some way partly responsible for their own deaths. If they are the kind of people that the Gardaí 'know' then they are the kind of people who have a certain familiarity with violence. Thus, their families are less likely to be upset when they become victims of drugs-related violence. Only when the violence extends beyond those 'known to the Gardaí' and touches innocent law-abiding citizens does it become a matter of serious public concern. In this process, being 'innocent' and being 'known to the Gardaí' become irreconcilable and incompatible statuses. Therefore, the phrase 'known to the Gardaí' operates as a kind of comfort blanket for mainstream Irish society. It relieves us of the need to feel sympathy for those who lose family members in drugs-related crime. But like all comfort blankets the relief that it provides can only be temporary. In the long term, our unwillingness to condemn such crimes turns slowly into an indifference to such deaths. Thus, drug-related murders become routinised.

The Politics of Class Reproduction

The issue of social class is important to the understanding of how the drugs business works and how it persists. The business takes hold in disadvantaged communities where residents lack education and employment and often live in poor-quality housing. As both McCafferty and O'Connell demonstrate in this volume, intersecting patterns of global and national economic change have resulted in social exclusion and socio-economic marginalisation of communities in these areas in Limerick.[40] Hagan argues that social exclusion provokes attempts by individuals and communities to re-capitalise their lives. Drugs-related crime is one of the most significant forms of this re-capitalisation. Hagan comments, 'In the absence of better sources of employment, drug dealing is a primary route to gaining material symbols of wealth and success in the neighbourhood.'[41] What drug dealing offers is a way out of poverty, but this promise is an illusion. This kind of crime is not a form of social mobility. What it offers in Limerick is death or prison. Drugs-related criminality undermines community life and the pattern of court appearance and prison sentences further isolates participants from legitimate employment and mainstream society. Indeed what is placed at risk is more fundamental than their life chances, it is their very lives.

As the use of cocaine increases in Irish society, the centrality of social class to the drugs nexus also becomes clear. Middle-class drug users have what appear to be considerable appetites for drugs and have the money to support their patterns of use. They are unwilling to go into disadvantaged areas that they consider to be dangerous in order to get their supplies. Hence, the drugs business moves to more user-friendly locations and in this way the act of consumption becomes separated from the locations of production and distribution. As a result, middle-class consumers become shielded from the social damage that their use of drugs inflicts on other people. Illegal drugs may connect Southill or Moyross to Colombia or Bolivia, but they are also what connects these areas to the citizens of richer and more privileged areas of Limerick city.

PART TWO

Living with Fear and Feuding
in Limerick

Living with Fear and Feuding in Limerick

Niamh Hourigan

In 1965, sociologist Liam Ryan conducted a study of one of Limerick's most deprived neighbourhoods. In his book *Social Dynamite*, he predicted that the anger, deprivation and social exclusion that he found there would lead to an explosion. These communities were, in fact, dynamite, primed to explode in the faces of the more middle-class citizens of Limerick city who made comments like, 'If you have the grace of God, keep out of the place.'[1] Ryan was not alone in his predictions. In his memoir, BBC journalist Feargal Keane describes his experience of reporting on the Limerick courts in the 1970s as 'shocking', writing:

> The defendants were almost exclusively drawn from the city's council estates. Their crimes ranged from theft of a church poor box to hideous gang rape. They were whey-faced and thin, coughing from cigarettes . . . They were destined for jail, followed by unemployment and jail again. The system regarded these young men with contempt and they returned the compliment . . . Meanwhile anybody who suggested that the city's crime problem might be getting a little out of control was roundly condemned. It was in Limerick that I first heard that favourite phrase of the politician 'You're after blowing that way out of proportion'. A journalist who hears that should realise he is onto something good. The reckoning in Limerick would come long after I left the city.[2]

The launch of the Regeneration programmes for Limerick's disadvantaged estates in 2008 was an effective acknowledgement by the state that the day of reckoning had indeed arrived. A series of savage gangland murders, coupled with random violent attacks on ordinary citizens in these areas which culminated in the burning of two young children in their car, made it increasingly difficult to deny that Limerick had a serious problem with violent crime.[3] However, despite the launch of a whole array of plans and documents for regeneration, very little understanding of the route by which social exclusion produces violent crime in Limerick has emerged.

Within the Fitzgerald Report for instance, descriptions of social exclusion in Limerick are detailed and unequivocal. Fitzgerald concludes, 'The picture that emerged during visits to these estates and discussions with residents and community workers was in many cases quite shocking. The quality of life for many people is extremely poor.'[4] However, even Fitzgerald seems unsure of how exactly this social exclusion generates feuding, intimidation and drugs-related organised crime. Tentative comments such as 'It has been suggested to me that criminals use young children to support their criminal activities because they cannot be prosecuted' indicate the limitations to his understanding of local criminality.[5] Given the short time-frame in which Fitzgerald researched his report, this weakness is understandable, but a vagueness concerning the link between social exclusion and violent crime pervades both the policy literature and the media commentary on Limerick's problems.

Within international social policy research, a strong link has been identified between social exclusion and violent crime.[6] In Ireland, attempts to map this link have emerged in two major fields of research. Within housing studies, Tony Fahey, Cathal O'Connell and Michelle Norris have examined how Irish government housing policy has contributed to spatial concentrations of the socially excluded in public housing. They argue that within these housing estates, crimes ranging from antisocial behaviour to violent assault are more likely to occur as a consequence of this spatial clustering of the disdvantaged.[7] In addition, criminologists Ian O'Donnell, Eoin O'Sullivan and Ciarán McCullagh have explored how the Irish criminal justice system imprisons the socially excluded while delivering less punitive punishments to white-collar criminals.[8] Again, their studies focus on wider societal factors such as the methods of crime statistics compilation by Gardaí, the ranking of the seriousness of offences within the Irish courts and the public perception of crime in Ireland. However, there is a clear absence of ethnographic research which examines how social exclusion generates violent crime at community level on a daily basis within the Irish state.[9]

Within American sociology, there is a long tradition of ethnographic research on gangs and organised crime which dates back to the work of Robert Merton in Chicago during the 1930s. He and his colleagues at the University of Chicago conducted a series of ethnographic studies which sought to understand the world-view of those involved in street gangs and organised crime.[10] This study of fear and feuding in Limerick city is rooted within this American ethnographic tradition. It seeks to provide insight into how the experience of living in Limerick's deprived estates has produced both the perpetrators and victims of one the most serious criminal cultures to have emerged in Ireland since the foundation of the state.

The research was conducted at three levels. Some 221 interviews were conducted with local residents, those on the fringes of criminal gangs, Gardaí, social, community and youth workers.[11] In addition, approximately one hundred hours of participant observation was conducted in a variety of locations, including streets, pubs, bookies, churches, community centres, playgrounds, shops and local public events.[12] Approximately one-third of the participant observation was conducted at night, while two-thirds was conducted during daylight hours. The observation data gathered at night yielded significantly different findings from data gathered during the day-time. Finally, the findings of the research were presented to four focus groups of residents from estates across the city.

In contacting interviewees, a 'networks of trust' approach was adopted.[13] The strongest assurances of anonymity and confidentiality were provided. The names of all interviewees quoted in this study have been changed and no identifying information appears in this text.[14] Within the interview cohort, attempts were made to generate a gender balance (though women were generally more ready to participate).[15] A range of different age groups were included, and the views of those on each side of the various local feuds were represented.

Because of the dangers of this type of research, the names of Limerick's major criminal families do not appear in direct quotes from interviewees. The term 'Reds' and 'Blues' are used to denote opposing family groups in local feuds.[16] This change is not designed to protect the identity of Limerick's criminal families, as their identities are well known through media reports and the 'true crime' publishing genre. Rather the names have been changed to protect the identities of those whose comments might identify them as being on a particular side within local feuds. Finally, it is important to note that during the three years of this study, the intensity of feuding and intimidation fluctuated considerably. While localised 'regimes of fear' were unravelling in some estates under pressure from policing and regeneration responses, new sites of intimidation and community violence were opening up in other parts of the city. Despite this fluctuation dynamic, however, the underlying structures of criminal hierarchies, the ideology of feuding and the mechanics of intimidation remained constant during the course of this research.

3. A History of Social Exclusion in Limerick

Niamh Hourigan

Limerick[1] is the third-largest city in the Republic of Ireland. It is situated on the banks of the River Shannon and has a population of over 90,000. The city dates from the Viking settlement of 812 and prominent city landmarks such as King John's Castle were constructed in the twelfth century. By the nineteenth century, Limerick had developed as a prominent hub for trade and manufacturing in Ireland.[2] The mainstay of this industrial development was bacon curing and other food processing, such as the production of condensed milk and sweets. Limerick also had large tanneries, flour mills, tobacco factories and clothing companies. This bustling trade produced not only a wealthy class of largely Anglo-Irish merchants and a burgeoning Catholic middle class but also an unusually large industrial working class. At the bottom of this social spectrum were the inhabitants of Limerick's slums, sometimes employed as casual unskilled labourers, more often not employed at all, who lived in the horrendous conditions later made famous in Frank McCourt's memoir *Angela's Ashes*.[3]

As Limerick city grew in the twentieth century, the merchant and middle classes gradually moved out to the new suburbs on the city's north- and south-sides. The labouring and working classes tended to remain closer to the city centre in neighbourhoods near the factories and the docks. This class developed its own distinctive culture which combined sport and musical activities with high levels of public devotion to the Catholic Church.[4]

The Catholic Church was located at the apex of this communal life, with the confessional devotions and lay organisations of the Redemptorist Fathers exerting a particularly profound influence on the world-view of these communities.[5] The lack of a university in the city contributed to a marked rigidity in Limeric's class structure. There were few outlets for the more able members of the working classes to achieve upward mobility. Prior to independence, the city had developed a reputation for industrial militancy which may have contributed to the establishment of the Limerick Soviet in 1919.[6]

However, it was the conditions of Limerick's slums which drew most attention from national and international commentators, even in the early part of the twentieth century. In 1909, travel writer Thomas Johnson described his growing horror as he walked through parts of the city:

> I could not help but wonder what strange notions of comfort the inhabitants of that city must have had to crowd their homes together in such as fashion when so many square miles of open country lay all round about. But, when I took a walk along those lanes and alleys, my wonder was turned to disgust when I found that these houses were not only crowded into congested areas but many were unsanitary and unfit for human habitation . . . Evidently on this planet it is not a crime to take advantage of a man's poverty and make a profit out of a death trap.[7]

Life was very tough for the residents of Limerick's slums. A typical tenement building could be shared by six families.[8] While some of these buildings had running water, almost none had sanitation or heating systems apart from open fires. Even worse was housing in the city's notorious lanes where large families lived in one-room cottages which not only lacked sanitation, heating and water but often did not have doors, windows or adequate roofing. The stresses of slum life created intimacy and interdependency, particularly during major life transitions such as childbirth and death. Families helped each other with clothing, food, and the celebration of major religious occasions such as christenings, first communions and weddings was marked by very high levels of mutual support.[9]

Despite this mutual aid, poverty also created potential for conflict. Fights could emerge over theft of scarce resources such as food or clothing, while the stress of conditions contributed to problems such as alcohol addiction and domestic violence. Throughout these communities, there was a strong culture of 'no grassing' to the authorities about petty thefts or local conflicts.[10]

Even after the establishment of the Irish Free State in 1922, this distrust of the police force remained, while at the same time it was recognised that Limerick continued to have 'an appalling shortage of decent housing'.[11] Some attempts were made at slum clearance between the 1930s and 1950s with the building of St Mary's Park and Ballinacurra Weston.[12] Although the quality of the housing improved in these areas, there was little change to the material conditions of resident families. It was still extremely difficult to get a job in Limerick. Individuals who had associations with particular factories tended to ensure their own children were employed in new vacancies. Mastriani writes:

> While most of the jobs in the older industries of Limerick did not require a high level of formal education, they were, in some sense, exclusive clubs of which those who had the right to join were quite proud . . . Since one could only enter most of the factories through a close family connection, there was also a great sense of community in these factories.[13]

The existence of these clubs meant that few opportunities existed for even the most ambitious young people from Limerick's most marginalised classes. While girls in their early teens could sometimes find work in factories, boys at the same age were most often employed as messenger boys by factories and local shops. Writing in the mid '60s, Liam Ryan found that the majority of the girls ceased working upon marriage and the boys found that they were unemployable once they had outgrown the messenger boy role in their late teens. He notes that:

> By the age of nineteen they feel that that they are men but they are still getting a boy's wage. Suddenly they are aware of the contrast with the apprenticeship boys who are now earning up to £15 a week. It is not easy for them to accept the situation and many seek a solution in emigration. Those who remain hang around on the street corners or hold up in the doorways of the bookmaker's shops, but nobody is going to employ them.[14]

Describing the childhood of the late Mikey Kelly, a reformed Limerick criminal and local politician, Galvin notes how small-scale criminal activity became a part of the struggle for survival by some members of this marginalised class. He describes how from the age of nine, Kelly

> stole vegetables and meat from city-centre shops to feed the family. Initially his father disapproved . . . But that gradually changed. With such a large family, their cramped living conditions, low income and the drinking, the fabric of the family was strained . . . 'I fed the family for two year' boasted Michael Kelly. 'My father was drinking at the time . . . They didn't mind the stealing because it put food on the table.'[15]

Although some of this small-scale crime was aimed at businesses in the city centre, some local neighbours were also victims. Kelly describes stealing food from local families and snatching money from local tradesmen.[16] There was a constant latent tension in these communities between the families whose fathers were employed, and who had enough to eat, and those who had almost nothing. It was this latter group who were most likely to slip into long-term criminality.[17]

Even as Limerick's industrial sector developed in the early 1960s, the problem of housing in the city continued to be the subject of national concern. Older local authority housing estates had become overcrowded, and in some parts of Limerick families were still living in slum tenements. In 1962, Minister for Local Government Neil Blaney caused a national furore by claiming that Limerick had some of the worst slums in the country.[18] While the city fathers initially poured scorn on these claims, the *Limerick Leader* estimated that there were about 868 unfit houses in the city and 624 families urgently in need of accommodation. Willie Gleeson wrote, 'Is it possible that in this year of grace 1962, there are human beings in this city – 97% Catholic – living in condemned houses in the matter of sanitation and ventilation that is the last word in things archaic? Again, the answer is yes.'[19] He describes hovels which are derelict, 'infested with rats and flies plus an abominable stench which pervades throughout every household'.[20] He concludes that

> Limerick's housing shortage is still acute. It is conservatively esti-
> mated that over one thousand houses are still needed to meet the
> city's requirements. Many families are in desperate plight for accom-
> modation and the problem is still the Corporation's number one
> headache.[21]

Successive modernising governments during the 1960s publicly pres-surised Limerick Corporation to improve housing conditions.[22] Two major housing initiatives were undertaken as part of this response, the development of Southill which began in 1967 on the city's southside and the construction of Moyross on the north-side in the early 1970s. However, because of the intensity of the housing crisis, Limerick Corporation appeared to focus on the provision of new housing units to the exclusion of other forms of community infrastructure.[23] Tony, who grew up in Moyross, describes the consequences of this poor planning:

> There were no shops in Moyross for my first seven or eight years
> there. We would have to walk ten minutes to the shops in Ballynanty.
> When I was about eleven a family opened a shop in their house in
> Cosgrove Park and another shop opened a few months later. There
> was no school, no community centre, no bars or pubs and no medical
> facilities. It was crazy really.[24]

Despite the lack of infrastructure in these new estates, the absence of playgrounds, schools, churches and even bus services, many families were very happy in their new homes. Eileen recalls how proud she was when she and her husband got their first house in Moyross. 'Cosgrove Park always looked so well and we could see the Clare Hills in the distance, it was beautiful. I was delighted when I came here.' Tony notes, 'we were five minutes walk from the country before Glenagross went up. We would cross the railway and be in the country. We had great freedom then.' Catherine, who moved with her family to Southill in the 1970s, recalls

> They were big houses, they were three bedroomed. A big hall, straight ahead was a dining room and in the living room there was an arch. Two fine bedrooms and a box-room. I must have been about six or seven and the first thing I can remember is the freedom of playing up here and there was all people playing who were my age.

The populations of Moyross and Southill during the 1970s combined the households of low-income workers with families who had been moved from the tenements of the city. Stacey comments, 'In my block, we had nurses, we had ambulance drivers. They would have been professional people, they were all working. There were dockers, ESB, CIE.' These working families were intermingled with tenement families who had less access to secure employment. Even in the mid '60s, Ryan identified that this group was having more difficulty in adjusting to life in the new estates. He comments

> And so they were uprooted and from being ten families in one house, or ten children in one cellar, they moved into beautiful big three-bedroomed houses. But they just could not cope with the new situation. They lost many of their roots. Their friends and neighbours of years and years were lost. They had no choice as to where they would go or when they would go.[25]

In analysing the sociological profile of these estates, Ryan argues that there was evidence of a deliberate attempt by authorities to mix the poorer families with the more affluent 'in the hope they would set the standard of the locality'.[26] However, interviews for this study indicate, that even in the 1970s, a marked heterogeneity had emerged, with some 'parks' and 'courts' being populated almost entirely by families of workers while other neighbourhoods had much higher rates of unemployment and disadvantage. In areas of the estates where the two groups were mixed, there was evidence of the conflict even in the 1970s centring on different cultural values, different modes of survival and opposing views of the state and its agencies.[27]

Despite this tension, there was relative stability in these neighbourhoods during the 1970s. The more advantaged families in these estates tended to dominate community activities. Karen describes how

> Sporting activities – football and athletics, for example – were run by parents in the community and there was never a shortage of kids to get involved or parents to help out. There was also a summer play scheme every year run by parents as well as older teenagers. We would be taken on day trips, swimming, given art classes. These were very successful throughout all my childhood in Moyross. It was very happy.

These community activists formed new organisations such as Southill and Moyross Community Councils. They launched successful campaigns for schools and bus services and raised funds for new church buildings. Cultural and social organisations such as scout troops, girl guides and church choirs were established. Some of these community leaders went on to have a prominent role in the broader city context, such as Southill's Tommy Allen, who became mayor of the city in 1981.

However, even during this relatively stable period, there is evidence of a struggle between these more affluent families who were providing community leadership and some of the more disadvantaged families in these estates. Without employment, men from these families were more likely to succumb to addiction or become involved in small-scale criminal activities. Teenagers from this group saw little reason to remain in school as they had little chance of future employment. Resistance to school was also based on the perception that no amount of education would be sufficient to overcome the stigma associated with living in Limerick's local authority housing estates. Ryan's study quotes one young boy:

> Secondary school! For God's sake, if you are from Parkland [Ballinacurra Weston] you might as well be on a football team for five years as be in a secondary school for five years. You just haven't a hope.[28]

A local teacher confirmed the presence of this stigma, commenting:

> I have seen lovely girls come to me for a reference and they say, 'If you put Parkland at the top we won't get anything.' And they ask me to put down some other address or place where there might not be a house half as good but the name isn't attached to the place.[29]

With little hope of a job, low levels of education and plenty of time on their hands, the activities of teenagers from these disadvantaged families became a source of tension between the advantaged and disadvantaged families in these estates as early as 1972. Boys, in particular, were inclined to hang around in public spaces in groups and intimidate other residents. They were involved in very small-scale antisocial behaviour such as throwing stones and name-calling. By today's standards, these activities appear mild, but local residents in Southill viewed them so seriously that they repeatedly demanded the construction of a Garda sub-station in the area during the 1970s.[30]

These calls, though unheeded by civic authorities, were evidence of a serious culture clash which was emerging between relatively advantaged working families and teenagers from the more disadvantaged families, who viewed the streets as the 'stage' where they could assert themselves, exert control and demand respect from others. This respect was based on generating fear among neighbours and an admiration among their male and female peers. Although Mikey Kelly described the day he moved to Southill as 'the worst day of his life', he acknowledges that he quickly sought to become a dominant force on the streets of the area by physically demanding, through fighting, this form of respect. Galvin comments, 'A powerfully built man, he was a good fighter, and he never shied away from a fight. "Thank God there was no such thing as weapons in those days," he said. But of course, there were weapons later, and eventually he graduated to them.'[31]

However, it is possible with hindsight to over-estimate the seriousness of the problems in these estates during this period. Many residents have positive memories of a place where the majority of citizens were law-abiding and where people went out of their way to help their neighbours and support the local community. In Moyross, Liam says, 'every summer each estate would get together and have a big clean up of the area; we would leave the key in the front door so we could go in and out as we pleased, kids would go into their friends using the front door key.' Most disputes caused by the bad behaviour of local children were resolved by consulting the child's parent, who punished the child accordingly. In any case, bad behaviour was rarely so serious that it required involving the Gardaí. Mick, who lived in Southill at this time, says, 'In the '70s there wouldn't have been anything as bad as a broken window, I don't really remember anything like that, I remember fighting and bitching between kids, you know, but that's all.' While Billy comments, 'I remember, we broke two windows playing football on the street and this was sorted out by all our parents being contacted and the windows being replaced and paid for by our parents.'

As the 1970s progressed and the first generation of local children began to mature, the streets of some of Limerick's local authority housing estates began to show signs of the emergence of an informal power hierarchy based on physical toughness and being a 'hard man'.[32] Those at the top of this emerging 'hard man' hierarchy had to continually fight off young contenders to maintain their position while the younger boys who wanted to make their name in this informal power structure had to be willing to fight the big names. Mikey Kelly's story is typical in that he admits, 'Up to the age of sixteen I lost more than I won, because I was always fighting older guys.'[33] However, it was through these fights that he achieved his status in the local street fraternity. This route to achieving local status and respect may not have involved going to school or participating in the formal economy but for people from the most excluded sectors of Limerick's disadvantaged estates, it was an immediate and relatively successful route to achieving alternative forms of status. The most visible sign of the emergence of this 'hard man' hierarchy was the increasing antisocial behaviour of teenage gangs which provoked concern among the more law-abiding residents of these estates. Some of these teenagers were also graduating from low-level antisocial behaviour to more violent crimes such as robbery and burglary.[34]

Behind the scenes, more serious criminal networks were also developing among those at the top of this hierarchy. Vincent comments, 'The Guards were so busy trying to keep the kids under control that the more serious boys were able to get on with their business in peace really.' Sean notes that there were 'always families who lived on the edge, they would have been hawkers, also involved in receiving stolen goods but successfully living on the edge and more affluent than their neighbours.'[35] It was these families who began to exploit these growing tensions and street conflicts for their own ends.

Intertwining with increasingly organised if small-scale criminal activity, a number of disadvantaged families had brought their practice of feuding with them to the newer estates. The pattern of tit-for-tat violence which characterised these feuds impacted on the quality of life of neighbouring families and provided another dimension to the growing complexity of the local criminal power structure.

As more affluent families in these estates became increasingly concerned about growing street violence and criminality, they used their community organisations as a forum to vent their anger at authorities who failed to take action. In the late 1970s, one local councillor publicly complained that the people of Southill were living in fear and terror. Cllr Frank

Leddin added that 'youths from seven to fourteen years of age were causing the most problems and that they were getting off lightly from the courts because of lack of criminal capacity'.[36] However, authorities did little to respond to their concerns and, subsequently, a number of changes occurred at global and national level which tipped the balance of power in these neighbourhoods towards residents with criminal orientations.

During the late 1970s and early '80s, Limerick city was hit by a series of factory closures which decimated its traditional industries. Large employers such as Matterson's, Rank's, Halpin's and the Limerick Clothing Company all closed their doors. The closure of these factories had a profound impact on the city's working class, both in terms of the sharp decline of their income and the undermining of the strong cultural identity which accompanied a job in these firms. There are striking similarities between this period in Limerick's history and the same period in English cities such as Sheffield and Newcastle, where factory closures led not only to economic decline but also to a sense of social and cultural isolation among former factory workers.

The decline of these indigenous industries was coupled with the closure of a number of factories owned by multinational corporations which had also been significant employers in the region, such as Ferenka and Wang. The working-class families who were the backbone of the more affluent groups in these estates were deeply affected by these changes. Many families slipped deeper into poverty, and the ranks of the 'disadvantaged' in Moyross, Southill, Ballinacurra Weston and St Mary's Park, in particular, swelled significantly.

Unfortunately, the most significant blow to the sociological profile of these estates came from government policy itself. Between 1984 and 1987, the Irish government instituted a tenancy surrender scheme in order to free up more local authority housing. Affluent tenants in public housing estates were offered a £5,000 (€6,349)grant to surrender their dwelling and move to accommodation in the private sector. This scheme was legitimised as a means of releasing limited public housing to those who were most needy on the housing waiting list. However, the impact of this scheme on Moyross and Southill, in particular, was devastating. Many of the more affluent families left the areas and moved to private estates in new neighbourhoods. The delicate balance between the advantaged and disadvantaged in these communities was demolished.

In the short term, it was the decline of community groups such as community councils, as well as church, youth and sporting activities, that was most evident. Tom from Southill comments:

> There is a photograph over in the church of the community council and you can pick the people out of it who went. There was from day dot here a very good community council and most of them went at the time. They would have been involved in the scouts, we had girl guides, we had *lots* going on . . . They were leaders, I could definitely say they were leaders and most of them went. There would have been one or two who stayed but then they didn't have the others to help them. So they gave up.

At a time when poverty and unemployment were increasing dramatically, the decline of these community organisations was a significant blow to these neighbourhoods.

The departure of the £5,000 grant tenants to the private sector created a serious political vacuum in these communities. These were the people who had asserted the dominance of law and order on the streets, who had complained about troublesome teenagers to their parents, who called the Gardaí and who campaigned for Garda substations, and now they were gone. The population of these estates who remained behind after the £5,000 grant had a much higher proportion of unemployed and single-parent households. The unemployment rate in Moyross in 1984, for instance, was 70 per cent.[37] The proportion of families who had serious problems in relation to addiction, domestic violence and money-lending also became much greater.

Disadvantaged teenagers in these estates found that they had a new freedom and a new scope to dominate the neighbourhood as the population became more vulnerable. A big increase in joyriding was the first sign that they were taking control of the streets through more robust forms of antisocial behaviour. Lorraine comments:

> I remember when I came back from England and this stolen car thing was a big thing at the time . . . people started to give up here you know because stolen cars was a big new thing for the Guards as well at the time, and you know, it was just an epidemic and then there was a big audience for it, everyone would go out and look and I don't think they [the Gardaí] took it seriously enough, even the residents didn't take it seriously enough.

However, as these teenagers graduated from joyriding to open substance abuse in public spaces, serious vandalism and burning houses, even the most vulnerable residents in these communities began to panic.

In April 1986, the local scout hall in Moyross was burnt out by a 'gang of about 35 boys and girls'.[38] In June 1986, an Englishman who had just recently moved to Moyross was intimidated out of his home.[39] The natural response of residents to these crimes was to complain to the Gardaí, but they weren't very satisfied with their response. To local residents, the Gardaí appeared to be either unable or unwilling to respond to the crisis. In terms of the scout hall fire, it was reported that 'the children are known but there's no witnesses', while the Englishman who left his house complained, 'I called the police but the youths just laughed their heads off. The police took their names and told them to move on. What really annoyed me was when the Garda asked me was there anything I had done to annoy them.'[40] It appeared that the type of policing in which the Gardaí had traditionally engaged was increasingly inadequate in dealing with the emerging crime problem in Limerick.

When the Garda Síochána was established in 1922 by the Irish Free State, the government was determined to assert the Irish police force's distinctiveness from the previous, colonial, Royal Irish Constabulary. To this end, the 'Guardians of the Peace' were to be, according to Ferriter, 'the servant of the people, not militaristic or coercive'.[41] Disarming and working with, rather than against, communities to achieve law and order was an essential part of this ethos. Unfortunately, the ethos played into the hands of Limerick's increasingly violent gangs. Unarmed Gardaí were reluctant, in some cases, to challenge young men with knives and baseball bats and in raw power terms the teenage gangs began to gain the upper hand in their own territory. The most disadvantaged residents were reluctant to call in the Gardaí, while the more affluent residents who remained in these estates complained of feeling abandoned by Gardaí during this period. As a community, people began to consider other routes to resolve their growing problems with antisocial behaviour.

In the midst of this chaos, the activities of local criminal families, those living 'successfully on the edge', increased significantly.[42] Criminal families who had historically been involved in selling stolen goods graduated to small-scale drugs and arms dealing, as well as more formal protection rackets. As teenage gangs became increasingly out of control and local residents gained no response from the Gardaí, it was to these crime families and their paramilitary connections that the communities turned for protection.

The relationship between Limerick's criminal families and teenage gangs is highly complex during this period. In some cases, criminal families exploited these teenagers for their own purposes, using them for lower-status tasks in their organisations. In some locations, however, these families also saw an opportunity to become the de facto source of authority for the entire community by stepping forward and offering to violently suppress the teenage gangs. Their version of law and order involved joining forces with dissident republican elements and engaging in acts of vigilantism. Terry says, 'I knew of one little fella and he had his head battered, another few guys were beaten really badly, all kinds of things happened to them and it just made things worse really.'

Vigilantism is a common response to policing failure in socially excluded neighbourhoods. Describing the same phenomenon in Philadelphia, Anderson comments:

> The police are viewed as representing the dominant society and as not caring to protect inner-city residents. When called they may not respond, which is one reason why residents feel they must be pre-pared to take extraordinary measures to defend themselves and their loved ones against those who are inclined to aggression . . . The code of the street thus emerges where the influence of the police ends.[43]

While the alliance between criminal families, republicans and the local community was short-lived as residents witnessed the harsh violence of vigilante rule, this moment allowed Limerick's criminal families to fully occupy the political vacuum vacated by the £5,000 grant families. By the end of the decade, these families had become the real source of authority in these estates and were much more feared by the general population than the police or other state agencies. The outcome for Limerick's crim-inal families was that they were able to build up territorial strongholds in certain parts of the city, creating pockets in estates which functioned as safe sites of operation for their criminal activities.

As Limerick's criminal families became more powerful, a third dimen-sion to the poverty-related crime in Limerick emerged. In the 1990s, a proportion of the houses vacated by £5,000 grant tenants were occupied by Irish families returning from Britain. These families had roots in the city and left sink estates in British cities to return to Limerick. Although they may have been hoping for a better quality of life on their return, they brought elements of Britain's sink estate culture with them which further exacerbated the problems in Limerick. Because of the complex inter-racial mix in UK public housing estates, some Irish families had experienced conflict with neighbours from other ethnic minorities. When these migrants returned to Limerick, they brought a different cultural perspec-tive on neighbourhood relationships with them. Fergus explains how he saw the other kids in his estate before he returned to Limerick:

> . . . the council could be quite tough on anti-social behaviour and you could be kicked out, so we'd be puttin' pressure on their [Pakistani]

> families to say nothin' and they'd do the same to us and so on . . .
> when I came back to Limerick, it was weird seein' all the white faces
> but I still didn't let me guard down.

Unlike Irish local authorities, British local authorities began to take a very robust line on antisocial behaviour in the late 1980s and early 1990s.[44] Because of their experience of these UK policies, returned migrant families in Limerick tended to view any complaint about the behaviour of a child in their family as a threat which might result in eviction. As a result, they responded to these complaints with reciprocal threats and intimidation rather than tackling the behaviour of the child. Thus, the informal neighbourhood practices for resolving problems caused by the antisocial behaviour of children which had operated effectively in some estates during the 1970s began to break down.

In his research in Philadelphia, Anderson notes how one family moving into a street can ultimately lead to the decline of the whole area.[45] This proved to be the case in some streets in Limerick's housing estates; where the disappearance of leaders along with the presence of returned migrants who embodied a new tougher value system, career criminals, feuding families and teenage gangs resulted in the deterioration of significant parcels of these estates.

The history of what happened in Moyross, Southill, Ballinacurra Weston and St Mary's Park in the 1990s is well known because drugs-related feuds between the Keane, Collopy, Ryan and McCarthy/Dundon gangs had achieved such prominence in national media.[46] In brief, during the early 1990s Ireland experienced an explosion in the consumption of recreational drugs. A burgeoning club culture which relied heavily on the consumption of speed and ecstasy, combined with rapidly increasingly affluence which boosted the demand for cannabis and cocaine, provided a lucrative new market for Limerick's career criminals. There is fairly wide consensus that Limerick's criminal families, those who had 'always lived successfully on the edge', initially made their contacts with national and international drugs networks through the horse trade. Horses had always been an important part of the local culture. The racing of sulkys (light-framed carts towed by a single horse) is a popular pastime in Limerick city. Some of Limerick's criminal fraternity bet large sums of money at these races in Tipperary, Laois and Clare.[47] It was through these races and the horse-trading that accompanied them that Limerick's criminal fraternity initially formed links with members of Dublin drugs gangs and drug importers into Munster.[48]

Garda figures provide a good overview of the scale of the increase in drugs-related crime in Limerick during the 1990s. In 1990, there were 73 drugs seizures in Limerick with a street value of £2,000 (€2,540). In 1995, the number of seizures had risen to 415 and the value of the drugs had also increased to £250,000 (€320,000). In 1999, there were 332 seizures of drugs worth £3,318,150 (€4.2 million).[49]

Limerick's criminal families had found themselves at the heart of a very lucrative business. They not only had the connections to national criminal networks and dissident paramilitary groups which allowed them to access supplies of drugs and guns, but they also had long experience of feuding, which gave them a reputation for violence and an experience of gun use which was unrivalled outside Dublin. They soon swept aside any regional competition and gained control of the provincial drugs trade. However, in order to run such a large business effectively, Limerick's criminal gangs required territorial strongholds.[50] They needed places where guns and drugs could be stored, where they could meet with their local dealers and where they could be relatively sure that local residents wouldn't inform the Gardaí. It is during this period that the intimidation of local residents in some estates reached new heights.

In 1992, Jim Kemmy, Mayor of Limerick, warned that 100 families were being forced out of their homes in Glenagross Park in Moyross. He complained that gangs were burning families out of their homes to such an extent that one in five houses were now boarded up.[51] How did these criminal gangs force people who had lived in these houses for years to abandon their homes? During the 1990s, children and teenagers became agents of intimidation operating for Limerick's criminal family gangs. Majella describes how this process operates:

> It can start with the youngest calling you names, a three and four-year-old calling you names or in your garden and riling you, playing in your garden or they are outside your garden, and there is a ball that's being hopped off your wall, hopped off your wall and hopped off your wall. That's mental torture and then it's like you go to the door and you're told to 'fuck off' and you're that and you're the other. So then you do what you think you're entitled to and you phone the Guards and then your window's gone in that night because you complained the child.

Calling the Gardaí often led to an escalation rather than a reduction in the campaign of intimidation, with windows being broken, rubbish being dumped in the garden and fires being set near the houses. Campaigns of intimidation against households tend to result in one of three outcomes. In some cases, the family is offered key money for their house. In this case, the family leaves with €5,000 for instance and the criminal family gang become the occupants of the house, using it as a base for operations or housing some of their members. No legal contracts are ever exchanged in this process. In other cases, families are not offered any money but are forced to flee because they fear for their lives. This process is deeply traumatic for the victims. Seamus describes one couple and their daughter who were forced out of their house:

> The daughter had to go and move but they never housed the mother or father, they automatically went with the daughter. The father never made it anywhere, he died within six weeks of having being intimidated, they couldn't take it anymore, and the mother died within seven months. So that couple were gone, they were very ill physically and mentally, they were wiped out by it.

In some cases, particular parts of each estate were targeted because of their physical structure. During the '70s and early '80s, 'Oak Park'[52] was one of the most stable parts of one Regeneration estate, with a large number of owner-occupiers and a low level of tenant turnover. Leanne comments, 'Oak Park you couldn't get a house in for love nor money. The people who moved into Oak Park, forty-three years ago, they would have been young families, all working, nobody unemployed. They loved their houses.' By the late 1990s, many of these residents had abandoned their houses due to intimidation. Sean says

> It would have happened late 1990s to 2003, everyone asked why did they want Oak Park? There was a very good reason – the layout of Oak Park. You had courts, where you have circles of courts, there was only one way in and one way out and you couldn't come from any other way . . . you could see everyone coming in and out.

This type of physical infrastructure was ideal as a territorial base for criminal activity. These areas were relatively inaccessible and the only access routes by car could be clearly monitored.

As the stigma of living in these estates increased and their reputation as sites of violence became more widespread, it became more difficult for Limerick City Council to convince the more stable families on the housing list to take up accommodation in these areas. As a result, the profile of residents became even more marginalised during the 1990s, with greater levels of relative poverty, unemployment, and single-parent households. The children of the disadvantaged not only saw no reason to stay in school but boys frequently couldn't get a place in a secondary school even if they wanted to attend. Limerick had a severe shortage of secondary school places for boys during the 1990s.[53] At its peak, one in twelve boys in the city had no school place. Galvin describes how the stigma of living in Regeneration estates impacted on boys' chances of gaining a school place:

> Every family was affected. And these children were not given priority the following year: their names were added to those of the children leaving primary school that year and they risked rejection again. The statistics show that one in twelve was rejected the second year and lost to the education system for ever. It was a recipe for disaster.[54]

During the late 1990s, the state began to recognise the seriousness of the problems which had emerged in Limerick. CCTV cameras were installed in some estates and a surveillance helicopter began to be used to monitor these areas. In 2001, the Criminal Assets Bureau was brought in to examine the activities of Limerick's criminal gangs. Increasingly, an Emergency Response Unit of armed Gardaí were called in to deal with the problems in Limerick's estates, and ultimately the Minister for Justice decided to establish a permanent armed response unit for the city.[55] By 2004–05, many of Limerick's most senior criminals were in prison. Yet the activities of the drugs gangs continued. In 2008, O'Rourke and Cusack estimated that the drugs trade at street level in Limerick was worth €30 million.[56]

Given the wealth generated from these activities, some of those at the top of Limerick's criminal hierarchies can now afford to leave their territorial strongholds, move abroad or buy new homes in country locations. These new homes not only provide them with a better quality of life but provide a welcome break from the intensity of local neighbourhood feuds.[57] Despite the departure of some senior gang members from the city, there continue to be some estates which are dominated by gang culture and areas where fear, intimidation and community violence continue to hold sway. In order to provide an understanding of how community violence is produced in these contexts, a micro-mapping of the social structure of disadvantaged estates in Limerick from a socio-cultural perspective is provided in Chapter Four.

4. Divided Communities

Mapping the social structure of disadvantaged neighbourhoods in Limerick

Niamh Hourigan

The macro-study of inequality in Limerick city presented by Des McCafferty in Chapter One demonstrates the sharp divisions between rich and poor within the greater Limerick conurbation. Within this context, it can be tempting to view disadvantaged communities in Limerick as uniformly marginal and dysfunctional, a classic example of social exclusion. However, this model fails to recognise the complexity of these neighbourhoods where vibrant, friendly, active communities can co-exist with drugs and feud-dominated estates. This approach doesn't explain how tireless and committed community leaders and law-abiding teenagers can survive almost side-by-side with those involved in criminal family gangs. The aim of this chapter is to demonstrate how the clustering of social groups in parts of disadvantaged neighbourhoods generates micro-social systems which create a marked distinction in how local residents experience living in their own community. In Limerick, understanding the functioning and successful parts of these communities is as important as recognising the problems in the dysfunctional pockets of these estates.

The large range of excellent quantitative research which has already been conducted on social exclusion in Limerick city was used as a baseline for this study.[1] The core areas for this micro-mapping were Limerick's four Regeneration estates (Moyross, Southill, St Mary's Park, Ballinacurra Weston); however, research was also conducted in other parts of the city.[2] The total population of the Limerick Regeneration areas based on the 2006 census is approximately 8,981.[3] Over 93 per cent of this population are of Irish origin and Catholic. Although the population of these areas has declined since 2002, there are paradoxically a very high proportion of residents who are under twenty-five.[4] This anomaly is due to the high level of lone parenthood in these estates. Barrett et al. found that 47–48 per cent of families in Moyross, Southill and St Mary's Park are lone-parent households, compared to a national average of just 17.9

per cent. The rate of early school-leaving ranges from 42 per cent in parts of Moyross to 55.4 per cent in St Mary's Park. In addition, rates of unemployment in some estates actually increased during the 2002–06 period, a time of considerable growth in employment nationally.[5] On a deprivation score which ranges between 1 and 10, all the Regeneration areas scored between 9 and 10, indicating that they are among the most severely disadvantaged neighbourhoods in the Irish state.[6]

Socio-Cultural Structures across Communities

A distinct social structure has developed within Limerick's disadvantaged estates in response to profound social exclusion. For instance, across all these estates, there is an unusually high level of intimacy between neighbours rooted in a mutual dependence. One community activist in Ballinacurra Weston, commented, 'If you've never been in want, you can never know what it is to really need other people.' Families tend to be most intimate with those who live on the same street or cul-de-sac as themselves. Billy comments how, 'I always know when my [elderly] dad has been out for his walk. He's very lazy, you know, but when he's been for his walk, he has all the news of the road, who's doing what and who's going where.' Joe comments, 'We know everything about our neighbours, too much, most of it by word of mouth. Anything that happens, we know about it, we know everyone's business.'

Because a considerable proportion of residents in some estates are not participating in the formal workforce, this network of neighbours often constitutes the largest part of their social world. Chloe comments:

> Everything is here for us, everything, everyone we know. If my mother said we were moving in the morning, I'd cry, I wouldn't go. I'd never leave Moyross even if I was famous, I'd always have a house in Moyross to come back to.

Many residents are deeply attached to their neighbours and find they experience pronounced anxiety if they move away. Mary says, 'I left Moyross after the grant and I came back. I couldn't settle where I was. I missed my neighbours so much, people in these other areas are so unfriendly, I'd die without my neighbours.'

The negative dimension of this intimacy is the lack of privacy which was evident in Liam Ryan's study of Ballinacurra Weston in the 1960s. He found that

> It is almost impossible to maintain privacy in the area, and everyone is well acquainted with his neighbour's business. Family quarrels are

fought in the street rather than in the home and in every street, there are one or two families who keep shouting and roaring till all hours of the night.[7]

In the contemporary context, this lack of privacy becomes particularly problematic during feuds, where personal information can be used against opponents as taunts or abusive graffiti.[8]

There is a second level of intimacy which is even more important in understanding the link between social exclusion and crime in Limerick. While residents in these estates knew their close neighbours intimately, they also had a remarkably sophisticated knowledge of the social geography of the wider population in their local area. The basic sociological unit of these communities is not the individual but the extended family.[9] Even for individuals who are working, the extended family is generally a more important source of identity and status than their career.[10] Although marriage is a rarity, the boundedness of the community remains an important factor in choosing a partner. Two interviewees commented, 'Nobody in Limerick marries outside a half mile.' Although adult intimate relationships can be unstable, blood ties between parents and children are of paramount importance in locating each man, woman and child's position within local family hierarchies. Kevin describes 'his buddy' Keith in the following terms: 'when I see a guy like Keith, or any guy on the street, I'm thinking of his family, his brothers, his mother, what crowd he hangs with, I don't really see him as separate, no-one is separate or on their own here.'

An individual can be treated with deference or contempt simply on the basis of their family relationships. It is not uncommon for an innocent family member to be punished for the crimes or debts of a sibling or a cousin by a criminal family gang. This knowledge of family relationships is largely passed down by grandmothers (nanas), who are the matriarchs of this family culture. John says 'in the whole of St Mary's Park we know who's related. The nanas are the best for that. My nana is great for it.'

In addition to family-based social position, the current status of boys, men and sometimes women involved in community violence and criminality is estimated through 'reputation'. Reputation is a complex measure of an individual's position within the local 'hard man' hierarchies which combines an estimate of their perceived toughness with their status within family and criminal gang hierarchies. Decisions about whether a person could be 'hopped' or 'clipped' [attacked] are made using a complex risk assessment of whether one is capable of physically tackling the individual along with the risk of embroiling one's own family in a conflict with the opponent's family.

For a child growing up in these areas, learning how to survive within this complex social geography is a time-consuming process, often taking up much more energy than formal education. It is a process which requires developing a personal image which combines physical toughness with quick thinking, a capacity for 'slagging' and/or verbal abuse, and a highly attuned awareness of danger. Children go to considerable lengths to acquire the mannerisms, accents and behaviours of the older toughest boys and girls on the street. Having acquired this street credibility, they are able to survive on their own estates. However, by embodying this form of dress, speech and behaviour, many teenagers find that they are rejected by more mainstream society, often being labelled as 'scumbags'. Surviving in broader Limerick society demands different skills, and middle-class citizens of Limerick stigmatise precisely the dress codes, behaviours and accents which these disadvantaged children have so painstakingly learnt. Consequently, children from the most disadvantaged families often feel ill at ease when away from the cocoon of the estate culture. Nora, who works with youth services, comments:

> You know, they can never leave their own parts of Limerick, we find it terrible sometimes, a young lad leaves because of a feud or a fight and he knows he is going to be attacked or shot so he goes to Dublin or Birmingham or Manchester but he finds he can't survive without everything he knows and he is back within a week, they never survive longer than a week.

The intimacy of these communities and the importance of family as the building block of their social structure is the chief similarity which is encountered across all Limerick's disadvantaged estates. However, a micro-level review of these communities reveals a marked heterogeneity within each community. In one of the early interviews for this project, Jim, an older man living on the city's north-side, commented:

> What you have to remember is that there is the 'advantaged among the disadvantaged' and the 'disadvantaged among the disadvantaged'. If your name is Blue or Red, there is no point in you going down to the community centre or the crèche or the youth club looking for help. They don't want to know about you.

This insight proved to be remarkably useful in subsequently tracing how social exclusion produces violent crime in Limerick.[11]

Based on an overview of census figures and the most recent quantitative research on social exclusion in Limerick, it is estimated that between 64 and 66 per cent of these communities can be classified as the 'advantaged of the disadvantaged' while 30 to 33 per cent are classified as 'disadvantaged of the disadvantaged'.[12] In mapping the social structure of these communities, the position of these two social groups will be considered in relation to two other categories of residents: core criminal families, and members of the Traveller community.[13]

Advantaged of the Disadvantaged

The 'advantaged of the disadvantaged' are defined first and foremost by their stable family structures. Even if lone parents are heading the household, they enjoy support from their extended family. While a sizeable number of this group are in employment, they are also relatively accomplished at enlisting support from state services. Their knowledge of the welfare system is extensive and they are effective at accessing services such as youth-reach programmes, subsidised crèche facilities, education and job creation initiatives. Kathleen, a community worker, comments, 'They always have their ear out for the next thing, you know, even down to "Is there something that my child can go to?" If there is, they'll bring their kids, they're very good.'

The 'advantaged of the disadvantaged' have aspirations towards upward mobility. They are anxious that their children stay in school for as long as possible and in some cases aspire to leaving the estate once some mobility is achieved. They are not involved in serious crime. For the 'advantaged of the disadvantaged', one of the biggest problems they face relates to stigma.

Stigma is repeatedly cited by this group as the major obstacle in trying to achieve upward mobility. Over half of interviewees in this category mentioned cases where someone was denied access to an employment or educational opportunity because of their address. Eileen's story is typical:

> My son went for a job cleaning a warehouse, just small stuff you know and the supervisor was really nice and interviewed him and gave him the job. Then he asked him to fill out all these forms. When he saw the address he made a face. A few minutes later, he came back and told him that the boss had given the job to someone else that morning. My son came out of that place really angry but also so sad, he had no chance, you see.

Address is also a problem for children applying for school places and grinds in other areas of the city, a common strategy among upwardly mobile parents. Stacey tells a typical story:

> I wanted to get my daughter maths grinds for the Leaving and I rang the teacher and she said fine until I told her the address and then she checked her diary and said she didn't think she could fit her in. Two weeks later, I got the child's aunt to ring the same woman giving her own address and she took her on, no problem.

The anger which is felt by the 'advantaged of the disadvantaged' when they repeatedly experience these types of incidents is palpable in interviews. Joe, an eighteen-year-old from Moyross, says, 'we've been left on the scrap heap, well out of the way and they don't give a fuck'. On a daily basis, this group struggle in the most difficult conditions to remain relatively law-abiding but when they move outside the strongholds of their own neighbourhoods they find themselves repeatedly encountering prejudice because of their address instead of encouragement because of their efforts.

Although the 'advantaged of the disadvantaged' have strong aspirations to achieve upward mobility, some members of this group experience considerable difficulty in making the leap into full-time employment. Getting a job involves not only battling the stigma of their address but also overcoming their fear of losing the social welfare safety net. Nearly half the women interviewed indicated that they were anxious to participate in community employment schemes but they also made it clear that they were reluctant to take up full-time work. By working full-time, they risked losing a whole range of entitlements, including medical cards, child benefits and rent allowances. Maeve, who runs training courses, says:

> They'll go so far, they'll get the training, they'll do any class on earth, but the minute it comes to 'if you have to get that job you have to lose your book', you'll lose your medical card and everything goes out the window. The dependency stops them from getting on in life. But it is understandable because most of the low-paid jobs that they could get won't compensate them for losing their entitlements.

Some of those who do go to work risk being called names such as 'snob' by their neighbours because their behaviour presents an inherent critique to welfare dependency. Mairéad, who now works in the community where she grew up, says, 'I've been called a snob and "Who's that snobby bitch?" and "Who do they think they are?" That's a big slag: Who do you think you are?'

In real terms, because of levels of early school-leaving, a significant proportion of children who grow up in these areas are already excluded from the workforce by the time they reach maturity. However, the upward mobility of any individual presents the spectre that social exclusion and poverty is the fault of the individual not the society, and therefore their success is met with anger and rejection. Ryan noted the dynamics of this process as early as 1965:

> The level of aspiration is extremely low, probably because if a youth wishes to aim higher than his friends, he has to accept derision or isolation from those who think it is stupid or disloyal to have ambitions above those common to the group as a whole.[14]

This rejection of the upwardly mobile is saddening because there is much evidence to suggest that social exclusion of residents in these estates is systematic and not due to failures or weaknesses of the individual.[15] This rejection results in the demoralisation of the individuals most capable of taking leadership roles in resisting criminal gangs and of organising community responses to exclusionary state and local government policies.

Disadvantaged of the Disadvantaged

Leo Tolstoy wrote that while 'all happy families resemble one another, each unhappy family is unhappy in its own way'.[16] Families who fall within the category of the 'disadvantaged of the disadvantaged' are generally unhappy, and their misery takes many different forms. However, there are three common features of their daily life which pushes them into this category: unstable family structures, addiction and money-lending.

Families within the 'disadvantaged of the disadvantaged' category tend to be quite unstable. Although the extended family is an important part of their lives, because of abuse and/or feuding, the extended family is usually as much a source of stress as support. Of those interviewed in this category for this study, over 70 per cent came from female-headed households. The lack of a constant male presence in the household to be a role model for socially acceptable expressions of masculinity is a significant loss to children, particularly boys.[17] A minority of women in this group had children by more than one father and they also acknowledged that the transition from one male partner to another in the home caused considerable stress to children. Parents from this category who were interviewed acknowledged that their children often spent more time on the streets than they did in their own home. Julia comments:

> My young fella treats the place like a hotel. When he gets up in the morning, he leaves as soon as he can and when he gets home in the afternoon, he changes and is off out again till half ten at night. I'd have to hide his shoes to keep him indoors. He never spends more than an hour in the day in my house.

Because these children gravitate towards the street, there is often a marked lack of parental control. Rachel says:

> I would have to try really hard to get into trouble. In fact, I don't think I could get into trouble. Before my dad left, I got into trouble for some things but now she [my mother] doesn't care. She gives me money for pizza and I like to stay out with my friends.

While women are more likely to be the victims of domestic violence, the status of men within the home is more insecure. Despite changes to the social welfare system, there is still a widespread belief that unmarried mothers should not have their partners in their homes. In response, men tend to have a low-key presence in the household during the day, and become more visible at night.

In terms of the state structures, the 'disadvantaged of the disadvantaged' have more intimate knowledge of the criminal justice system than social services. They demonstrate extensive knowledge of An Garda Siochána, the courts and the prison system combined with a keen awareness of their own rights. Maureen, who works with social services, describes her work with two boys within this category:

> These are the ones on the outskirts of the gangs. Their mother was after getting thrown out of one place and she'd been picked up by the Gardaí and the two boys came up to the office here and they were telling us about their mother's rights. They knew them well, one was eleven and the other was thirteen.

A significant proportion of parents in this category appeared to be grappling with a serious addiction or attempting to manage a partner or family member with an addiction problem.[18] The reasons for the high levels of addiction within this group are readily identifiable. The most disadvantaged residents in these estates have lives which are punctuated by considerable stress linked to poverty, stigma and antisocial behaviour. In his research on health and inequality, Wilkinson highlights the toxic impact of this type of stress on the disadvantaged:

> To feel depressed, cheated, bitter, desperate, vulnerable, frightened, angry, worried about debts or jobs or housing insecurity; to feel devalued, useless, helpless, uncared for, hopeless, isolated, anxious and a failure; these feelings can dominate people's whole experience of life, colouring their experience of everything else. It is the chronic stress arising from feelings like these which does the damage.[19]

Drug, alcohol and gambling addictions provide, in the short term, considerable relief from this stress.[20] However, the negative consequences of the behaviour become quickly evident to the addict and their families. Gaining access to drugs, alcohol or money for gambling absorbs a huge amount of time and energy and eventually becomes a significant source of stress in itself. In addition, the mood-altering dimensions of addictive drugs lessen the individual's capacity to deal with the normal demands of daily life. This increasing inadequacy leads to a huge rise in stress levels and can result in a whole range of abusive and self-harming behaviours.[21]

In terms of broader family structures, these addictions absorb much of the parent's emotional and psychological energy, leaving little time for the responsibilities of rearing children. Dunn et al. found that in the US, addicted parents are three times more likely to neglect their children than those with no serious addictions.[22] In Limerick, there is also considerable evidence that addiction breeds child neglect. Families in the 'disadvantaged of the disadvantaged' category are entitled to the same welfare supports as more advantaged families, but they keep state agencies at a distance because they fear the interference of child protection services. Fionnuala says:

> I hate to see them comin' around, wantin' to know everythin' about you an' askin' an' askin'. Why do you do this an' why do you do that? I bet no-one's askin' them about how they manage their kids. So I just lave 'em off, I stay away from them. I love the kids.

Because of this resistance to state interference, the 'disadvantaged of the disadvantaged' are often less informed about their entitlements than their more advantaged neighbours.

The range of addictions (drugs, alcohol and gambling) in these families put enormous pressure on their income. Money which should be used to pay for food, rent and utility bills can end up at the local off-licence, bookies or in the local drug-dealer's pockets. Many of these families are forced to turn to moneylenders in order to supplement their income. Even in the 1960s, Ryan found that the presence of money-lenders was a significant factor in pushing a family into absolute poverty. He quotes one resident:

> It was fierce. You could be short of money – I knew one woman who borrowed £5; until she paid back that £5 in one piece she had to pay £2 a month interest. She was paying it for one and a half years and had paid back £30 before she cleared the debt.[23]

In tracing how social exclusion pushes families into crime, the presence of parasitic moneylenders in these communities is one of the most neglected elements of the contemporary social policy debate.[24] Christmas and occasions such as First Communions often provide the initial reason for getting into debt. Sheila, who works in one estate, describes how:

> It was the day before Christmas and I gave this woman a lift in my car, very cold day and when she is getting out of the car in the city, she tells me she is going across town to borrow €30 from a money-lender to get Christmas things. If she had only told me the day before, I could have a taken her somewhere to get her the money but they've no self-esteem you see, she wouldn't believe that anyone would lend her the money and how much will she pay back for that, maybe €90?

Timmy describes what happens to those who fail to repay their debts to moneylenders:

> They take their allowance book or whatever book they have and hold it and go down every week and wait for them to get the money and bring it out. I seen it, you know, people who couldn't get loans off the legal moneylenders. If you missed a week or something like that, you pay double and if you couldn't pay double you might get a right beating over it.

Therefore, although a disadvantaged family might be in receipt of the same amount of social welfare as an advantaged family, because of addiction and moneylending, in real terms they experience much greater poverty.

For children from these families, life can involve a daily struggle with hunger, inadequate clothing and constant cold due to lack of heating. Valerie describes how one ten-year-old boy on the fringes of the gang engages with the youth service because he is hungry:

> They kept asking does he want something to eat and he says yeah, yeah and he sat there and he started with his carrots and he ate every-thing but his whole demeanour, his whole defiance, hating being there; but he has to be because he's hungry, because he knows that the service have to feed him because they know if they don't feed him they don't know if he's ever going to be fed.

For children from this category who are often neglected and abused, the gang structure offers the chance to escape deep poverty and have status and respect in the community. This is a potent combination and youth service workers find it very difficult to entice children away from gangs. One social service worker Coleman concludes

> I have a few kids on the edge of these criminal gangs. They are just
> there with them. There is the youth service killin' themselves trying to
> break the cycle. But they want to be in. They don't want to be any-
> thing else. There is nothing else for them, they're the real
> disadvantaged.

While media analysis of crime in Limerick has focused on high-profile
criminals, it is the 'disadvantaged of the disadvantaged', who may number
between 2,000 and 3,000 persons, that provide the reservoir of new
members for Limerick's criminal family gangs. It is children from this
group currently experiencing poverty and neglect who will form the basis
of the next generation of criminal gangs.

Core Criminal Families

Recognising the distinctions between the 'advantaged of the disadvantaged' and the 'disadvantaged of the disadvantaged' is a critical first step
in mapping the link between social exclusion and violent crime in
Limerick. However, in 2008 it was estimated that there were sixteen core
criminal families made up of 350 men, women and children who also live
in these estates. From a sociological perspective, the profile of Limerick's
core crime families is not uniform. Some of the most powerful crime families in Limerick city have much deeper roots in their neighbourhoods
than others.[25] Some families are involved in sophisticated organised-crime
networks while others are more focused on local feuds.[26] Most families
combine feuding with more lucrative criminal activities. However, there
are some commonalities in evidence. Firstly, these families have historically been involved in commercial activities on the margins of legality. As
a result, the families enjoyed greater affluence than their neighbours even
before the explosion of the drugs trade in Ireland in the 1990s.[27] This
affluence, coupled with their willingness to use violence, provided the
origins of their powerful position within these communities.

The 1990s drugs explosion dramatically increased their income and
led to the expansion of the criminal networks beyond immediate family
members.[28] Some of these families now operate sophisticated criminal
organisations which have access to guns and advanced surveillance technologies.[29] They carefully maintain their dominance in the local
community, actively punishing those who show disrespect. Bill tells a
story which reveals clearly the kind of fear which core criminals provoke
in their more vulnerable neighbours:

> I was in the local barbers on Saturday morning and there was a huge
> queue. It was a rugby day so there were about ten guys waiting for

haircuts. Anyway, I was havin' a chat with one of the lads when one
of the Blues walks in. He's got a bullet-proof vest on and he says I'm
next. So without a word, everyone else gets up and leaves. One auld
fella had to go home and change. He wet himself, he was so scared.

Because of the level of intimacy in these communities, everyone knows
the identity of core criminal families and, on a daily basis, they need do
relatively little to maintain their dominance in their local neighbourhoods.

Within sociological literature, there is a long tradition of characterising
criminality as a 'creative' response to social exclusion; when one is denied
opportunities in the conventional economy, one simply creates new opportunities within the illegal economy.[30] Because Limerick's crime families
have traditionally embodied this creative response to social exclusion,
there is a curious ambiguity in some residents' response to the core
members. Eileen says, 'these families always provided the community with
what they needed.' Freddie speaks with pride, saying, 'I was at one of their
weddings, I know them all, they're a very close family.' However, the same
residents are often shocked to discover that the drugs trade in Limerick is
now valued at an estimated €30 million.[31] It is accepted wisdom within
these communities that core crime family members are safest, while those
located on the fringes of the kinship network are more likely to be attacked
in feuds or drug-related conflicts. For some core crime family members,
having the means to move away from disadvantaged estates has become
one of the most significant benefits of their new-found wealth.

Travellers

Many of the most deprived urban neighbourhoods in Limerick city are
home to families of settled Travellers. There are also large halting sites
located near Moyross and Southill. According to Limerick Regeneration,
Southill has two Traveller halting sites with twenty-four families and three
settled families. Ballynanty/Moyross has one halting site with seventeen
families and one settled family.[32] Within the international media in particular, there has been a marked tendency to blame Limerick's notoriety for
criminal activity and feuding on this ethno-cultural group.[33]
Approximately 8 per cent of interviewees for this study were of Traveller
origin.[34] Data collected during this research suggests that there is no
causal link between Traveller culture and criminal activity in Limerick.
This does not mean that Travellers are not involved in these activities.

Based on the information gathered in interviews for this study, it
would appear that there are a number of Traveller families who have

links with Limerick's criminal families. However, there are also Traveller families who have no association with this criminal activity. Of the core crime families, according to interviewees, some have Traveller ethnicity in their background, other families do not have any connection to Traveller cultures. The presence or absence of Traveller ethnicity does not appear to make any significant difference to participation in feuding. Within the national media, a love of horses and an emphasis on family loyalty are stereotypes associated with Limerick's feuding families.[35] These are stereotypes also associated with the Traveller community in Ireland.[36] However, as Kelleher and O'Connor's chapter demonstrates, the love of family and horses is found across the social spectrum in disadvantaged estates. Therefore, the presence of these cultural characteristics cannot be used as a basis for drawing a causal connection between Traveller ethnicity and the serious criminality which has emerged in Limerick city.

Conclusion

Within Devereux et al.'s chapter on media coverage of crime in Moyross, they outline the anger which many local residents feel when their neighbourhood is constantly referred to as a 'troubled estate'. The micro-mapping of the social structure of disadvantaged estates presented in this chapter suggests that there is good reason for this anger. During this research, I found that in parts of each estate where the 'advantaged of the disadvantaged' were clustered, neighbours gave each much more support than is evident in middle-class estates in Ireland,[37] a feature also highlighted by Humphreys' chapter. However, in pockets where the 'disadvantaged of the disadvantaged' are clustered, community violence and criminality are much more evident. These are the communities where it is easy to intimidate local residents, where children are less supervised and where young people experience few sanctions if they do become involved in antisocial behaviour. These are also the neighbourhoods where local residents are most wary of the Gardaí and social services because of their own addictions and problems.

International research on social exclusion demonstrates how those who are excluded can become involved in violent crime;[38] however, the micro-social structure of communities outlined here shows clearly why only a minority of the excluded become enmeshed in criminality. In this context, tarring all residents of disadvantaged estates with one brush is not only deeply unhelpful but counter-productive, as it perpetuates a stigma which locks more advantaged families into poverty. The research presented in the next chapter on community violence and organised crime traces how the 'disadvantaged of the disadvantaged' slide into criminality, a process which ultimately results in the oppression of their neighbours and the emergence of localised 'regimes of fear'.

5. Organised Crime and Community Violence

understanding Limerick's 'regimes of fear'

Niamh Hourigan

In November 2003, a media furore emerged in Ireland when a murder case against a young Limerick gangland criminal collapsed because of what Justice Paul Carney called a 'case of collective amnesia'. *The Irish Times* reported that 'six witnesses, some of whom had initially given detailed statements to Gardaí identifying the defendant, either refused to answer questions or said they could not remember the murder.'[1] When one of these witnesses was subsequently tried for perjury, he outlined his rationale in stark terms, stating, 'I can come out of prison but I can't come out of a box.' In response to this statement, the presiding Judge Carroll Moran acknowledged that a 'regime of fear' existed in some parts of Limerick.[2]

In view of the research presented in this chapter, this was a perceptive statement because Moran's comment recognised not only that fear was a significant obstacle in getting witnesses to testify against criminals in Limerick but also that the generation of this fear was systematic. In certain estates, criminal gangs had used their propensity towards violence and their surveillance of the community as a means of becoming the de facto governing authority in the area and their power had significantly undermined the capacity of state agencies to assert the legitimacy of law and order.

This chapter seeks to map how poverty, criminality and powerlessness have produced regimes of fear in Limerick. The study focused on Moyross, Southill, St Mary's Park and Ballinacurra Weston as well as other disadvantaged parts of Limerick city.[3] Five dimensions were identified which interweave to produce fear and generate systematic community violence in these areas. Firstly, the role of the 'hard man' culture in generating status and shaping youth transitions to criminality among the 'disadvantaged of the disadvantaged' is examined. Secondly, three levels of participation in criminal gang activity which were evident during the research are outlined. The mechanics of fear are then interrogated by examining how surveillance and intimidation of local residents obstructs the operation of the criminal justice system and produces a model of community violence. The position of the prison system within regimes of fear is examined in terms of surveillance of communities from within prison. Finally, the role of globalisation is examined in terms of the city's position within a global drugs commodity chain, and the exploitation of technologies and global cultural forms by Limerick's gangland criminals.

Getting Respect: masculinity, violence and crime

The historical overview of crime and social exclusion in Limerick presented in Chapter Three demonstrates how residents in disadvantaged estates experience considerable difficulty in achieving upward mobility through mainstream Limerick society. Because of their address, residents can be stigmatised when applying for jobs and because of patterns of early school-leaving, a significant proportion of young people from these communities do not progress through the education system. For men, this economic marginalisation and social stigma is coupled with their hugely insecure position within the family home. Even the Irish state's Department of Social Welfare acknowledges that in relation to fathers:

> A powerful exclusionary dynamic comes from the state itself as the social welfare system creates a financial benefit for mothers to claim lone parent benefit and for fathers' names not to be put on the birth certificate, in effect for them not to be seen to officially exist.[4]

Economically excluded, culturally stigmatised and insecure in their position as fathers and partners, these men have no legitimate source of pride or esteem available to them. Yet their need to achieve status, to be admired and respected is the same as everyone else's. As a result, they have created a different system of status. This status is linked to being a 'hard man' who embodies toughness and a capacity for violence, a figure who then elicits fear in his more vulnerable neighbours.[5]

Sociologist Richard Sennett has described how lack of respect is one of the most significant 'hidden injuries of class.'[6] By being a 'hard man', however, participants in Limerick's gang culture subvert this process.[7] Citizens of mainstream Limerick society may continue to view these men as 'scumbags', but within their own communities they are deeply feared because they embody a form of masculinity linked to toughness and violence. Paul describes one of the most feared men in his cul-de-sac in the following terms: 'I don't even want to mention his name or look at him. I get nervous just talking about him.' For a man who is otherwise despised in Limerick society, eliciting this level of fear in his neighbours confers status and does indeed generate a form of respect, respect based on fear.

The task of maintaining this 'hard man' status on a day-to-day basis is considerable. Mary describes the pressure her son feels to maintain his tough image

> He never relaxes, he's always watchin' out, waitin' for the next thing. He worries more about his own crowd than the opposition. Its fear that they won't respect him, that they'll think he's weak and if they do, in his head, he's finished.

Recognition within the 'hard man' hierarchy yields significant power dividends. Stella describes some of the men in her local estate in the following terms:

> They'll never work to be powerful. They'll never go to school to be powerful. They'll never achieve anything in life, they know themselves, the only way they can achieve anything is to sell drugs or intimidate the livin' daylights outa someone and get an utter feelin' of power out of them, of getting' rid of people.

Thus, status and fear-based respect constitute the primary motivating factor for gang participation. Although the financial rewards of gangland activity are significant, particularly for the 'serious players', because of the rate of imprisonment, few gang members get to enjoy these rewards over the long term.[8] However, the status associated with being a 'hard man' and in particular with being a 'serious player' within criminal gangs is transferable and operates as effectively within the prison system as it does on the outside.

Both Elijah Anderson and Phillippe Bourgois, who researched gang cultures in the United States, highlight status and respect as the most significant reward for gang participation.[9] Anderson writes

> Possession of respect – and the credible threat of vengeance – is highly valued . . . In service to this ethic, repeated displays of 'nerve' and 'heart' build or reinforce a credible reputation for vengeance that works to deter aggression and disrespect, which are sources of great anxiety on the inner city street.[10]

In researching community violence in the UK, Hill found the same rationale in operation among gang members, stating:

They've nothing else in their lives apart from their desperate need to feel a sense of power over others on the street. Their days and nights revolve around whether they feel 'disrespected' by their peers or whether some petty grievance or other has flared up into a score that needs to be settled.[11]

During this research, there was evidence that this search for fear-based respect and positioning in local toughness hierarchies is not confined to boys and men. Girls and women linked to these gangs are increasingly copying these behaviours by emphasising their own toughness and fearsomeness. This trend mirrors the findings of a range of other studies internationally which highlight the emergence of female gang participation.[12]

The probability that a child will embrace this fear-based respect as the only form of status available to them is closely linked to the micro-social structure of disadvantaged communities outlined in Chapter Four. If a child grows up in an area where the 'advantaged of the disadvantaged' families are clustered, he or she is likely to engage with the school system and extra-curricular activities on offer. In these estates, the behaviour of local children is monitored and residents actively vet, when they can, the allocation of vacant units by local housing authorities to prevent families who embody the fear-based respect value system entering the neighbourhood.[13]

For a child who is growing up in an area where the 'disadvantaged of the disadvantaged' are clustered, the likelihood of embracing the fear-based respect model is much greater. Evidence of the 'hard man' culture will be visible daily on the streets, even in the posturing and street language of young children. Families in these neighbourhoods are often too vulnerable or too troubled to challenge this street-based toughness hierarchy. Parents who arrive in these areas tend to focus on teaching their children how to cope with this street culture rather than openly challenging the toughness hierarchy. Teresa described how she felt when she moved into one very disadvantaged part of a Limerick estate:

> The day after we arrived, I sat down with my husband and I said if we are going to survive here we are going to have to raise them tough. I'd be out on the street and I'd be shouting at other mothers, if they only knew how soft I am but if they did know, we'd be fucked.

In his study of gang activity in Philadelphia, Anderson describes disadvantaged areas where the 'hard man' culture is in operation as being governed by what he calls the 'code of the street'. He writes that a child growing up in this environment is confronted with a

> . . . local hierarchy based on toughness where the premium is placed
> on being a good fighter. As a means of survival, one often learns the
> value of having a 'name', a reputation for being willing and able to
> fight. To build such a reputation is to gain respect among peers . . .
> toughness is a virtue, humility is not.[14]

He argues that by the age of seven, a child growing up in these areas
must come to terms with the code and either begin to embrace the dress,
accents, behaviour and manners demanded by this code or resign themselves to being a perpetual victim of street violence and local gangs.[15]

The defining feature of Limerick estates where the 'code of the street'
is in operation is the prevalence of antisocial behaviour by young children. By being be able to break windows, set fires, burn cars, litter and
verbally abuse neighbours without being checked, children signal that
they are aspiring to enter the 'hard man' hierarchy. Their activities also
send a clear signal to local residents who do not embody this toughness
that the streets are not controlled by the forces of law and order but by
other elements.[16] Even when residents are not sure who these 'other elements' are, they feel vulnerable to random attacks and experience
considerable anxiety as a result.[17] It is important to note that some of the
most notorious incidents of community violence which have occurred in
Limerick in recent years, such as the attack on Gavin and Millie Murray,
have not been premediated or gang-related attacks but random violence
perpetrated by 'out of control' teenagers in parts of these estates governed by the 'code'.[18]

Senior gang participants who live in these areas may do little on a
daily basis to participate in 'code of the street' violence. They have
already proved their status within the 'hard man' hierarchy and because
of the intimacy in these neighbourhoods everyone knows that they are
located at the apex of this system. The antisocial behaviour of children
simply 'creates the water for the fish to swim in', in the words of local resident Seamus. He means that it is within this context of lawlessness that
gang participants are then able to engage in their more serious criminal
activities relatively unobstructed.

Family Gang Criminal Hierarchies

Family creates an important distinction to the way in which the 'code of
the street' operates in Limerick compared to North American contexts.
In American cities, young men and women tend to join gangs as individuals and their status within the gang is largely determined by their
own physical toughness.[19] However, the status of the individual is not as

important in Limerick's gang culture. Because family is at the core of Limerick's organised crime networks and feuds, family relationships played a huge role in determining the individual's position in local hier-archies and they act as a mitigating factor to the status generated by 'code of the street' community violence. During the course of this research, it was possible to identify at least three distinct layers to family gang criminal hierarchies in Limerick: serious players, foot-soldiers, child gang participants.

The Serious Players

There are only a small number of really important powerful families in these neighbourhoods and it would be almost impossible for an individual with no blood relationship to these families to become a 'serious player' in the local criminal hierarchies. Core crime families have graduated since the mid '80s from petty crime and receiving stolen goods to controlling much of the importation and sale of drugs in the south of Ireland.[20] Despite the material benefits from this criminal activity, daily life in these families is punctuated by constant stress and turmoil as they struggle to maintain control over the 'code' territories of these estates and pursue their two major criminal activities: drugs trading and feuding. As one local Limerick solicitor shrewdly commented, 'Limerick's criminals were able to gain such dominance in the national drugs business because of their capacity for violence and familiarity with weapons. These were skills gained during local feuds, some of which pre-date the recent drugs boom in Ireland.' Because of their position in the drugs trade, Limerick's core criminal fam-ilies need territorial strongholds. They require pockets of estates where they can store guns and deal drugs from certain houses. Therefore, it is not surprising that they exploit the random violence and lawlessness gen-erated by the 'code of the street' for their own purposes.

Apart from the strategic benefits of creating territorial strongholds, it is possible that the desire for community control evident among the 'serious players' is also linked to feuding itself. The full socio-psycholog-ical impact of feuding will be examined in Chapter Six. However, in understanding the 'serious players', research on stress disorders experi-enced by soldiers in war zones does provide some insights into their behaviours. Classic symptoms of these stress disorders include aggression, poor impulse control, paranoia and hyper-vigilance. Hyper-vigilance refers to a constant scanning of the local environment for threats.[21] Muiris explains how, as a child growing up in a feuding family, he learned to be constantly vigilant for threats:

> You know all my childhood was spent on the look-out, it was like growing up in a friggin' war-zone. Nights were the big time for attacks so I'd spend all night looking out the windows at the back while my brother would look out the front. I saw one of my family being shot in the end. I really try not to think about it. It's too fuckin' awful. No child should have to see that.

The habit of hyper-vigilance learned in childhood is almost impossible to break for many adults from feuding backgrounds. Jane, who grew up in a feuding family, explains

> I can never relax, you know, it's terrible but I'm used to it. I've never known anythin' else. I'm used to fellas goin' mad, I'm used to hidin's, I wish I wasn't but I am. I'm used to watchin' my back all the time and I always watch myself. I won't be seen caught talkin' to the wrong person. Of course I fuckin' won't.

Tadhg, who grew up in a similar context, says:

> I'm always waitin' for the next thing. I keep my eyes peeled. I always know what's goin' on and I'm keepin' an eye out all the time. People don't fuck with me coz they know better. But you know, sometimes I'd like a break. I can't go anywhere, I can't leave the house. I can't just have a normal life and sometimes I'd like that.

The hyper-vigilance of the 'serious players' in Limerick criminal family gangs contributes significantly to their capacity to control local communities and the fear with which they are viewed by neighbours. Because they are constantly 'waiting for the next thing', they closely monitor their neighbours, watching for any signs of resistance to their dominance in their behaviour. Even direct eye contact can be perceived as evidence of resistance to gang control. These individuals rarely have jobs or hobbies which interfere with this mission to control their immediate environment. Although most residents of Limerick's disadvantaged neighbourhoods will never have a direct engagement with the serious players, they remain the most feared stratum of Limerick's criminal family gangs.

Foot-Soldiers

Beneath the serious players in Limerick's criminal hierarchies is the second stratum, foot-soldiers.[22] These foot-soldiers are predominantly young men between the ages of fifteen and twenty-five. There appears to be at least three major routes to becoming a foot-soldier.[23] Extended family kinship networks provide the first source of recruitment.

Although there are only a small number of core criminal families in Limerick, they are related via blood ties to a much larger circle of families. It is these blood ties which provide the initial bond between the young man and the criminal family gang. Foot-soldiers recruited from this extended family circle understand that because they are on the fringes of the family, they will never enjoy the status of core family members. Mick, who is on the fringes of a gang, explains:

> My mother would be related to some of them and I kinda play that up. It's never really the same [as being a core crime family member] but still it's somethin', isn't it?

Foot-soldier gang participants who have distant blood relationships to the core criminal family appear to be particularly vulnerable to revenge attacks in local feuds.

The second source of foot-soldier recruitment is children in local street gangs who are actively seeking to graduate to the next level of criminal activity.[24] Some of these children have no blood relationship to the family gangs but they recognise that gang members have status and are feared within the local neighbourhood. Coming from deeply disadvantaged families, they are accustomed to neglect, abuse and violence. Therefore, the way of life offered by gang membership presents no major deterrents, and for them the rewards of money and being part of the politically dominant force within the neighbourhood are significant.[25]

In most cases, these disadvantaged children will have already been acting as agents of surveillance and intimidation for criminal families. What distinguishes these children is their evident desire to be part of the family gang network. Sharon describes one of her son's friends in the following terms:

> Now one of my kids would be really good friends with one of these lads, let's call him Tom. Now Tom is a nice enough kid but his dad has moved on long ago. His mam has got a new fella who doesn't like him very much and gives him the odd clip round the ear. Sometimes he sleeps rough on the streets, sometimes he stays here or with other friends but I know he's lonely and you see when he's with the gang, he has a kinda escape from all that. Instead of feelin' sorry for him, we're all afraid of him and in his head that's better than pity.

The third route to the role of foot-soldier is through addiction itself. Since 2006, the number of foot-soldiers with active addictions appears to have increased significantly as the use of heroin has risen sharply in Limerick.[26] In this case, the young man or woman becomes acquainted with the gang initially as a customer. After a period of time, they are asked to undertake small-scale dealing or act as a drugs mule in exchange for drugs or to pay off debts to dealers. Because of their active addictions, these foot-soldiers are among the most reluctant and least reliable gang participants.

Foot-soldiers in criminal family gangs have to engage in the most risky and least lucrative of gangland activities. As a matter of course, they are expected to transport and deal drugs. However, they can also be asked to carry guns and conduct shootings, beatings and serious intimidation for criminal family gang members. If a foot-soldier fails in these activities or turns state's witness, they themselves can be beaten or shot.[27] More importantly, serious players are hyper-vigilant with them, always watching them for signs of dishonesty or disloyalty to the criminal family gang.

Child Gang Participants

At the bottom of Limerick's criminal hierarchy are members of its most distinctive stratum, child gang participants.[28] These children live in pockets of these estates inhabited by disadvantaged families and governed by criminal families. The child gang participants are one of the most important elements in the criminal network because they operate as the 'eyes and ears' of foot-soldiers and serious players on a daily basis. The children encountered during the course of this research who were involved in this type of activity ranged in age from three to fourteen and included boys and girls. Some of the children participating in these streets had blood relationships to foot-soldiers or serious players while others had no blood ties to criminal families.[29] Participants were engaged in behaviours which ranged from mild forms of intimidation such as verbal abuse to the most serious forms of intimidation. Some of their activities, such as knocking on doors, throwing stones, and spraying graffiti, can be mistaken by authorities for 'play', the type of behaviour engaged in by children and teenagers across the social spectrum. However, in their own estates, the neighbours who are the targets of these behaviours are not chosen at random but selected on the basis of their vulnerability or the likelihood of their obstructing gang activities.

It was clear from talking to teachers, neighbours and care-workers that these children had little understanding of the consequences of their behaviour. However, they do appear to recognise that they have become part of the informal power network that governs the streets of the area and they derive a certain thrill from this knowledge. Even when they have no links to criminal gangs, the addictive excitement generated by antisocial behaviour appears to be the most significant reward for engaging in these activities. Many of the children observed were infrequent attenders at school. The thrill of participation in antisocial behaviour plays a considerable role in alleviating the boredom they experience in this context.[30]

In some cases, local residents indicated that the antisocial behaviour of local children was being actively encouraged by parents through a simple process of praise and reward.[31] When victims of their behaviours complained to their parents, the mother or father might react with hostility to the complainant, effectively encouraging the child to continue in the behaviour. Sarah explains:

> If someone complains them, they say, 'Don't mind that stupid bastard, son'. Then the child thinks that's an adult and he's a stupid bastard and my mother is telling me to call him a stupid bastard so I can keep doin' what I'm doin' and my mam will think that's fine.

In other instances, it would appear that parents were too enmeshed in their own addictions and problems to sanction the child or were themselves afraid of the child.

Under Irish law currently, it is difficult to prosecute minors for intimidation.[32] Two Gardaí interviewed indicated that they believed that disciplining a six-year-old who is engaged in antisocial behaviour is not their job. In their view, it is a child protection issue. However, child protection services are reluctant to remove children from family homes as the process of putting children into care tends to exacerbate trauma and distress for the child. While a number of diversionary and case-conference-based approaches to antisocial behaviour have been developed in Limerick, these strategies tend to focus on the reasons for the child's behaviour without actively stopping the behaviours themselves. The full implications of child gang participation for policing and child protection services will be considered in Chapter Seven.

The Production of Fear

While forms of power exist in all human societies, fear only emerges in situations where there are significant power inequalities and the weaker actor becomes afraid of the more powerful actor.[33] Although one of the founders of sociology, Max Weber, defined power as 'the chance of a man or a number of men to realise their own will in a communal action even against the resistance of others',[34] political sociologists have historically tended to focus on the power wielded by nation states. French sociologist Michel

Foucault challenged this tendency by developing his 'analytics of power' which recognises that power systems can exist 'in unexpected places and in unexpected ways'.[35] He insists that power only becomes identifiable when it is witnessed in operation as it works 'to produce particular types of bodies and minds in practices which remain invisible from the point of view of the older [state-centred] model of power'.[36]

It is Foucault's theories of power which have been most useful in understanding the operation of Limerick's regimes of fear. He argues that 'power is not an institution, nor a structure, nor a possession. It is the name we give to a complex strategic situation.'[37] Caught between core criminal families, social workers, Gardaí and local housing authorities, the residents of Limerick's disadvantaged estates find themselves living in one of the most complex 'strategic situations' in the Republic of Ireland. Subjected to constant surveillance and assessment by state agencies, the more disadvantaged residents are already predisposed to be fearful and doubt their capacity 'to realise their own will'. However, the role of state agencies in shaping their experience of powerlessness is secondary to the feelings of terror they experience as a result of being constantly monitored by criminal family gangs.

In his book *Discipline and Punish*, Foucault writes how 'docile bodies are produced by organizing individuals in practices of surveillance which train comportment according to classifications of normal and abnormal behaviour'.[38] Although Foucault's original research focused on prisons, the systems of surveillance operated by Limerick's criminal family gangs operate with the same aim of producing 'docile bodies' that conform to their own warped models of normal and abnormal behaviour. Their 'docile' neighbours are those who do not challenge their dominance, do not inquire about the nature of their criminal activities, do not inform the state about their activities, do not liaise with the Gardaí and do not show any signs that they expect a better quality of life.

It is through an intense system of surveillance that criminal family gangs are able to transform their neighbours into docile bodies. Among disadvantaged residents in these areas, it is widely believed that criminal families use scanners to listen to phone-calls in the estates and monitor information relayed on police communications systems.[39] Some criminal families have installed sophisticated camera and security systems around their homes which monitor the surrounding environment. However, the bulk of surveillance is conducted by the men, women and children linked to criminal families simply as part of their daily activities.

It is important to remember that the parts of these estates which are territorial strongholds for gangs have often been pre-selected because they have a layout which is easy to monitor, such as a court or a cul-de-sac. As rates of unemployment and single parenthood are high and rates of school attendance are low, the majority of local residents are at home all day in these closely confined spaces. It is, therefore, relatively straight-forward to monitor their movements. On seven separate occasions during this research, a resident halted a private conversation on the street for fear of being overheard. Fourteen interviewees indicated that they were very fearful of being seen talking to community Gardaí. On three occasions during this research, an interview in a private home was halted because the interviewee was concerned that someone was listening 'out the back'. Gang members are relatively unapologetic about this level of surveillance. Lochlainn, a fringe member of a local gang, says, 'We just want people to shut the fuck up and let us do our own thing. If they [the neighbours] draw the shades [Gardaí] down on us, they'll know all about it. The Guards are just another fuckin' gang.'

Foucault also highlights how power systems not only control the external behaviour of individuals but also creep into the internal world of the individual, colouring their perception of reality. He explores how people internalise the values of the power systems which they encounter and how this process impacts on their self-image, their aspirations and their behaviour. During interviews, local residents demonstrated a marked awareness of this pressure to internalise the world view of crim-inal family gangs. Single mother Ann observes:

> You know what they really want is for you to be down on yourself, so that you don't believe you can have any other life. They want you to keep your head down and just put up with it, even if there are gun-shots comin' in your window and you're lyin' on the floor with your kids, even if they're all shoutin' and roarin' at three in the morning and your baby is cryin' an' upset. What they want is for you to keep your head down and just shut the fuck up and accept that that's your life, full stop.

Central to this process of internalising the world view of criminal gangs are the physical conditions in the parts of the estates under their control. In parts of disadvantaged estates where criminal family gangs have most control, litter is strewn everywhere, walls have graffiti sprayed on them featuring terms such as 'scum', 'filth' and 'pigs' and a high proportion of houses are boarded up, derelict or burnt out. In some cases, loose horses roam on green areas, though Limerick City Council has taken steps to impound horses.[40]

Theorists of social exclusion have described as 'broken window syndrome' the anxiety which residents feel when the physical conditions of their neighbourhood deteriorate to this extent.[41] Lupton and Power argue that lack of confidence in the security of an estate can contribute to a downward spiral in the world view of the residents which impacts on other aspects of their lives. They comment

> Residents who lack a sense of control over their living environment and day-to-day security and who lose trust in others also often lack confidence in their ability to control other aspects of their lives, such as job prospects and housing choices. A sense of powerlessness and alienation can develop, and is evidenced by high levels of depression.[42]

During the course of this study, there was evidence that criminal family gangs actively recognised the efficacy of 'broken window syndrome' in subduing their neighbours and took steps to maintain the physically dilapidated condition of areas under their control.

From the gang member's perspective, dirt and dilapidation sends out a number of powerful messages which help underpin the power base of the family gangs. Firstly, physical dirt is a deterrent to outsiders, particularly agents of the state such as community workers, to enter the area. More importantly, dirt and vandalism send out a powerful message to local residents that they deserve no better. At some level, local gang leaders recognise that resistance to their authority requires a certain level of self-esteem on the part of local residents. Therefore they actively discourage any signs of pride in the local environment which would demonstrate increasing esteem and an emerging sense that 'we deserve better'.

Interviewees for this study indicated that a number of strategies were repeatedly used by criminal family gangs to maintain these living conditions, including strategic illegal dumping,[43] and using children to litter, graffiti and vandalise residents' homes. In a few cases, residents who took steps to improve their homes in the most disadvantaged parts of these estates were actively targeted by criminal gangs. Of all the incidents encountered during this study, Pete's story most clearly demonstrated the link between the physical condition of neighbourhoods and gang-control. His friend Tony recounts how:

> Pete[44] has been living here since he was a kid. All his family have gone on and moved out but Pete's a bit strange you know, but very nice an' all that. Anyway, Pete lives in a pretty tough part of this estate, lots of kids in gangs around, you know, they torment him and he never cleans the house so it's got loads of rats. So one day Pete decides that he's

gonna clean up his house. He spent the whole day paintin' his front, real nice, clearin' all the mess and dog shit out of his garden, cut the grass an' everythin' and fixed his gate. That night he got his windows put in for it. Smashed the whole fuckin' lot, the bastards. They just didn't want him gettin' ahead of himself or givin' anyone else ideas.

Pete's determination to care for his own home sent, without his realisation, a message of resistance to the family-based gangs who controlled the area. By cleaning up his environment, he was saying effectively, 'I care about myself', 'I care about my home', 'I think I deserve better'. This assertion of self-esteem is perceived as a threat by family gangs because it presents the spectre that their part of the estate will return to the control of local residents who have enough self-esteem to act on these messages. Therefore, it was necessary to publicly quash Pete's efforts in order to demonstrate that aspirations to a better environment were impossible to achieve.

In examining the operation of Limerick's regimes of fear, it is important to remember that there is a relatively high turnover of housing in Limerick's most deprived estates. Therefore, the social geography of different parts of these estates is constantly changing as more advantaged families move out and disadvantaged families move around and form new households. In this shifting population, criminal family gangs are constantly working at the task of maintaining control over some parts of these estates. If a troubled family leaves because of a feud or the burning of their home, a particular part of the estate might improve while correspondingly other parts may decline if a new family moves in who has close links to drugs and feuds networks.

Because local residents are aware of the high levels of surveillance by criminal gangs and have internalised the oppression within this power system, it is relatively easy for these families to subsequently engage in more advanced forms of intimidation which support their criminal activities. In Britain, Maynard identified three levels of intimidation in operation in disadvantaged estates.[45] At the most basic level, he found that a sizeable proportion of disadvantaged families viewed the likelihood of intimidation as being so strong that they would never consider giving evidence to police. This perception was also powerfully evident in Limerick. Bill comments, for instance:

You know I go out the door and I don't look right nor left, I don't want to know what's goin' on and I don't want to see it. If you see things, you're fucked, you draw them all down on you. The Guards looking for information and the drugs guys wantin' to make sure you

> don't talk to the Guards, they'll make your life hell and if you open
> your mouth, you may as well be fuckin' dead.

British and Scottish crime surveys estimate that fear of reprisals accounts
for between 3 and 4 per cent of all crimes not reported to the police,
'rising to 14 percent of assault and robbery cases, where the victim and
offender are more likely to know each other and opportunities for intimidation are therefore greater'.[46] Ten interviewees for this study who were
asked about levels of unreported crime agreed that the figures for their
neighbourhoods would be at least as high as Maynard's estimates.

The second level of intimidation involves actual physical assaults or
damage to property to deter victims and non-victim witnesses from either
reporting a crime or giving evidence in court. Maynard estimated that 13
per cent of crime reported by victims and 9 per cent reported by witnesses
led to this type of intimidation in high-crime housing estates in Britain. In
disadvantaged estates in Limerick, physical assaults ranged from a 'clip
round the ear' to Jim's description of how 'I got four shades of shit kicked
out of me. I was in hospital for a month afterwards. I still have problems
with my health. I sleep with a baseball bat in the bed now.'

Damage to the physical property of residents was also a common
form of intimidation and included serious vandalism to cars as well as
burning residents out of their houses. Residents can be burnt out simply
because gangs want them out of the way, because they refuse to accept
key money or because there is a suspicion that they have informed
Gardaí about criminal activities. Mavis tells how:

> You know, I was ran outa my house by those scum and I absolutely
> loved that house. I put my heart into makin' it nice. We had lovely
> times in it, an' all our memories are there. We brought our kids up
> there an' we had birthdays and christenings and great days. That was
> back in the harmless times. We had a beautiful kitchen an' all, and
> it's all gone now, burnt. I'll never get over it as long as I live.

The shells of burnt-out houses which remain after these incidents stand
as testimony to the continuing power of criminal family gangs and their
capacity to disrupt the lives of neighbouring families.

Despite the introduction of new legislation to allow evidence gathered
via electronic surveillance to be entered in court,[47] the Irish criminal
justice system remains heavily reliant on witness testimony in order to
gain criminal convictions.[48] By establishing intense regimes of fear which
effectively discourage individuals to testify, criminal family gangs have
successfully obstructed a significant dimension of the Irish criminal

justice system. While the Gardaí in Limerick have a high rate of conviction, extensive witness intimidation ensures that a number of serious criminals remain at large and, when caught, are convicted for relatively minor crimes.[49] One local Garda comments, 'Nearly every day I have an incident where there are concerns about witness intimidation. It's the first obstacle in any major investigation.'

When a high-profile testimony against a crime family does result in a punishment shooting such as the murder of Roy Collins in 2009,[50] this act succeeds not only in punishing the family in question but deterring anyone else who might consider giving testimony. Local residents in these areas share a fairly widespread belief that despite the good intentions of the Gardaí, they do not have the power to shield them from the family-based gangs. Terry comments:

> There is nothing' a Guard could say to me that would make me talk. Are they gonna hold my hand in the middle of the night with the windows comin' in on top of me and someone startin' a fire outside? Are they gonna walk me and my kid to school every day? I don't fuckin' think so.

In 2009, both the Director of Public Prosecutions and the Garda Commissioner acknowledged the weakness of witness protection within the Irish criminal justice system.[51] In conducting this ethnographic research in Limerick's disadvantaged estates, it became clear that the significance of the extended family within these communities generated a cultural obstacle to effective witness protection. While it might be possible for the state to protect one witness and their immediate family, it is realistically impossible for state agencies to protect or uproot thirty or forty extended family members in order to protect them from gang intimidation. Yet, within the logic of feuds, these extended family members are legitimate targets. Thus, in communities where family members are viewed as interchangeable and individuals can be punished for the misdemeanours of their relations, effective witness protection becomes almost impossible.

In reviewing the operation of regimes of fear in Limerick, the parallels between community violence and some forms of domestic violence are striking. Contemporary research on domestic violence highlights how physical acts of aggression often occur at the apex of a process of intimidation which has been ongoing for some time and includes verbal abuse as well as psychological oppression.[52] The process of community violence which underpins Limerick's regimes of fear operates in a similar manner. The high-profile murders which achieve national media attention often occur as an endgame to a process of intimidation which has been ongoing for a much longer period. This intimidation may have included numerous minor acts of vandalism, verbal abuse and psychological oppression. Understanding the degenerative nature of community violence in Limerick is essential in mounting an effective criminal justice response to intimidation and rebuilding oppressed communities.

Prison

The social world of the men, women and children at the heart of Limerick's regimes of fear is very small. Because of poverty and the complex geographies of local feuds, the movement of the most disadvantaged families within the city and county is quite contained, though some of the serious players are highly mobile. Tommy, a youth worker, comments:

> Some of the bigger players are swanning off around Europe to do deals, that's the bigger guys. The small minnows who are ending up in prison haven't been outside Moyross or Southill. They are afraid to go into town, they can't go into the city centre, they just stay on their own estate and go to house parties.

Despite the confined nature of their social world, there is one state institution which is relatively familiar territory: the prison system. As in many western societies, the Irish prison population contains a disproportionate number of society's most excluded individuals.[53] Indeed, in examining social exclusion and gang participation in Paris and the United States, Loic Wacquant has found that prison makes up one of the most significant parts of the social world of the disadvantaged, where many young men tend to end up either 'six feet under the ground or in jail'.[54]

The life experience of the most disadvantaged families in Limerick conforms closely to this model. Research conducted for the Bedford Row Project, the prisoners' family centre in Limerick, demonstrates that for some families, prison conviction is a shocking and deeply traumatic experience. They quote one prisoner's mother who says, 'You have to keep telling yourself it is not your fault. You have done nothing wrong. You did not send him out to do it. But if something happens you don't stop loving them and being there for them.'[55] Another mother comments, 'When my daughter heard that her brother was going to prison she was physically sick for four weeks. My youngest daughter can't go near the prison, she can't bear to see him locked up and not being able to cope.'[56]

However, for other families, particularly those deeply enmeshed in feuding, prison is a more familiar part of life experience. Daithí comments

Some of these guys would have been in and out of prison all their lives. Their dads would have been in prison, their uncles would have been in prison. Nearly every adult male they know would have done time at one stage so, you know, it's no big deal. They know where the prison is, they know how the system operates and they know who's who in there so they just get on with it and do their time.

Although prison is an important part of this social world, its confinement offers no respite from the intensity of local feuds or the demands of proving status within local 'hard man' criminal hierarchies. If anything, a prison sentence can lead to an intensification of these experiences.

Within Limerick prison, authorities have been forced to take account of the dynamic of local feuds in assigning prisoners to cells in various wings. Máirtín, who was inside for a year, describes how this operates:

They put all the Reds together and all the Blues together. When a guy from the wing I was in wanted to go to the gym or the medical wing or anything else, they had to lock down the rest of the prison to make sure he didn't meet anyone from the Blues' side. If he did, he'd have to take them on. If it was known that he'd met one of them and didn't take them, he'd be fucked, our side would beat the crap out of him.

Hilda, who has worked in the prison system, highlights the emphasis on prisoner safety in assigning prisoners to particular wings based on the structure of local feuds. She comments

They are very careful about people coming in and they are very astute about who's who and they do find out very quickly if they've put someone in the wrong place. I don't know where they get their information from. I know the Gardaí would let them know and they have their own files. Also they've seen some of them so often they know automatically where they are located. But guys who are not in the feud but from the county, or sex offenders, they have to really watch themselves.

Feuding also restricts the efficacy of the prison's rehabilitative services, according with to findings of the Bedford Row study

In Limerick prison, gangland feuds can also be an obstacle to attending classes. Tensions are high in the prison. Prisoners from different gangs reside in different wings of the prison to avoid feuding between gangs. Prisoners in the new wings have to go to the old wings to attend classes. At times, it is not safe to go there.[57]

Status within the criminal hierarchy on the outside transfers to the hierarchy inside the prison.[58] Factors such as relationship to core family gang members and personal toughness are reproduced in order to determine the individual's position within the prison hierarchy. Those working within the prison system are keenly aware of these hierarchies and recognise the distinction between the 'serious players' and the 'foot-soldiers' within that prison system. Hilda says, 'I'd be tipped off by prison officers about who is a serious player or not. I try to meet them as a normal person because I think some of them come into the system with labels, and sometimes status because of those labels.'

A young man arriving into the prison system who finds himself in a wing with his own side of the feud still has to find his niche within the hierarchy. As Einat and Kaminski have shown in other contexts, the process of initiation into prison hierarchies can be traumatic, even for those surrounded by close associates.[59] Prionsias, who has also worked within the local prison system, comments:

> A young lad who comes in would be bullied, he'd be tested. He could be physically assaulted or bullied, he certainly would be psychologically bullied and name-called to see how he responds and reacts, and depending on how he's able for that will depend on whether he's able to survive in that wing or not. There are some quite severe assaults. Vulnerable people are bullied all the time in there. What you really have to do very quickly is learn to harden up and, above all, not show any vulnerability.

Testimony from prisoners' families in Limerick gathered by Kelleher et al. suggests that some younger inmates never come to terms with the prison hierarchy and experience constant stress while inside prison. One inmate's mother commented:

> He never came out of the cell for 24/7. He would not go to the yard. He was intimidated and felt that there were people who would get at him. He was not able to cope with prison. He was suicidal and threatened to take his own life. There were very few medical services. He stayed in the cell 24/7 for months solid.[60]

Another woman explained, 'Rory is not coping well at all. One time recently I went up to the prison and he was suicidal. Nobody would tell me anything.'[61] Indeed, the inmates who appear to cope best with the initiation into prison are those who recognise the need to establish their own status within the 'hard man' hierarchy at an early stage. Kelleher at al. quote one ex-prisoner who comments:

> It is not a safe place. I have nightmares about jail still. There are drugs and people get raped. I got an education in crime when I was in jail. You have to prove that you are not a fool. When I went in first I said 'who is the hardest man here'. I went up to him and knocked him out. I got my privileges taken away but I had little trouble with other prisoners.[62]

Some interviewees suggest that there was a certain level of status associated with a prison sentence in terms of building one's reputation for toughness within the criminal hierarchy. Joe, who has worked with prisoners for a number of years, comments:

> There seems to be a code of honour that it's a good thing to be in there doing life for murder. They seem to have this whole idea that it's normal or it's okay and I feel that their world is very small. It's Moyross or Weston or Limerick prison. It's very very small.

However, for those less directly involved in serious criminal activity, the process of imprisonment seems to be associated with great shame and embarrassment.

The Bedford Row Project report suggests that while a prison sentence can build an individual's 'reputation' in the largely male-dominated 'hard man' hierarchies, prisoners' families, particularly women and children, carry a considerable burden of stigma as a result of the conviction. One prisoner's mother comments, 'When I go to the doctor and the secretary calls my name, I feel that everyone is looking at me. I have so many mixed feelings. Why are people judging my family because of what my son has done?'[63] Another woman comments: 'My son being in prison is difficult for my other children who have not been in trouble. They get labelled too.'[64] Despite the stigma which prisoners' families experience, there is evidence that many families make a big effort to support the prisoner during his sentence. One social worker noted that feuding families are particularly supportive:

> Their whole family seems to gather around them, they have huge family support. Their mothers, sisters, wives, you see them going in there and it's amazing to see the unity and it's never like 'oh he's an eejit, he got himself in there'. It's accepted as part of life and they get on with it.

Even families less accustomed to the prison system appear to try and help prisoners by giving them money and by making an effort to look well and act in a positive manner during prison visits.[65]

Because so many 'serious players' in Limerick's criminal family gangs are in prison, the hierarchies inside the prison system appear to play an important role in the operation of regimes of fear on the outside. Diarmuid, who has friends in a gang, comments:

> Even though the big boys are in prison, they are still in charge. You have to have people in charge on the inside and people in charge on the outside Sure they've nothing else to do in there but think about things and plan stuff. And the lads would be too shitless to do anythin' without their say so.

A local solicitor concurs:

> When the so-called big players are in there, they are still running the show. They are very highly regarded, that is probably out of fear as much as anything else and nothing happens without their say so. They have to be consulted about almost everything and a phone-call from the prison can stop a crime in mid-process. It has stopped crimes which are already under way.

The primary means of communication between the inside and the outside world is the mobile phone. Four interviewees for this study who had been inside indicated that until 2007 there were large numbers of mobile phones in Limerick prison. Mick comments

> In fairness almost everyone had a phone. It wasn't hard to get them in and out and the lads used them to keep in touch with what was goin' on. Sometimes we'd know about stuff, like shootins' and that long before the Guards. But when that fuckin' wanker in Portlaoise went on Joe Duffy, there was a big crackdown and it was much harder after that to have a phone.

Mick is referring to John Daly, who was serving nine years for armed robbery in Portlaoise prison when he decided to ring the Joe Duffy *Liveline* show in May 2007 to defend himself against *Sunday World* journalist Paul Williams. His phone call resulted in a major clampdown in the Irish prison system, with 1,300 items of contraband being seized. Daly subsequently received many death threats from fellow inmates and was murdered in Finglas after his release.[66]

Ex-prisoner interviewees for this study estimated that the number of phones in Limerick prison has reduced significantly since this clampdown. Within the prison hierarchy, phones have now become highly prized items. Timmy comments:

There are still phones there, they are well protected and they are given to young guys as well to look after and if they lose them they can be severely reprimanded by their own men. So the serious players won't be caught with phones but the guys around them will take the rap because you can get an extra three months on your sentence now for being caught with a phone.

Concerns about the implications of mobile phone use within prisons became a prominent issue in Ireland during 2009, with the Minister for Justice exploring the possibility of establishing mechanisms for jamming signals within prisons.[67]

Because of the connectivity which exists between prison and the outside world, events on the outside can heighten tensions in the prison, while fights in prison can have serious consequences for families living on the outside. Seán, who spent two years in prison, provides a good example of the way outside events impact on the inside.

I'm thinking of a time when a relation of a fairly serious player was shot. By Jesus, you could have cut the fuckin' tension with a knife inside. Everyone was nervous, their side was nervous and our side wanted to fuckin' kill one of them and the screws could see it too. They are on the lookout the whole time just waitin' waitin' waitin' for somethin' to happen, for the big blow up.

Fergus describes how conflicts on the inside can have consequences for relations of inmates on the outside

There was this young fella who came in and he was a right fuckin' eejit. Big mouth and no fuckin' sense. Anyway, he starts givin' lip, and he said somethin' to one of the serious guys. And he just looked at him and said really quietly, 'Is your cousin livin' down in Oak Park?' And that was it, his cousin had to pack up and leave the house coz he was afraid he'd be attacked.

The connectivity between the prison and the outside world means that members of criminal gangs can create 'docile bodies' through surveillance even when they are inside the prison system. Residents in some parts of these estates believe that they can never escape the watchful eyes of the 'serious players'. Although it is almost impossible to measure the level of surveillance which is being conducted by inmates of the prison on those living in disadvantaged estates, over 50 per cent of residents interviewed believed that their estates continued to be monitored by those on the inside. Suzanne comments:

> They know every fuckin' thing that goes on, not all the small stuff
> but definitely all the important stuff and the thing is that they are still
> in control even when they are on the inside. They are still the big
> players and we feel it, we know it and we're still afraid of them. We
> just fuckin' dread it when one of them gets out.

Perhaps the most convincing evidence of surveillance comes from the
wives and girlfriends of prisoners themselves. Six women interviewed
during this study had partners who were or had been in the prison
system and it had a profound impact on their behaviour. Aisling
describes one of her neighbours whose partner has just gone inside in
the following terms:

> Her fella now, he'd be quite a serious player and she's absolutely shit-
> less since he went in. Apparently he's goin' off his head in there coz
> he feels he can't control things. She's terrified that if she puts a foot
> out of line, if she's seen talkin' to a guy or in the pub, or anything
> like that, there'd be hell to pay. So she never goes out, she barely
> leaves the house.

The wives and girlfriends of prisoners monitor their own behaviour
closely and take particular care that they are not publicly linked with
other men. If a prisoner believes that his partner has been unfaithful, she
may be beaten or attacked when he is freed. The negative consequences
of prison release are also very evident in the Bedford Row study, where
family members reported that men were often released without any
warning or preparation either for themselves or their families.[68] For
women who have strained relationships with their partners, the consequences of these sudden releases can be dangerous.

Foot-soldiers and those on the fringes of feuding gangs are also
careful to monitor their behaviour as the hyper-vigilance of the 'serious
players' remains in operation even when they are in prison. Liam, who
works with youth services, comments, 'they are afraid they'll meet the
opposing side or even be seen saluting the wrong person or being seen in
the wrong place. If that goes back inside, something could happen to
them, they are afraid of their lives.' Thus, despite imprisonment, the
power of the serious players within the gangs and their capacity to
monitor communities on the outside remains intact.

These findings raise questions about the current reliance on imprisonment as the primary solution to unpicking Limerick's regimes of fear.
Efforts to protect juries, victims and witnesses within the criminal justice
system and utilise electronic surveillance evidence are all designed to

convict criminals and put them inside the prison system.[69] Because Limerick's family gangs have successfully adapted to the prison structure, the imprisonment of 'serious players' and their foot-soldiers does not appear to significantly obstruct community surveillance. These findings would suggest that solutions which focus on the recruitment of minors into criminal activity need to receive greater attention within proposed solutions to this problem.

Globalisation

It is very easy to characterise the problems which have emerged in Limerick as the product of local cultural factors, combined with bad planning and extreme social exclusion. However, it is clear that Limerick's regimes of fear are not only the product of local circumstances but also specific changes at national and global levels. In order to assess these broader processes, the impact of globalisation on disadvantaged communities was examined in this final section of the research. Held and McGrew note that globalisation

> ... refers to ... enduring patterns of worldwide interconnectedness. But the concept of globalisation denotes much more than a stretching of social relations and activities across regions and frontiers. For it suggests a growing magnitude or intensity of global flows such that states and societies become increasingly enmeshed in worldwide systems and networks of interaction. As a consequence, distant occurrences and developments can come to have serious domestic impacts which local happenings can engender significant global repercussions.[70]

At the most basic level, the link between Limerick's criminal gangs and globalisation is based on commerce. Limerick has achieved its international notoriety for violent crime because of its position as a node in a global commodity chain which involves the trade of drugs and guns.[71] During the 1990s, the demand for recreational drugs in Ireland increased exponentially, linked to the burgeoning popularity of global club culture.[72] Limerick's gangs, already involved in low-level criminal activities, offered an entrepreneurial response to this demand. As a result of their success as drugs suppliers, they have become one of the dominant criminal forces in the south of Ireland.[73] Using a familiarity with weapons already gained through local feuds, these gangs became key local players in a global commodity chain by forming links with drugs networks in Britain, Holland and Spain.[74] Some journalists have also alleged that these gangs are not just involved in selling drugs in the

Republic of Ireland but also engaged in the trade of guns to gangs outside the jurisdiction.[75]

The vast majority of gang participants who are living in disadvantaged communities in Limerick are not explicitly aware of this global dimension to their activity. As fringe gang member Joe comments, 'I couldn't give a fuck where the shit comes from.' Andrew Papachristos found a similar absence of awareness among drug-dealing gang members in Chicago. He writes:

> Hector stands at the end of a long and familiar global commodity chain. The little plastic bags in his palm contain $10 chunks of crack cocaine that look like jagged disfigured sugar cubes. By the time the drug hits the streets of Chicago, it has been touched by more than a dozen people in three countries. Hector has no interest in its global supply chain. His daily concerns and activities centre on a few city blocks, his aspirations reaching just as far.[76]

However, according to interviewees, a small number of more senior members of Limerick gangs appear to be keenly aware of their position in the global drugs commodity chain. Their willingness to travel and indeed sometimes relocate to the UK, Holland and Spain in order to maintain supply to the Irish drugs markets indicates that they can be characterised as 'hyper-mobile global actors' who have facilitated the integration of Ireland into the global illegal economy.[77] It is significant that in the flurry of scholarship which celebrated Ireland's short-lived Celtic Tiger boom within the global economy between 1995 and 2007,[78] no major scholarly analyses have been undertaken of this influential segment of Ireland's trans-national capitalist class.[79]

Not only have technologies linked to globalisation such as mobile phones and surveillance equipment made gang participation easier, web-based technologies have also provided new sites where Limerick gang members can 'perform' their masculinity and 'hard man' status. In August 2009, the *Limerick Chronicle* reported that contributors to the Internet discussion forum Limerick Blogger had been threatened for making anti-gang postings. In an adaptation of the usual threat of 'I know where you live', one gang member had apparently threatened 'I have your IP address'.[80] Members of Limerick's criminal gangs have also posted their own web pages on social networking sites such as Bebo, My Space and Facebook. These pages are used to make threats, display weapons and proclaim dominance in local feuds.[81] The video website YouTube has featured live footage of gang members making threats, joy-riding and burning cars.[82]

In these postings, Limerick gang members not only proclaim their dominance within local neighbourhoods but often seek to align themselves with the more glamorous dimensions of global gang culture. Andrew Papachristos notes how global technologies have contributed to the dissemination of glamorised though ultimately inaccurate images of gang participation:

> The increasing mobility of information via cyberspace, films and music makes it easy for gangs, gang members and gang wannabes to get information, adapt personalities and distort gang behaviours. Most often, these images of gang life are not simply exaggerated: they're flat-out wrong. Flashy cars . . . and wads of cash are not the gang world norm. Hustling to make ends meet, trying to put food on the table while staying out of jail . . . and dealing with the humdrum of school, unemployment and child support are more typical.[83]

John Hagedorn argues that it is impossible to understand contemporary gang culture without recognising the influence of the music, dress-codes and behaviours associated with rap and hip-hop music which emerged from US urban ghettos in the '80s and '90s. He comments, 'what we are witnessing in hip hop is the creation of a powerful global identity based on street experiences that are filled with multiple meanings, contradictions and intense cultural struggle.'[84]

The popularity of these cultural forms was powerfully evident among young people in Limerick's disadvantaged estates. Dean would be typical: 'my fav is Tupac, I don' like none of that Coldplay shit.' Limerick has produced its own indigenous forms of rap and comedy satires of Limerick rap have also achieved popularity.[85] It is easy to dismiss this hybrid cultural form as being simply derivative of US rap culture, but genuine Limerick rap provides disadvantaged teens with a means of re-imagining their social exclusion. At the most basic level, Limerick rap celebrates the hyper-masculine behaviours and protest masculinities which define status on the streets of disadvantaged communities in Limerick.[86] However, what is striking about the content of this rap is that it focuses almost completely on the theme of power over women, Gardaí and members of opposing family-based gangs. Given the intense social exclusion and powerlessness which exists among the most disadvantaged in Limerick, it is not surprising that a musical form where performers constantly portray themselves as powerful has such appeal. However, two counsellors expressed fears that immersion in US rap culture when accompanied with drug consumption might be contributing to increasing volatility of gang members and a distorted relationship with their local reality. Timothy, who counsels young men in this position, comments:

> The younger generation are far more chaotic, they'd risk anything. They are always getting hyped up on tablets and coke and then they're listenin' to this rap and it makes them really hyper, ready to snap really. They are far more dangerous than their fathers because they are less in control of themselves and because of the drugs an' the hip-hop music and movies they watch, they are a bit more separated from reality here.

In terms of the world view of the 'disadvantaged of the disadvantaged' across estates in Limerick, there was a notable absence of references to national culture and the national public sphere. Hardly any interviewees reported reading a national broadsheet newspaper or watching programmes on the national television service, RTÉ. The absence of the national public sphere from disadvantaged communities in Limerick highlights not only their depth of social exclusion but also the degree to which they have become detached from mainstream Irish society.

This absence of the 'national' also helps explain why Limerick gang members are so unaffected by the 'moral panics' which emerge in the national media after high-profile murders and attacks.[87] Timothy provides particular insight into this phenomenon:

> There is one guy I'm working with and he'd be a pretty big player and when that guy was killed up in Roxboro [Roy Collins] and there was this whole media thing about it and it was in every paper and he said to me 'you know the guys who did that are probably oblivious to all this. They haven't a clue what's going on, they'd have no interest and they wouldn't read a paper.' He said they are probably 'out of it' right now, this very minute. These fellas aren't goin to be worrying about who's sayin' what on the television.

The lack of awareness of the national public sphere highlights the complex way in which the socially excluded in Limerick's disadvantaged estates have engaged with globalisation.

The Irish policy makers who celebrated the success of the Celtic Tiger boom between 1995 and 2007 appeared to give little consideration to how those who were excluded from its rewards would respond to their marginalisation.[88] Keohane and Kuhling highlight the specifically Irish forms of consumption-based status which emerged in Ireland during this period:

> . . . the house becomes the sublime object of the ideology of com-
> modity fetishism as does the practice of the elaboration of the
> interior . . . New houses are perceived by their owners, and indeed
> by others, as a 'beautiful thing'. [They seek] recognition, status, self
> esteem that in the eyes of the community they are seen to be doing
> well.[89]

There is evidence that members of Limerick's criminal gangs also internalised this value system but found illegal means of attaining these
high-status consumer goods. Through their public display of luxury cars,
expensive home improvements and lavish family celebrations, they
demonstrate their own form of conspicuous consumption, albeit a form
of consumption which comes at a heavy cost to themselves and their
communities. One local resident, Sinéad, perceptively comments, 'I see
them coming around in their BMW jeeps and their Mercedes, I see them
coming around and sometimes they are just checkin' their operations,
they are just here to say, look at me, look at what I've got, look at what
you've given me.'

Having placed so much emphasis on the acquisition of high-status
consumer goods during the Celtic Tiger period Irish society offers little
in the way of moral rationales outlining why these goods should not be
obtained through criminal means. When questioned about the moral
dimensions of their behaviour, one gang member commented that customers want drugs and they are simply supplying the consumer demand.
When the illegality of drug-dealing is raised, he highlighted the evident
disrespect for the law among Irish political and financial elites which
came to light during the tribunals of the 1990s and more recent banking
crises. He comments, 'Why should I give a shit about the law? Look at
all those fuckers of politicians and developers creaming it for the last
twenty years, what about all those tribunals? Did those fuckers respect
the law?' At the same time, the legitimacy of the Catholic morality which
had considerable influence in disadvantaged communities in Limerick
during Liam Ryan's *Social Dynamite* study in the 1960s has also diminished. Secularisation and, most importantly, revelations of child sex
abuse have significantly undermined the legitimacy of church-based
moral frameworks in these communities despite the high levels of trust
evident in local clergy and sisters. As Joe Lee points out, Ireland lacks
any 'traditional civic culture'.[90] As the moral authority of political, economic and church-based elites declines, community leaders in
disadvantaged estates have little in the way of moral frameworks to offer
young people in response to the corrosive logic of the gangs which

stresses criminality as the only route to the acquisition of desirable consumer goods and achieving local fear-based respect.

Conclusion

The regimes of fear which have emerged in Limerick are not unique. The same mechanics of fear are evident in parts of west Dublin and other parts of Ireland where extreme social exclusion is coupled with drugs-related criminality. Understanding how fear can be used to obstruct the operation of the criminal justice system is an essential part of mounting an effective state response to intimidation and community violence. Evidence from this study suggests that problems in relation to the antisocial behaviour of minors may need to be addressed at a more robust level than local authority housing divisions or child protection services.

This study also suggests that, in Limerick at least, criminal gangs have adapted very effectively to the prison system, using foot-soldiers and surveillance to continue to direct criminal activities from the inside. As a result, unpicking these regimes of fear may require a response that looks beyond the imprisonment of key individuals and focuses more on the demand and supply side of the drugs nexus. At the level of demand, middle-class drug users need to be made aware of the impact of their drugs consumption on disadvantaged communities. On the supply side, early intervention measures which target disadvantaged children at pre-school age must be developed as a matter of urgency in order to draw these minors away from the lures of drugs use. Finally, the criminal problems which have emerged in Limerick city are linked not only to drugs but also to the specific socio-cultural understandings which inform feuding in the city. The research presented within the next chapter focuses on this interweaving issue.

6. The Sociology of Feuding
Limerick gangland and Traveller feuds compared

Niamh Hourigan

This chapter seeks to provide a sociological analysis of feuding in the Irish context and compare the structure of Limerick 'gangland' and Traveller feuds. There is relatively little scholarly analysis available on contemporary feuds in Ireland despite the growing intensity of feuding during the last fifteen years. Two studies were undertaken in response to Traveller feuding in the Midlands,[1] but no sociological research has been conducted on how feuding interweaves with the particular criminal justice challenges which exist in Limerick city.

Within this chapter, the process of feuding is defined and the place of feuding within Irish history is examined. The reasons for increased Traveller feuding in recent years are explored and the origins of the major feud(s) in Limerick are outlined. The bulk of the chapter is devoted to developing a sociology of feuding based on research conducted in Limerick and a separate interview series conducted among Travellers in Ennis, Mullingar, Dundalk and Waterford.[2] The similarities between Limerick feuds and Traveller feuds, in terms of weak relationships to law and order and the centrality of family honour in providing a legitimating rationale for feuding, are highlighted. The dynamic of tit for tat and the 'pressure to perform' experienced by young men in feuding families is also outlined. Finally, the impact of feud-related trauma on the men, women and children who are members of feuding families is discussed. In the conclusion, the importance of feud-related identities is highlighted as a significantly neglected factor in policy debates on regeneration in Limerick city and Traveller policy initiatives. In this context, the potential for innovative conflict resolution and criminal justice responses to feuding in the Republic of Ireland is reviewed.

What is a Feud?

The *Oxford English Dictionary* defines a feud as 'lasting mutual hostility between two tribes or families with murderous assaults in revenge for injury'.[3] The *Columbia Encyclopaedia* describes a feud as:

> formalised private warfare, especially between family groups. The blood feud is characteristic of those societies in which a strong central government either has not arisen or has decayed. In modern times, the feud, outlawed in most countries, has persisted where public justice cannot be easily enforced and private means are a simpler recourse.[4]

At the most basic level, feuds consist of long-running conflicts between families, clans or gangs. Feuds begin because the members of one family group perceive themselves to have been wronged or insulted in some way by another family group. Intense feelings of resentment are usually manifested through acts of revenge which provoke retaliation and ultimately generate a long-lasting cycle of violence between the two parties.

Feuds are most likely to emerge in communities where the forces of law and order are either weak or perceived as being remote from the feuding population. Roger Gould comments:

> In contexts in which the state's role in dispute resolution is weak, people are more likely to protect their interests with deadly force, either aggressively, defensively or pre-emptively. This pattern has been widely documented in traditional societies and in marginalised urban communities in the contemporary industrialised world. In such situations, group membership has enormous value in that it constitutes a mutual-defence pact.[5]

When an individual does not perceive the criminal justice system as a viable source of protection, they either have to provide their own protection or find shelter within their kin network. These kin or clan relationships were as important in ancient feuds as they are today for some marginalised communities in contemporary Ireland.[6] Grutzpalk comments, 'the system of tribal blood feud worked on the basis of a balance of terror. Individual safety was guaranteed by the clan or not at all. As an ancient Greek you were not free to choose your personal ties. You either belonged to a group or no one would worry for your safety'.[7] Durkheim concludes that participation in feuding in these contexts becomes almost compulsory as it demonstrates the loyalty of the individual to other members of the group and is linked to status and prestige in the broader kin network. There is little reward for non-participation as members of feuding families who are not involved in violence are still vulnerable to attack from the opposing side. Individuals with no strong family ties in feud-dominated communities can become victims of the random violence of all family groups.[8] This classic feud logic is still evident in the Limerick feud(s) and within some kin networks in the Traveller community.

History of Feuding in Ireland

While elements of the Irish media tend to characterise feuds as a form of conflict which is exclusive to those on the margins of Irish society,[9] it is probable that many Irish citizens of Catholic descent have feuding and faction-fighting as part of their own family histories.[10] There is evidence that Irish Catholics during the nineteenth century were reluctant to consult what they perceived as an 'alien' colonial administration in order to resolve internal disputes within communities. As a result, organised faction fights and less formalised family feuds became the commonplace method of resolving disputes about property, broken engagements, bullying and conflicts linked to ancient clan-based tensions.[11]

Nineteenth-century British colonial administrators in Ireland viewed these feuds as irrational, 'a remnant of the old barbarous system of clanship, which still continues in practice', according to one senior figure.[12] However, feuding and faction-fighting remained a widespread social practice throughout Ireland in the nineteenth century and was particularly prevalent in Munster. O'Donnell concludes:

> Faction-fighting was a legacy of a distressed and subject people . . . denied education and otherwise effectively cut off from the mainstream of current affairs . . . the frustration of being denied a part in the government of their own country or a meaningful place in its industry and commerce . . . it is not altogether surprising that the frustrated people turned to faction-fighting not only as a test of clannish strength or for a settlement of family feuds but also as an escape from the trials and tribulations of their inferior status and as an act of defiance towards the authorities they despised.[13]

While the practice of faction-fighting appears to have died out during the twentieth century, family feuds remained a relatively commonplace feature of life in rural Ireland and in the more deprived communities of Ireland's cities.[14] The persistence of feuding in some working-class urban contexts appears to be linked to the continuing importance of the extended family as the central organising structure of these communities. In addition, the culture of 'no grassing' to police about local disputes, a post-colonial legacy, generated a degree of distance in the relationship between some marginalised communities and the Irish policing authorities.[15]

Traveller Feuds in Contemporary Ireland

Although there are no official statistics relating to Traveller feuds, there is some evidence of a significant increase in feud-related violence within the Traveller community in recent years. Dillon notes that between 1996 and 2006 at least a dozen Traveller men were killed in feud-related violence. He says, 'considering that Travellers make up 0.6 per cent of the total population this equates to 2,000 homicides [in the settled community] in Ireland over a ten-year period. It is an incredible statistic.'[16] During the summer of 2008, Gardaí in Waterford recorded over a hundred incidents related to a local feud,[17] while nationally in 2008, six major Traveller feuds 'either sparked off violence, led to specific Garda crack-downs or ended up in court'.[18]

Based on interviews conducted for this study,[19] it would appear that the reasons for this increase in feuding are complex. Since the 1960s, the state has pursued an assimilationist policy in relation to the Traveller community which has strongly encouraged/forced them to abandon their traditionally nomadic lifestyle and embrace sedentarisation.[20] The advantages of the strategy for the settled community are obvious as it minimises conflict with Travellers around the movement of encampments and property rights.[21] However, Traveller activist Michael McDonagh explains how even when mobility is reduced, the nomadic mindset remains a central organising feature of Traveller culture. He states

> When Travellers speak of travelling, we mean something different from what country people [settled people] usually understand by it . . . Country people travel to get from A to B, but for Travellers, the physical fact of moving is just one aspect of a nomadic mindset that permeates every aspect of our lives. Nomadism entails a way of looking at the world, a different way of perceiving things, a different attitude to accommodation, to work and to life in general.[22]

A review of policy documents on Travellers from the *Commission on Itinerancy* (1965) onwards suggests that little consideration was given to the impact which this imposed sedentary lifestyle would have on Travellers' nomadic mindset, specifically in terms of conflict management between families.

Historically, relationships between Traveller families were rooted in the understanding that each family was mobile to some degree.[23] In the settled community, conflicts between neighbours are usually constrained by the knowledge that both families will have to live in close proximity with the opposing family after the conflict. However, the modes through which

Travellers engaged in conflict were based on the cultural understanding that they would, after the conflict, be able to move away from the opposing family. Although it was possible for the state to settle a nomadic group within one generation, it was evidently not possible to change culturally specific patterns of resolving inter-family conflicts in the same period.

Ní Shúinéar's 2005 study on conflict within the Traveller community outlines the strain which living in close quarters has placed on inter-family relationships within the Traveller community. One respondent comments:

> Seldom seen is wonderful at times, right! When I'm with you all the time, all your naggly little bits and pieces come as well with it and stuff, where my other relations are living over in [in the other side of the country] and I only see them an odd time and it's always a celebration.[24]

Another informant comments 'you cannot get a big number of Travellers to agree in one place. Settled people will move out because there's too many Traveller families. And the Traveller families will move out because there's too many Traveller families.'[25]

Ní Shúinéar argues that Travellers historically dealt with inter-family conflict by moving on and avoiding it. She quotes one interviewee who says:

> Traditionally, the way of dealing with conflict was to avoid it. That's exactly – I know it sounds really simple! But that's exactly how it worked. You were moving, you were very transient. Now because Travellers are changing and becoming more sedentary, they have great difficult with dealing with conflict when it's face to face, and the only way of dealing with it, is, lash out.[26]

Since the introduction of the Housing (Miscellaneous Provisions) Act 2002, the traditional option of moving away from conflict has been removed as a Traveller family who moves on to public or private land faces criminal prosecution.[27] A number of interviewees who worked with the Traveller community have indicated that they believe the 'Trespass Law' has had a deeply negative impact on feuding. Mairéad comments, 'There is some law that's bad law and that's one of them, it has placed some Traveller families under huge pressure. When there's conflict, they have no way out, no escape route, so things just escalate and get more intense. No wonder things are as bad as they are now.'[28]

Apart from moving on, it would appear that the two traditional sources of conflict resolution with the Traveller community, elder intervention and fair fights, have also become less effective in recent years.

The role of elders or 'negotiators' in resolving conflict was highlighted by a number of Travellers interviewed for this study.[29] However, McGearty et al. found that

> The role of elders in the Traveller community has changed just as it has in the settled community and this has changed their effectiveness as conflict management agents. There is evidence that younger people are making more decisions for themselves and the authority of the elders is less influential.[30]

The practice of the 'fair fight' as a mode of conflict resolution has also undergone significant changes that render it less effective. Ní Shúinéar notes that historically the 'fair fight' was a 'political event' and 'an extremely serious legal undertaking' which could end tensions between two conflicting families.[31] The organisation of 'fair fights' has been transformed in recent years. Large sums of money can now be won or lost on 'fair fights'. The results of the fighting are broadcast immediately via mobile phones and the results of 'fair fights' can be the source of conflict rather than the resolution of a conflict. One of Ní Shúinéar's informants notes:

> There is a movement from two men going out and boxing the head of one another, and shake hands and say 'That's all. That's solved.' That's not reality anymore. Reality now is where grudges are held in, planned out how you'll get vengeance back, and you know, individually, alliances among, within family groupings, of maybe twenty or thirty young people saying 'Anything happens to any one of us, we all move together and attack.'[32]

Despite increased settlement of Travellers, the community continues to have a very weak relationship with the forces of law and order in Ireland.[33] Along with African asylum seekers, Travellers are the minority group which complains most frequently of harassment by the Garda Síochána.[34] In their submission to the Garda Diversity Strategy, Pavee Point, the Traveller nongovernmental organisation (NGO), state: 'There is a history of generally poor relations between the Gardaí and the Traveller community, characterised by mistrust and hostility on both sides. Many Travellers feel that their community is over-policed and under-protected and that it is policed at the behest of the settled community.'[35]

Some Travellers interviewed have indicated that they preferred not to consult the formal criminal justice system when resolving internal disputes. Historically, fear of encountering prejudice and racism from police forces on both sides of the border has been mingled with a conviction that resolution of internal disputes should be kept within the community.[36]

Dillon comments, 'Travelling people generally prefer to sort out their affairs among themselves. The police, solicitors and the court system of "country people" are regarded with suspicion.'[37] However, Traveller organisations argue that there is a general reluctance among Gardaí to resolve internal disputes among Travellers, a situation which contributes to the culture of feuding. The Pavee Point submission concludes:

> In some cases where violent conflict has occurred within the Traveller community, Travellers have described instances where the Guards have failed to respond to emergency calls for assistance or have stood back and allowed, or in some cases encouraged, people to take the law into their own hands. It suits some Travellers for the Guards to adopt a 'hands off' approach in this context. However, there are other Travellers for whom this is not helpful, but they often feel that they cannot articulate their need for Garda protection publicly.[38]

Therefore, the combination of cultural change, the strain of sedentarisation and a weak relationship to law and order have contributed to an increase in feuding within the Traveller community in recent years.

Limerick Gangland Feuds

Because some of the participants in Limerick gangland feuds have links to families of settled Travellers, there has been a perception in some media outlets that the Limerick feuds are simply an extension of the generic Traveller feuding model. For instance, an article in *The Observer* in Britain highlights the role of 'a family of settled Travellers with criminal connections stretching from the west of Ireland into Britain which set up a violent feud'[39] in Limerick, while an article in the *Sunday Independent* described one Limerick feuding family as possessing 'a reputation of exceptional brutality. They have links through marriage in some instances, with a number of Travelling families.'[40]

Until the mid 1980s, there is no doubt that Limerick feuds bore some resemblance to classic feud models,[41] with small incidents re-igniting long-standing tensions between local families. Mikey Kelly[42] described typical examples of this conflict before his death:

> We were feuding with the McCarthy family from The Cooperage . . . They hit my brother in town one day. He was attacked for a fag and 20p. I met up with him and he was distraught. He told me what had happened and I went down the lane and had a go at the four of them . . . Things escalated and it was tit for tat.[43]

Indeed, interviews conducted for this study indicate that the small-scale feuding, which never really died out in older areas of Limerick, escalated to new heights when some families were moved from older communities to new estates on the outskirts of the city. As outlined in Chapter Three, the combination of a densely concentrated population of economically marginalised people and a weak police presence in these estates created an environment where feuding flourished. However, the widespread criminalisation of the activities of Limerick's feuding families since the early 1990s has brought these feuds much closer to the North American model of inter-gang conflict.[44]

It is beyond the scope of this chapter to describe, in detail, the history of the current feud(s) in Limerick, as each event within these feuds is deeply contested by participating families. For a recent account, I refer readers to press reports and books within the 'true crime' genre.[45] For the purposes of the analysis presented in this chapter, it is necessary to understand that the critical events which sparked the current feud(s) in Limerick occurred from 2000 onwards[46] and involve members of a number of well-known Limerick families.[47] The feud has been linked to a number of serious murders and assaults on feuding family members, bystanders, witnesses and those who, through bad luck or conflict, have got in the way of the feud.[48]

The scale and intensity of the current feud(s) in Limerick city dwarf any feuding conflicts within the Traveller community in the Republic of Ireland. The feuding in Limerick is distinctive in terms of its longevity, the total numbers of families involved and the interweaving of feuding with organised criminal activity. While much of the current feuding dates back to events in the early '90s (with the attempted murder of Christy Keane and the subsequent shooting of Eddie Ryan in 2000 often being cited as a pivotal moment),[49] some members of Limerick feuding families will cite events which happened much earlier as contributing to the current feud(s). A number of the key figures in contemporary Limerick feud(s) weren't even alive when the feuding began, yet the feud remains a master narrative in their extended families, and membership of feuding families functions as a master status,[50] dominating all other aspects of personal identity. In describing his work with one Limerick criminal, Seosamh, a local counsellor, says the following:

> You have to ask who began the feud. Where does Tommy Red[51] come into the feud so what is really his tradition and history with the feud and how much of the narrative of the original feud does Tommy Red know and how much does he want to know? It's quite remote from

him really so why does Tommy Red fan the flames of something he knows shag all about and why . . . because it adds to his status . . . so again we are back to power and respect and reputation.

In Chapters Three, Four and Five, it was outlined how code-of-the-street violence had emerged in some estates in Limerick city due to state neglect and the remote nature of policing authorities, particularly during the late 1980s. This code led to the emergence of a local tough man hierarchy where status became linked to one's capacity to elicit fear in others, a status which had to be maintained by engaging in violent acts. Limerick's feuding families can be found at the apex of this tough man hierarchy. Mentioning the names of the feuding families is enough to generate fear in many ordinary citizens interviewed for this research in these estates. This status is very valuable in a local context, and thus, there are some individuals that have a vested interest in the perpetuation of the feud(s). John, a community worker, notes:

> I think it's the names, and the names instil more fear than the actual feuding because of the fear of what they can do or this macho talk about what they have done, their status in the community. Feuding by its nature transforms, over the long term, into something else and then your own identity becomes so interlinked with the feuding status part that your identity becomes totally enmeshed with the master status of the feud. Basically, there is no you outside the feud, coz what else do you have?

The telling and re-telling of the narrative of the feud within extended families mean that feuding becomes part of the fundamental value system of young people growing up in feuding families. Sharon, a local resident, describes how

> . . . the Guards were down making an arrest and they had the squad car down and as usual, the kids were up kickin' the tyres and chattin' to them and I heard one garda say to this young fella' about five sayin' so 'what do you want to be when you grow up?' and he turned to him, cool as you like, and said, 'I want to kill one of those fuckin' Reds.'

It would appear that as the feud(s) rumbles on and as each family suffers its own losses, boys, in particular, are conditioned to expect that they will have to play their part in the feud and avenge attacks on their family members. Kevin, who works with young people, says, 'I know one family where the boys would have been brought in when the uncle was murdered and told you will have to avenge his death. They weren't even ten at this time.' This pressure to perform experienced by young men, in particular, can become acute in situations where the more senior male figures in the family are either dead or in prison. In these instances, not only does the boy become a significant target for the opposing family but he, himself, will experience enormous pressure to perform his duty by his own family. Carol, who works with troubled teenage boys, says:

> I've had guys sitting there in front of me, where you are sitting now. Big tough guys wearing bulletproof vests and God's truth, they are shittin' themselves. They are the most frightened people you will ever meet. And some of them might only just be out of St Pat's (youth detention facility) or prison or what have you, but they know that they are expected to perform and they have to get on with it, even if they don't want to, otherwise they're fucked.

Success in these contexts is measured by one's performance in the feud(s). Selina, a woman who is related to a feuding family, comments, 'Well, you're expected to perform in your job aren't you, your performance is measured. Well, theirs is as well, it's just that what they've got to do is much harder.' The longevity of the Limerick feud(s), the importance of the narrative of the feud within the identities and value systems of feuding families, means that feuding now constitutes a significant criminal justice and socio-cultural problem in parts of Limerick city.

Family and Family Honour

The extended family is the central organising structure of the Traveller community. Michael McDonagh explains:

> Working at your family ties is the key to Traveller identity so we will turn up at all meetings of the extended family, for weddings, for funerals or when visiting the sick in hospital. If you even look at what happens in hospital when someone's sick or dying, everyone gathers together and visits the hospital, and the nurses are going haywire over the huge number of Travellers there.[52]

While family dominates the domestic sphere of life for most Irish people, it is participation in the workforce and occupational structures which provides income and informs status and identity.[53] In contrast, for Travellers, family not only provides intimacy but also status, identity and income, the rewards settled people generally associate with their occupations.[54]

In circumstances where the status of the family is threatened and there is a weak relationship to the forces of law and order, it is essential that individuals demonstrate their loyalty to the family by their willingness to defend family honour.[55] Conflicts can emerge over commercial transactions, control of space, the transgression of sexual boundaries, bullying, etc., but it is the rationale of 'protecting family honour' which transforms these individual incidents into long-running and violent family feuds. Mary, a middle-aged Traveller woman, explains:

> Family is everything, you see, and you can't let the side down, you can't let things go because others will think they have got the better of you, they will think that they're better than you. So you have to show that you can defend yourself and you have to rear your sons to show that they can defend the honour of the family. We'd die for each other, it's the most important thing.

One of Ní Shúinéar's informants describes succinctly the link between personal identity and protecting family honour for Travellers:

> It's not so much that one person has been insulted and you're taking up for them. It's almost like you're taking up for yourself. And that's the difference between doing that and deciding to take up for somebody because they're related to you, or because they're your brother. It's almost like: your family – you – have been insulted. You have been insulted. Because of your name. So you're not actually taking up for somebody else. You're taking up for yourself.[56]

Therefore, as the individual's identity is critically linked to the status of their extended family, the defence of family honour becomes a matter of both personal and collective importance.

As discussed in Chapter Four, family is also the central organising structure of some communities in disadvantaged areas of Limerick city. Family relationships are particularly important in feuding contexts. Although there are only a small number of core feuding families in Limerick, these families are related to a much larger kin network. During periods where feuding tensions are heightened, members of this broader kin network can become targets, particularly if it is difficult to get access to core family members. Mavis describes one incident where

> One of the girls down the road, she's two kids, but one of them, well, his father is one of the Reds. Anyway one day we hear that one of the Blues has been clipped [attacked] an' they're comin' to get this youngster. He was 'bout thirteen at the time. Well, she managed to get him away but she was scared to come back.

Likewise, if an individual on the fringes of a feuding family decides to turn state's witness, they are exposing all the members of their extended family to risk of reprisal. This fear of reprisal against family members presents a major obstacle to the policing of feuds.

Although feuding conflicts in Limerick city are long-standing, patterns of alliance and hostility between individual families are constantly shifting within a broader division between major kinship networks.[57] Family honour is also frequently cited as a legitimating rationale for the feuding by participants in this context. Tomás, whose family is related to one of the main feuding families, explains, 'We have to keep our side up the whole time, we can't let them get the upper hand on us. It's about pride really.' However, using the term 'family honour' to describe this ideology can be deceptive. Within European anthropological literature, family honour is defined as the 'maintenance of good reputation in general and, more specifically, masculine and feminine honour codes'.[58] This definition bears little relationship to the rationale which informs Limerick feuds. Pitt-Rivers describes the model of family honour which he encountered in Mediterranean feuds as 'one's worth in one's own eyes and in the eyes of others'.[59] This perspective on family honour which is linked to prestige rather than a moral value system is closer to the legitimising rationale of Limerick feuds.

Status which is heightened by feuding can be valuable when engaging in criminal activities. Essentially, because of their fearsome reputation linked to feuds, members of feuding families are less likely to be challenged by neighbours and community leaders as they engage in criminal and violent activities. Seoirse, a local community worker, argues that the perpetuation of the feud in this context becomes simply a way of life, a way of demonstrating continuing supremacy in local tough man hierarchies:

> So if you and I start a feud and we're in our twenties and twenty years down the road is the feud still about what you and I started it about? It's not because you have twenty years of societal change, you have twenty years of people coming and going, and you have umpteen relatives who really have no idea what it all started over but everybody's caught up in it because the tradition is that we don't talk to that crowd, we fight with them.

For the sociologist examining the Limerick feud(s), a central question becomes: where does the feuding violence end and the drugs-related violence begin? Those who have worked with feuding families have a very clear sense of the distinction between the two forms of conflict. One local solicitor comments, 'the feud and the drugs stuff are sort of accidental cousins. One is linked to the other and yet they are definitely not the same thing.' Siobhan, a health worker, notes

> Drugs crime has a focus and it's drugs and money and that's where it sits. Feuding is subjective because who began the feud, what did the feud stay going over and now ten years down the road, what is the feud over . . . so the starting point of the feud is never where the feud ends up, whereas the starting point of the drugs is drugs and money and it ends with drugs and money but if you put a feud in there, a feud is an issue between two families. It might never end.

Based on interviews with those living with feud-related violence in Limerick between 2007 and 2010, a typology of four different links between feuding and drugs-related violence can be identified:

- Some incidents are strictly feud-related and have nothing to do with drugs apart from the fact that all participants may have links to the trade of illegal drugs.
- Conflicts over drugs turf or the sale and distribution of drugs can reverberate back on the feud and heighten feuding tensions.
- There are some incidents where the agendas of the feud and the drugs business coincide.
- In some instances, the feud can provide a useful excuse to engage in conflict when a drugs-based outcome is actually the objective.

Thus, the violence of feuding becomes enmeshed very easily with the violence which John Hagedorn argues is an inevitable consequence of the illegal drugs trade.[60] He comments:

> Drug selling is a private matter between participants, with enforcement of contracts a matter of raw power. Violence in the drug business can be conceptualised as social control and self-help in an area of commerce that the state has decided not to regulate as it does other business.[61]

Though feuding has become closely intertwined with drugs-related violence, it represents a distinct criminal justice problem which has contributed in a very significant way to the deterioration of community life in some parts of disadvantaged estates in Limerick.

Trauma and Stress

The process of maintaining family status within a feud is a violent and dangerous enterprise and takes precedence over all other realities for feuding families. Within the Traveller sample interviewed, a number of respondents stressed the difficulty of meeting their family's daily needs when feuding tensions were heightened. Lack of sleep because of severe stress, as well as restricted mobility because of fear of meeting members of opposing families, were themes that emerged in a number of interviews.

Maura, head of a Traveller Training Centre, comments: 'you just feel so sorry for the families and the individuals involved because they're traumatised . . . they are afraid to sleep at home . . . and when you can't take care of your basic needs how can you expect to take care of their higher order needs?' Keith, who works with young Travellers, describes the impact of feuds on Traveller teens in his programme as follows:

> The kids are either out of here because they're scared to be here or those who do come in are only on proviso that they are safe here . . . in the last feud a member of staff here would have been in a house calling to see the family and the whole room was full with weapons. The window blocked up, the door blocked up and they were just there, waiting for it to happen basically. How can normal life go on in that situation?

The restrictions which feuding places on 'normal life' were also very evident in the Limerick sample. In 2009, the *Irish Independent* reported how two children from a Limerick family involved in a local feud each had missed over 200 schooldays within one year. Their older brother had been shot dead during feuding violence and their solicitor argued that both children were deeply traumatised by the experience. However, the appalling trap which feuding creates was most evident when the solicitor commented, 'the children's mother was too traumatised to come to court, is on medication, and sits at home all day praying for the death of the person who killed her son.'[62] Therefore, for these children, already traumatised by feuding, there is no end to the violence. When their brother's death is eventually avenged, their family will once again become the target of a new wave of violence and so the deadly tit-for-tat logic continues the feud.

It is this corrosive tit-for-tat logic which generates the trauma and stress experienced by families involved in Traveller and Limerick gangland feuds. Participants in feuding experience protracted high-level stress punctuated by deeply traumatic violent incidents. James, a social service worker in Limerick, comments:

> Within the logic of tit for tat there is no respite, if you're in ascendance, if you're the family who has been involved in a hit you are waiting for reprisal. If you're the family that's been the subject of the hit, you are planning your next move so the families who are caught up in it have no respite. It's just relentless torture, relentless stress punctuated by horrible violence.

Not surprisingly, many of the participants in feuding demonstrate signs of what Judith Herman describes as complex post-traumatic stress syndrome.

She argues that prolonged and repeated trauma creates distressing and severe psychological problems, including disassociative states, affective and anxiety disorders, hyper-vigilance, re-enactment, re-victimisation and suicidality.[63] It is interesting to note in this context that Limerick has both the highest rate of suicide and the highest rate of self-harm in the Republic of Ireland,[64] while Mary Rose Walker's research demonstrates that the suicide rate within the Traveller community is also much higher than the national average.[65]

Given the numbers of teachers, social workers, psychologists and community activists who highlighted the theme of trauma within both the Limerick and Traveller interview series, the material presented here is an attempt to map the various manifestations of feud-related trauma in men, women and children in these communities. The research draws on participant observation and interviews in Limerick, focus groups with Travellers and interviews with four psychologists working in various capacities with Travellers and within disadvantaged communities in Limerick. Rather than offering a definitive guide to trauma and post-traumatic stress, it is envisaged that this research might be the starting point for further, more extensive research on feud-related trauma.

In 2008, the Canadian child psychologist Stuart Shanker visited parts of Limerick city at the behest of the Limerick Enterprise and Development Board. In a presentation which he subsequently gave on his experiences there, he argued that some of the children he met in those estates were as traumatised as those he encountered on the Gaza strip.[66] Behaviours which were highlighted by teachers as indicative of this trauma included extreme forms of acting out, violent behaviours, intense psychological, emotional and verbal abuse of others, as well as inappropriate touching of themselves and others. Paul, a first-class teacher in one local primary school, comments:

> There are kids in my class and they just should not be here. It's not that they are stupid or intellectually incapable of doing the school work, they are just far too traumatised to participate in the school system. They are witnessing things every day that any sane adult couldn't cope with, their basic physical and emotional needs are not met because the family is so distressed or troubled and they are coming in here and they are literally spinning off their heads. Never mind reading, they can't sit down, they can't concentrate on one thing for more than a minute and the classroom situation just makes it worse. You wouldn't ask a war veteran to sit in a class of twenty kids for five hours a day, they'd go mad. Well, these kids are going crazy!

Research on community violence in the United States demonstrates that witnessing this form of violence generates a range of behavioural and mental health problems in children and leads to increased risk of youth offending.[67] Turner and Lloyd also found that getting traumatic news about the victimisation of relatives, a common facet of life in feuding families, can also have a profoundly damaging impact on children.[68]

As children caught up in feuds move towards adulthood, those working in the prison system and disadvantaged youth programmes present an even more worrying picture of how trauma and post-traumatic stress impacts on the behaviours of young adults. Lorita Purnell highlights hyper-vigilance, difficulty concentrating, poor impulse control and emotional distancing as particularly common symptoms of post-traumatic stress.[69] All these symptoms were highlighted by psychologists working with both communities but were especially emphasised by counsellors in Limerick city. The hyper-vigilance evident in members of feuding families was a striking theme within the Limerick interview series. Kieran, who has worked as a counsellor in the prison system, notes:

> Hyper-vigilance would be in a lot of the feuding clients that I'd meet. Like where they'd sit in the room would be very important to them and they constantly check the windows and doors. Within the confines of the whole prison, it's very restrictive and with the different factions you can't mix them.

Seamus, a psychologist, describes a typical meeting with one of his clients in Limerick:

> A noise, the very minute you'd hear a noise, Timmy[70] would have leapt out of his skin, he'd be like a wild animal whose ears are pricking up, right because, 'What's that, where's that coming from?' He'd be up at the window and he'd be looking out the window and he'd be like 'What's that down there, who own's that and where's that goin' ... so what would be a half an hour meeting with you to have your problem looked at ... could be maybe a two-hour meeting with Timmy because Timmy is checking me out as well and asking me questions like 'What the fuck are you doing here?' and 'Who the fuck are you?' and 'What do you give a rat's ass 'bout me for?'

The hyper-vigilance which is evident in feud participants in confined situations also leads to a significant level of self-restricted mobility. Kieran describes how one of his clients

> ... was afraid to go outside the door ... If he needed anything in town, his mother would have to drive him to the door of the shop that

he would have to go into and he would go in and get his tracksuit or whatever and then come out, go straight back into the car and straight back home. He didn't feel safe walking on the street, walking in town. He didn't feel safe being seen talking to anybody in case it was the wrong person. If I ever saw anybody suffering from post-traumatic stress it was him. And this guy was eighteen and he was the father of two children.

From interviews with psychologists and social service practitioners involved with feuding families, there is evidence that those involved in feuds are always on alert, always waiting for the next attack. At no point do they believe that they can relax, as Kieran describes:

> I notice with a lot of clients that I worked with, they were constantly looking around them, much more than I would be noticing. There was one particular guy and I saw him in a different room to the one that I'd normally use and he had to walk all around that room checking it out, he had to look out the window. He just could not relax. This was a different environment and you could see he was asking himself, 'am I safe here, am I alright?' He was ok with me because he knew me well but he did not feel safe in the room. I asked him about it and he said 'what is this place, why are we here?' He wanted to know everything about it. He must have asked me twenty questions and he never really relaxed and we never got deep into the session.

Given the heightened state of tension within which feud participants exist, it is not surprising that any small challenge from a neighbour, partner or child can lead to an explosion. Kieran concludes, 'They are effectively Vietnam War vets and then at certain times, they explode and it's just waiting for that explosion . . . the question is what happens when that explosion comes.'

Tragically, there appears to be little within current state response to feuding which recognises the level of trauma experienced by feud participants. Seamus concludes:

> Is it prison on one side or 5 B [psychiatric ward in Limerick Regional Hospital] on the other? Neither in my mind work because what we end up treating is the presenting issues rather than the root. And neither establishment is going to treat the root but will treat the presenting issue. So if, from the prison side, you have good behaviour, you're back out, probably a bit quiet for a while until something else triggers. In terms of 5 B, once the drugs have calmed you down and you're okay, you are back out again. Then when you're back out, you concoct your

own mixture of legal and illicit drugs and off you go until the next thing, so really what I'm saying is neither is actually serving a purpose.

Even leaving the city, in the case of Limerick feud(s), does not appear to alleviate the post-traumatic stress experienced by feud participants as they seem to take the feud with them in their consciousness. Kieran tells how:

> I had another client and he went to America and he told me he was in pubs in America and he was looking around behind waiting for one of the Reds to come in so he has post-traumatic stress without a doubt and he just couldn't relax over there. So he couldn't get out of it, he brought it with him wherever he went.

Anecdotally, there appeared to be a very high level of consumption of prescription medication among women in these contexts, both in Limerick and in Traveller feuding families. Seamus describes how the feud impacts on his client Timmy's relationship with his mother:

> The mother probably won't see anything wrong with Timmy[71] but will fret every night he goes out until he's back home. Lord, I wonder what some of those mothers go through, how they get up and face a day, but probably they are so drugged out of it themselves with doctors' prescriptions that they don't fully take in what's going on.

Not all of the men, women and children who demonstrate signs of being deeply traumatised are directly involved in local feuding. However, the prominence of themes of trauma and post-traumatic stress in both interview series would suggest that this is a severely neglected dimension of the current policy debates on feuding in Limerick and in the Traveller community.

Conclusion

Feuding is becoming an increasingly significant criminal justice problem yet understandings of feuding from sociological, psychological or criminological perspectives are relatively underdeveloped. Feuding within the Traveller community is clearly on the increase and in response to this problem in the Midlands, conflict resolution structures have been developed. The *Midlands Traveller Conflict and Mediation Initiative* has brought together a variety of stakeholders with a view to tackling the problem in the region.[72] There is also evidence that Gardaí in the Midlands have developed more sophisticated understandings of Traveller conflict which have improved the policing of feuds. One Garda sergeant in the Midlands commented

> After the investigations . . . it was very important for us as a strategy
> that both sides were arrested on the one day, that we didn't say, 'well
> arrest all of this crowd today and the other side next week', that would
> have driven everybody mad. Everybody got the same slice of the cake
> and got treated the same way.

This response, which recognises the need for even-handedness in dealing
with feuding families, suggests that it is possible to improve criminal justice
responses to the problem. Thus, strategies can be developed which ensure,
at the very least, that policing responses do not worsen feuding tensions.

It is unclear, however, whether these more nuanced responses to
feuding emerging in the Midlands will inform criminal justice responses
throughout Ireland, particularly in counties such as Clare and Waterford
where Traveller feuding is becoming more problematic. The findings of
this research suggest that developing understanding of the distinctive
dynamic of feud(s), particularly Traveller feuds as opposed to gangland
feuding, needs to become a dedicated part of training for recruits to An
Garda Síochána. Secondly, as initiatives to increase the diversity of the
police force develop, the recruitment of Gardaí from the Traveller community should be a priority. The recruitment of more Traveller Gardaí
would have a number of benefits. Firstly, it would decrease the remoteness
of the police force from the Traveller community and diminish the 'them'
and 'us' mentality which was evident in a considerable proportion of the
Traveller interview sample. Secondly, the recruitment of Traveller Gardaí
would greatly improve the knowledge and understanding of feuding
within the police force. However, it is critical in this context that Gardaí
recruited would represent a range of families within the Traveller community rather than a single kinship network.

Traveller NGOs such as Pavee Point and the Irish Travellers Movement
need to become more directly involved in the development of culturally
appropriate conflict resolution strategies.[73] In the future, it will be difficult
for Traveller organisations to continue to make claims for the recognition of
distinct Traveller culture and Traveller rights at a collective level without
also taking some responsibility around solving problems linked to Traveller-
specific conflicts at a collective level. In no way should all Travellers be
asked to bear the blame for the activities of feuding families. However, it is
imperative that Traveller organisations begin the process of developing
political structures within the community itself which function at the level
of the extended family. These structures are necessary to build links
between relatively integrated Traveller families and Traveller families on
the very margins of Irish society who are more likely to be involved in

feuding violence. It is only through the existence of political structures built around the extended family unit within the Traveller community itself that any long-term solutions to inter-family feuds can emerge.

Finally, the orientation of Traveller adult education needs to shift in order to address feuding within the Traveller community. The Traveller education initiatives which develop in the future[74] need to consider how Traveller adult education programmes can contribute to the reduction of feuding. Strategies might include the provision of programmes on anger management, personal development, conflict resolution and domestic violence. Finally, Traveller adult education services should be overtly designed to function as a *positive* point of contact between the Traveller community, the Gardaí and the HSE.

The feud(s) in Limerick constitute a very different sociological phenomenon. In response to the intensification of feuding in Limerick, the criminal justice system has instituted a number of initiatives aimed at tackling the organised crime elements of the problem rather than the feuding itself. These initiatives include moving the Central Criminal Court to Limerick, the deployment of the Criminal Assets Bureau in Limerick, the establishment of a permanent armed 'Emergency Response Unit' in the city and the investment of considerable resources in community policing. Limerick is now one of the most heavily policed cities in Ireland,[75] yet the understandings of inter-family conflict which underpin the feuding still play little or no role in criminal justice responses. Indeed, apart from the prison service which, because of prisoner safety issues, recognises the central importance of feud-related identities, understanding of the very distinct problem which feuding (as opposed to organised crime) constitutes in Limerick has not developed within the criminal justice system.

There have been a number of small-scale attempts to generate conflict resolution responses to feuding, but these initiatives have been informal and irregular. In 2004, local Fianna Fáil TD Willie O'Dea organised a meeting in the city which was attended by almost all the major participants in the feud. There have also been attempts to intervene in the feud by members of the clergy, local solicitors and members of Limerick City Council. It is, as yet, unclear how much long-term success has been generated by these initiatives.[76] Local residents, community and criminal justice stakeholders interviewed for this research were not optimistic about a long-term end to feuding in Limerick. Terry, who worked in the prison service, comments

> I'd often ask some of them, who I know would be in the feud, is there
> going to be any reconciliation and they'd say that 'there are too many

people dead now . . . when more of us are back out again, you'll see it all again.' I've been told that by more than one person so the tension is still very much there.

In terms of the hierarchy of feuding families, there was cynicism as to whether any conflict resolution was possible between core families. Donal, a community worker, comments:

I think attempts [at conflict resolution] are worth trying. I wonder at times do they fully understand what they are walking into and yes, there are women on the fringes who wish to get out and that goes back to the feminine side of things, that goes back to the worry, that goes back to seeing a son or daughter hurt, all that traumatic stuff compounded together. I suppose you realise how futile all of this stuff is, the morning you stare into a hole in the ground and you say, What has that done for our family and where has that put us in the middle of the feud? Maybe at some level, a rationale kicks in there and sort of says, I'd love out, but who holds the power to make that decision? Not them, unfortunately.

There is some anecdotal evidence that when conflict erupts spontaneously between families at the lower levels of the feuding hierarchies, there is some potential for short-term conflict resolution strategies. Sheila, a social service worker, tells how:

I remember a time when things just up blew out of nowhere between two families on the fringes. A young lad got badly hurt and his family were baying for blood. But the mother didn't want any retaliation and a local Garda went in and brokered a peace so the thing wouldn't turn into a bloodbath. And it held, to my surprise, to be honest, it held.

The success of these small-scale informal interventions suggests that there isat least some potential for conflict resolution at the lower levels of feud(s) in Limerick.

At the top level of the feuding hierarchies, core families have more to lose from the resolution of conflicts. Though feuding takes a huge toll on their family life, the widespread acceptance of the logic of the feud(s) provides a legitimising basis for a range of their activities. This logic also negates in a very powerful way the logic of the Irish criminal justice system. Jonathan, who works with youth services, explains:

So if I go out and attack you, just randomly like, you can go to court and give evidence against me. You might be a bit afraid in the run up to the case but if I'm convicted you don't have to worry about that anymore. I'm in prison, I can't hurt you and I can't hurt anyone else. All's well that ends well. In a feud, if you testify against someone, you have to face all the intimidation by the accused and his family before the court date; even if he/she gets convicted, the rest of his family will still be out to get you. You might be willing to take this risk for yourself but in this situation, the rest of your family are also legitimate targets so witness protection is impossible. It's bullshit, how can you protect twenty or thirty family members?

Unlike a witness in an individualised case, the process of giving evidence for a feud-related crime does not make your life or your community any safer; in fact, it makes you a target. Therefore, a witness does not receive the major *benefit* associated with giving testimony in an individualised situation. In addition, your actions not only expose you to serious risk but expose all your family members to the same risk, to the extent that meaningful witness protection is impossible. Therefore, the *cost* of giving testimony, to yourself and your relations, is much greater than in an individualised crime situation. Given this structure, it is not surprising that policing feuds and the protection of witnesses to feuding violence in Limerick has become extremely difficult.

For some time, the state solicitor in Limerick, Michael Murray, has been advocating creating criminal justice responses to feuding which borrow from the continental system of jurisprudence.[77] Given the findings of this research, there are very sound sociological and criminological reasons to support this proposal. These continental systems, which involve appointing investigating or prosecuting magistrates, have proved an effective means of protecting witnesses in Mediterranean contexts where extended family structures also interweave in a complex manner with organised crime. So far, police in Ireland have tended to look towards North American or British contexts for responses to gang behaviour. However, in sociological terms, the gangs which operate in these contexts are bonded by racial ties which operate in a totally different manner to the family bonds which mark the boundaries of Limerick feuds. The family-based criminal networks which operate in Mediterranean contexts are undoubtedly much more sophisticated than Limerick's family gangs. However, the criminal justice responses which are designed to circumnavigate tight family bonds in these countries should be considered in developing Irish criminal justice responses to gangland feuding.

A comparison of Traveller and Limerick gangland feuding highlights a number of significant commonalities. The weakness of law and order in these communities and the importance of the extended family unit as a source of personal and collective identity provide the basis for feuding in both cultural contexts. However, there are also a number of key differences between these two forms of feuding which suggest that distinct solutions will be required. While conflict resolution, education and culturally sensitive policing may reduce Traveller feuding, the longevity and the serious nature of the gangland feuding in Limerick city suggest that only major criminal justice reforms which are rooted in a sociological understanding of how family-based organised crime operates will generate a lasting solution to the problem.

7. Lessons from Limerick
policing, child protection
regeneration,

Niamh Hourigan

The object of the study of fear and feuding in Limerick was to provide a richer sociological understanding of the mechanics of intimidation which were being used to create 'regimes of fear' in some parts of the city. The study was not designed to specifically critique social policy or criminal justice responses to these problems. Nevertheless, during the three years when this ethnography was conducted, some wide-ranging policy responses were enacted by the state. Observing the successes and failures of the policing, regeneration and child protection policies on the ground became an unavoidable part of the project. The material presented in this chapter offers some preliminary evaluations of these policy responses with a view to identifying strengths and weaknesses in their current configuration and charting the potential for further development.

Policing and Criminal Justice Responses

In his 2007 report *Addressing Issues of Social Exclusion in Moyross and other Disadvantaged Areas of Limerick City,* John Fitzgerald noted that 'dealing with issues of criminality' would be 'fundamental to creating the conditions for other interventions to be successful and for restoring the confidence of local communities'.[1] It was evident from his report that he had fully comprehended the profound impact which drugs and feud-related criminality had on these communities, though his understanding of how this criminality operated was relatively underdeveloped. Nevertheless, the criminal justice policy changes which have been enacted since the Fitzgerald Report constitute a very significant state response to the problems in Limerick city. Fitzgerald recommended:

- Increased involvement by the Criminal Assets Bureau in Limerick
- The creation of a 'highly visible Garda presence' in these estates with 'a minimum 100 additional Gardaí . . . whose sole function will be policing these areas'.[2]

In fact, these measures were building on a number of criminal justice interventions which had already been undertaken, including CAB investigations in the city which had been ongoing since 2001, sittings of the Central Criminal Court in the city, as well as Operation Anvil, which involved the seizure of guns and weapons from criminal gangs.[3] Since the Fitzgerald Report, a number of additional criminal justice responses have emerged, including the establishment of an armed 'Emergency Response Unit'[4] in the city and the enactment of the Criminal Justice Bill (2009), which created a number of gang-related offences.[5]

During the three years of this study, it was evident that community policing initiatives had constituted one of the most effective policy responses to fear and feuding in the city. Why? As a policy response, the arrival of the increased numbers of community Gardaí happened relatively quickly.[6] Secondly, the work of community Gardaí constituted a frontline intervention 'on the ground' rather than a new bureaucratic initiative based on guidelines, regulations, etc. Community policing functions as a targeted response to a specific problem and, as such, has generated real improvements to crime rates[7] in the city and improved relationships between the Gardaí and local communities. One Garda comments:

> Well the biggest improvement that I would have seen in my time is getting the Gardaí out of the squad cars. The cycle units have made a big difference. A lot of the Gardaí involved are young and approachable and they can talk to the kids . . . It's less threatening and gives them a different view of the Force. Some of the female Gardaí have also been a big help in getting rid of this macho thing.

During the three years' ethnography, Gardaí did become much more visible on the ground. Their presence was evident not just in the activities of community Gardaí, but also in the visibility of the Emergency Response Unit, whose presence was regarded as reassuring, particularly by elderly people. The installation of improved CCTV systems funded by Regeneration has also increased residents' sense of safety.[8] Maureen comments:

> The cameras have made a big difference. Now it's easier to prove what's going on but people have to co-operate, they have to ring the centres and the Guards have to follow-up. When everyone does their bit it really works, when they don't, well, it's not so good.

The participation of community Gardaí in local residents' fora and other community organisations had also led to improved relationships between residents and the police and much greater personal familiarity between individual Gardaí and individual residents. In communities where everyone knows everyone else, a personal relationship with a Garda can be very important. Kevin comments:

> I find it's much easier when you know them. You can go down to the station and say 'Can I speak to Tommy or Jim or Sinéad?' and you know that they know you and they're not goin' to think you're just some scumbag. That does make a difference.

This increased level of trust is also evident in Humphreys' chapter in this volume where Gardaí were the second most trusted group in Corpus Christi parish in Moyross after local clergy. However, some of the younger interviewees like Mike complain about the intensity of policing in these areas, saying, 'if we even hang around together, they want to know what we're up to. It's just . . . it can be a bit intense sometimes . . . you feel like you're bein' watched all the fuckin' time.'

However, the success of community policing measures has not been universal throughout the city. Understandably, in areas where the 'disadvantaged of the disadvantaged' are clustered and the regimes of fear are most effective, it is much harder for community Gardaí to form good local relationships. Imelda, who lives in one such area, says, 'I'd still be terrified if anyone saw me talking to the Guards even if it was a woman Guard, they know every fuckin' thing that goes on round here and you never know who's watchin' or how it will come back on you.'

In some areas, not only is it more difficult for young Gardaí to build good relationships but they also have to endure hostile responses from residents, particularly local teenagers. Community Gardaí working in these contexts need to have sufficient interpersonal skills to overcome verbal abuse and at the same time behave in a friendly manner to local residents. They must have the self-esteem to assert themselves in situations where they may not be wanted or liked. Not all young Gardaí have these qualities and it must be recognised that community policing in some of these contexts may be a task more suited to more experienced members of the force. One Garda acknowledged this problem:

> You know, we have to have so many caps on the ground because of Regen but not all of them are suited to this work. It's really tough out there and some of them just can't cut it. In fairness, there are others who are great, but it takes a particular type of person to be able to cope with the demands of the job and there are only so many of those types around.

It is critical that Garda management and Garda training systems begin to recognise the particular interpersonal challenges that exist for community Gardaí in these contexts. From a political sociology perspective, Gardaí who police in some parts of these estates are working in contexts of 'contested sovereignty'.[9] What does this mean? In the vast majority of places where An Garda Síochána operate within the Republic of Ireland, they are viewed as the legitimate police force, the physical embodiment of the sovereign power of the Irish state, even by citizens who don't necessarily share the state's value system as enshrined in law. However, the micro-study of fear and feuding demonstrates that criminal gangs who operate out of marginalised estates have sought to establish themselves as the sovereign power in the local area. Through their daily activities linked to regimes of fear, they seek to demonstrate to all local residents that while they may tolerate the comings and goings of state officials, in real terms they are in charge.

It is critical to recognise the distinction between night and day in terms of contested sovereignty. During the day, agents of the state such as Gardaí, social and youth workers come and go from these estates in relative safety. However, at night, almost all these state agents disappear and the real sovereign power holders in the estates, men and women involved in criminal gangs, foot-soldiers and children who act as their 'eyes and ears', become much more visible. It is at night-time that these individuals enact their sovereign power, rewarding those who co-operate and sanctioning residents who have got in their way or those who might be vulnerable. From a methodological perspective, the research gathered in these estates during the day-time presents a completely different picture to the image of estate life which becomes evident at night.[10]

Policing in contexts of contested sovereignty generates a number of distinct challenges, some of which have yet to be recognised within the Irish criminal justice system. Firstly, community Gardaí operating in these contexts may be confronted with local residents who view them as the enemy, as 'just another fuckin' gang', in the words of one teenager. Therefore, they may experience disrespect, verbal abuse and a certain community resistance to their activities. More importantly, those involved in criminal gangs are inclined to popularise the view that the Gardaí and the state don't care about local residents. Every small incident which isn't taken seriously or pursued fully by Gardaí is viewed by local residents as a sign that the state doesn't care about their safety and that, as a consequence, they are at the mercy of the gangs.

Given this context, it is essential that Gardaí respond fully to call-outs and deal comprehensively with minor issues. In some instances, residents may turn to local gang members, the real sovereign power holders, to resolve an issue when the Gardaí don't act. Vinnie's[11] story elucidates how, even in the current context, challenges remain:

> I was out washing the van one day and this young fella from down the road comes over to me an' asks me for a lift into town. He was out of his fuckin' box so I wasn't goin' to give him a lift. Anyway, that night my tyres got slashed. The next day the community Gardaí came round an' they said they'd look into it and they'd see what they could do. That night my windows got broken. I rang looking for the Guard the next day but they weren't working . . . Monday morning I rang looking for the Garda again but the Guard was sick this time so I rang my brother to ask him 'what should I do' and he said, 'Why don't you get one of the Reds on to it?' he said. Now, I'm not gonna do that coz I know better but lots of people round here would do exactly that in my shoes!

Though Vinnie resists the temptation to resort to the vigilantism of the gangs, the weakness of the Garda response in this situation adds to the power and legitimacy of the gang members in the local area and actually undermines the sovereignty of the state.

Given the improvements which have already been made in terms of policing in Limerick, one of the main areas where local Gardaí could further develop their response is in terms of accessibility. During the course of this study, it was evident that criminal gang members were actively circulating stories about police radios being scanned in order to deter local residents from contacting Gardaí. Although Gardaí brought in a new secure communications system in early 2010,[12] further publicity campaigns need to be conducted about its existence. Residents need to understand that their complaints will not be communicated back to gang members. In this context, the physical accessibility of some of the local Garda stations located close to Regeneration estates needs to be improved.[13] Gardaí have put huge work into building good relationships between local members of the force and the community. However, sometimes it can be difficult for local residents to get access to Gardaí they know because some local stations are open for limited hours and the phones in these local stations are only manned during these times. Given the critical importance of the local community Garda resource in terms of policing, further consideration should be given to opening stations for longer periods, particularly at night, and having the phones in local stations manned at night.

From the Garda perspective, a number of Gardaí complained about the 'revolving door' within the local prison service. They argue that it is disheartening for themselves and witnesses, when they put enormous efforts into getting a conviction, often to find that the perpetrator of the crime has been released relatively quickly back into the community. They argue that the 'revolving door' within the prison system de-motivates witnesses and undermines their work in communities.[14]

At national level, the Criminal Justice Act (2009) constitutes the state's most significant legislative response to the activities of criminal gangs in Limerick and Dublin. The Act introduced a number of key offences designed to specifically target the activities of gang members. These offences included 'witness intimidation' and 'directing a criminal gang'.[15] Most importantly, in terms of the findings of the fear study, the Act makes it possible for Gardaí to use surveillance evidence in court. This change represents a significant step forward in facilitating prosecution of gang members and unpicking 'regimes of fear'. By lessening the need for witness-based evidence, this legal change makes it possible for the state to pursue charges against gang members without asking their neighbours and victims to put themselves and their family's lives at risk. It is perhaps too early to evaluate the effectiveness of these new measures, but early indications suggest that the powers enacted in the Criminal Justice Act have significantly improved the capacity of the criminal justice system to respond to gang-related organised crime.[16] However, the single biggest gap in the state's criminal justice response to gangland activity and feuding in Limerick concerns the absence of targeted responses to the criminal acts and antisocial behaviour of minors. Because of current weakness on this issue, gangs are continuing to recruit a steady stream of young participants and the success of measures targeted at adult criminals is being undermined.

Antisocial Behaviour and Child Protection

Possibly the most significant finding of the micro-study of feuding and fear in Limerick concerned evidence of exploitation of minors, children between the ages of three and fourteen by criminal gangs in Limerick city. Residents of disadvantaged estates experience more fear and trauma on a daily basis because of the antisocial behaviour of children than the more serious activities of feuding gang members in their communities. This fear is generated not only by individual acts of intimidation but also by the perception that the children involved in these incidents are operating under the auspices of criminal gangs. Reasons for targeting individual families might include links to opposing feuding families, a local gang wanting their home for surveillance/trading purposes or the suspicion that the householder had been in contact with the Gardaí. As Sheila says, 'You never know who's behind them, and if you take them on, what are you gonna draw down on top of you? Livin' fuckin' hell, that's what!' Not all antisocial behaviour is gang-directed; at least half of the activity described during interviews appeared to be linked to the general lawlessness in parts of these estates governed by the 'code of the street' outlined in Chapter Five.

At the moment, the criminal justice system is almost completely powerless to respond to this problem. The Children Act (2001) increased the age of criminal responsibility for children in Ireland from seven to twelve.[17] This change brought the juvenile justice system in Ireland into line with other European countries and means that children under twelve in Ireland are basically exempt from prosecution. The only exception to this rule relates to children aged ten or eleven 'who can be charged in relation to serious offences such as murder, manslaughter, rape or aggravated sexual assault'.[18] In a report on *Anti-Social Behaviour and the Law* commissioned by Limerick Regeneration, Leahy et al. comment:

> As a result of the introduction of Section 129,[19] the Garda Síochána are now effectively powerless to charge a child under 12 due to his or her age. The Gardaí must take the child to his or her parents or guardians, and if this is not possible to the HSE, which may result in the child being taken into care if the parents or guardians cannot be located.[20]

The Criminal Justice Act (2006) does set out very specific steps for dealing with the antisocial behaviour of children between the ages of twelve and eighteen.[21] These steps include the issuing of behaviour warnings, meetings with parents and the creation of good behaviour contracts.[22] If these measures are unsuccessful, and during the course of this research they did not appear to have much success, the child may be directed to enter a Garda Diversion Programme.[23] There are a number of Garda Diversion Programmes across Limerick city, some of which are very successful, others less so. Critically, Garda Diversion Programmes can only accept children over the age of twelve who are not at the stage of being prosecuted in court. Given that the age of children involved in antisocial behaviour was steadily decreasing during the course of this three-year study, the most troubled children have moved beyond the scope of Garda Diversion by the time they reach the age of twelve. A range of diversionary strategies has been piloted for the under-twelves in Limerick, but it is unclear as yet how these programmes will impact on the problem in the long term.[24]

If local Gardaí are not satisfied that a child would benefit from a diversion programme, they can apply to the Children's Court for a Behaviour Order which might prohibit the child from behaving in a certain manner or from being in specific places.[25] During the course of this research, there was evidence of a reluctance to use behaviour orders as a response to serious antisocial behaviour simply because they are almost impossible to enforce. The penalty for not complying with a behaviour order is a fine (not exceeding €8,000) or detention in a child's detention school.[26] However, for the vast majority of children in this situation, they and their parents are so enmeshed in addiction and criminality that the state has no chance of successfully imposing a fine. Secondly, places in children's detention facilities are already so over-subscribed that the chance of a child being sent to such a service is relatively remote.[27] Thus, within the current system, the Gardaí are relatively powerless to sanction children engaged in serious forms of antisocial behaviour and the juvenile justice system offers no adequate alternative response to the problem.

Apart from criminal justice responses, local authorities who manage public housing have a regulatory role in terms of antisocial behaviour of their tenants. Under the Housing Act (Miscellaneous Provisions) (1997)[28] tenants can be evicted from local authority housing because of the antisocial behaviour towards other residents, using an Exclusion Order. During the course of this research, there was considerable dispute among participants about the success of local authorities[29] in managing antisocial behaviour. Local housing officials argue that they have to manage a very high proportion of local authority housing.[30] Limerick City Council have taken a number of steps to tackle this problem, including the issuing of verbal and written warnings as well as taking back homes from tenants.[31] They have appointed a number of antisocial behaviour officers and established a dedicated hotline to report troublesome behaviour.[32] However, residents in some estates have argued that some housing management decisions have made antisocial behaviour worse and destabilised previously settled areas. Thus they tend to view local authorities with mistrust and suspicion.[33]

There would appear to be even greater suspicion of the Rent Supplement Scheme administered by the Health Service Executive.[34] Because rent supplement is provided to tenants of private landlords, the HSE has no power to regulate the behaviour of tenants availing of this payment. Local authority officials argue that the scheme undermines their work on antisocial behaviour while also highlighting that they have no power to regulate the behaviour of owner-occupied homes. In this context, the practice of trading homes through the use of key money has made it more difficult to regulate antisocial behaviour as officials attempting to manage local authority estates with privately owned homes have difficulty identifying owners.

Given the serious linkages between antisocial behaviour, community violence and criminal gang activities in Limerick, it is questionable whether the housing departments of local authorities are the appropriate body to target this issue. The findings of this research would suggest that they are not the appropriate agencies for this work. Expertise within housing departments of local authorities tends to be linked not surprisingly to housing rather than the criminal justice and child protection issues which lie at the heart of the very serious antisocial behaviour problems in the city. Although the structure of local government in Limerick is currently under review, it is unclear how the creation of a new super-authority for the city and county will impact on housing management policy and antisocial behaviour in the city.[35]

The child protection services currently run by the Health Service Executive also have a 'duty of care' towards troubled children who are involved in antisocial behaviour. Under the Children Act (2001), a troubled child whose behaviour is difficult but not criminal can be diverted to HSE services. Following a family conference, the child can be directed to attend a special care unit.[36] The Children Act (2001) also provides a statutory basis for a range of conferences (Garda conference, family welfare conference, family conference) which are designed to identify the causes of the child's behaviour and develop an Action Plan to prevent its reoccurrence. Section 115 of the Children Act introduced a whole series of community sanctions which can be imposed on the child and are supervised by probation and welfare officers.[37] There are provisions to impose sanctions on parents of these children which include parental supervision orders, fines and court orders to control their children, though these provisions have not been widely implemented.[38]

Finally, under the Child Care Act (1991), the child protection services of the HSE have an obligation to identify children at risk. Once a child at risk has been identified, the HSE may apply to the courts for a number of different types of care order.[39] Despite the scope of these orders, a number of the social workers which I interviewed viewed taking a child into care as a last resort, for two reasons. Firstly, taking a child into care can be very distressing for both the child and the parents, even in contexts where the home is abusive.[40] Thelma, one social worker, comments, 'To be honest, it's really the last option because it's so traumatic for everyone. We already have so many kids in foster care in Limerick and it's rare enough that the process makes things any better for the child. Often it just makes things worse.'

The other reason social workers were reluctant to take children into care was evidence of a growing crisis in the care system itself during this period. For example, in June 2010 an audit of two local HSE offices in Dublin by HIQA (Health Information and Quality Authority) showed that hundreds of children in care were being neglected by the HSE. Writing in the *The Irish Times*, Carl O'Brien concludes:

> If the Health Service Executive (HSE) was a parent, many of its children would be taken away and placed in care. That's the only conclusion to be drawn from the monumental scale of failure uncovered in our child protection and social work services in recent months. We know that hundreds of children are living with unapproved carers; that overworked social workers are unable to respond to thousands of cases of suspected abuse or neglect; that more than 100 vulnerable young people in care or in contact with social services have died of brutal causes.[41]

In terms of the specific problems in Limerick, there was evidence that over-bureaucratisation and lack of resources also contributed to the weakness of the HSE response to antisocial behaviour in disadvantaged estates. However, it would appear that the current weakness in state response to antisocial behaviour is also rooted in a lack of understanding of the motivations for the child's behaviour *from the child's perspective*.

Why do children engage in antisocial behaviour?

Limerick is a particularly important site to study antisocial behaviour in Ireland because problems in relation to the behaviour of minors have been noted since the early 1970s. Numerous youth intervention strategies have been launched and piloted in the city since this period. Within the Irish social policy literature on antisocial behaviour, the prevailing understanding of antisocial behaviour focuses on the boredom experienced by children and the need to provide resources, facilities and activities for children as means of combating antisocial behaviour. For instance, O'Connell comments:

> For older children and teenagers, the space and opportunity for socialising, rather than the equipment, is the most important consideration. This group has almost no facilities provided for them and the only places in which to hang out in the evening are green areas and street corners.[42]

Therefore, the solution to antisocial behaviour using this logic is to provide more facilities and resources for children.

Since the launch of Limerick Regeneration in 2007, vast resources have been devoted to youth intervention projects, summer camps, sports and music schemes and improved facilities for young people.[43] Although much of the proposed building work for Regeneration has not yet taken place, the provision of facilities and resources for young people is one area on which Regeneration has focused huge attention. At a conservative estimate, several million has been spent on these projects. At the end of 2010, there were twenty-four major youth intervention schemes in Limerick and ten sports development officers in the city.[44] Yet despite this scale of funding, there has been only a 25 per cent reduction in referrals to Garda diversion schemes and the impact of these projects on the under twelves is very unclear.[45] Antisocial behaviour continues to be a significant problem in the city and a severe problem in some disadvantaged estates. As late as November 2010, one family described their difficulties in a local newspaper, claiming that 'a gang of children between 6 and 10 had terrorised residents.' One woman commented 'They are going around putting in windows and running riot. You can't confront their parents because their will be retribution.'[46] The failure of their youth intervention approaches to deliver a more comprehensive reduction in levels of antisocial behaviour in the city, given recent resource allocation, suggests a fundamental weakness in understandings of the problem.

Using the participation observation material gathered during this research, and interviews with social workers, teachers and childcare workers in local communities, my research indicates that acts of antisocial behaviour tend to be committed most often by children drawn from the 'disadvantaged of the disadvantaged' category or from families who are deeply enmeshed in drugs-related criminality. These were the children engaging in antisocial behaviours ranging from littering, graffiti, graphic verbal abuse of neighbours (often using terminology of a sexual nature), damaging cars, setting small fires, breaking windows and, in some cases, burning houses. How does this process make these children feel? Firstly, the process of engaging in antisocial behaviour and running away is hugely exciting. Secondly, the fear and apprehension which these acts generate in the neighbourhood makes them feel very powerful. This combination of power and excitement generates 'one massive fuckin' buzz', in the words of one interviewee, and this buzz is highly addictive.

While characterising the rationale for antisocial behaviour as an addiction to a 'buzz' may seem to be a radical analysis, there is relatively strong support for this analysis within American criminological and sociological research. In 1988, Jack Katz published a book entitled *The Seduction of Crime* where he argued that understanding the 'sensual experience' of committing deviant acts was as important as recognising the rational rewards of these behaviours such as money or stolen goods.[47] He highlighted the 'sneaky thrills' experienced by shoplifters, for instance, and commented, 'quite apart from what is taken, they may regard getting away with it as a thrilling demonstration of personal competence, especially if it is accomplished under the eyes of adults.'[48]

Even more compelling in terms of understanding the 'buzz' of antisocial behaviour is Stephen Lyng's concept of edgework. His initial research sought to examine the experiences of sky-divers as actors engaged in voluntary risk-taking behaviours. He expanded the model to interrogate the experiences of those involved in urban graffiti and joyriding, activities associated with antisocial behaviour in Ireland. Edgeworkers, he argues, are those who actively seek out stress. He comments:

> Stress seeking is viewed as a way to fulfil a need for arousal or for stimulation, as a way to develop capacities for competent control over environmental objects, as a form of tension reduction behaviour with addictive qualities related to the build up of intoxicating stress hormones and as 'indirect self destructive behaviour' that functions as a defence mechanism against depression and despair.[49]

He notes that ultimately the voluntary risk-taking behaviour leaves the edgeworker with a heightened sense of self and a feeling of being powerful. He observes:

> Participants in virtually all types of edgework claim that the experience produces a sense of 'self-realization', 'self-actualization' or 'self-determination'. In the pure form of edgework, individuals experience themselves as instinctively acting entities, which leaves them with a purified and magnified sense of self.[50]

Lyng's colleague, William Miller, has devoted particular attention to the application of the edgework model to juvenile delinquency. He argues that children and adolescents are particularly likely to be seduced by edgework because they experience so much powerlessness in other contexts in their daily lives. He notes

> As a result of their powerless social status, many children are forced to endure serious oppression (e.g. physical punishment, humiliation, unequal opportunity, physical/sexual abuse, and neglect). Furthermore,

> children rarely have the opportunity for authentic self-directed behaviour . . . Ultimately, no matter which parenting style is adopted children are subject to the authority of adults.[51]

He notes that edgework is accompanied by at least four distinct sensations which offer the potential to challenge this experience of powerlessness. These sensations are: (1) self-determination, (2) fear of failure, (3) excitement and (4) hyper-reality. He concludes

> Delinquency, as a form of edgework, may represent an attempt to escape an otherwise oppressive, constraining and alienating social world. Delinquent activities can provide juveniles with a sense of excitement and personal autonomy that allows them to momentarily transcend a routine, alienated existence that is controlled by adults. It is the intense feelings of fear and excitement and the sense of control that make the edgework experience, in this case delinquency, particularly seductive.[52]

Although scholars of edgework have long acknowledged the potentially addictive dimensions of these behaviours, little consideration has been given to the implications of an addiction to edgework for social policy responses to antisocial behaviour.

Aviel Goodman defines an addictive behaviour as a process

> . . . whereby a behaviour that can function both to produce pleasure and to provide escape from internal discomfort is employed in a pattern characterised by (1) recurrent failure to control the behaviour and (2) continuation of the behaviour despite significant negative consequences.[53]

The excitement of engaging in the antisocial behaviour appears to generate a mood-altering 'high' typical of the highs identified in other addictive behaviour research.[54] When I suggested to youth workers and social workers at a HSE workshop that I thought there might be an addictive element to antisocial behaviour,[55] a number of frontline workers subsequently provided corroborating examples from their own experience. For instance, Joe, who works with youth services, says:

> Take the kids I work with. They're out there in these estates, they don't have school, they're bored, they know that they haven't a chance out there in the real world and then they get this colossal buzz out of doing all these dangerous things and they get a buzz from seeing how much they can terrorise vulnerable people. Is it addictive? You fuckin' bet it is and once they hit early teens, you throw a load of drugs on top of that so now 'I'm doing all my mad stuff and I'm high', it's like a bloody runaway train.

If the addictive element of antisocial behaviour is recognised, then the underlying reasons for the weakness of current state policy responses become clear. Effective treatment programmes for addictive behaviours including alcoholism, drugs, gambling and sexual addiction all stress the importance of stopping the addictive behaviour *before* treating the underlying causes of the addiction.[56] However, current Irish policy responses address the underlying cause of antisocial behaviour rather than actively stopping the behaviour itself. State policy on antisocial behaviour currently combines three major disciplinary approaches:

- PSYCHO-THERAPEUTIC RESPONSES which focus on problems within the family such as substance addiction or abuse which might contribute to poor parenting and acting out behaviours. However, the work of therapists and youth workers does not involve actively stopping the behaviours themselves when they are taking place in estates.

- DIVERSIONARY RESPONSES which seek to replace the buzz of antisocial activities with more orthodox socially acceptable activities such as sports and community activities. For children who are not deeply troubled, this approach does appear to be effective. However, for children who are more addicted to the high of the antisocial behaviour experience, the buzz of these activities is not sufficient to replace their antisocial behaviour buzz. Seán, who has worked on some of these programmes, comments:

  > You take a kid who's involved in seriously wrong behaviour and you are trying to get him on a football team or out doing water sports. For the goodish kids that'll work, for the more troubled kids, it's like trying to tell someone who is used to doing a line of cocaine every day that what they really need is a nice bar of chocolate.

  Therefore, these more troubled children will often return to the addictive behaviour after participation in these programmes.

- JUSTICE/SANCTIONING RESPONSES which sanction the parents or the child. As Goodman's definition indicates, part of the addictive model is that these behaviours continue despite negative consequences. As the negative consequences currently being imposed by the juvenile justice system and HSE aren't particularly effective, these models appear to generate little long-term change. Children tend to continue with the problematic behaviour or graduate to more serious forms of criminality.

There have been calls from senior Gardaí in Limerick for parents to be held accountable for the actions of their children.[57] However, given the levels of dysfunction in these families, it is difficult to envisage how this 'holding to account' could operate in any meaningful way. It is unlikely that a district court would be willing to jail a parent for the antisocial behaviour of their child. This solution would adversely impact on the child's welfare. Fining parents or deducting welfare payments has the same result, unfortunately, again without actively breaking the addiction of anti-social behaviour.

I would argue that in estates where the antisocial behaviour is very problematic, the state needs to consider a different type of response. At a raw power level, the state has to actively stop children engaged in antiso-cial behaviour. The process of stopping the behaviour does not necessarily have to involve criminalising the child. However, the state must actively set a boundary in terms of the child's behaviour when parents are incapable or unwilling to do so. Failure to set this boundary results in the repeated traumatisation of residents in some parts of these estates. I would recom-mend the appointment of an antisocial behaviour officer or unit to be based in estates where serious anti-social behaviour problems exist. These officers would have to be based in local communities on a full-time basis. Workers in this unit would have to be prepared to provide a 24/7 service and would probably be more active at night than during the day-time. The task of these officers would be simply to take children who are involved in antisocial behaviour home. If the antisocial behaviour officer takes the child home and finds that the home is abusive or the parent/guardian unavailable, they can then contact the social worker and the child can be placed in care. If the child goes back out on the streets having been taken home, they should be taken home again and again until the pattern of addictive behaviour is broken. In this way, the child learns that he cannot engage in antisocial behaviour. Secondly, parents who are tacitly sup-porting these activities also learn that their children cannot engage in these behaviours. For parents who are trying to encourage their child to stop their activities, the work of the antisocial behaviour officer could be of enormous support and benefit. In some severe instances, these officers may need the assistance of the Gardaí, but these officers should not be members of the Gardaí. Only when the pattern of addictive behaviour has been broken do the more therapeutic responses which focus on the under-lying causes of the behaviour have any chance of being successful.

Child Protection: the problems evident in Limerick

The state's failure to adequately tackle antisocial behaviour issues which have emerged in Limerick city is symptomatic of much broader problems which exist in terms of child protection services. Unlike the community policing response, where significant and tangible changes were evident in Limerick during the three-year period of this research, there was no improvement evident in service provision for seriously troubled and neglected children. In fact, because of the significant increase in heroin addiction in these communities, there was some evidence that child neglect issues actually got worse during the course of this research.[58]

What was astonishing as I spoke to local residents, teachers, community activists and social workers themselves was the number of suspected cases of serious neglect and abuse which were known to the HSE and hadn't been investigated or dealt with adequately. Ellen, a local teacher, comments:

> I don't know what the HSE is at. I've had kids in my class who are really neglected, dirty, unwashed kids, kids who know they won't be fed all weekend and are asking their six-year-old classmates for food on Fridays. I've had kids who had clearly been beaten. I don't know how many times I've reported suspected abuse. All I hear from the HSE is 'we don't have the power to do anything', or 'we don't have the resources to do anything' or 'we're so overloaded that we won't be able to investigate for months' . . . What *can* they do? That's what I'd like to know.

The theme of inaction by social workers crops up repeatedly in the research, not only in interviews with local residents but in those with social workers themselves. One senior social worker comments:

> The problem as I see it is simply this: at the moment, within the service, the threshold of intervention is just too high. By the time we get to the point of intervening in a seriously neglected or abused child's life, it is nearly always too late to make any real difference. It becomes a matter for the psychiatric services or the criminal justice system or, sometimes, the undertakers . . . What we need is preventative action, a system which identifies children at risk and moves in to protect and support before the damage is done, not after. This is the big failure at the moment and it makes me want to pull my hair out.

A general recognition that the threshold of intervention by child protection services is too high was not only evident in research for this study but was also the major finding of research conducted for the National Care Planning Project (2005). The pilot research for this project was conducted in Southill in 2004 and the problems linked to late intervention continued to be evident between 2007 and 2010. Sinéad Brophy, who evaluated this project on behalf of the HSE, comments:

> The lack of a 'whole system' approach to promoting good child care appears to have resulted in very late interventions with families of concern, which by their lateness then require more radical solutions than may have been necessary with earlier focused preventative interventions.[59]

One social worker argues that the bureaucratic culture of the HSE itself makes this problem worse. She says, 'There is a culture of closure in the HSE. They are constantly trying to make problems go away, or define them in such a way so that they are not their responsibility.'

The lack of adequate service provision in terms of child protection is not unique to Limerick. In May 2010, the Ombudsman for Children, Emily Logan, published a report in which she found that the HSE had failed to protect children at risk in Irish society and, specifically, had failed to implement the Children First: National Guidelines for the Protection and Welfare of Children.[60] She found that

> Much needs to be done to improve protection and promote children's rights and welfare. This is not simply a matter of resources. Some of the problems identified – variable practice, lack of internal and external scrutiny and a failure of inter-agency collaboration – indicate a need for a fundamental change in culture and attitude towards child protection more generally.[61]

The inadequacies of child protection services have contributed significantly to the poor image of the HSE and HSE social workers which was evident in communities in Limerick during my research. Helen Buckley[62] highlights this image problem for social workers, stating in *The Irish Times*:

> Whether we care to acknowledge it or not, it is a well established fact that HSE social workers are regarded with fear and hostility in many communities, particularly those that are most deprived. This fact was evidenced by a report published by the office of the Minister for Children in 2008. The negative image of HSE social workers, largely based on misinformation about their powers to remove children, challenges their ability to engage families in a non-coercive way.[63]

Given the extent of this national crisis in child protection, what were the specific problems evident in Limerick?

OVER-BUREAUCRATISATION: The area of child protection is over-burdened with regulations while being under-resourced in terms of staff equipped to engage in frontline interventions. Mick, who works in child protection, provides the following example:

> You take a child involved in antisocial behaviour who you think it at
> risk. Well, the only way to get action for that child is to submit a child
> protection notification. But only a very small proportion of all original
> referrals actually get approved by the Child Protection Notification
> Committee based on budgets, etc. It's only at that stage that you can
> have a case conference and get some action and the process of getting
> it approved takes for fucking ever. I've been talking to some of these
> new child protection officers in church organisations who see their job
> as notifying the HSE of every suspected case of abuse. I feel like sayin'
> to them, you're wasting your fuckin' time, man.

It is unfortunate that the current state response to the crisis in the child protection system is to introduce even more regulations rather than focusing
on the critical issue of resources and frontline interventions, issues that have
also been highlighted as central to the improvement of child protection services in the UK.[64] It is suggested that any future revision of child protection
regulations be undertaken with a view to streamlining and speeding up the
system rather than adding even more layers of bureaucracy.

LACK OF 24/7 CHILD PROTECTION SERVICE: Child protection services in
Ireland currently run Monday to Friday between nine and five.
Unfortunately, nobody seems to have informed children involved in antisocial behaviour that they should confine their activities to office hours.
Indeed, child protection workers are generally most available when antisocial behaviour is at its lowest ebb (early morning) and least available at
night and weekends when these behaviours are at their peak. Again, this
mode of distributing resources is totally inappropriate to the current situation. The absence of weekend and out-of-hours services has been
repeatedly criticised in recent years.[65] In terms of child protection services,
it means that children find themselves in the care of 24/7 service providers
such as hospitals and the Gardaí, services which are not designed to
provide for their needs.[66] This research suggests that an out-of-hours social
worker service needs to be established as a matter of urgency.

LACK OF RESOURCES FOR SPECIAL CARE PLACES FOR CHILDREN AND
TEENAGERS IN CRISIS: The numbers of places in special units and detention schools in Ireland is very limited, and repeatedly those in the criminal
justice system are forced to release children at risk or place them in inappropriate care settings because of the lack of adequate service provision. In
a typical case in July 2010, a youth who had been involved in a serious
assault and was under a care order was placed in St Patrick's Institution
because the HSE had no appropriate place for him.[67] Limerick already has
one of the highest numbers of sixteen to eighteen years olds on remand or

serving sentences in St Patrick's Institution.[68] Given the funding which is being made available to tackle other aspects of youth disadvantage in the city, the absence of these special care programmes is hugely problematic.

VETTING OF FOSTER CARERS WITHIN EXTENDED FAMILY NETWORKS: There is a marked preference within the care system for fostering children within the extended family network.[69] However, in situations where extended families may be deeply enmeshed in feuds and drug-related criminality, it is critical that the system recognises that these extended family contexts may be as abusive and exploitative as the child's family of origin. Given that feuding and criminality are based on the family unit rather than the individual in Limerick, it is critical that foster parents for children within extended family networks be thoroughly vetted *before* the child is placed in their care.

THE CURRENT CONFIGURATION OF THE CHILD PROTECTION WORKER ROLE. Most of the social workers interviewed during the course of this research were highly committed individuals who saw their main role in communities as providing therapeutic support to troubled children and families. However, the community's perception of social workers was very different and focused almost entirely on their negative sanctioning powers: their powers to remove a child from its family. There is a fundamental conflict between these two roles. Research on therapeutic relationships indicates that they require a firm basis of trust before any meaningful change can happen.[70] However, because clients view social workers as hostile agents of the state, their social worker is often the last person they want to trust. In fact, a number of parents told me that their main strategy with social workers was to tell them exactly what they thought they wanted to hear with a view to getting rid of them as quickly as possible.

This phenomenon of 'disguised compliance' has also been highlighted by Harry Ferguson, Professer of Social Work at the University of Nottingham, who comments:

> We have failed to acknowledge the sheer scale of resistance and hostility that professionals have to bear in child protection. In one study of three social work teams, I found that in 34% of cases, social workers defined the parents or carers as involuntary clients who did not want a service.[71]

However, in line with Humphreys' research, I found that local residents did trust local clergy and sisters and were inclined to tell them many of their problems. The findings of this research suggest that the therapeutic dimension and sanctioning dimension of the child protection role need to be separated. It would perhaps be more useful if initial therapeutic work could be conducted by family support workers who have no sanctioning powers. If their interventions fail, then the child protection worker should become involved.

CONSISTENCY IN SOCIAL WORKER ALLOCATION: One of the most common complaints about the social work system from residents in disadvantaged estates was the turnover of social workers themselves. Maureen comments:

> I know some of them really try their best but you are just gettin' to know them and they're gone and then you have to start again with someone else and tell them all your shit. To be honest, it gets a bit wearin' after a while. It would be much easier just to deal with one person, then you'd know who to trust.

The importance of assigning a single social worker to individual cases over the long term also emerged in relation to children in the care system.[72]

GAPS IN SOCIAL WORKER TRAINING: There were significant gaps evident in the training of newly qualified social workers. These gaps were hugely problematic because, as Terry who works in the HSE comments, 'we are throwing the youngest, most inexperienced social workers into the hardest jobs on the frontline, making the situation worse. The first gap evident was in the lack of awareness of the negative perception of social workers within communities. Two young social workers whom I encountered had arrived in these communities with huge idealism and a detailed knowledge of social policy. They also appeared to expect that they would be welcomed with 'open arms' when engaging in their therapeutic work and were almost entirely unprepared for the hostility they encountered from local residents. Noelle, who works with social services, comments:

> My own experience would give me grave reservations about the way we are training our social workers. We are giving them extensive theoretical knowledge that they don't really need on a daily basis while they lack basic interpersonal skills to cope with the demands on the job. They can tell you all about child protection policy but when a parent says 'get out of my fuckin' face ye fuckin' do-goodin' bitch', they are flummoxed. Unfortunately, skills to cope with the latter situation are much more important in this job. They need a lot more practice training before they are let off on their own. They need to be intensely mentored and supervised for the first two or three years of practice after college.

There was a marked difference between young, newly trained social workers and some of the more experienced workers in terms of their ability 'to get alongside' their clients. Terry says, 'even with the current configuration of roles, more experienced social workers can *plámás* their way around the system and build up trust . . . the younger ones tend to come back and just say the family didn't engage.'

There was widespread recognition from social workers operating in frontline situations, who I interviewed, that training models need to be changed. Noelle says:

> I think there are two groups we can learn from in terms of social worker training. If you look at the training of primary teachers, teaching practice is the central element even after graduation. Basically, teachers go into schools and their examiner comes along, watches them in action and says you're doing that wrong and that wrong and that wrong . . . They nail them on the weaknesses of their practice. While we have practice teaching for students at university, we need more supervision of practice for the social workers who've just left college. We could also learn a lot from the Guards in terms of how to reassure people when they see you as a hostile agent of the state. These things can be taught and young social workers need to learn them. We have to take more responsibility for changing the image of the profession.

Finally, the question of how social workers engage with the therapeutic dimensions of their own work was also raised. Tomás, a psychologist who works extensively with social workers, comments:

> In psychotherapy, you go into a situation where you want to help someone with their problems but can only do this effectively when you recognise that you have a load of problems of your own that need to be worked on. So you are one flawed, fucked up person, talking to another flawed fucked up person. Working on yourself is part of the process. However, some of these young social workers seem to be going into situations with the idea of they are here to change the world without really being aware of their own issues and problems. It creates a huge power imbalance at an interpersonal level with their clients. In fairness, the 'old hands' are much more self-aware and it makes a huge difference to their practice.

Clearly, some of these issues need to be addressed at the level of social work training programmes in the universities. However, there is also evidence that the weakness of HSE management structures in terms of child protection services is exacerbating these training weaknesses.

SUPERVISION AND MANAGEMENT OF SOCIAL WORKERS BY HSE: The inadequacy of HSE management structures which focused on managing rather than mentoring young social workers was the most frequent complaint articulated by social workers themselves. Siobhán comments:

> The workloads are ridiculous; the bombardment rate here in Limerick
> is just massive. A lot of social workers are managing numerous kids in
> care but if you have three really troubled kids, that's a full-time job.

Problems in terms of the distribution of workloads in child protection were highlighted by the Ombudsman for Children in 2010, who noted significant regional imbalances in terms of the relative distribution of social work posts in light of caseloads.[73] Apart from workloads, social workers complained that they received very little supervisory support from the HSE even when working in situations where there is deep dysfunction, abuse and violence, such as Limerick feuding contexts. Tony says, 'Time and again, I see that young social workers are just being managed, they are not being properly supervised. These guys need a lot of mentoring and support to cope with the situations they face, and they are just not getting it.'

Finally, the safety of social workers as they worked in local communities was highlighted as an issue that needs more attention. Noelle concludes, 'It's mad, we are sending young social workers, often female, alone into highly volatile situations and yet we would never send a young Garda on their own into the same context, they work in pairs. There is something seriously wrong with the system.' These comments suggest that, along with changes to social worker training, the supervision and management structures of child protection workers within the HSE needs to be overhauled.

CREDIBILITY AND RATIONALE PROBLEMS: There was a marked distinction between the credibility of criminal justice stakeholders in the communities I researched in Limerick and the perceived credibility of social service workers such as social, community and youth workers. This credibility gap appeared to be linked to the differing rationales underpinning their work rather than the performance of individuals. When those within the criminal justice system sanction gang members, they use a legal rationale. This rationale states that those who break the law are transgressing the rules of the Irish state which draw on moral perspectives of right and wrong behaviour. While fringe gang members whom I interviewed are prone to accusing the Gardaí of all kinds of corruption, they generally acknowledge that their own behaviour does transgress the law. Therefore, the Gardaí as the agents of law and order have a legitimate reason for their actions.

However, social and youth workers appear to devote much of their time when working with teenagers on the fringes of gangs to convincing them that their activities are not just wrong but also irrational. When questioned about the reasons for their intervention with a difficult teenager, workers will most frequently say that the child clearly has some psychological/family/learning issue which means that they don't recognise the very logical reasons why they should abandon their errant ways and integrate into mainstream society. Essentially, the understanding which underpins these interventions is rooted in notions of reason and rationality: getting involved in criminal gangs is an irrational act which will end in death/prison while 'getting straight' through courses/jobs etc. is the more rational response to their situation.

The young men who I interviewed during this research don't accept the logic of this perspective and, having spent three years researching in these communities, I don't accept its logic either. It would appear that youth workers may have to recognise that for young men who are deeply socially excluded in Irish society, becoming involved in criminal activity and working as a foot-soldier for a criminal gang is actually the most rational response to their situation, even if it is morally wrong.[74] These are young men who have very low levels of education, no training and no realistic chance of getting a job. Even in situations where they increase their skills, they still have to overcome the 'scumbag' stigma which is linked to their mode of dress, accent and address. Few if any of these men will marry and, in broader Limerick society, they enjoy no status and face a lifetime on social welfare.

In contrast, being active in a criminal gang provides such a youth with money and status in his community. He is more feared by his neighbours and more attractive to some girls. His membership of the gang may even shelter him from the random 'code of the street' violence in his area. Young men who eschew the lure of the gang are still faced with a life of poverty where they continue to be viewed as a 'scumbag' by many people in Limerick society. They have little chance of marrying and in some cases their unwillingness to be involved in criminal activity can mean they will be viewed as a soft target by tougher members of the local community. This is evident in Kelleher and O'Connor's chapter in this volume, which focuses precisely on men in this category who fear being out in public spaces or being in pubs where they may get into conflict with criminal gang members.

Humphreys' research on health outcomes (Chapter Ten) demonstrates that the general population in these areas have a high mortality rate and the phenomenon of early death is not unusual in disadvantaged estates in Limerick.[75] Therefore, the reasoning that non-participation in the gang will make your life better, longer or safer doesn't all correspond to reality. The 'irrationality of criminality' ethos undermines much of the good youth work done in these communities because while gang members will acknowledge that their behaviour is wrong from legal and moral perspectives they generally insist with good reason that their choices are entirely rational.

It is critical to recognise that meaningful therapeutic work with youths in these situations needs to start from a position of trust and mutual respect. When a youth worker insists that the solution to a young man's problems is to simply recognise the irrationality of his own behaviour, they are failing to acknowledge the complexity of that person's reality and the real prejudice that he faces in broader Limerick society. It is suggested that rehabilitation programmes that start from moral standpoints such as restorative justice models might be more useful with some youths than approaches which seek to invalidate their perfectly accurate assessment of their own life situation.

There has been a huge amount of criticism of the child protection system in Ireland in the last five years, yet the research on fear, feuding and intimidation in Limerick does offer some new insights in terms of this national debate. In 2010, 434 migrant children had disappeared from care contexts in the Republic of Ireland.[76] In the wake of the death of Daniel McAnaspie, there was evidence that at least thirty-seven children had died in HSE care.[77] The vast majority of these children are the powerless victims of neglect by the Irish state. What is striking about the children involved in antisocial behaviour in Limerick city is that they are not powerless. In fact, they are feared by their neighbours, teachers and sometimes even their own parents. Declan, a local teacher, comments:

> I look at these kids and I think finally the state's neglect of its own children is coming back to bite it in the ass . . . Somebody was bound to see this neglect and exploit it and that's exactly what the criminal gangs have done. It's ironic we get load of bigwigs down recently telling us they are going to smash the gangs and yet the state is powerless in the face of these kids.

Evidence of the activities of children being exploited by criminal gangs in Limerick presents a new urgency to the national question of child protection reform. Failure to enact these reforms will almost certainly have an adverse impact on the state's most wide-ranging response to criminality and disadvantage in Limerick city, the Limerick Regeneration project.

Regeneration: the story so far

The term regeneration means to be 'renewed, reformed or re-constituted'; it can also be used to refer to spiritual rebirth.[78] This term was adopted by the Irish government as the title for its major area-based intervention[79] project in Limerick city which was launched in 2007.[80] The antecedents of the Regeneration project are wide-ranging, but a number of interviewees have highlighted the burning of two children in a car in Moyross in 2006 as a particularly important catalyst for it.[81] The media response to this incident is the subject of the chapter by Devereux et al. in this volume. Plans for this area-based intervention in Limerick were initially based on a report on social exclusion in the city written by John Fitzgerald.[82] This report highlighted the importance of tackling criminality in the city in the first instance.[83] By making inroads into drugs and feud-based crime in these communities, a space would be created for a whole range of other interventions aimed at tackling social exclusion.[84]

The areas targeted for Regeneration in the city were Moyross, St Mary's Park, Southill and Ballinacurra Weston.[85] Following cabinet approval of Fitzgerald's report, the state established the Limerick Regeneration Agencies which set to work creating detailed plans for these interventions.[86] These plans, when launched, became the subject of some controversy as they placed huge emphasis on rebuilding the physical infrastructure of these estates through public-private partnerships with less emphasis on the social problems highlighted in Fitzgerald's original report.[87]

As the debate raged within the media and local communities about the merits of this housing-based approach, external events intervened. The global economic downturn of 2008 pushed the Irish economy into deep recession, creating a particular crisis in the construction industry.[88] The potential to use public-private models to fund Regeneration diminished significantly within months as banks and housing developers shifted to crisis-management modes. Even the capacity of the state to fund Limerick Regeneration's plans was questioned.[89]

In the short term, management within Limerick Regeneration mounted a rearguard action, re-orienting the project to focus more on social regeneration.[90] As a long-term strategy, they continued to lobby the Irish government for funding for physical rebuilding projects, a process which has met with some success. In July 2010, the Irish government approved €337 million for Limerick Regeneration.[91] Given that much of the envisaged building work has not yet begun, it is impossible to fully evaluate at this stage the impact which Regeneration will have on social exclusion in the city. However, after three years of social regeneration initiatives, some strengths and weaknesses in the current configuration of the project are already evident.

Positive Outcomes Which Have Already Emerged From Regeneration

TACKLING STIGMA: Within the fear and feuding study presented in this volume, the stigma associated with living in disadvantaged housing estates in Limerick was repeatedly highlighted as a problem by the 'advantaged of the disadvantaged'. From the outset, attempts were made by Regeneration agencies to unpick this stigma and present a more positive image of life in these estates.[92] These efforts have already yielded dividends. A survey of local press during the summer of 2010 revealed a range of positive articles about events in Regeneration estates. These events included an awards event for leaders of summer camps,[93] the opening of a community garden in Moyross,[94] a charity football match between Gardaí and the monks of Moyross[95] and awards recognising the work of youths involved in the Limerick South Community Youth Intervention (LSCYI).[96] Not all of these events originated with Limerick Regeneration, but the agency has played an important role in creating a space for positive press coverage of disadvantaged communities in Limerick.

The Regeneration team have also been effective in drawing attention to positive role models from these estates. In this context, highlighting of the achievements of local Munster and Ireland rugby player Keith Earls must be commended as his celebrity status is linked to a positive form of robust masculinity, the type of role model which is particularly needed in the context of 'code of the street' violence.[97]

SUPPORTING THE 'ADVANTAGED OF THE DISADVANTAGED': While researching in these communities between 2007 and 2010, I was struck by how much the 'advantaged of the disadvantaged' have benefited from some of the social regeneration projects already undertaken. For families who are relatively stable and parents who are ambitious for the children, the sporting, educational and music-based initiatives launched by Limerick Regeneration have been very beneficial. These projects have given these children access to resources and supports which did not exist prior to 2007.[98]

ADVOCACY FOR LOCAL RESIDENTS: One of the major problems facing Regeneration communities in 2007 was the complexity of the local government structures in Limerick which involved three different local councils. Limerick Regeneration workers have played an important role in acting as advocates for some local residents in these communities with local councils. This advocacy role has undoubtedly contributed to tensions between the Regeneration Agencies and local authorities, but nevertheless constituted a significant part of the contribution of Limerick Regeneration to assisting residents in these estates to improve their living conditions.

HIGHLIGHTING PROBLEMS: As an area-based intervention, managers in the Limerick Regeneration Agencies have no power to solve problems which are rooted in weaknesses which exist in policy formulation at a national level. However, managers in these agencies have played an important role in highlighting some of the problems which exist. The role of the agency in commissioning a report on potential responses to antisocial behaviour under Irish law is particularly useful in this context.[99]

Areas Which Regeneration Has Yet To Achieve

IMPROVING SERVICE DELIVERY FROM THE HSE: The Regeneration agencies have argued that one of their main roles is to ensure effective service provision in local areas.[100] I would argue that while this role has been fulfilled in terms of criminal justice issues, the positive impact which Regeneration has made on the work of the HSE and child protection services is much less evident. The development of a child-tracking system, LANS (Limerick Assessment of Needs System), has been the major child protection project championed by Limerick Regeneration. However, it is unclear whether the tracking of children in disadvantaged estates in Limerick will have any impact on the delivery of child protection services. A quote from Brendan Kenny of Limerick Regeneration in 2009 suggests that he sees the benefits of LANS in terms of the creation of more diversionary strategies:

> The programme isn't geared at taking children into state care . . . that is a matter for the HSE. The idea is to track and monitor children who are at risk and steer them away from criminality. There is a problem with children under 12 running wild. In some cases, their families are involved in criminality. In other cases, they are not . . .[101]

While the launch of LANS is significant, the existence of a tracking system does not alter the current legal and policy weaknesses in services for seriously troubled children.

EXPERTISE ISSUES: The weakness of the Regeneration Agency in improving the delivery of child protection services is linked in the first instance to its status as an area-based intervention project which has no input into national regulatory structures for child protection. However, the initial orientation of the project towards physical rather than social regeneration may have exacerbated this weakness. At its inception, Regeneration was largely conceived of as a housing project based on a report of a former city manager and managed predominantly by those with expertise in housing and urban regeneration projects. While the Regeneration teams included workers with a range of expertise on social issues, the senior management team within the agency should, given the current emphasis on social regeneration, include at least one senior manager who has highly developed expertise in the fields of child protection. In-house expertise on this issue would greatly improve the capacity of Regeneration management to engage more robustly with child protection service providers at local and national level.

DRUGS: Patterns of drug consumption in some Regeneration communities have changed considerably since the inception of the project in 2007.[102] In terms of the activities of criminal gangs, it is difficult to know whether the increased levels of heroin use in Limerick constitutes a gang response to economic recession or an attempt to undermine Regeneration itself. Either way, this strategy may be quite successful on both counts.

The success of state agencies in responding to the heroin problem has been mixed. In 2010, it was announced that despite the existence of the Limerick Regeneration project, Limerick city was to lose eleven drugs workers due to cutbacks in the Limerick Youth Service, ALJEFF (the Addiction Treatment Agency) and Limerick Foróige, leaving just one youth drugs worker in the city.[103] The Health Service Executive has announced plans for a new methadone treatment clinic in Limerick[104] but it is clear that Regeneration agencies need a revised drugs strategy to minimise the numbers of young people who are becoming addicted to heroin. The rise in heroin addiction in the city is also creating a range of problems in relation to increased street crime, begging and child neglect, problems which have impacted on some Regeneration estates as well as other parts of the city.[105] Thus, the management of Regeneration need to consider whether changing patterns of drugs use in the city require the agency to formulate a revised drugs strategy as part of its work.

DIFFUSION OF PROBLEMS TO OTHER AREAS: Finally, it is important to recognise that because Limerick Regeneration focuses on four specific parts of the city, some of the problems which previously existed in these estates have diffused to other areas in response to the success of Regeneration measures. In his original report, John Fitzgerald identified criminality as the core problem in Limerick, and the success of criminal justice and Regeneration measures appears to have indeed provoked some senior gang members to leave Regeneration estates.[106] Given the changes in the city's social geography which have occurred in part as result of Regeneration, it is essential that the agency collaborate closely with local authorities in order to monitor how the project is impacting on the Mid-West region as a whole.

Conclusion

In his initial report, John Fitzgerald notes that the success of criminal justice agencies in tackling drugs-related crime in the city 'will be fundamental to creating the conditions for other interventions to be successful and for restoring the confidence of local communities'.[107] In terms of reducing criminality among adults, the success of the Gardaí and the criminal justice system supported by Limerick Regeneration has been notable. Crime rates have been reduced and the quality of life in some Regeneration estates has improved significantly, according to some interviewees. However, measures to tackle child protection issues which are critical to eliminating the reservoir of labour exploited by criminal gangs have not been as successful. It is child abuse and child neglect which will breed the next generation of criminals. To be fair, the child protection system at national level is in crisis and it is my view that any solution to Limerick's antisocial behaviour problems requires legal, policy and resource changes which can only be enacted by national government. It is simply not possible for the Regeneration agency, which is focused on an 'area-based intervention' and where expertise is largely oriented towards housing, to develop a solution to a problem which has yet to be resolved at national level.

8. Neighbourliness and Community Spirit in Moyross and Southill

Life narratives

Máire Treasa Nic Eochagáin and Frances Minahan

Moyross (*Máire Treasa Nic Eochagáin*)

I have no bad side of neighbours to talk about. I mean neighbours now inside of this whole park, as far as I would know people. A long long time ago when I was fairly new to the place, we were coming out from Mass one morning and there was a group of women and they were talking about a family nearby. I didn't know the family, I may have known their name but I didn't know much about them because I was working outside the place. There was a huge discussion going on about this woman who had become seriously ill and the whole thrust of the conversation was 'Well, her husband doesn't have to worry, he shouldn't have to worry. Look I'll take the children to school, Mary will get the sandwiches ready for them the night before. Kathleen will have an evening meal ready for them when they come home. Teresa will do the washing.' And the six or eight women around me had all of this family's domestic affairs under control and were all so willing to help out and I stood there with my silly ideas of privacy and not interfering and so on and when the group had more or less scattered, I walked with one of them who was coming my way and I said to her, 'you must know this family very well' and she looked at me, she really looked at me as if I were growing horns, and she said 'I don't know them at all but we all have to help.' That put me in my place and I never forgot it. This was the Moyross that I had some dreams about and I had notions about the place before I came here at all.

When I got to know the woman [who was ill] a long time after, I quickly found out that she had looked after so many children in the community. She had run a club for them and she was just one person. Firstly, it was little children and then the bigger ones began to say, 'Can we join?' and she hadn't the heart to say you can't. And she took them places and there was so little money but she never saw a child turned away. Children that would have been looked upon as quite difficult particularly if they were older, twelve or fourteen, she gathered those quietly around her and said 'I need help. I'm trying to run this club and I need help.' And she put them in charge of various little groups and they would die for her. One of her own children said long before she was able to talk she was hearing the word 'community' because she heard her mother use it so often. And she said that sometimes when they would ask as children for something, their mother would sometimes say to them, 'No we can't do that, we have to think of the community.' I thought that was so lovely and that would be the thinking of many people here. That would not be the thinking of everybody – that would be fairyland, it would be wonderful if that were true – but it is the thinking of quite a few people here.

In the length of time I'm here, roughly ten years, I took a year out. I went away because I was offered a year in America because I had some idea at the time of working in South America on a voluntary basis and I wanted to go down there and see if I could find my niche. I told my neighbours when I was going and why I was going and when I came back, I didn't even have to dust this house. Now most people would say that's not possible but it was. And on, when I retired, I took the whole year off again and went to China to teach English on a voluntary capacity. And my neighbours here, I won't forget, you know these tiny things that stay in your memory. I was leaving here at four o'clock in the morning. A friend came to collect me and take my bags and here, as I was just going out the gate, were my two neighbours who'd got up to say goodbye. And the same story when I came back, my house was in perfect order and they had come in and out of it and looked after it all the time.

If you have never been in want, it is very difficult to put yourself in the shoes of someone who has a very small income. It wouldn't occur to people of means that you couldn't afford to buy salt, that's just a small little thing for most people but imagine what it would be like if you had to spend a week without salt. I think people who have small incomes are generally aware of the needs that other people might have and you see it here all the time. I have a neighbour and she is next door to someone who is bedridden. But every Sunday, that woman, when she is preparing her own meal for her family, will always send a Sunday dinner over to this woman who is housebound in order to give her son a free day because it is he who takes care of her. He comes and goes and lights the fires and so on. And I think that's a gorgeous thing. It's not so much that she is giving a poor person something but she is giving somebody freedom for at least one day in the week and that's not often available to carers. The same neighbour, who has anything but a big income herself, also helps another neighbour who has recently become a widower. I've noticed that whenever she is making an Irish stew or something she knows he likes, she will send one of the children to call him or she'll send the dinner over to him and I think that's just wonderful. I hear of the same things happening round Kileely and Ballynanty so it must have something to do with the culture of little, reaching out to other people who also don't have a huge amount.

Many moons ago, I had visitors coming for Sunday lunch, the usual one o'clock, and in the middle of the cooking the gas went and I had to run to my neighbours with the potatoes, and 'Will you finish this' and 'Will you finish that for me' and all of my neighbours were just so good and so helpful to me. Now that would never happen in a more affluent area. At one time I was renting a house off the Ennis Road and one Sunday morning I got up and I realised I had no milk. I must have come home late on the Saturday night from somewhere. I went to the little shop only to find it closed. There was nowhere in that whole place where I could knock on the door and say, 'Please could you lend me a half jug of milk.' I knew most of those people. Each of them would have given me the milk but I know for sure I would have been the talk of the road and the comment would mostly be, 'Well wouldn't you think she could plan her life better than running out of milk for Sunday morning.' If you are in need you will find yourself having to borrow but it's a good experience. I think [in middle-class areas] it's a fear of being looked down on. I knew that Sunday morning that I would get the milk but I would be looked down on, that I couldn't look anybody in the eye again.

Neighbours have an eye for you, even the ones I might not have to borrow from. We go down to Mass together, we walk, we chat to each other on the way. We have a lovely custom in the church, after Mass, we gather in the yard outside and we all have a great chat there in groups and you see people and you are very aware if you haven't seen someone for a couple of weeks and you might say, 'How are you, I haven't seen you for a while' and it's not about checking up on the person. It's about how the person really is and I think that's a very good thing in an area and it builds community in the simplest of ways. We would have a number who would come down to Mass here [in Moyross] from Kileely and Ballynanty. It's not that there is anything wrong with St Munchin's parish but it's very scattered. Here, we are very connected. The Chinese don't say I will contact you, they say I will connect with you.

We have had dreadful things happen in the community and it diminishes everybody and most of all it diminishes the people that have perpetrated the wrongdoing, whatever that happens to be. It brings a lot of pain into the community because there are such a big number of people here who work constantly, in every way they can, for the bettering of the community, for the good of the community. And then, some of those big awful crimes that happened have pulled us all down so far that you feel now we have to start right at the bottom again and try and build up what has been lost through this dreadful act, whether it be murder or wounding somebody or hurting them badly and so on.

But of course, there is a background to that, that did not happen just gratuitously or by accident. I would have known some of those families when they were small children and I'm sad to have to say that neither the state nor the society cared two pins what happened to them. I have seen a number of families where parents have died or left and no-one came in to help them and now a number of those children have grown up to be criminals. They were bright, clever children and by the time they reached thirteen or fourteen they knew there was no hope for them, and then of course we have all this difficult situation of our young people going outside the area and needing to work and answering an ad and the moment their address appeared the offer of the job is withdrawn and some very lame excuse given. Now a child who has to suffer that excuse and is turned away, that child is turned away with dreadful bitterness in their heart and maybe a week later or maybe six months later, that person who owns a big store in town is greatly surprised to have their plate-glass window put in. Now look at the cost of that, to that person, to society, to all the customers and all because a young person was really hurt when there was no good reason for it.

Young people in Moyross are as good as young people anywhere. Our pipe band has won world competitions, not just national competitions. They've gone all over the world and they have been such ambassadors for Moyross. A few years ago, President Mary McAleese gave out fifty-five awards, the Gaisce awards, to young people who had done well in so many areas. She suddenly said to those that were there, 'why is a small place like Moyross going home with eleven of the Gaisce awards out of fifty-five, that's one fifth of the total for the whole of the country?' Now, there aren't many people who are as open as she is and they aren't prepared to give the young people who come from Moyross the same recognition for the same giftedness. If they do well in their exams very little is heard about them, but if one of them breaks a window we all hear about it. I just want them to be given fair recognition, not preferential treatment, just give them their due desserts.

How do people come back [from the arson attack on children Gavin and Millie Murray in Moyross]? Mostly, through community groups. We have a group called Moyross Partners, and issues and activities that are needed and new ventures are all discussed and planned at those kinds of gatherings. And you have smaller groups like the Residents' Forum, where everything that happens in the community is discussed and that's where you can offer support to each other. Even the very fact that you can sit down as a community, as a group, and discuss what's going on, that's a tremendous support.

People talk it out. It's done in the little informal groupings around the area. Of course, there is a lot of disappointment at a time like that and that disappointment practically brings the community to its knees, but I think because there are great structures here and there are possibilities for gathering together that deflates some of the most bitter disappointment. It gives people hope that there are still others like themselves, still willing to go again, to do things, to plan things, to try and keep things going and if possible to make them a little better. I think that's possibly the best way you can get over things like that. Like the whole community put a lot of effort into making a big collection for Millie and Gavin and that was taken charge of by responsible members of the community, people that the whole community would trust. There is a trust fund now for Millie and Gavin and there is no possibility that one fiver will be taken out of that for something useless and frivolous unlike, unfortunately, what has happened in some of the higher echelons of our society. There is much more accountability here for any kind of funding that comes in for any single group. They account for what they spend down to a postage stamp. There is no possibility that any government will come in here and find black holes and spaces in the books and where did this piece of money go and no answer.

When I first came here I would say most of the initiatives for various things that happened here came from groups like the Little Sisters of the Assumption who very sadly will be leaving the community. They brought people together and one of the very first headlines under which we were brought together was 'What is my dream for Moyross?' and that was so good. And then, little by little, people in the community that had an interest in developing the community, they were sent for training. And many of them did their community leadership training out in UL and that pays off great benefits to any community and many of those people now are in leadership positions within the community. And even those who aren't are contributing in their own way at local gatherings. The

church has always been a centre here. It astonished me when I came here
first. In other places, people to go to the church for holy reasons. Here
people go to the church for Mass and that, but they also go if they are in
difficulties as one of the first ports of call for 'I need help'. And that
amazed me. Now it might have a little to do with the fact that St Vincent
de Paul and the church were seen as working together. It may have been
something like that.

There have been people in this community who have stood up to the
criminal fraternity and said, 'you are not us'. There is a great sense that if
you are in difficulty through the activities of criminals, there is a community there to help us. I suppose cameras have helped in a big big way but
cameras aren't much good if people don't alert the centre. And that's quite
simple, people are no longer afraid to do that, people are no longer afraid
to talk to a Garda on the street for a moment or to make contact. We have
a local Garda here, he's one of our community Gardaí here, and I think
there is a great sense of trust here between the local community and
himself. We have other Gardaí as well but we might not know them as well
as we know this man. I don't think people would hesitate to call Gardaí
from anywhere and report a crime because why should a community
allow people to commit crime even if there is an excuse for them having
gotten into criminality in the first place? It doesn't excuse everything they
do from there on. In your heart, you can have real pity for them that this
is what has happened to a normal decent family. They just weren't some
strange people who came down from the sky, they were our very neighbours and I suppose a sense of never being able to get anywhere was part
of their thinking. I don't know that, I'm just surmising that.

When you see yourself in a position where you think you have no
hope, there is a big temptation to get into crime. But then look at all the
young people we have all over the area, who have gone on to second
level, to third level, who have got good jobs, have a wonderful name for
themselves and are upright, responsible citizens. Wouldn't anybody be
proud of them? If only we could get help very early on. If governments
could just look not five years ahead but twenty-five years ahead, they
could save the state millions and they could bring an awful lot more hap-
piness about for communities by intervening right at the very earliest
stages. When we first had a house or two damaged by young people who
had no sense of community, why were those young people not dealt with
at that time and dealt with adequately? People here at the time would
have said things like the Gardaí can't manage and I would say, 'Why
wasn't the army brought in?' I remember a Garda saying to me that the

government will never use the Gardaí against the people. But my response is, why do you allow people who have gone into crime to act against the people? It doesn't make sense to me.

When I first came to Moyross we had no structures but now we have structures. The Sisters of the Assumption were really the people who provided the inspiration and the initiative, for women particularly. They were providing little classes to teach people to cook and so on, to teach people all kinds of little skills but most of all, they were doing self-development programmes and those were the ones that paid off best. Because as soon as women, in particular, got a sense of their own worth, it became huge for them and very powerful, particularly in situations where women were beaten and eventually had to separate. It was tremendous for them to discover I myself have worth, I have great dignity and I am a person in my own right. I think that was huge. I helped organise a course for bereaved and separated people at one stage which had a self-development dimension. And on the way there, we stopped for a break and one of them said to me, 'Now, Máire Treasa, I want you to listen to me, I mean I really want you to listen to me, I think an awful lot more of myself coming back than I did going down there.' Now that's reward enough for me. If I could hear that out of every house in Moyross, I would be in heaven.

My dream for Moyross, strangely enough, has very little to do with Regeneration. Even though it will be a very good thing in the long run provided that for every euro put into bricks and mortar and new houses there will be at least an equivalent euro put into developing the people who live in Moyross, that is hugely important, and people would feel good about themselves. You can teach very young children how dangerous it is to go near moneylenders, you can teach people a lot of skills which will make their lives much better, you can teach them that they can have respect for themselves and others. That's my dream for Moyross.

Southill (*Frances Minahan*)

I have been living and working in Southill for a number of years and from the beginning I have experienced the neighbourliness and friendliness characteristic of this community. The first evening we arrived we forgot to get milk, and a neighbour – who happened to be a past pupil – came to the rescue. This set the tone for the giving and receiving which has typified our experience here. Community spirit and care for one another is so obvious here, especially in times of need or difficulty like sickness or bereavement. People really care about one another. About two years ago, a young innocent man was murdered and the neighbours really looked out for his family. They cared for them in very practical ways like bringing food to the house or inviting them for dinner. I'm also thinking of a woman who cooked a meal each evening for an elderly neighbour and very few knew about it. There is a lot of quiet support for people. In times of real difficulty, we are there for one another. I experienced this caring myself when my mother died.

There are difficulties sometimes so that community spirit isn't quite as public as it is in other areas. During tense times, you would be aware that people are just staying indoors and are not as visible in the community as other times. People understandably wouldn't be inclined to talk if something serious happens. For safety reasons, people have to be very careful. Sometimes people can be perceived as being guilty by association – even a remote association. That adds to the complexity of life here. But people here also have a great sense of humour and fun. We've had some great social gatherings that revive the spirit in everyone. Humour and fun help people to cope with the more stressful side of life. If you were to take life at surface level here, you'd say there's a lot of fear, a lot of negativity, a lot of hopelessness. While this is real it's only one part of the picture.

Over the years, there has been a history of broken promises with some outside agencies and that certainly has dampened or dulled the spirit in people. Many fear that Regeneration may be yet another broken promise. In this time of recession when plans aren't moving as fast as hoped, people fear that yet again their hopes for a brighter future will be dashed. However, there are also people who are determined that this won't happen. There are some very committed community groups here – for example, the O'Malley Park/Keyes Park Residents' Forum. This is a great group of residents who have stuck together through thick and thin over the past few years and given hours of their time to thinking, planning and representing the views of the community.

They are people who never want to leave Southill. They belong here. They have put great effort and energy into homemaking and they have been very happy. They just don't want to leave and they are adamant that nobody will force them to move from here. There are other families who feel they want to get out and make a fresh start and they want to leave all the hassle behind them and live a 'normal' life, where they can let their children or grandchildren out to play in safety in a housing estate which is clean and well maintained. In fairness, that's so understandable, they are asking for nothing more than any other citizen in the country.

There are times when you can see that hope has once again been dashed and people get on with their own lives and just don't see the point of getting involved. That's a pity because continuously you hear people say that twenty years or thirty years ago this community was alive with involvement. The African saying, 'It takes a village to raise a child', was true here. In earlier times, the community here was able to take a more active role in raising their children together. So many people have said that such was the sense of community here that if a neighbour's child was in trouble or getting up to mischief a word from a neighbour would sort it out. Now that's the foundation and residents want to go back to that foundation and have the safety and the normal requirements and privileges of any citizen. But it takes courage and confidence to even dare believe that change can happen. It also takes courage to believe in change in a community where it may not be accepted or appreciated by some people, for all sorts of reasons. Low community self-image, lack of hope, fragmentation – I think they all go together. Low self-image means people haven't the energy to trust or get involved and there's a sense of oppression and divisiveness. Low self-image affects morale in the community. It becomes a situation then where anything goes, whether it's the illegal dumping of rubbish, antisocial or criminal behaviour. Low self-image can lead to a lot of negativity in all aspects of life. This can make it very difficult for residents who have represented their community, championed Regeneration and encouraged others to believe in it. They find themselves caught in the middle very often when promises made by the authorities don't materialise.

All of human life is here and we all share the same human nature. The capacity for gifts and weaknesses is in all of us. In the context of Regeneration, the University of Limerick offered a six-week course to community representatives which renewed energy while also being most informative. Supports like this can strengthen team spirit in people who are involved and also boosts confidence. It also made me more aware of the great range of talents, skills and abilities which exist within the community here. People's academic intelligence and their achievements here have been kept hidden for too long. We don't hear enough about our students who have won scholarships, who are university graduates with Master's degrees and PhDs. There are also lots of sporting heroes; two of our weightlifters have had great achievements both at national and world level and we've a European champion boxer, obviously. One of the local sports trainers said recently, 'you know we really need to publicise this more as the positive part of the community. It's a really good news story.' There is a sense here that the good news stories need to be made public, now more than ever.

People in this community have a great capacity to enjoy the simple things in life. We had a great night in the Community Centre for the 'Young at Heart'. People are still talking about it and saying how it connected them to what life was like in the early days of Southill, the good old days, which are not so long ago. Occasions such as this – and many more examples could be given – renew the positive energy in the community. Sometimes people are always preoccupied about the next step in life and the future and they forget to enjoy today. Maybe because of the difficulties, that doesn't happen here. People are able to enjoy today if today turns out to be a good day.

Many people think about leadership in terms of skills but it's really more about what's within us. For some people, leadership can start with a small step like taking part in a church service or becoming a volunteer for a community event. Leadership can often start from these small beginnings. The next step can be doing something different, something more demanding, but that capacity for leadership is in everybody here at different stages of development. It is also important to recognise that the potential for the positive or negative is in all of us. Aristotle said, 'What lies in your power to do, lies in your power not to do, the choice is yours.' It's easy to be critical when thinking about those involved in certain activities but the fact is that the potential for good or evil is in all of us. In that way, I think this community is a microcosm for our world.

Maybe because the circumstances here are a bit exceptional in some ways, people are forced sometimes to think about the positive and the negative more frequently. They have to think about their own behaviour, about being positive or negative, and they are forced into a consciousness of this. It is interesting that while in this community there are people who have chosen a negative path, I'm struck all the time by how many really good people I meet. The circumstances can push people down a negative path but they also sometimes push people towards exceptional goodness. Maybe in this situation, people are forced to consider more the question 'What do I believe? What are my values when the chips are down?' These circumstances mean that people sometimes have to consider these questions very deeply. A time comes in all our lives when we are faced with similar questions. It's just that the circumstances are different for each one of us.

Criticism of Regeneration serves the negative element here well, because then people don't believe, they don't have hope and that makes them very vulnerable. There is a bit of risk involved in saying, 'I believe it will happen' and sometimes it can be easier to stay stuck and say, 'Oh it's the same old story. I'll believe it when I see it.' You can hide behind that or make the choice to risk believing in the future, a different future. I think it's linked up with identity. Any one of us can stay in a victim identity and stick with that. There is a familiarity about having that victim identity, but if you begin to open your world, either at a personal level or at a community level, you begin to look at your world in a way that holds hope and possibility for a different future. If people can break away from that victim identity, it can have an enormous impact on all parts of life, like the small pebble that has a ripple effect through the pond. Changing just one aspect of your thinking opens up so many other possibilities. That is where I imagine some of us who work in the community can accompany people in making one tiny change in their way of thinking. In terms of working and living in the community, I see my role as being about encouraging and supporting others in their active involvement in the community. That role involves facilitating the emergence of leaders in the community.

I've been thinking more about hope in recent times. We can be pessimistic or optimistic about a particular problem but that's different to hope. Hope is about believing in the tomorrow and we can never let go of that at any level in our lives. I see the church's role as supporting people in hope, helping them realise that there is more than today. They need to believe that there is *more than* what is happening right now in their own world or in the community here. We are *more than* whatever is happening. That's what we're about. It's about holding the hope, believing that tomorrow can and will be different. It's not about being unrealistic. In certain circumstances and in dark times, when people reach out to others that alone can create hope. It is about being with the person and being connected. I think the worst thing that can happen to any one of us in our situation is to be cut off, to be disconnected from other people. And that again can be part of the darker side of our reality – people can feel intimidated, cut off and afraid. That's where going out, being part of a club or a group, is so important. It doesn't change the reality out there but it changes us on the inside. It makes us feel more connected to each other.

In difficult times, that sense of support and connection is crucial. You know that lovely Irish quote, 'Ar scáth a chéile a mhaireann na daoine.' That's very alive here. That thoughtfulness, that sense of community, solidarity and support is very powerful. Whereas in a community where families are more self-sufficient that may not be the case and it's a quality that cannot be bought. There are different kinds of richness and there are huge riches here in terms of community spirit. My wish is that the people of Southill will have all the supports they need from each agency in order to develop ownership, responsibility and leadership to make their dreams come true.

PART THREE

Key Research
Perspectives

9. Men on the Margins
Masculinities in disadvantaged areas in Limerick city

Patricia Kelleher and Pat O'Connor

Large numbers of men benefit materially, socially and politically from patriarchy, but the advantages described as the 'patriarchal dividend' are not spread equally among men.[1] In other words, not all men are equally privileged. In this context, a key issue is how do men negotiate their identities as men within disadvantaged areas? This raises questions about the social and economic structures in which they live as well as about their cultural definitions of masculinities. Connell suggested that, 'Masculinities are constructed, over time, in young people's encounters with a system of gender relations.'[2] Thus gender 'is something people do' and it varies across time and place.[3]

This chapter is an exploratory study of masculinities enacted within locally disadvantaged contexts. Drawing on in-depth interviews with young men, it suggests that they, for the most part, enact marginalised masculinities, excluded from the public space in these local communities by drug disorder and by pre-teen and teenage protest masculinities; and from the economic area by their own poor educational levels and an inability to attain breadwinner status. A minority of the men in this study had moved towards a re-envisioning of masculinity, mainly through caring, with sport being one of the few ways in which the majority enacted masculinities in an unproblematic way. Many of them had lives marked by personal trauma and difficulties. However, their ability to access support was limited by a definition of masculinity that precluded confiding. In summary, this chapter seeks to explore the extent and nature of their difficulties in 'doing' masculinities.[4] It also outlines some of the interventions which could be put in place to bring young men in such disadvantaged communities in from the margins.

Methodology

This study of men on the margins is set in disadvantaged areas of Limerick city. Limerick city is one of sharp contrasts in terms of the

169

spatial distribution of relative affluence and deprivation.[5] DeCleir points out that economic disadvantage and social exclusion are highly concentrated in four of the sixteen housing estates built by the local authority in Limerick city.[6] Limerick Regeneration comprises two Regeneration Agencies, and was established by the government in June 2007, following on from the Fitzgerald Report published in April 2007. It was established to address what Fitzgerald had described as 'chronic and concentrated' in Limerick city.[7] A Draft Plan to address the needs of these areas was launched in October 2008 and Master Plans were published in September 2009.[8]

Large numbers of households in these areas are welfare dependent, unemployed and consist of lone parents. The unemployment rate is two-and-a-half to three-and-a-half times the national average. At a time when lone-parent family units with one dependent child under fifteen years made up 21 per cent of family units in the state as a whole, they made up between 57 and 64 per cent of families in these areas.[9]

The criteria for the selection of the young men in this study included age and location: i.e. they were aged between eighteen and thirty-three years and grew up or lived in one of the disadvantaged areas which are now the remit of Limerick Regeneration. Key practitioners agreed to refer young men to the study and eighteen young men volunteered to be interviewed. Hence, it is not a random survey, but an exploratory study whose purpose is to give voice to young men living in disadvantaged areas. The young men were interviewed during May and June 2007. The average age of the young men interviewed was twenty-two years. All of the men were white and Irish-born. All but two were currently unemployed. None of the men were married or had ever been married. Half (nine) of the men interviewed had children. Between them, they identified fifteen children as theirs. Three of the nine who had children were living with the mother of their child(ren). Five of the men who had children were non-resident fathers and one other man was a lone parent with the main responsibility for his child.

More than half (ten) of the eighteen men interviewed were living in their parents' house (including three of the non-resident fathers). Four of the eighteen men were involved to some extent in pushing out the boundaries for the enactment of masculinities: in two cases, their partner was the main earner; one was in receipt of carer's allowance and a fourth was himself a lone parent.

The interviews, which were semi-structured, lasted on average one hour. The analysis consisted of thematic qualitative analysis of the interview data – initially focusing on key concepts drawn from Connell's work and later on other themes that emerged inductively from the data in interaction with the literature. In the text, participants' identities are protected by the use of fictitious names and by removing or altering any identifying information not essential to the analysis. The key issue underlying this study was the question of how men negotiate their masculinities within the context of economic and social marginalisation. The study presents the experiences of social marginalisation as seen by these young men in their struggle for dignity and survival under three themes:

- School days and uncertain futures;
- Everyday life: lack of access to public space;
- Other sites for 'doing masculinity': paid work, fatherhood, confiding, sport.

School Days and Uncertain Futures

The right to education is outlined in the Declaration of Human Rights (1948). Good literacy and numeracy skills are important for everyday living. However, 30 per cent of pupils in primary schools in disadvantaged areas in Ireland have serious literacy difficulties (about three times the national average). This is a human rights issue.[10] Educational credentials in what the American sociologist S.M. Miller calls the 'credential' society affects access to employment, social mobility and pay levels.[11] In Ireland, since the 1980s access to top jobs in skilled manual work and in professional, administrative and managerial work is based primarily on such educational credentials. Critically, the need for such credentials has extended to apprenticeships, one of the traditional ladders of working-class mobility from low-paid insecure jobs to skilled employment.[12] O'Neill points out that lacking economic, social and cultural capital, children living in areas which experience cumulative disadvantage face considerable difficulties managing the school environment.[13]

Almost all of the young men interviewed found school difficult and many 'hated' school, particularly secondary school, and found the transition to secondary school particularly difficult. Many of these young men lacked basic reading and writing skills and could not cope with the broad range of academic subjects which were part of the curriculum of second-level education. Many were not able to cope with homework: 'I was in the lowest class and never did homework. I always got someone to do it.' (Colm) It was clear that these young men needed a more nurturing and supportive environment, which would help them to learn: 'I left school in the first year of secondary school. I had difficulties learning. I had difficulties spelling and did not get any help.' (Mark)

It is not surprising that they did not have the confidence, or felt that they did not have the intelligence, to remain at school. Dylan, who left school at fifteen , asserted: 'I had not got what it takes. I was no good at school.' Young men like Declan who had a learning difficulty experienced particular difficulties: 'I was not diagnosed until after I left school . . . I knew that I had difficulties. I got bullied and harassed at school because of my learning difficulties.'

For many of these young men, social and environmental stress in the community spills over into their personal and family lives and affects their capacity to absorb and retain knowledge. The impact of murders and sudden deaths of family members are particularly poignant. Brian was fourteen when his father was shot in tragic circumstances: 'When my father died, I could not hack it [school] anymore. I was fourteen and got a job in a Community Training Workshop.'

Thirteen of the eighteen young men in the study left school at fifteen years or younger, making what O'Donnell and Sharpe call 'career-less transitions' where only insecure, low-paid jobs are open to them and where it is difficult for them to have a stake in society.[14] The remaining five men passed the Junior Certificate and left before completing the Leaving Certificate or qualifying for a trade. This contrasts with the fact that the majority of Irish young people complete the Leaving Certificate, although boys, especially those in disadvantaged areas, are less likely to do this. Without educational credentials, apprenticeships are not available to them.[15]

The themes emerging in these young men's accounts of their school days were reminiscent of Willis's 'lads' and Mac an Ghiall's 'macho lads'.[16] Thus, as in these studies, some coped with the school environment by being rebellious and refusing to accept the teacher's authority: 'We were all messers. I was thrown out of school. I had got suspended a few times. They said that they would take me back if I signed a form for good behaviour. I wouldn't sign it.' (Joe)

Many of the men had subsequently benefited from special educational and work training projects where learning was organised in more informal ways in smaller groups. The existence of community-based projects specifically designed to help young adults rebuild their careers has enabled some young men to re-enter education. Joe, who is now nineteen, left school at fifteen and ended up in low-paid jobs. He is currently studying for the Leaving Certificate Applied and would like to get a trade, preferably as a plumber. He is hopeful that he will succeed:

> The project is very different than school where you are just sitting in
> a classroom. Here it is relaxed. You call the teacher by the first name.
> They are your friends. You know that they care about you. There is
> need for a lot more projects like this. A lot of people are waiting to get
> in. (Joe)

Vince, who is now twenty-three and has also returned to education: 'I am
now doing the Leaving Cert and would like a job in computers.'(Vince)
Jason commented on the fact that teachers in the project understood the
pupils, were attentive to them, helped them to learn and made learning
interesting:

> It is the way they run the place. They know what is going on
> [meaning they understand the everyday life of people]. The project is
> welcoming. They ask you how you are. They have a great sense of
> humour. I know a lot of people who want to get into the project, but
> there is a waiting list. (Jason)

Although some young people are aware that education is one of the most
important means of accessing a decent wage, they feel that they have left
it too late to return to education: 'I am sorry now that I did not stay on. I
would not go back to school. It is too late to do that.'(Kevin)

Because of lack of formal qualifications the jobs to which many of the
young men have access are uninteresting and low-paid and some cannot
find work at all. Much of their day consists of 'hanging around, doing
nothing in particular'. Several mentioned that they would stay in bed until
mid-day. Many spent many hours watching sport on television. A typical
afternoon could involve 'watching television in a mate's house', while at
weekends: 'I'd phone a few friends and get them over for a few cans. We
would put on the Play Station and You Tube.' What came across in the
interviews is that these young men experience the 'emotional wounds of
class inequality', what the sociologists Sennett and Cobb refer to as 'the
hidden injuries of class', where injurious games of self-justification elevate
one group by ostracising and 'othering' minority groups and groups on
the margins.[17]

Everyday Life: lack of access to public space

Classic ethnographic studies such as Liebow's study in 1967 and Whyte's
study of 1943 show how important the street is for unemployed men.[18]
However, the young men in this study feel that they have to 'negotiate
multilayered aspects of risk and danger in relation to violence in public
space'.[19] Their difficulties in accessing public space arise from two sources:

firstly, drug-related disorder in their communities, and secondly, the activities of teens and pre-teenage boys, which it is suggested can be seen as indicative of protest masculinity.

Feuding and Drugs-Related Disorder

Inter-family feuding has long been a feature of life in Limerick and precedes the emergence of the illegal drug trade of the 1980s and 1990s (see Chapter Six of this volume). As the trafficking and selling of illegal drugs became a source of considerable wealth, feuding among families escalated and deepened. Inter-family feuding is now a feature of life in many of the deprived areas in Limerick city, as the families that are involved in the drugs trade seek to retain or extend control over 'drug patches'. Hand grenades, pipe bombs and explosives feature in different disputes. Revenge killings are common and lives are being destroyed and communities devastated.

Young men interviewed in this study talked about how families are drawn into the feuds in a variety of ways. Young men, alienated and susceptible, agree to carry and to sell drugs to earn what they see as a decent wage when few other opportunities are open to them. They are the small dealers, couriers or mules, who smuggle drugs by 'stuffing' or swallowing them. They are what Vince, one of the young men interviewed, calls the 'penny boys' or the 'runners', the people who take the risk of being caught. Paddy echoes this viewpoint:

> Many of the small dealers tried to work [looked for work]. They were in little jobs [low-paid work]. There was a stigma. People did not like that they were from here. Because of this, they started selling drugs to get a bit of money. It was normal. Now they get shot at and arrested.

While some people are selling drugs to feed their families, others have greater expectations and are involved in responding to the escalating needs created by a consumer society: 'Young men want money for show. Young fellas want cars and money. They want tackies, trainers, clothes, the best of stuff. They want the brand names.' (Declan)

Also involved are drug addicts who sell drugs in order to support their addiction. The struggle for control over 'patches' and drugs has exacerbated gangland feuds between a select number of local families. This in turn has led to revenge attacks ordered by gang bosses. Many people who have nothing to do with the feud can get caught up in it because of who they are related to: 'You cannot lead an ordinary life. There are too many people looking for revenge. There is no end to the feuds. There are too many people dead.' (Dave) Niall explained: 'A friend of mine was stabbed in the lungs, because his nephew was involved in the feud.' There are numerous accounts of serious violence:

> I knew a fellow who was smoking heroin. He did not have the money to pay for it. He got a beating. If they couldn't get him, they'd get his brother. He turned to someone else to borrow the money. He did not know that they were part of the feud. He is caught in now and cannot get out. In fact his whole family is caught in the feud. (Jason)

Violence and destruction have caused devastation on many streets: 'A bomb was found in a house beside me. Two or three houses down from me have been burned down twice.' (Owen) 'There are only two houses left on the block I live in. Six or seven have been burned down. The whole block at the back of us has been burned.' (Paddy) When tensions are high, normal life is disrupted over innocuous incidences: 'Stupid things are happening. A fight can start over a girlfriend. It gets out of hand and cannot be stopped.' (Dylan).

Among the young men in the present study, even walking around the community, going to visit relatives in other areas, going into the city centre or even going to the pub is restricted – not least because 'someone would think that you are dealing in drugs'. Some of the men do frequent local pubs but many of them expressed a fear of doing so because of the prevalence of violence: 'It is too dangerous to go to the pub. I stay at home with my girlfriend and watch television. At weekends we get a few cans.' (Dave) Jason also avoids pubs: 'When I have drink on me, it encourages me to slag them [drug dealers] off. This is a dangerous situation to be in.'

Many people who have nothing to do with the feud get caught up in it because of who they are related to or who they borrow money from and: 'Once you are involved, you cannot get out . . . You cannot lead an ordinary life. There are too many people looking for revenge. There is no end to the feuds. There are too many people dead.' (Joe)

Many of them had very happy childhood memories of these areas: 'I was brought up in Moyross. I enjoyed it' (William); 'My father used to take me fishing and camping' (Philip); 'We used to go to football matches' (Owen). However, they are very aware of how drugs have now devastated the communities in which they live: 'St Mary's was a great place to grow up. There were regattas on the river. You could hang around for hours. But this has all changed. We have not got that these days. The feuds have destroyed the city.' (Niall)

Nevertheless, the local area was and is important to the young men interviewed and there is a strong sense of place, a place which they know intimately. The majority of them have siblings and extended kin living nearby and are strongly attached to these communities. Despite the horrific violence and intimidation – 'our kids cannot leave the house . . . It is not safe out there' (Tom) – only two of the eighteen men would like to move out of the area.

Protest Masculinity

The importance of the street for youth gangs has been described in many classic sociological studies and also emerged in this study.[20] Connell suggests that many young men use the street to make a claim to power in the absence of any real educational or occupational resources. This he calls 'protest masculinity'.[21] Protest masculinity is a 'tough guy' assertion. It is the assertion of a masculinity in a context where many of the traditional routes of respectability have been closed off. It is not, however, only the material gains that are sought after in protest masculinity. The symbolic meaning of activity is also important. Protest masculinity provides young men with recognition, an identity and a place in the world that has been denied to them.

Severe neighbourhood harassment and disruption can be caused by activities related to pre-teen and teenage protest masculinity. As they observe and emulate the older lads, many of the pre-teen and teenage boys graduate from setting fire to rubbish and drinking in fields to robbing houses, robbing cars, joy riding and prison. The older lads in turn see the crime and drug bosses as heroes and want to be like them. At a basic level, participation in a young gang relieves boredom. Mark, who is now eighteen years, recalls his participation in gangs at a young age: 'At twelve and thirteen we used to drink and smoke cannabis. Fuck all else to do. Fuck all here. We just hung around drinking and having a laugh.'

Joyriding is overwhelmingly an activity of older teenagers who temporarily take control of the public domain, transcending their feelings of powerlessness and boredom through 'displays of risk, excitement, masculinity and even carnivalesque pleasure'[22] in an 'extended present' in which they can forget the stark realities of an uncertain future.[23] Such activities create a sense of excitement, enact ritualistic defiance and, most importantly, are an opportunity to publicly demonstrate skills before audiences and so gain social status and 'street cred' in a context where their lives are characterised by educational failure, bleak prospects and high alcohol and drug use. It is what Lyng describes as 'edgework'.[24] In edgework there is an emphasis on skill and performance which if not successful can lead to injury and death: 'You have to keep control, make sure that you do not hit anything. People come out to watch the hand-brake spin. Young fellas come out of the cracks in the walls looking at the spinning.' (Chris)

The risk involved creates a heightened sense of self and a feeling of 'omnipotence'. McVerry sees joyriding as the ultimate expression of alienation.[25] Over time young people graduate through a series of stages from watching joyriders to actually driving cars:

> Young fellas are hanging around saying – 'What will we do? Rob a car.' When I was young I used to rob cars . . . At first I used to watch the older lads robbing cars. It is exciting. Everyone gathers around. Girls stand at the corners looking on. Then I was a passenger in the car. Then I drove. (Paddy)

Finally, many of the cars are burned out. Most of the young men interviewed, even if they had been involved in the past, would not now condone 'joyriding' since it adds to the total disorganisation and turmoil in disadvantaged areas: 'Cars are speeding up and down, horses and sulkies flying up and down the road, jeeps are speeding beside the horses to see how fast the horses are going, young children are on quads. The place is mad.' (Niall)

A lack of confidence in and antagonistic relations with the Gardaí have long been shown to be associated with social marginalistaion.[26] Aggressive patrolling and indiscriminate street searches by the Gardaí and what are perceived as unacceptable attempts to solve crimes were experienced as harassment by some of the young men in this study. On the other hand, the invisibility of the forces of law and order (as reflected in the absence of Garda stations in these areas) reinforced the perception of the Gardaí as not 'making much of a difference'; 'The Gardaí have little control. They can't do much. They can't catch the drug dealers.' (Paddy)

Caring for animals, especially horses, was seen as one of the few non-criminal outlets for these young men (as in other working-class areas). Paradoxically, however, in response to publicity about 'wandering' horses, this outlet had effectively been eliminated by the Gardaí, thus further denuding their lives: 'Everyone loves horses. I love horses. All I wanted was horses. The Gardaí and pound took them.' (Paddy)

Four of the men in the present study indicated that they had spent time in prison. Some had been to prison on several occasions. Three received sentences for drink-and-anger related crimes and one for stealing cars. All four are making a determined effort to remain crime-free. Although a prison sentence was initially seen as a 'badge of honour', generally young men found it difficult to serve the sentence. Colm, who is now twenty-eight and has two children, was 'locked up' for being drunk and disorderly. He found prison very difficult: 'It was terrible. You had no privacy. It was crazy.'

Tom, who is twenty-three, got involved in crime through drink and received an eighteen-month prison sentence. He has two sons and intends to remain out of crime. Niall, who is now twenty-nine, says:

> When I was young I was very angry. I was in a gang. I thought I was the bee's knees, high on cider. After a few times in jail, depression kicked in. I knew that I had to do something about my life. Prison copped me out [did his head in]. Once when I was up before the courts, I asked the judge not to lock me up and the judge gave me a chance.

The access of these young men in the present study to public spaces was limited both by the activities of those involved in drug-related crimes and by the protest masculinities of the teens and pre-teens in these areas. This had implications for their ability to enact masculinities since it effectively excluded them from a variety of public areas.

Other Sites for 'Doing Masculinity': paid work, fatherhood, confiding, sport

In Ireland even today masculinity has continued to be defined particularly in terms of paid work and the ability to be a 'breadwinner'.[27] For Connell, potentially at least, men could transform elements of the enactment of masculinities by their pragmatic acceptance of women as key breadwinners and by undertaking domestic and childcare work.[28] Brannen and Nilsen also suggested that 'new forms of masculinity constitute positive and transformative resources for young men in the context of negative structural conditions'.[29] In this section, we look at the extent to which these young men identified paid work, fathering, confiding and sport as sites for the enactment of masculinities.

These unemployed men faced considerable difficulties in 'doing masculinity' in socially acceptable ways within a societal context where having a job was still the most acceptable way to be a man, and where poverty and the lack of material resources were likely to affect their ability to do this and to establish a home or to get married. The vast majority of the young men interviewed do not have work in the traditional meaning of having a 'job'. As young adults, they see themselves as personifications of failure precisely because they share the values of the wider culture in wanting to have a 'decent' job to support a family. Unemployment or low-paid work damages confidence and undermines the breadwinner role: 'It emotionally affects a man that he cannot support a family. Men value themselves in work. Without work many feel useless. It is an emptiness feeling.' (Declan)

Even the two young men who are full-time carers in the home would like to be in paid work outside the home: 'I would love to have money to provide for my kids. When my kids are asked, "What does your father do?" I would like them to be able to say that I do something' (Niall). Having no paid work both profoundly affects their sense of self and makes it difficult for them to support a family financially. Kiernan draws attention specifically to the economic barriers which unemployed men encounter in making a conscious decision to have children.[30] Dylan, aged twenty-two who has no children, would like to settle down: 'I would love to be able to support a family. I feel that this is not possible at the moment. I have not a decent job. I have no qualifications.'

Many of the young men also encounter discrimination and disrespect because of where they live: 'Your address affects your chances of employment. If I want to apply for a job I have to give my sister's address. I was advised to change address on my application form, as it would discriminate against me when applying for a job.' (Declan) Nevertheless there was a suggestion that some felt entitled to paid work: 'Now we have not a fair chance of getting a job.' Thus five of the eighteen young men, without being asked, stated that competition from migrant workers affects their chances of getting paid work and is also lowering pay levels. Their perception is that foreign workers are 'working for half nothing' and 'messing up the whole system', although they stressed that they 'were not blaming them'.

None of the eighteen men interviewed for the present study has ever married. One man commented on the fact that marriage in his community is a very rare event. In Ireland, there has been some shift in the amount of housework and caring work that men do. Nevertheless, 70 to 80 per cent of Irish men do no cooking, cleaning or laundry on a weekday – and this changes little over the weekend.[31] The majority of the young men in the present study still saw women as having the main responsibility for children – and the ability to 'do a runner' was one of the few aspects of a patriarchal dividend that they saw men as having: 'The man can get up and walk. Children are more women's responsibility. Women have it hard. Men can get up and take off.' (Chris)[32]

Nevertheless, there is some evidence in the present study that traditional gender patterns are changing and that these men are taking on a greater role in doing housework, although it would appear that it is more a 'helping hand' than a decisive shift. Thus, sixteen of the eighteen men in the present study 'help out' in the house, with only two men stating that they would not do housework: 'I help out at home. Things have changed. I do the hoovering upstairs and polishing. I do the shopping every Friday.' (Tom) In the present study where the woman was the sole earner in the household there was an acceptance that the men would undertake domestic and childcare work. Also, one man was a carer and carried out the main household and caring work. Thus, there was some suggestion of the emergence of what Brannen and Nilsen called 'new forms of masculinity' in the lives of four of the eighteen young men.[33]

In the current study, nine of the eighteen men interviewed had children, five of them were non-resident fathers. These five non-resident fathers wished to retain an involvement with their children. One of them has an agreement with his ex-partner to jointly care for their children and has the children overnight three nights a week; three have/had cases in the family law courts and there is palpable anger among some of these men against the legal system: 'Unmarried men are discriminated against. They get an unfair deal. They do not have rights, yet have to pay maintenance.' (Colm) Many had difficulty coping with their former partners after the relationship ended. There is also a lot of distrust between women and men. Chris felt that having the children gave women power over men: 'For the first while she let me take the kids. Now she is using the kids to control me.'

Taking on a changing role in the family poses serious challenges to men, not only to develop the skills of housework and caring, but also to develop the capacity for relationship competence and emotional communication.[34] Nevertheless, all nine men that had children acknowledged the positive impact that becoming a father had on them. Having a child challenged them to have some level of stability in their lives and to take some responsibility for their children. Many mentioned their determination to 'stay out of trouble' because they now have children.

Although men are just as capable as women of confiding, such confiding is more likely to occur between women than between men.[35] Franklin has shown that confiding between men is related to wider structural and cultural factors, including constructions of masculinity involving 'aggression, competitiveness, stoicism, rational thinking and independence'.[36] arguably legitimated by the existence of heroic, taciturn exemplary models of masculinity in American Western movies.[37] Cleary found that many of the young Irish men she studied who had attempted suicide were unable or unwilling to confide in anyone because of fear of rejection, guilt or simply an inability to articulate such feelings.[38] In a study by Begley et al., although the majority of Irish men aged eighteen to thirty-fourfound it useful to talk to someone, more than two-thirds said that they sometimes had a drink or tried not to think about a problem when they were worried or upset.[39] Sixteen of the eighteen young men in the present study stated that they would not confide in anyone if they had an emotional difficulty. Confiding in others, especially other men, was seen as a weakness, reflecting fears about emotional vulnerability and even perceived homosexuality: 'It is pansy stuff. I am not one for shared love stuff' (Vince); 'I would not talk about things bothering me. Men keep it all in. Fellas are frightened to talk to other fellas. They are afraid that the fellas will talk about it to someone else. I would try and sort it out myself.' (Dylan)

Thus these young men did not have a construct of masculinity that allowed them to access emotionally supportive relationships. The cost of not confiding can be high and may be associated with depression and/or violence.[40] Such cost seemed particularly likely to occur in a context where there was a lot of unresolved anger around 'revenge' killings and other kinds of loss and trauma: 'I was holding everything on my chest. I was trapped in a hole, no light. You would let no one know. It was eating me up slowly' (Niall); 'Men can't say how they feel. In the pub, they start roaring and shouting. They take the aggression out on someone else – what the fuck are you looking at?' (Dylan). The only style of communication some of the men appeared to value was a didactic one. Thus their difficulties around confiding in others extended to counselling (even when mandated by the court for alcohol abuse): 'No counsellor can help me. I have been talking to her for five weeks. It is all me telling her.' (Mark)

Boys in Ireland as elsewhere are more likely than girls to be heavily involved in sport.[41] It has been widely suggested that sport is a site for the enactment of masculinities, not least because sport, for those who are good at it, allows for the display of physical skills, toughness, control and detachment.[42] Indeed Connell suggested that sport – particularly physical-contact competitive team sport – was almost as important as sexuality as 'a site of masculinity formation'.[43]

For the men in the present study, sport was one of the few sites for the enactment of masculinities. Twelve of the eighteen men in the present study were involved in sport – some at a very high level (including playing under-age soccer for Ireland). Many trained regularly, some even taking a leadership role in getting others involved in it:

> I love sport. I train every Tuesday, Thursday and play matches on Sunday. There are about fifty involved in the soccer. I got fellas involved in the soccer that you would think would not kick a ball. I knocked at doors to get them up out of bed for a match. To keep fit is very important. (Dylan)

William 'loves' sport and is proud of the local facilities: 'Moyross has an all-weather indoor soccer pitch, snooker, boxing club. I love soccer and hurling.' (William) However, facilities for these activities were unevenly available in these disadvantaged areas. Thus one area had no soccer club-house. In another area, although there is a 'soccer academy', there is no soccer pitch and young people have to be transported outside the area by coach for soccer practice.

Summary: conclusions and recommendations

The eighteen young men in this exploratory study grew up in areas which are characterised by socio-economic disadvantage. The majority left school early and some left school with their individual needs unmet. Young men without educational credentials make what O'Donnell and Sharpe refer to as 'career-less transitions' to insecure, low-paid jobs or are unable to get paid work.[44] An additional obstacle to getting work is the discrimination they experience because of where they live and competition for low-paid work from migrant workers.

Many of them benefited / are benefiting from education projects that are person-centred, have small classes and where a relational, informal approach to learning is adopted. These models are participatory, affirm the self-esteem of the young men and also foster closer and stronger relationships with their teachers. These models contrast with that of many services, which operate along hierarchal lines, are impersonal in nature and provide for little consultation with the users of services.

Control in the communities in which they live is exercised by a small number of families who control the distribution of drugs and other criminal activity. The escalation of violence resulting from the drugs trade has devastated such communities. The people who are suffering most are the ordinary families. They are the neighbours of the drug barons, and are virtually imprisoned in their own communities. In the words of one man: 'Drugs have broken us. Drugs changed everything in our community. Through greed and power, the whole town is torn apart.' (Paddy)

The local area is important to the young men interviewed. There is a strong sense of place, which they know intimately and are highly connected to through kinship. Low-level everyday violence and intimidation creates fear and anxiety. Because of the violence, men feel restricted walking around their community and frequenting local pubs. Visiting pubs and relatives in other working-class areas in Limerick city is also not to be taken lightly. The public spaces that men were used to occupying are no longer available to them. Nevertheless, despite the violence and the loss of access to public space, it is interesting to note that only two of the young men would like to move out of the area in which they live.

It is not surprising that teens and pre-teens are susceptible to getting involved in antisocial behaviour that is severely disruptive to the community, including neighbourhood harassment and disruption by setting rubbish on fire and drinking in fields. As they grow older and emulate the older lads, they graduate to robbing cars, joyriding and prison. The older lads in turn see the crime and drug bosses as heroes. Success in this context is seen as flirting with danger and taking risks, yet steering clear of the Gardaí.

Alongside difficulties in getting work and with the education system, the young men in the present study struggle with a multitude of other factors. These include the traumatic death of friends and relatives, and social and emotional difficulties. Many of them in their teenage years lived 'for the present' but now realise that they need somehow to create a future.[45] When they reach their early to mid twenties, they are marooned in a social and cultural environment where it is extremely difficult for them to construct a life that 'makes sense' in any terms. They are 'bystanders' of two cultures – what they see as an alien mainstream culture and a hard-core criminal subculture which permeates those communities. The traditional male roles of breadwinner and protector of the family are not open to them. Many of them are ready to engage with projects and services. However, there are few interventions for young men in their early twenties. The need for a radical overhaul of how services have traditionally been delivered is acknowledged by the chief executive of the Limerick Regeneration Programme.[46] In delivering services he also points to the need to put in place better systems of co-ordination between different agencies. The present study indicates the need for a complex variety of interventions, which would include the following:

FACILITATING ACCESS TO A SAFE PUBLIC SPACE: Ensuring that these communities are made safe needs to be a key priority of law-enforcement agencies. There is also a need to enhance the visibility of public services and their delivery within these communities. In addition, a comprehensive protection and support programme is needed for both men and women who wish to leave the community.

EDUCATION AND WORK TRAINING: Finding and keeping a job is one of the most effective ways to prevent re-offending. There is a clear need for more special education projects for young adults at local level which focus on keeping them out of crime and are linked to progression routes to apprenticeship training and employment. In delivering programmes, the methodologies developed by special education projects in the community can provide some guidelines. Most importantly, there is need for one agency to take responsibility for co-ordinating a response to the needs of young men.

BEREAVEMENT COUNSELLING: Many young men and their families experience unresolved grief resulting from the violence, injury, death and loss. Bereavement counselling and group-work need to be accessible to young men and delivered in a way that is acceptable to them.

RELATIONAL AND EMOTIONAL COMPETENCIES: Many of the young men find it difficult to confide in others. Some also find it difficult to see relationships other than in control terms – with, for example, 'doing a runner' being seen as one of the few advantages that they have in life as compared with women. This raises questions about their cultural constructions of masculinity – ones that could be usefully challenged.

SPORT: This is one of the few areas where the young men in disadvantaged communities enact masculinities. A further development of the facilities to enable them to do this is recommended.

Based on this exploratory study, it is suggested that many of the difficulties these young men face stem from the interaction between the capitalist economic system and a cultural construction of masculinities. In this context, projects that encourage structural as well as cultural transformation need to be encouraged. This requires structural changes in the educational and occupational systems as well as access to safe public spaces. But it also requires cultural transformation since masculinities which inhibit, for example, accessing supportive relationships and undertaking parental responsibility are also unhelpful. These are formidable tasks but ones which the activities of the Regeneration Agency can play a key role in facilitating.

10. Social Capital, Health and Inequality
What's the problem in the neighbourhoods?

Eileen Humphreys

A key characteristic of Limerick is the high level of social inequality at spatial level in the neighbourhoods that make up the city and suburbs.[1] For a variety of reasons including 'mistakes' in planning the city, Limerick city and suburbs are characterised by distinct neighbourhoods which are segregated along social class lines, are physically bounded (poor physical connectivity across neighbourhoods of varying socio-economic status) and with little interaction across the social class divide. While poverty is bad for society, poverty with strong social inequality is worse.[2] If living standards for the most disadvantaged have improved in absolute terms over time, even though the relativities between the most affluent and most deprived have remained more or less the same,[3] why does inequality matter so much and why is it associated with such negative consequences?

Social inequalities, which have structural causes, negatively affect social cohesion and social capital by increasing the social distance between people and groups in society and reducing the likelihood of shared social associations being formed.[4] Countries and regions with high levels of trust in people in general and high levels of civic engagement, such as Scandinavian states and the north of Italy, tend to be more equal in terms of income distribution.[5] High levels of trust and civic engagement (reflected in engagement in voluntary associations) are indicators of a developed 'social capital'. The decline in social capital in the US and its associated social isolation – reflected in the image of 'bowling alone' – suggesting a lack of community spirit[6] – are linked to growing inequalities of income.[7] Lack of social cohesion, often used interchangeably with social capital, is associated with a variety of social ills including high rates of crime, suicides, non-marital births and teenage pregnancy, drug abuse and poor physical and mental health in populations.[8] The association between structural social inequalities and health is linked to the psycho-social explanation of health inequalities. It is argued that strong social inequalities negatively affect social cohesion and social capital which, in turn, leads to psycho-social stress at the individual level, affecting the biological pathways, producing ill-health in populations.[9]

This chapter examines selected aspects of the social capital in neighbourhoods in Limerick city and suburbs, and the contention that positive outcomes are associated with higher levels of social capital.[10] It is based on two separate studies undertaken in Limerick. The study sites include areas which, consistently since 1991, have been classified as the relatively most deprived neighbourhoods and the most affluent neighbourhoods in the city and suburbs.[11] These neighbourhoods provide an example of the highest levels of social inequality at a spatial level within a relatively small geographic area on the north-side of Limerick city.

The first study, undertaken in 2005, focused on measuring and describing the social capital in the neighbourhoods, and explored the associations between social capital, quality of life and the socio-economic development trend of the neighbourhoods.[12] It included both relatively affluent and disadvantaged neighbourhoods. The second study, undertaken in 2007/8, focused on an ageing population in four parishes on the north-side of the city, known collectively as Thomond Parish Cluster.[13] Similarly, the parishes include areas which are among the most prosperous and most disadvantaged in the city (and the state). A unifying theme in both studies is the relevance of place to people's lives and outcomes such as health. A further related theme is social class as a defining factor in communities of place in Limerick.

The context of the research is that the planning of Limerick city and suburbs (involving three local authorities) has impacted on the social capital of communities as well as on the quality of neighbourhood and community life – in the first instance, by establishing the social pattern of the neighbourhoods. In terms of the debate on whether the relative successes or problems of the neighbourhoods are explained by the people or the place, the indications from this body of research are that the social capital at neighbourhood level is being shaped both by the characteristics of the people who live there, including social class, and conditions of place. Problems arise from the clustering of people and households who are poor into relatively segregated places. This, in turn, affects the conditions of place – the infrastructure, the services and its external image in the city, the region and beyond.

The level of social capital (and its prevalent type) is a good indicator of the quality of life in the neighbourhood. However, it does not follow that the social capital is the factor which causes neighbourhoods to be better or worse places to live. The findings of these studies in Limerick and a wider body of research suggest that positive community social capital at neighbourhood level tends to occur with, rather than cause, the positive outcomes associated with it.[14] The social capital of neighbourhoods is also affected by wider trends of regional growth and decline, trends in labour markets (availability of job opportunities) and housing supply/housing policy. Opening up new opportunities to neighbourhoods, such as a new mix of housing, facilities and work places, can result in inward mobility of people with different characteristics to established residents (for instance, in terms of levels of education, income, age, health profile). Over time, depending on whether or not people stay, the social capital of such areas changes.

Focusing on the health of populations, the study of an older population in the four parishes shows that as well as characteristics of people (age, gender, social class), neighbourhood conditions and aspects of social capital influence health outcomes. The relationships are complex in terms of how neighbourhood affects health. The findings of this research provide support for the view that poorer people living in more affluent neighbourhoods will tend to have better outcomes in terms of health than those in poorer neighbourhoods – i.e. the social mix of 'place' matters to outcomes.

Definitions of Social Capital and Key Literature

There are many definitions of social capital. In these studies, social capital refers to: 'features of social organisation, such as networks, norms and trust that can improve the efficiency of society by facilitating co-ordinated action'.[15] Social capital from an 'Putnamian' perspective concerns: (i) social networks which bring people together; (ii) supportive attitudes or norms, particularly trust in people in general and the belief that people 'look out for each other' (referred to as generalised reciprocity); and (iii) outcomes flowing from such networks and norms and from working together in a co-ordinated way. One problem with this formulation of social capital is that it is viewed only in a positive light. However, several researchers have highlighted that social capital can have a 'downside'.[16] The downside includes its potential to exclude outsiders or people who are different from the mainstream community. Social networks can also be used for antisocial and deviant purposes (e.g. to operate criminal networks, to enforce intimidation, to prevent the reporting of criminal activities by members of a network of acquaintances or a community).

There is now some consensus that there are three dimensions of social capital,[17] namely: (i) bonding social capital, which refers to the 'strong' socially homogeneous ties of family and close friends. These 'strong' ties are most important in providing social and emotional support to individuals in everyday life. In small territorial communities (neighbourhoods), bonding is associated with shared identities, a strong sense of place and neighbourliness; (ii) bridging social capital, which refers to the socially heterogeneous or 'weak' ties connecting people into horizontal associations. These ties cut across social groups and, by bringing people into contact with others unlike themselves (heterogeneous social ties), can be effective in bringing access to wider resources and upward mobility. In communities of place, bridging social capital is associated with the activity level of voluntary associations (e.g. the proportion of the population involved in voluntary associations) and their role in building up relationships of trust across social groupings; (iii) linking social capital, which refers to links between people and groups in vertical ties or power relationships. In small-scale communities of place, this generally refers to links beyond the community into formal organisations at higher levels in the power hierarchy (city-wide, regional and national decision-making structures). Vertical links provide access to external resources including economic and financial capital (e.g. funding for local initiatives), information and decision-making processes. This is the type of social capital associated with a community's capacity to influence decisions that affect them.

Health of populations is better where the social capital is high.[18] People with more active participation in voluntary associations and regular contact in social networks have lower incidence of common mental illnesses.[19] Correlations have been found between poor social networks and mortality from various causes.[20] Research on the links between social capital and health outcomes is not conclusive in that some researchers have found no such association.[21]

In terms of place, there is a growing body of evidence for the thesis[22] that neighbourhood affluence exerts an independent effect on health, net of individual level socio-economic resources.[23] For instance, recent research in the US concluded that there appears to be 'a health advantage (for poorer people) associated with living in the most affluent neighbourhoods'.[24] Other research found that neighbourhood affluence exerts a significant positive effect on health (after controlling for individual level socio-economic, demographic and health-related background factors). However, this research indicates that 'individual-level income has a considerably greater effect on individual self-rated health than neighbourhood affluence'.[25] Similarly, in a review of the evidence of neighbourhood effects on personal outcomes for children and adults, it was found that neighbourhood effects are significant but are much smaller than the effects of family characteristics such as income, socio-economic status or educational attainment of parents.[26]

Objectives and Theoretical Frameworks of the Studies

The research on which this chapter is based focused on different objectives. The study to evaluate the social capital of Limerick city neighbourhoods was based on Putnam's concept of social capital referring to shared values of trust ('most people can be trusted') and reciprocity ('people look out for each other') and involvement in social networks, including associations which bring people from different backgrounds together to deal with common problems. It sought to explore different types of social capital and 'measure' the overall level of social capital of the neighbourhoods. It also explored whether there is evidence of a relationship between the levels of social capital and the socio-economic development profile and trend in the neighbourhoods.

The study of ageing in communities of place concerns, inter alia, the importance or otherwise of the structural and contextual conditions of neighbourhood to the health status of people. It focuses on the extent to which characteristics of neighbourhood (place), including the social capital, matter to the health status of older people. It is argued that concentrations of affluence or poverty at neighbourhood level affect health outcomes for residents over and above their individual characteristics.[27] The theory is that poorer people yield a health benefit from sharing neighbourhoods with more affluent individuals linked to: (i) better functioning institutions and better services in more affluent neighbourhoods, and (ii) the adoption of mainstream behavioural norms (by poorer people) via social learning effects. The theory is that people in lower social classes living side by side with people higher up the social hierarchy tend to emulate the behaviours of people in higher social classes, raising the standards of, and mobility opportunities for, the lower social classes.[28] These ideas, particularly related to the positive impact of social diversity at the neighbourhood level in terms of improving the life chances and opportunities for poor people, as well as the view that social diversity in itself is enriching, have been present in the academic literature for a long time.[29]

Promoting social diversity is increasingly in vogue in advanced states such as the US, the Netherlands and the UK, as part of the policy response to the complex problems of poor neighbourhoods. However, Atkinson argues that while 'intuitively, many people support the idea that social diversity is a social good and brings wider benefits', this contention is 'barely tested in academic research' and there is empirical research that does not support this.[30] Linked to this, it is argued that research needs to establish what kinds of social diversity 'might work best, where and in what combinations'.

Study Methodologies

The study sites were selected to represent different typologies of neighbourhood in the city and suburbs. The selection criteria in the first (social capital) study included: (i) different characteristics of relative affluence/relative disadvantage based on the Haase Index;[31] (ii) different levels of residential mobility (high, medium, low mobility) based on a variable included in the 2002 census (proportion of the population changing address in the last year). The study sites were the extremely disadvantaged neighbourhoods of Moyross and St Mary's Park, and average and affluent neighbourhoods respectively in the Inner City and Dock area and Castletroy/Monaleen in the suburbs. The disadvantaged neighbourhoods are examples of relatively low (St Mary's Park) or medium levels (Moyross) of residential mobility, while the average and affluent neighbourhoods have high levels of residential mobility.

In the study of health status of an older population resident in different types of communities of place, the Four Parishes study spanned ten electoral districts on the north-side of the city. The parishes comprise: (i) Our Lady of the Rosary parish, the most prosperous area of Limerick city with an ageing population, centred on the North Circular Road and Ennis Road; (ii) St Munchin's parish, a large, socially-mixed parish concentrated towards a lower socio-economic profile; (iii) Christ the King parish comprising most of the 1970s middle-class suburbs of Caherdavin; and (iv) Corpus Christi parish coinciding largely with the 1970s local authority housing estate of Moyross.

Both studies involved a quantitative research strategy and cross-sectional research design. Both were centred on a social survey based on independent samples by neighbourhood, and a probability sampling approach. The surveys involved a structured questionnaire administered through face-to-face interviews with people in their own homes. Details of the areas studied (neighbourhoods/parishes), total population, sample size, response rate and key characteristics are shown in Tables 1 and 2 below.

TABLE 1: NEIGHBOURHOOD SOCIAL CAPITAL STUDY –
POPULATION, SAMPLE AND KEY CHARACTERISTICS

Neighbourhoods Names/size	Areas included	Sample size achieved and response rate	Key characteristics
Castletroy/Monaleen/ Annacotty (part) (suburbs) 1,670 households (estimate)	Part of the Ballysimon electoral district. Study area concentrated around the University of Limerick but including some of the older parts of Castletroy, into the new estates in Monaleen and Annacotty	100 respondents, 6% of households; 87% response rate	Affluent area but disimprovement in profile of relative deprivation between 1991 and 2002 census periods. High mobility area; high rates of home ownership and private rental; large student population.
Moyross (part city/ part suburbs at the time of study), 1,100 households (Census of Ireland 2006)	Moyross estate which comprises 12 parks. Partly within the electoral district of Ballynanty and partly (3 parks) within Limerick North rural electoral district (inside the county boundary at the time of study)	101 respondents, 9% of households; 98% response rate	Large-scale local authority housing estate (1970s); very disadvantaged, slight improvement in the relative deprivation score between 1991 and 2002; medium residential mobility rates
King's Island (city), 972 households (Census of Ireland 2006)	St Mary's Park (St John's A Electoral District); Lee Estate and Assumpta Park (St John's B, electoral district) and a small area near the core of the city (St. John's C).	98 respondents; 10.3% of households	Traditional inner city community. The largest residential area (St Mary's Park, 443 households) has been consistently the most disadvantaged ED in the state since 1991; low mobility area, especially St Mary's Park.
Inner City/Dock area, 1,630 households (estimate)	Covers Steamboat Quay, Harvey's Quay, O'Connell Avenue, South Circular Road and city centre. Covers 4 electoral districts: Shannon A, Dock A, Dock C (part), Dock D.	100 respondents; 6.1% of households	Mixed area, classified generally above average to affluent; disimprovement in relative deprivation in parts of the area between 1991 and 2002; concentrations of new apartments / private rental; large immigrant population in Steamboat Quay (30%); high rate of residential mobility.

TABLE 2: AGEING POPULATIONS IN THE FOUR PARISHES –
POPULATION, SAMPLE AND KEY CHARACTERISTICS

Neighbourhoods Names/size	Areas included	Sample size achieved and response rate	Key characteristics
Our Lady of the Rosary, 1,160 people 65 years and over (Census of Ireland, 2006)	North Circular Road, Ennis Road, part of Mayorstone.	218 respondents; 19% of study population; response rate 71%	Most affluent part of the city and the state; ageing, prosperous population.
St Munchin's parish, 1,007 people 65 years and over (Census, 2006)	Thomondgate, Kileely, Ballynanty, part of Caherdavin, part of Mayorstone, parts of Ennis Road, Farranshone	151 respondents; 15% of study population; response rate 56%	Large sprawling parish; mixed social class base but oriented towards lower socio-economic profile; large, ageing population.
Christ the King Parish, 288 people 65 years and over (Census, 2006)	Original suburban estates in Caherdavin built from the 1970s, part of Limerick North rural electoral district; formerly in the county but recently incorporated within the city boundary (limited boundary extension)	146 respondents; 51% of study population; response rate 68%	Middle-class estate; built in the 1970s; many employed in new industries in Shannon; small ageing population.
Corpus Christi parish, 58 people 65 years and over (estimate)	Mainly coincides with the Moyross local authority housing estate – details above; in Ballynanty electoral district (part) and Limerick North Rural (part)	27 respondents; 47% of study population; response rate 68 %	Extremely disadvantaged. Worsened in relative deprivation between 2002 and 2006; large exodus of population in this period; small older population; bias in the elderly population towards a higher social class profile compared with the estate as a whole, linked to presence of two communities of sisters who are now elderly.
Total sample		542 respondents; 65% response rate	

Key Findings

Selected findings of the research in the neighbourhoods and parishes are presented below. These focus on aspects of the social capital of the neighbourhoods and outcomes associated with it, in terms of quality of life in the neighbourhoods/parishes and health status in an ageing population. The findings of both studies indicate a strong sense of belonging to community. With the exception of the Inner City and Dock area, which has a high concentration of non-national residents, the majority of residents have a sense of belonging to community. Sense of belonging to community is strongest in King's Island (85%). It is weaker in Moyross (69%) but perhaps is surprisingly strong in Castletroy/Monaleen (74%), in that most residents surveyed are not natives and the average length of residence there was five years. It is very low in the Inner City and Dock area (25%) (Figure 1).

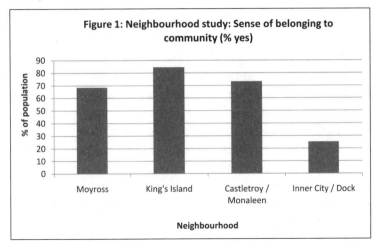

CASES AND TESTS: N All=378; Chi. sq.=0.000; Phi=0.466, p<0.001

Findings from the Four Parishes study indicate that the sense of belonging to community is even stronger among the older population. It is strongest in Christ the King parish (93%), followed by Our Lady of the Rosary parish (91%) and weakest in the most disadvantaged parish of Corpus Christi (70%). In the oldest parish, St Munchin's, over 80 per cent of the older people feel a sense of belonging to community.

The extent of knowing and trusting neighbours and the extent of agreement that 'people look out for each other' (reciprocity) were explored in both studies. It is in the lower mobility and disadvantaged neighbourhoods that people know most of their neighbours – for instance, in King's Island 78 per cent know 'most of the people living there', while this is 66 per cent in Moyross. Only 10 per cent of people in the highest mobility area, Inner City/Docks, indicate that they know most of their neighbours.

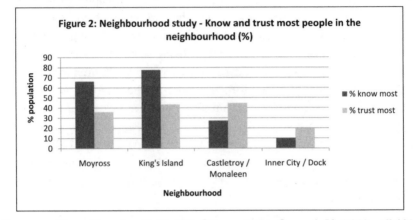

CASES AND TESTS: Knowing: N All=398; Chi. sq.=0.000; Cramer's V=0.360, p<0.001
Trusting: N All=382; Chi. sq.=0.000; Cramer's V=0.218, p<0.001

In Castletroy/Monaleen, the highest proportion of the population states that they trust 'most people living in the neighbourhood'. However, based on a wider range of similar neighbourhood-based studies of social capital, it is not only the absolute level of trust that matters.[32] Rather, the differential (gap) between knowing and trusting is an important measure of the social capital. The gap between knowing and trusting is greatest in a negative direction in trust in King's Island (78% know most, while 43% trust most people living in the neighbourhood) followed by Moyross, where a higher proportion know (66%) compared with the proportion who trust (36%) people living in the neighbourhood. The opposite is the case in the more affluent and higher-mobility neighbourhoods (Castletroy/Monaleen and Inner City and Dock area) where residents trust people to a much greater extent than they know them (a positive gap).

A similar pattern is in evidence in the Four Parishes study. It is only in Corpus Christi parish (Moyross) that older residents know people (59% know most) to a greater extent that they trust them (44%), producing a negative gap (−15%) between knowing and trusting people in general. In Christ the King parish – the middle-class suburban community – the proportion trusting people to a greater extent than knowing them is highest (+31%); the next highest is the most prosperous parish of Our Lady of the Rosary (+21%). The findings indicate a sense of reciprocity overall with a majority in all neighbourhoods agreeing with the statement that 'this area is a place where local people look out for each other' (Figure 3).

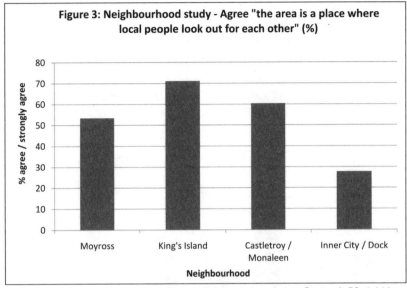

Figure 3: Neighbourhood study - Agree "the area is a place where local people look out for each other" (%)

CASES AND TESTS: N All= 372; Chi sq. p=0.000; Association Cramer's V=0.229, p<0.001

Reciprocity is strongest in King's Island, where over 70 per cent agree that 'local people look out for each other', followed by Castletroy/Monaleen (60%). It is weakest in the Inner City/Dock area where only 28 per cent agree and the majority (54%) disagrees with the statement. With older people in the four parishes, sense of reciprocity is even stronger. In Christ the King parish, 90 per cent agree that 'people look out for each other', followed by Corpus Christi (84% agree) and Our Lady of the Rosary (80% agree). It is somewhat weaker in the parish of St Munchin's (73% agree and 24% disagree).

Internal community cohesion (a measure of 'bonding' social capital) is explored by asking the extent that people agree the area 'is a close/tight-knit community'. Compared with other neighbourhoods, it is on King's Island (the most deprived neighbourhood in the city) that the highest proportion of residents agree that this is a 'close/tight-knit' community (69%). In the high-mobility Inner City/Dock area, the lowest proportion agrees that this is a 'close/tight-knit' community (only 20%). In Moyross, the proportion of residents who consider the community 'close/tight-knit' is also small (25%). Commenting on this, respondents stated that they 'keep more to themselves', they 'don't go in and out of each other's houses' and 'wouldn't keep keys of a neighbour's house'. Some residents consider parts of the community as 'close and tight-knit' – for instance, among older residents that came to live there at the same time. Some feel that 'close/tight knit' community is a negative characteristic, commenting, for instance, that the neighbourhood is 'clannish' and 'closed'. The social capital literature similarly distinguishes between 'close' (which can be a positive characteristic) and 'closed' (negative) communities (Figure 4).

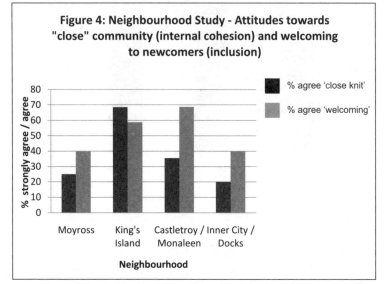

Figure 4: Neighbourhood Study - Attitudes towards "close" community (internal cohesion) and welcoming to newcomers (inclusion)

CASES AND TESTS: Close: N All=375; Chi sq. p=0.000; Association Cramer's V=0.258, p<0.001

Welcoming: N All=374; Chi sq. p=0.000; Association Cramer's V=0.194, p<0.001

Inclusion is explored by asking the extent to which residents agree that the area is 'welcoming to newcomers'. Moyross and the Inner City/Dock area are least inclusive on this indicator while Castletroy/Monaleen is most inclusive. In Moyross and the Inner City/Dock area, compared with other neighbourhoods, the smallest proportion (40%) agrees 'the area is welcoming to newcomers' while the largest proportion disagrees with this statement in Moyross (33%). In Moyross, some residents commented that newcomers are not welcome until they know more about them since the estate tends to get tenants that 'nobody else wants'. Allocation of housing on the estate is a contentious issue. Residents in some parts of the neighbourhood consider their area a 'dumping ground' for families who are not wanted elsewhere. In the Inner City/Dock area, the impression is one of a community in transitory accommodation and they do not make efforts to welcome people who are not likely to stay, while the immigrant and the indigenous populations here generally do not mix.

Focusing on the same indicators in the study of older people in the four parishes, the communities hold attitudes more supportive of the notion of 'close' community than the earlier study (Figure 5). Such attitudes are perhaps more typical of the views of an older population grouping compared with the general adult population.

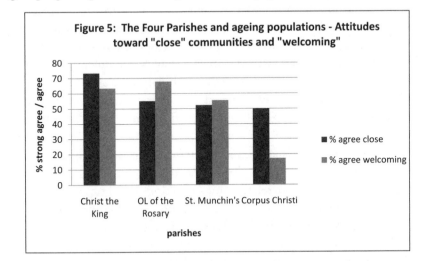

Figure 5: The Four Parishes and ageing populations - Attitudes toward "close" communities and "welcoming"

CASES AND TESTS: Close: N All=541, Chi sq. p=0.000; Association Cramer's V=0.258, p<0.001

Welcoming: N All=541; Chi sq. p=0.000; Association Cramer's V=0.194, p<0.001

It is in Christ the King parish that the largest majority agrees that the area is a 'close/tight-knit community' (73%) and the smallest proportion disagrees with the statement (18%). Exactly half of the population of Corpus Christi parish (Moyross) agree that the area is a 'close/tight-knit' community. However, it should be noted that the vast majority of the older population live in more settled parts of Moyross. Attitudes on the extent to which the area is 'welcoming to newcomers' are generally less positive among older people in the four parishes compared with the earlier survey. Attitudes on this indicator are least favourable in Corpus Christi (Moyross) where only a small proportion (17%) agrees and the majority disagrees with the statement (65%).

Commenting on the statement regarding newcomers on the estate, from the point of view of older residents in Corpus Christi, allocationof housing is considered to have been mismanaged over the years in Moyross, where houses were let to problem families who subsequently 'took over' parts of the estate. As housing units became available and were let to problem tenants, other residents left because of criminal and antisocial behaviour. In other parishes, there are some concerns regarding housing being bought by the local council for rent, or by private landlords, and properties being let to problem families. Older people express fears of neighbourhood deterioration generally and fears for their safety and security. There are also experiences of 'bad neighbours' in some areas. Some older residents in areas constructed as social housing estates refer to the 'damage' to the communities resulting from the availability of the surrender grant (in operation from 1984 to 1987).[33] It enabled those with the most capacity for upward mobility, often the community leaders on local authority estates, to move out, leaving behind a more disadvantaged population. As such, the estates failed to mature and the mobility disrupted existing family and friendship networks.

Trust in institutions is an important indicator of social capital in that it focuses on attitudes which are supportive or otherwise of people engaging in vertical power relationships ('linking' social capital) – in particularly with institutions and agencies responsible for the delivery of services in local communities.[34] While the detailed findings are not presented here, the proportion expressing positive trust in selected institutions, by neighbourhood (social capital neighbourhood study), are shown in Figure 6 below.

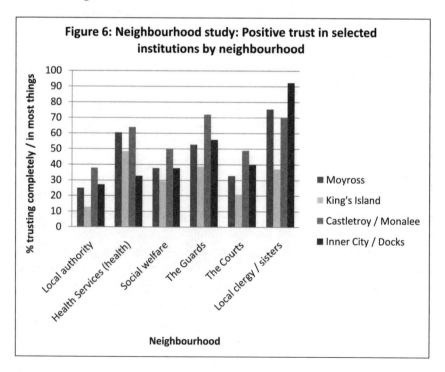

Figure 6: Neighbourhood study: Positive trust in selected institutions by neighbourhood

Some common patterns are in evidence in the neighbourhoods in terms of institutions attracting relatively high and relatively low levels of trust.[35] Trust is at the lowest level in relation to the local authority compared with other institutions – ranging from lowest level of trust in this institution in King's Island (13%) to the highest level of trust in Castletroy/Monaleen (38%). In Castletroy/Monaleen and Inner City and Dock, a higher proportion trusts than distrusts the local authority (27% in Castletroy/Monaleen and 23% in Inner City/Dock area state they trust the local authority 'not *much/not at all*'). In both Moyross and King's Island, trust in the local authority, the courts, social welfare (and the Probation Service – data not shown above) is negative, in that more people distrust these institutions than trust them. With the exception of the inner city neighbourhood (King's Island), trust is at the highest level in relation to the local clergy and sisters compared with other institutions. In the more affluent and high mobility neighbourhoods (Castletroy/Monaleen and Inner City/Dock area), trust is positive in relation to all institutions.[36]

In the Four Parishes study, trust in institutions is at a higher level which, perhaps, is not surprising in an older population cohort. Similar to the earlier neighbourhoods' study, relative to other institutions the highest level of trust is in the local clergy and sisters, followed by the Gardaí. The lowest level of trust in all parishes is in the local authority (Figure 7).[37]

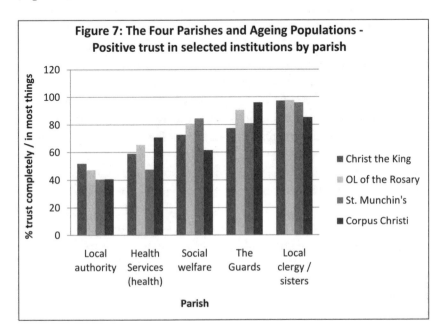

Figure 7: The Four Parishes and Ageing Populations -
Positive trust in selected institutions by parish

It is in Corpus Christi (Moyross) that residents have the highest levels of trust in the Gardaí. Growing trust in the Gardaí was already in evidence from the earlier study. Generally, this is associated with the introduction of community policing and a more visible Garda presence on the ground in Moyross in recent years. Lower ratings of the police in St Munchin's and Christ the King parishes are associated with the opposite – generally the lack of a visible Garda presence 'on the beat', concerns among older people for their own safety and security, and fears associated with antisocial behaviour. In relation to the local clergy and sisters, some commented in the earlier neighbourhood study that while they lacked trust in the institution of the Church (and some of the hierarchy), they trusted and respected people in the local clergy and sisters. In disadvantaged parts of Moyross and areas like Ballynanty, the communities of local sisters based on the estates are seen to have worked hard to support people in need in the communities, and to promote community development in Moyross, even though most residents do not engage in religious practice. A minority of older people, however, also relate negative experiences of the institutional church. These include negative experiences in school, which older people often associated with their relative poverty (i.e. they were neglected because they were poor).

In both Corpus Christi and St Munchin's parishes, a higher proportion distrusts the local council (48% in Corpus Christi and 46% in St Munchin's) than trusts them (41% in each parish). Negative attitudes of trust in the local council in Corpus Christi (Moyross) and St Munchin's (including some disadvantaged neighbourhoods such as Ballynanty, Kileely and Thomondgate) is associated with a sense of neglect of the estates by the council over many years such that some parts greatly deteriorated to become very difficult places in which to live. In more affluent areas, relatively low trust in the local authority is associated with residents' perceptions of poor planning decisions for the city in general and the north-side in particular.

Using various indictors in the dataset, overall measures of social capital and different aspects of the social capital were developed based on aggregating the social capital of residents to the level of neighbourhood (scored from –2 (lowest) to +2 (highest)).[38] The indicators used are summarised in Table 3, while findings on selected indicators have been reported above. The overall measure of social capital is the average of 'bonding', 'bridging' and 'linking'.

TABLE 3: MEASURING THE SOCIAL CAPITAL OF THE NEIGHBOURHOODS:
SELECTED INDICATORS

Dimensions	Bonding	Bridging	Linking
Attitudes	Trust in people in neighbourhood; Reciprocity ('looking out for each other'); Internal cohesion ('close' community)	Trust in community leaders; Trust in community organisations	Trust in institutions; Attitudes towards local governance
Networks	Knowing neighbours; Presence of 'strong ties'– close family, friends and neighbours in the area; Regular interaction by meeting, 'phone etc. with 'strong ties'	Involvement in voluntary and community organisations	Awareness of voluntary organisations classified as 'linking' social capital (e.g. residents' associations, neighbourhood watch; organisations involved in statutory/community partnerships); involvement in such organisations.

In terms of overall levels of social capital, this is positive only in Castletroy/Monaleen and King's Island. In King's Island, strong social capital reflects higher level of bonding (sense of a 'close community' and strong supportive networks of family, friends and neighbours) and in Castletroy/Monaleen, positive but less bonding and more bridging social capital (trust and involvement in voluntary associations). Bonding social capital is the most developed form of social capital in all areas, bridging is less developed and linking social capital is the weakest form.[39] Weak linking social capital, especially in the disadvantaged communities (King's Island and Moyross), particularly reflects the low level of trust in institutions. Even though structures and processes have been put in place to engage community in decisions that affect them (e.g. local action centres associated with the PAUL (People Against Unemployment in Limerick), Partnership in Limerick, the Community Development Programme, structures linked to the City Development Board), weak linking social capital is indicative of the distance of the grass-roots population of these areas from mainstream agencies and institutions.

The lower mobility and more disadvantaged communities (King's Island and Moyross) have higher levels of bonding social capital. Unsurprisingly, the high mobility and particularly the transient Inner City/Dock area have low levels of bonding social capital. Bridging and linking social capital are highest in Castletroy/Monaleen (affluent but high mobility) compared with other neighbourhoods. Bridging and linking social capital are low and negative (more people lack than possess it) in the disadvantaged neighbourhoods. Linking social capital is lowest in King's Island, the most disadvantaged neighbourhood in the study (Figure 8).

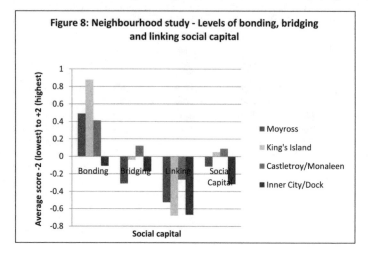

Quality of life in the areas, as well as quality of the social relational aspects and community social capital, were explored in both studies. The survey included questions related to satisfaction with the neighbourhood as a place to live, perceptions of the extent to which certain issues are problems and the extent of local problems in the neighbourhood setting. Where the social capital is high, the expectation is that the quality of life is good.

Levels of satisfaction with the neighbourhood are highest in Castletroy/Monaleen where 86 per cent consider it a very/fairly good place to live and only 3 per cent consider it a fairly/very bad place to live (Figure 9). Moyross has the worst rating where less than half (47%) consider it a very/fairly good place to live and more than one-fifth (21%) consider it a fairly/very bad place to live. While King's Island is also disadvantaged, residents' satisfaction ratings are high, with the vast majority of residents (77%) considering it a very/fairly good place to live.

Focusing on the four parishes, satisfaction ratings by older people with their neighbourhoods are even higher. In Our Lady of the Rosary parish, 99 per cent rate their neighbourhood as a very/fairly good place to live, followed by Christ the King parish (93%). Consistent with the earlier study, satisfaction ratings are lowest in Corpus Christi (Moyross), where 73 per cent rate it as very/fairly good and 23 per cent rate it as fairly/very bad. At the same time, this is a much higher resident satisfaction rating than recorded in the earlier survey. Again, it should be noted that older people tend to live in the more settled and 'best' areas of Moyross.

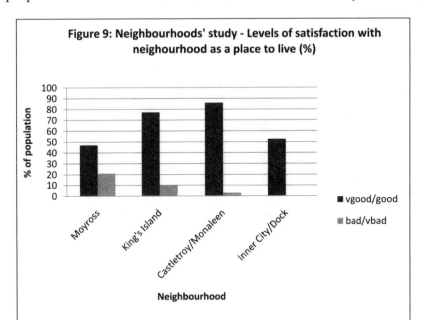

Figure 9: Neighbourhoods' study - Levels of satisfaction with neighourhood as a place to live (%)

CASES AND TESTS : N All=396; Chi sq. p=0.000; Association Cramer's V=0.271, p=0.000

The types and extent of neighbourhood problems were explored in both studies.[40] Findings in relation to specific issues are described below. The problem identified by the largest proportion of residents of the disadvantaged estates (Moyross and King's Island) is that of the poor external image of the neighbourhood – or that the place has a bad name. This was identified by 91 per cent of residents of Moyross and 75 per cent of residents of King's Island as a very big/big problem. Overall, Moyross and King's Island have a more severe problem across all problem types compared with the more affluent areas of Castletroy/Monaleen and Inner City/Dock. For instance, almost half the residents of Moyross (48%) and 60 per cent of the residents of Kings' Island indicate that the 'area being poorly maintained/run down' is a very big/big problem. Approximately 75 per cent of the population of both Moyross and King's Island indicate that 'young people hanging around with nothing to do' is a very big/big problem. 'Bad neighbours/problem families' is a very big/big problem for 22 per cent of the population of Moyross, while this affects 10 per cent of the population of Castletroy/Monaleen and 7 per cent of the population of King's Island.

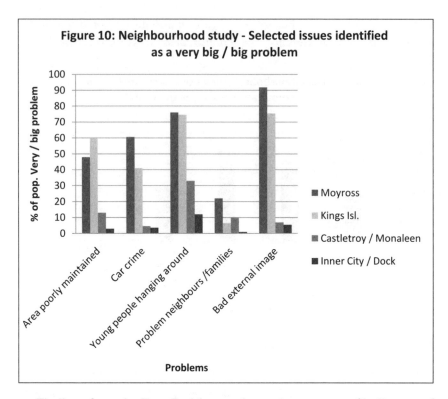

Figure 10: Neighbourhood study - Selected issues identified as a very big / big problem

Findings from the Four Parishes study on the same set of indicators of neighbourhood problems show some consistency with the earlier study. The greatest variation between the parishes concerns the problem of 'bad external image'; whereas all residents (100%) of Corpus Christi parish (Moyross) consider this a very big/big problem for their neighbourhood, it is not at all a problem in the most affluent parish (less than 1% indicate it is a problem). Poor external image applies in pockets of St Munchin's parish (6% indicate it is a big/very big problem) and by a smaller proportion again of the older population in Christ the King parish (4%). 'Young people hanging around with nothing to do' is a bigger problem in Corpus Christi (Moyross) but is also identified as a very big/big problem by approximately one-quarter of the older population of Christ the King (mainly middle class suburb) and St Munchin's (24%) and by a smaller proportion in the very affluent parish of Our Lady of the Rosary (8%). Some older people commented that gatherings of young people in groups around residential areas seem 'threatening'.

In the neighbourhoods study, multivariate analysis of the dataset can identify the factors, independent of each other, which explain high levels of social capital and types of social capital (bonding, bridging, linking).

This analysis confirmed that relatively lower mobility neighbourhoods (King's Island and Moyross) are associated with higher levels of social capital. However, these lower mobility neighbourhoods are also the most disadvantaged. The positive association with social capital here results from much stronger 'bonding' social capital (in King's Island and Moyross). In terms of characteristics of people associated with social capital, consistent with other empirical research, it was found that higher levels of education, being in middle and older age groups, home owner-ship, longer residence in areas and being married or living with a partner are positively associated with social capital.[41] Higher levels of education and being in older age groups were found to be positively associated with bridging and linking social capital.

This study also showed that characteristics of place matter to the levels of social capital – high levels of use of community and social facilities by local residents and high ratings for the quality of neighbourhood as a place to live are positively associated with all types of social capital (bonding, bridging and linking). Strong concentrations of problems and poor neighbourhood facilities negatively affect the social capital.

In the four parishes, the more affluent neighbourhoods (Our Lady of the Rosary Parish and Christ the King) have a better profile in terms of the presence and quality of local services, less concentration of neigh-bourhood problems, higher levels of trust in people and institutions and higher levels of engagement in voluntary associations. The most affluent parish, Our Lady of the Rosary, however, has poorer community facilities and a weaker sense of community than the middle-class Christ the King parish.

In terms of social capital and its influence on health, people with atti-tudes of strong social trust, reciprocity and institutional trust have a better health profile (i.e. they have higher scores on the scales used to measure health).[42] Similarly, those with larger social networks, more frequently in social contact with relatives and friends, and engaged in voluntary associ-ations, have a better health profile. Consistent with other research on health inequalities, health status by social class (high, middle and low social class based on occupational groupings) broadly follows the social gradient.[43] Those in the highest social classes (professional, managerial and technical occupations) score highest on the various scales used to measure health status, those in the middle social classes (non-manual and skills occupations) score the next highest and those in the lowest social classes (semi-skilled and unskilled occupations) tend to have the lowest scores across the various scales of health. Variation by social class is greater on scales designed to measure mental health, where scores are lower here for those in the lowest social classes.

Variation by parish (with 'place' used as a proxy for social class) also follows the social pattern. The highest scores, indicating best health, are in the most affluent parish (Our Lady of the Rosary), the next highest in the parish of mid to high socio-economic status (Christ the King), lower scores in the socially mixed area leaning towards lower socio-economic status (St Munchin's) and lowest scores in the most disadvantaged parish (Corpus Christi).

Analysis of the dataset was undertaken to identify the factors, independent of each other, which explain variations in physical and mental health in this older population. As expected, the results confirm that men have better physical health than women in old age and that physical health (but not mental health) declines as people get older. Level of education is the only indicator of socio-economic status found to be associated with physical health status (with higher levels of education associated with better health status). Being in the lower social classes (unskilled occupations), however, is associated with poorer mental health. In terms of place-related factors, accessible essential services (such as GP surgeries, shops, social facilities) at neighbourhood level are positively associated with physical health. Living in relatively more disadvantaged areas (based on the Hasse Index at ED level rather than parish) is associated with poorer mental health.

Certain factors of social capital also matter to health outcomes. Social trust in people in general is associated with better mental health, while institutional trust and the sense that people 'look out for each other' are associated with better physical health. These attitudes were more prevalent in the affluent communities. The findings also establish that the mental health status of the population is good (i.e. scores on scales to measure mental health are high into the oldest age groups). A possible explanation of this is that those with poorest mental health have less chance of surviving into old age (thus those who survive tend to have good mental health). The literature establishes the linkage between poor mental health and morbidities, leading to various causes of premature death. This research also found, as stated above, that low social class and living in relatively disadvantaged areas are associated with poor mental health. This explanation links into the social inequality argument on variations in health outcomes in populations and the psycho-social hypothesis.[44] Because the aspects over and above individual characteristics affecting health tend to favour those in higher social classes (living in neighbourhoods with better services and higher levels of social capital), there is an accumulated disadvantage to those in the lowest social classes living in the poorest areas. It seems that those in the lowest social classes have less chance of surviving into old age and there is evidence that they tend to have poorer physical and mental health in old age.

Conclusions

Disadvantaged neighbourhoods are not devoid of social capital. Older working-class communities and low-mobility disadvantaged communities, in particular, have highly developed bonding social capital. Bonding social capital brings positive outcomes for people in the form of social support from informal networks and can create a 'social comfort zone' as a result of being with people who are socially similar and with shared values. There is no doubt that sources of informal support in the community enhance the quality of life in poor communities. However, bonding social capital is not associated with upward mobility nor with changing the trajectory of disadvantaged neighbourhoods. For instance, while King's Island has the highest levels of bonding social capital, the largest residential estate on King's Island, St Mary's Park – in some respects, seen to be 'a great community' – has been ranked consistently as the most disadvantaged electoral district in the state in every census period since 1991.[45]

The evidence from this research is that disadvantaged neighbourhoods lack the bridging and linking social capital associated with upward mobility of individuals and positive developmental outcomes in territorial communities. Lack of bridging and linking social capital seems to be part of the problem of the most disadvantaged neighbourhoods. Conditions in disadvantaged neighbourhoods tend to reinforce this. Living in neighbourhoods with serious problems, including antisocial behaviour, tends to have a negative effect on peoples' attitudes of trust towards public institutions (whom they regard as responsible for not dealing effectively with the problems of the neighbourhoods). This, in turn, makes it more difficult to mobilise residents to work together towards change, and engage with public agencies in the process. The inclination of some residents, particularly those with aspirations to 'get ahead', is to leave if they have a choice. The evidence is that there has been a strong exodus of population out of many of the disadvantaged estates of Limerick in recent years – based, for instance, on population losses from the estates over last two census periods.[46]

While mature middle-class and more affluent neighbourhoods (such as Christ the King parish) tend to have high levels of social capital at community level, highly mobile communities, like the redeveloped inner city area of Limerick, tend to have low levels of social capital. Low levels of social capital in high-mobility neighbourhoods is reflected in different ways compared with low social capital in disadvantaged neighbourhoods – for instance, not in terms of negative trust in institutions (as the disadvantaged areas) but rather in weak neighbourhood-based social networks and low participation in community/voluntary organisations. The types of individuals resident in areas like the redeveloped inner city of Limerick (young, in work, mobile) tend to rely much less on neighbourhood for sources of social support and identity. While certain deficits of social capital can be part of the problem of disadvantaged neighbourhoods, reducing the complex problems of such areas to simplistic notions of social capital – such as 'lack of community spirit' – is not correct. Consequently, problems of most disadvantaged neighbourhoods cannot be addressed through efforts to rebuild the social capital.

What about social inequality? The findings of the research on health inequalities and ageing populations in local neighbourhoods provide evidence of the social gradient in health based on indicators of socio-economic status (social class and levels of education) and place of residence. Social capital is also part of the explanation. Theories associated with the social inequality argument and its effects on outcomes for individuals such as health status can appear to be contradictory. As outlined briefly at the beginning of the chapter, the argument is that strong social inequalities in society negatively affect the social cohesion and social capital, leading to many social ills at societal level, including poor health outcomes in populations. Those lowest down the social hierarchy tend to have the poorest health. However, it is argued that poorer people living in more affluent rather than poor neighbourhoods tend to have better outcomes in terms of health status (by definition in a context of social inequality).

Overall, the conclusion is drawn that both poverty (especially living in conditions of concentrated poverty) and social inequality at societal level contribute to poorer health outcomes for individuals. The different explanations of causal processes are not necessarily contradictory, but it is extremely difficult to establish the contribution of each (material deprivation versus the psycho-social explanation) to poorer health status. Social capital factors are also part of the explanation but they operate mainly indirectly (through characteristics of people and place) to impact on health. More affluent people and neighbourhoods tend to have advantages here but the patterns are highly differentiated, linked to other conditions such as mobility levels, demographic and traditional or historical factors of place.

Discussion and Lessons for Public Policy

Social capital, while it is not the cause of prosperity and better functioning neighbourhoods, is an important indicator of the quality of neighbour-hood life. Some aspects of the social capital of poor communities – namely, strong bonding and support from informal networks – improve quality of life and help poor people and families to cope on a day-to-day basis. However, strong bonding in poor neighbourhoods can also support nega-tive aspects of community, including criminality in families and their extended networks, and be exploitative of a vulnerable population. Furthermore, deprived neighbourhoods 'held together' with strong bonding social capital and low mobility provide examples of places which have failed to change in terms of socio-economic development and, like parts of King's Island, produce inter-generational poverty.

In terms of lessons for public policy, the results of this research indi-cate that it is essential to address the strong patterns of social inequality in society as the long-term strategy and to work towards that objective. That requires much better co-ordination of various types of sectoral policy interventions – education, training, access to employment oppor-tunities, health, welfare and fiscal policy – as well as housing and area-based interventions.

The findings of this research suggest a number of measures to alleviate the consequences of poverty and social inequality. Promoting social diver-sity in neighbourhoods to address the problem of spatially concentrated poverty could be part of a solution. However, the effects in terms of upward mobility of the poor will tend to require a medium- to long-term time horizon. In the short term, as demonstrated in the current experi-ence of Limerick, de-concentration of poverty could be painful and generally is politically unpalatable (i.e. very few, including many people living in poor communities, support a policy of population dispersal of poor people).

In order to create a better environment for the types of social capital associated with upward mobility (diversity of social networks) to develop in communities, public agencies and other stakeholders need to be mindful of positive and negative effects of planning decisions on community social capital. While long-term gains are expected from greater social diversity in residential areas (particularly, it would seem, for poorer people), there are also losses. Initiatives to 'break up' poor estates, via mixed types and tenures in housing policy, will tend to result in loss of the family and support networks which make survival possible for some poor people and families. Poor and vulnerable households may also find themselves outside of the reach of the targeted services in areas such as education, youth services and family support to address problems associated with their relative disadvantage. Dispersal of the population of poor neighbourhoods may simply move the problem and, in some cases, negatively affect and destabilise settled communities. As such, initiatives to break-up spatial concentrations of poverty need to take into account potentially negative impacts and understand where and in what conditions more social diversity might work.

Focusing back on place, diversity of use of space in the neighbourhood setting – residential, commercial/retail, amenity – is important with a view to creating more 'complete' and sustainable neighbourhoods, economically and socially. Drawing on wider literature, mixed development tends to create more permeable places. It creates conditions where people from within and outside the neighbourhood can meet (bridging social capital) – because for instance, there are reasons such as work, shopping, leisure, for outsiders to go into the neighbourhood as well as residents to use the space.[47] Initiatives to promote a social mix within schools, and across all types of activities where people get together within and outside the neighbourhood – social, cultural and sporting associations – are of great importance in building bridging social capital. Successful strategies need to take a broad perspective in order to build up social, economic and institutional linkages between disadvantaged neighbourhoods and the wider urban and sub-regional opportunity structure. The focus needs to be on outward-looking strategies to build up neighbourhood/city-wide and regional connectivity.[48]

The findings of this research also point to the importance of interventions to improve conditions of neighbourhood (public services, shops, amenities) and this, in turn, points to the need for more diversity (of incomes). Residential neighbourhoods with concentrations of people with low socio-economic status do not have the purchasing power to sustain a base of essential services of high quality. They also tend to be less attractive as sites for such services, including public, amenity as well as commercial services. Such deficiencies, coupled with negative perceptions, reflected in stigma of place, will tend to reinforce each other to have a downward spiralling effect on relatively disadvantaged neighbourhoods.

11. Behind the Headlines

Media coverage of social exclusion in Limerick city – the case of Moyross

Eoin Devereux, Amanda Haynes and Martin J. Power

In a media setting, and within the public mind, Ireland's 'Third City' has acquired an intensely negative reputation over time.[1] While there are many historical precedents for the maligning of the place's image, it is generally agreed that it reached a new low within media practice in the 1980s with the ascription, in some media quarters, of the label 'Stab City' to Limerick. The blanket representation of Limerick as a place of crime, social disorder, poverty and social exclusion has continued, and it has been amplified in recent years, particularly in the context of the feuds between rival drugs gangs, most of which have been played out in the city's marginalised local authority estates such as Moyross, St Mary's Park, Southill and Ballinacurra Weston. Understandably, a variety of interest groups have expressed concern over the ways in which Limerick generally and marginalised areas in particular have been misrepresented by the mass media.[2]

Our focus in this chapter is not on the veracity or otherwise of individual stories about Limerick, but rather our task is to get behind the headlines and to examine, in detail, the making of media messages concerning one socially excluded area in Limerick city, namely Moyross. We focus on the role of print and broadcast media professionals in the (mis)representation of this area. Our research takes place in the context of a wider sociological debate about the ways in which mass media can contribute towards the further stigmatising of the socially excluded and the places in which they live.[3] We critically examine the ways in which media professionals understand the many complex problems facing Moyross. Media professionals such as journalists, reporters, editors and sub-editors play a crucial role in shaping and determining how the social world is understood. While we privilege the role of the media professional in shaping and determining media coverage, we also take the views and experiences of local community activists vis-à-vis media coverage of their locality into account. This chapter is drawn from a more extensive study on media coverage of Moyross and is largely based upon data gathered through the use of semi-structured interviews with media professionals and from focus groups with community leaders. The main focus of our chapter is to examine how the media's portrayal of Moyross is variously understood by both media professionals and by community leaders. In stressing the pivotal role played by media professionals in framing and shaping public perceptions about Moyross, our research is located within a production research paradigm. We begin by describing the key tenets of this paradigm and summarise the key findings from our content analysis of print and broadcast coverage of Moyross before examining the main themes of the chapter.

Media-Making: understanding media professionals

Although media studies has been dominated in recent years by analyses of content (discourse) and audience reception, there is a long-standing tradition within media sociology of examining the world of the media professional and of the activities of news journalists in particular.[4] Early sociologists such as Weber and Park recognised the pivotal role played by media professionals such as journalists and editors in shaping our understanding and perceptions of the social world.[5] What has come to be known as 'production research' places the spotlight on the initial 'making' of media messages or texts. Drawing upon a range of ethnographic research methods including interviews and participant observation, it investigates the culture of media organisations and the activities, experiences and ideologies of media professionals.[6] It seeks to explain how and why particular discourses, ideologies or frames come to predominate within media coverage. The production research approach carries with it the promise of revealing more about the realities of doing media work, the constraints within which media professionals operate and the intended meanings that are encoded into media texts.[7]

The production research approach acknowledges that the creativity or agency of media professionals such as journalists and reporters is constrained by a wide range of factors internal and external to their respective media organisations. Internal constraints might include the routines of production; ownership structure; editorial line; culture or ethos of a particular media organisation. External constraints might include the economic power of advertisers or sponsors; the laws and regulations imposed by the state concerning libel or defamation; the willingness (or not) of the politically and economically powerful to co-operate in the production of certain kinds of media texts and the potential for negative reaction from audience members.[8]

Elements of the production research approach have been used to good effect in attempting to understand why certain kinds of explanations of poverty and social exclusion come to predominate within a media setting. Devereux, for example, has used this approach to understand how *The Irish Times* reported on the 1998 Sudanese famine crisis and how RTÉ television portrayed poverty, exclusion and long-term unemployment.[9] The latter study drew upon extensive interviews and observation of RTÉ personnel and sought to explain the thinking behind how RTÉ represented poverty, exclusion and long-term unemployment in 1990s Ireland. In a similar vein, Iyengar[10] attempted to explain how US television networks sought to explain poverty, unemployment and racial inequality. Eschewing any pretence of journalistic objectivity or neutrality, Iyengar demonstrates how the makers of television news make use of either episodic or thematic frames in explaining the phenomena of poverty and unemployment to their audiences. His study shows how the practice by media professionals of explaining poverty in episodic terms is more likely to result in audiences believing that poverty is caused by individual rather than societal or structural failings. Unemployment by contrast is reported on more regularly and is framed in thematic terms which in turn affect how audiences perceive of the issue. Iyengar's research underlines for us the importance of understanding the conscious and unconscious practices that shape media work and that ultimately have an impact on how audiences understand particular phenomena.

Mediating the Message about Moyross

In our analysis of media representations of Moyross we concluded that coverage was highly problematic and in fact could be seen as contributing to the further stigmatisation and pathologising of the people and the place. Our findings add weight to our conviction that media texts are never neutral or objective in representing the social world.

Coverage of the area is overwhelmingly negative. Some 70 per cent (298) of our sample of print media articles, for example, had crime as their primary theme. Even allowing for the fact that 84 of these articles were concerned with the Millie and Gavin Murray story[11] and its aftermath, crime remains the most common context by which the public hear about Moyross. The second most common theme in print media reporting at this time was that of Regeneration. This was the primary theme in only 10 per cent of all articles examined. Even in covering a process that might ultimately re-shape Moyross in a positive way, media professionals resort to negative frames. A number of the headlines concerning Regeneration use stigmatising language – e.g. Moyross is variously referred to as a 'troubled city suburb', a 'feud estate', a 'crime-ridden housing estate' and a 'gangland estate'. A much smaller number of articles were concerned with more positive stories about the efforts of the Moyross community in the face of the challenges posed by social exclusion. In our total sample of 420 articles we identified only 10 that were primarily focused on community spirit in Moyross.

While Moyross is regarded as being newsworthy (mainly in negative terms), it is noticeable that media coverage of the area, as a rule, does not provide much by way of explanation as to why social exclusion and marginalisation exist in Moyross in the first place. In both print and broadcast media, stories are more likely to be episodic than thematic. With some notable exceptions, we found that media coverage is focused on the factual reporting of episodic events, rather than providing any analysis, context or critique, such as are reserved in the main for editorials and features. Structural explanations are largely confined to brief excerpts from sources' comments which are regularly presented as lists of causal factors. For example, in the articles that are primarily about Regeneration only three can be regarded as engaging in any meaningful way with the structural causes of Moyross's problems. A *Limerick Leader* editorial (29 May 2006), a feature from the same newspaper (26 May 2007) and an editorial from the *Irish Independent* (30 October 2006) all offer readers an analysis of the causes of the area's difficulties. While the *Limerick Leader* focuses on political neglect, the *Independent* focuses on the impact of illegal drugs. The homogenising tendencies of media coverage report on Moyross as if it were a single entity.[12]

As further evidence of the pathologising discourses evident within media coverage of Moyross, we argue that the language regularly and routinely used by media professionals is problematic. For example, a number of articles employ the metaphor of a war zone to describe the estate. Moyross is described as 'troubled', 'notorious', 'a blackspot', a site of endemic problems or a 'time-bomb'. Thirty-eight newspaper articles define Moyross as troubled ('troubled estate' and 'troubled Limerick suburb' and 'troubled area' being the most common descriptions) and sometimes, in doing this, grouping Moyross and Southill together. The term 'troubled' is routinely used by media professionals but not by their sources, which leads us to conclude that it is a powerful media construct. It should be noted, however, that it is not inevitable that the media use the epithets 'troubled' or 'troubled estate' in reference to Moyross. Live 95 FM's documentary on Millie and Gavin Murray successfully managed to narrate a tragic story about the arson attack and its aftermath without ever once referring to Moyross in this fashion.

Findings and Analysis

> . . . that's how people have access to information on Moyross. They wouldn't know anything about Moyross if it wasn't for the media. (Journalist-participant, hereafter JP)

It is worth acknowledging at the outset that the journalists whom we interviewed feel that Moyross has changed in the last couple of years and with the coming of Regeneration. They hold that the level of crime in the estate has declined. Resulting both from this perceived trend and from the advent of the Regeneration project, it is to be expected that one might see a change in the coverage of Moyross from the time during which our data was collected to the present day. Indeed, a number of the journalists mentioned what they perceive as the beginnings of a shift in the kinds of stories that are told about the area. 'At least every week you'd hear about a shooting, at least, in Moyross . . . That definitely has quietened down dramatically in the past year.' (JP) However, as we will see, the imperative to cover crime and the perceived newsworthiness of crime occurring specifically in Moyross remains strong. Moreover, for the focus group participants to whom we spoke, unrepresentative media coverage is very much a current issue.

The residents and community activists to whom we spoke were critical – to varying degrees – of the ways in which the local and national media represented and stigmatised Moyross. While the local print and broadcast media fare somewhat better in terms of local perceptions of how their area is represented, there was still a clear sense of coverage being problematic and unbalanced. The lack of detailed knowledge of Moyross by the national media came in for particular criticism. Residents were critical of the way in which some journalists used a very limited range of sources and repeatedly used archive visuals to portray the area. In contrast to the dominant (negative) themes within media coverage, our interviewees offered alternative accounts of the lived experience in Moyross. However, while the residents expressed resilient pride in their local community – in spite of their area's negative media image – they were also very conscious of the damaging role that the media play in shaping external perceptions of the area and the self-image of local people.

Representations of Moyross

There was agreement among our interviewees that Moyross has been and continues to be represented in a negative light, despite the aforementioned perceived beginnings of more positive coverage. The image of Moyross, constructed in the public mind, was held to be one of an area overcome by crime and antisocial behaviour. 'It means crime to people. It means crime, it means murder . . . Particularly in the two years that you are covering Moyross was a very negative place in Limerick.' (JP)

> Outside Limerick it triggers fear and it triggers a place where people associate it with trouble, with crime, with violence, with feuds, with gangs, with drugs and it's a place, definitely outside of Limerick, it's the place where people wouldn't want to live and even within Limerick city . . . people don't want their new neighbours to be from Moyross. But certainly around the country . . . I think it's not a place that's got a great name, it's not a place that people would connect with opportunity or progress. (JP)

It is noticeable that our community interviewees seemed very conscious of external perceptions of their area: 'people see Moyross, or St Munchin's, or St Mary's Park as a community, which as long as they are kept where they are, they are not a problem to us, we have no problem with them, they are lovely people.' (community-participant, hereafter CP). One resident suggested that those living outside Moyross misperceive it as a 'total disgrace' and a 'no-go area' as a direct result of the media coverage. Others expressed similar opinions about such misperceptions:

> The biggest problem that we have is the perception that one bad apple and the whole bag is rotten and the bottom line is the bag isn't rotten down here . . . there was a lady coming for a job . . . she made a statement in the interview that she had come out the night before with her child, a seven-year-old child, and said this is where you will end up if you don't go to school. Now this was a professional person . . . and it just goes to show you the perception that people have out there. (CP)

The residents highlighted the excellent character of the majority of Moyross residents and felt strongly that there are very positive aspects to Moyross, which are seriously neglected in media coverage and which ultimately impact upon external perceptions of the area:

> They haven't seen what we have . . . There's such beautiful places out here. These are the good things: the schools, our church, our library, the activity, the adult education classes, our pipe band. I mean, they're

never shown like that . . . But if there is a shooting or a mugging or a robbery – Moyross, Moyross, Moyross. (CP)

Pushing Good News

Interestingly, the journalists we interviewed spoke of a specific sense of obligation, to tell good news stories about the Moyross area. They spoke of feeling a responsibility to give coverage to positive events, which might provide the audience with a more balanced perspective on the area. Often this obligation was framed as a response to efforts on the part of the community to alter their own circumstances or image. Such efforts were seen to be deserving of media attention: 'that has to be shown up as well when a neighbourhood or an estate is trying to turn around and trying to show its good side that has to be reported as well because you can't show one side of an estate.' (JP)

This is of particular interest in light of the overwhelmingly negative coverage that we found in our sample. While we acknowledge that the journalists to whom we spoke regard the time period to which our sample relates as peculiar, one would nonetheless expect a greater reflection of their self-professed desire to report on positive events in the coverage of that time than is apparent.

The constrictions and limitations of working for highly commercial news media organisations provide a framework for understanding the negativity of media representations of Moyross. A number of factors limit the capacity of journalists to realise a desire to tell good news stories. These limitations relate to news values, journalistic practices and to the role of the editor and sub-editor. Later we will also argue that a dearth of time may also impact on journalists' opportunities for critical self-reflection.

All but one of our journalist-participants (a broadcast journalist) agree that it is more difficult to gain coverage for positive than negative events. The journalists to whom we spoke talk about having to 'push' good news stories: 'and I said [in an email to her editors]. Look if something bad happened in Moyross we would put it on the front page. This wasn't just positive, this was outstanding.' (JP)

Bad News Sells

Exploring the role of the editor and sub-editor is key to understanding the obstacles that journalists face in gaining coverage for such events. Repeatedly we are told that, not only in general, but with specific reference to Moyross, stories about criminality are more likely to be accepted by editors and sub-editors than positive news stories. Our participant-journalists acknowledged the news value of negative stories. There was general agreement that bad news is perceived as more commercially viable and that, as such, negative stories are more likely to be published and to receive prominent coverage:

> When it bleeds it leads. If something negative happens in Moyross its on the nationals . . . if it's a negative story it is closer to getting to the front page than a happy clappy story in relation to Moyross . . . but I think that's across the board in the local media. (JP)

One of our focus group participants suggested that residents are more likely to be approached as sources where their comments are negative:

> . . . they don't want to listen to the people like us that's willing to say the positive side of Moyross. If I can say something bad I'll have a reporter down to me and I'm great and I'll be on the television, I'll be on the radio and everything. And if they go to Mary and she has something good to say, well you're not going to put Mary on, you're going to put me on, because I am the one that's running the place down. (CP)

Local versus National

Community participants were considerably more negative regarding the national media: 'the national media and the national papers will not take up on a good news story because they have no interest' (CP), and with one exception they were particularly critical of televisual representations. 'The television is the worst of all, I think' (CP). As we will demonstrate later, our journalist-participants also held that national media are less likely to provide positive representations of Moyross than their local counterparts. Both sets of interviewees shared a perception that tabloid coverage is the most problematic. 'National tabloids are 95 per cent negative' (CP) and both paper or broadcast-based tabloid formats were cited as more likely to sensationalise. One of our journalist-participants explained that tabloid formats may have less space to cover good news stories because of the prioritisation of celebrity news:

> I think you can see from looking at the tabloids as well they have less space because you know they'll go bigger on Jade Goody type stories and you know I suppose sexier stories as well, sexier women, but the amount of space they have also will determine what they use. (JP)

Indeed, while all the newspaper journalists emphasised the degree to which the final shape of their stories is impacted by the role of the editor and sub-editor, it was the journalist who contributed to tabloids who found this relationship most problematic:

> I have sources who know me and trust me but you know it's still very hard to explain to people that there's a sub at work here or you know who's writing headlines and stuff . . . there are times when I am filing copy I'll say – and I'll know myself now at this stage what they're going to change – and I'll say if you're changing that take my name off it or don't use my stuff, you know. It's very difficult because it is, it's what I do and it's my wages as well, but at the same time I want, and I have to be able, to stand over what I write.

While assertions of negativity were made with equal reference to both local and national newspapers, most residents believed that local print and broadcast coverage of Moyross also included a greater quantity of positive material than their national counterparts. One interviewee stated, 'I would say locally, the actual local coverage, I would say by the *Limerick Leader* and by the radio locally, is probably 60:40 good coverage' (CP). Community participants were generally positive regarding Live 95 FM. They perceived the station as willing to promote events that the community bring to their attention.

Nonetheless, some felt disappointed by the local coverage of events, holding that not all local media give sufficient coverage to positive events in Moyross and, across the board, positive events are given less prominence: 'It wouldn't get the front page and the headline' (CP). 'We had the ball, the Moyross ball, in October, the *Post* [the *Limerick Post*] wouldn't cover it. They wouldn't put in the photographs that were sent in. Neither would the *Independent* [the *Limerick Independent*] . . . the *Leader* did' (CP). Across the board, however, commercial considerations are key to undermining the commercial value of positive news.

The Ease of Stereotyping

There was a sense among our journalist participants that there was some truth behind the negative stereotyping of Moyross. Although the journalists to whom we spoke seemed more attuned to the negative aspects of life in Moyross than the everyday banality of most residents' lives, most did recognise that the focus of media attention was overwhelmingly on the negative at the expense of a balanced depiction of the area.

The stereotype of Moyross as the 'troubled estate' is a frequently used template.[13] The term Moyross acts as a cognitive trigger[14] for audience members, providing them with familiar storylines about the area and its residents, which serve to reinforce commonly held beliefs about the people and place. Both community participants and journalists recognised the template: 'Moyross is the rock star of deprivation [laughter from others], you know, crime and gangs' (CP).

> I think there has been, in the past, some truth to caricatures, there often is, but I think the caricature has suited the media and . . . when a particular image is in the public mind and it will sell newspapers or, alternatively, it will bring in viewers or listeners, they have a tendency to feed into that stereotype. (JP)

One of the journalists holds that this stigmatised identity extends to Limerick city in general. He holds that stories about Limerick are framed in terms of an association with a history of criminality. While crime occurring in other provincial cities is commonly depicted as an aberration, crime occurring in Limerick is normalised, he asserts:

> I genuinely believe that every country needs a waste paper bin, in media terms, and I think, unfortunately, Limerick has become the waste paper bin and, because it has a simple image in the minds of people outside of Limerick, it is one that a lot of people, perhaps even subconsciously, like to reinforce in their coverage. (JP)

The participants reject the idea that the behaviour of residents as a group exceeds the limits of expected deviance or differentiates them from residents of other areas. They suggest that there are worse places in Cork and Galway, but these cities are represented less sensationally because they are tourist attractions, a point of view shared with the journalist quoted above.

Impact on Residents

The preponderance of negative media coverage has a powerful impact on the residents' interactions with external actors. 'I know there's a lot of people who won't go into Moyross because they are probably nervous. But it's like us if we read a paper and see something in Dublin . . . Do you know what I mean, it's all down to the papers like.' Residents cited real impacts of Moyross's stigmatised identity on their interactions with external actors, resulting in prejudice and differential treatment. Residents cite a number of services, in relation to which they perceive that they have been denied equal access, including taxis, insurance cover and costs, mortgages:

> . . . there was a couple of instances where if somebody was looking for a mortgage and wanted to buy a house here that was coming up

for sale here and wanting to stay in the area near their family and wanting to borrow maybe forty or fifty thousand, and they would not give them a mortgage for fifty but they could give them a mortgage for 250 to buy a house 300 yards away. (CP)

One lady in particular, she was in her seventies, and she ordered a taxi from town with her groceries and she said Moyross. That man pulled up outside Watchhouse Cross [on the outskirts]. That lady was living up in the very top of Moyross. She had to walk with six bags. (CP)

The community participants to whom we spoke resisted the negative image of their locale:

I have always maintained, and I have maintained it a thousand times over, that the most important thing as far as I am concerned is not the people outside of Moyross, what their opinion is of us . . . the most important thing that we have to hold on to is our opinion of ourselves. Under no circumstances should we have a downgraded opinion of ourselves. (CP)

However, some residents spoke of how people internalise the stigmatised image of their estate, impacting their self-image in turn.

She gets really upset, she gets really annoyed and I say look, do you want to leave the area if you feel that bad about it? . . . She hates to think that because where she is living is being run down. It's kind of a pride. It hurts a person's pride. Me, it's water off a duck's back, I don't care any more. (CP)

They also cited examples of others who have succumbed to pressure to change or hide signifiers of their identity as Moyross residents:

I know people who have changed their accents and you probably do too, from Moyross, one girl on a media studies course inside in town . . . she is very in tune or rooted to where she comes from, she put her hand up straight away, [she said]: 'that's how I felt when I was a teenager: if I was to get ahead I'm going to have to change my accent.' (CP)

The Troubled Estate

Our analysis of print media coverage confirmed that Moyross was frequently labelled as a 'troubled estate', reinforcing a stigmatised and homogenising identity. A number of the journalists to whom we spoke used this term themselves in their coverage of the area. When we put this practice to them, they acknowledged it as problematic, but were nonetheless unapologetic about its use. 'I suppose I have called it troubled estate–depending on the story. It is problematic, of course it is, that it suffers from a label, those type of labels. I suppose troubled estate is what it is at times, so that's why that phrase is used, you know' (JP). Residents are acutely aware of this kind of labelling:

> .. no matter what story that comes up, you will find the 'troubled estate', 'the ghetto', it is categorised, it is stigmatised, and no matter what story, if they are giving a story about something that happened, if it's from Moyross they will always make sure that it is known that this is a stigmatised area. (CP)

Notably, only one of the journalists had taken a conscious decision not to use the term in his work. He summarises succinctly the reasons for eschewing the use of this kind of label: 'The obvious danger is that you never get away from it. I mean, can you ever see a situation where someone replaces constant reference to the trouble with the joyous, the joyous estate of Moyross, that's never going to happen. So that very shorthand is dangerous.' (JP)

It may be that the ubiquity of this label in both broadcast and print media coverage reflects its unconscious use. However, there is a case for arguing that in addition to pushing stories about positive events, journalists who are concerned about the impact of their reporting on Moyross might also reflect upon the manner in which they frame the area in general. It will be difficult to change the public perception of the locale if journalists continue to reinforce the area's stigmatised identity through use of such labels, even in relating good news.

Moyross's News Value

It was clear from speaking to our journalist-participants that Moyross's association with criminality and deprivation in the public mind (and more recently the resulting Regeneration project) is the primary source of its interest for the media. There is a sense here that media organisations tend to view the audience as located outside of Moyross, and the media as providing a window into this place from which the audience themselves are socially distant:

> People have a kind of a morbid interest in this family feud, the gang feud that goes on in Limerick. I think because it's almost like something out of 'The Sopranos'. So from that point of view it is interesting, I mean, people are watching 'CSI', watching programmes

like 'The Wire' and so they see a lot of that happening in Moyross.
And it's true up, like, up till very recently that definitely was the case.
I think that Moyross does have that appeal. Unfortunately it's a neg-
ative appeal. (JP)

Although one of our journalist participants specifically cited her interest in
Moyross as focused on educational developments, this is still framed as
resistance to media organisations' primary focus on the area's association
with criminality. 'I've considered it [Moyross] newsworthy because I have
in my time attempted to do other news stories in Moyross, apart from the
ones that would oblige me to be there in terms of crime and antisocial
behaviour.' (JP)

In our analysis of media content, we found that many good news
stories about Moyross, unrelated to criminality or antisocial behaviour,
still made reference to these issues, diluting the positivity of the overall
article. One of our participants makes specific reference to the underlying
news values that explain this phenomenon; it is the very juxtaposition
between the stigmatised image of the area and the positive event that
makes the story newsworthy: 'it has been newsworthy for even the
smallest little things that the estate does. Now, perhaps it got that attention
because the wider picture was one that wasn't a great picture.' (JP)

One of our journalist-participants notes that it is not good news about
Moyross that receives little coverage, but good news in general. The negative media depiction of Moyross, which all our participants agree has had
such an influence on its public reputation, is not so much the consequence
of inaccurate as unbalanced reporting. As our journalist-participants
incisively noted, it may not be that other areas in Limerick receive significantly more positive coverage, but that they manage to stay below the radar
of media whose profit motivations orient them to prioritising bad news.

Market Matters

As mentioned above, local media are likely to give additional space to
positive events. The victories of the community, in terms of sports or educational developments, were often constructed as local, not national news,
and therefore more appropriate to local media: 'I think at a local level
people feel . . . if something positive is happening we try to put that out
there as well, and to let people know about the good stories, because at
the end of the day they are our readers or they are our listeners.'
However, while newspaper journalists spoke of their own support for the
coverage of positive events in terms of a principled stance, they spoke of
their media organisations' coverage of positive events in terms of profit

motivation as well as remit. It was their perception that local media give more space to positive events in Moyross in publications that are seen to have a bigger market in the area: 'they are also looking at audience and readers and loyalty.' (JP)

Parachuting Journalism

Journalists contributing to local media tended to locate the reasons for more negative national coverage in reduced local knowledge and sensitivity to impact. 'I don't want to be unfair – local media is far from perfect – certainly nationally, particularly in Dublin, it is easy to caricature somewhere that is a little bit away from you.' They held that national media organisations were more likely to represent Moyross in a stereotypical, oversimplified or even inaccurate fashion, specifically because they lack the local knowledge of regionally-based journalists: 'When there are the really big stories like the time of the Millie and Gavin thing or some of the bigger murder-type stories when there are people down . . . they are down to do a job, they are under pressure with time, they've a different impression of a place and it does, it's definitely different.' (JP) Several participants in the focus groups were conscious of journalists' sometimes limited experience of the area or issue on which they are reporting: 'It's only since Regeneration has come to this city that it has been said that there is a north-side and there is a south-side. I know it's always been there.' (CP)

Remote Journalism

While bigger stories will attract journalists to the locality, many stories are now researched remotely by phone and email. This applies not only to journalists working for national media organisations, but also those working for local media. 'The bigger the story, I would be out there. If it was a smaller story I would be doing it over the phone and a photographer would just go out there separately' (JP). While local journalists may cover a smaller geographical area, their remit may be so broad as to confine them to the office: 'Sometimes it takes a big story for us to get out of the office, because of all the bits and pieces that we are covering. It's a real pain' (JP). The dangers of this increasingly ubiquitous news practice, are of course, a greater reliance on sources rather than first-hand observation, on official sources (who are more readily identifiable and contactable) and, according to one of our journalist-interviewees, on a smaller number of sources. In the context of such practices it may be more difficult to develop an alternative to the dominant interpretation of events.

Images

In print journalism, the selection of images to accompany articles is a key area of influence of the sub-editor. Images can have a significant impact on the meanings readers associate with an article. They are part of the text with which the audience engages: 'Predominantly because . . . the news has been bad news coming out of Moyross it always has been predominantly a bad picture to go alongside it' (JP). Negative images can play a role in reinforcing the stigmatised identity of Moyross. Residents have complained, in particular, about use of images that are unrepresentative of the estate in its entirety. Although newspaper journalists held that archival images are used only occasionally, there was a recognition that this practice does occur and can be particularly problematic in terms of unrepresentative depictions. Our analysis of television content also identified repeated use of a limited range of depictions of Moyross in this medium, including images of burnt-out houses and wandering horses. An interviewee in the area of broadcast journalism held that television journalists do not commonly use archival footage. They stated that periodic issues with access can increase reliance on archival footage. In addition, the stories in our broadcast sample related to the arson attack on Gavin and Millie – participant-journalists noted that archival images will be employed when referring back to a past event.

Despite these explanations, residents participating in our focus groups have criticised more recent use of stereotypical images in contemporary current affairs programming. Some participants hold that media professionals choose not to film better areas and cited an example of a recent episode of RTÉ's 'Nationwide' regarding a positive story about a successful local FETAC horse project. 'And it was very positive I have to say . . . But the images they showed with it was just horrendous . . . for something that was such a positive story . . . all the boarded-up houses'(CP). Journalist-participants also recognised this phenomenon:

> . . . if you go out there you will see horses, you know, but you don't see them all the time, but . . . I would imagine some people when they're watching their television news at home at night are expecting to see the horse walking past in the background, you know, if the reporter is doing a piece to camera in Moyross. (JP)

One participant suggests that it is difficult to visually illustrate more positive developments in the area. He states: 'TV doesn't cover stories without the pictures and community development largely takes place without the pictures . . . it doesn't make for sexy TV.' (CP)

Tarring Everyone with the Same Shorthand

In a study of seven local housing estates, including Moyross, published in 1999, Corcoran notes that, 'Differentiation does not . . . begin and end along the perimeter of the estate. In fact, in all of the estates a complex intra-estate differentiation occurs . . . they themselves exhibit considerable internal stratification.'[15] Moyross specifically was found to exhibit physical and symbolic divisions; residents made distinctions between the area as a whole and what they regarded as a minority of 'Parks' which were subject to more intense social problems.

The continuing existence of distinctions among parks is supported by Humphreys' chapter in this book. Her analysis draws on two large-scale studies, one conducted with the general population of Moyross and a second conducted with older residents, whose residences were concentrated in 'more settled' areas of Moyross (Cosgrove, Cliona and Dalgaish Parks).[16] With this study, she found that this latter sub-population of residents are more likely to perceive the area as a good place to live (73%), as a place where people watch out for neighbours (84%), as forming a close community (50%); and report higher levels of trust in their neighbours (44%), than the general population of Moyross.[17]

While other chapters in this volume have documented the critical and very real impacts of living in proximity to serious criminals (see the chapters by Hourigan) and the manner in which their activities can come to dominate the everyday lives of their neighbours, it is also important to hear about residents' other experiences and, indeed, about the experiences of residents living in other parks. Our focus group participants told us some of these other stories of Moyross: 'even after all these years, I mean I never had a problem, thank God, out here. Never did now. So, they're not actually targeting the good parts – the good parts of Moyross, the good people of Moyross' (CP). Humphreys' chapter confirms broader experience of these 'good relationships' (indeed finding that Moyross has higher levels of bonding capital than other areas in Limerick, such as the more affluent areas of Castletroy and Monaleen). However, community participants also suggested that the heterogeneity of the area was not reflected in media discourse: 'All I see emphasised is a horse and big stones and burnt-out houses. There isn't a burnt-out house in Cliona Park . . . There's one burnt out house in Cosgrove Park. They haven't gone down there . . . spotless clean' (CP).

Our content analysis of media coverage uncovered homogenising tendencies whereby distinctions between the different parts and parks and events that happen therein are subsumed under the umbrella label

'Moyross'. We argue that in the public's imagination this practice serves to extend the experience of living daily with criminality, which does dominate the lived experience of some parks, to the whole area. The journalists to whom we spoke recognised this phenomenon and, indeed, many suggested that Moyross's stigmatised reputation is equally extended to Limerick city in the national consciousness: 'I think it certainly, it does tarnish the whole area but it's like the bigger picture then, how Moyross then tarnishes what happens to the whole of Limerick like' (JP). However, they saw little opportunity to resolve this issue. Our journalist-participants explained that Moyross is a geographical identifier to which the audience can relate: 'I suppose well at this stage I suppose it's because a lot of listeners and readers know where Moyross is but that's because there's a reason for that I suppose' (JP). Moreover, such level of detail was not seen to be of interest to national audiences: 'the splitting up of Moyross into its constituent elements or of Southill into its constituent elements isn't something that . . . trying to imagine myself living in Wexford, that I'd be particularly interested in.' (JP)

As a number of our journalist-participants pointed out, there is little value in simply transferring the stigma with which Moyross is currently associated to specific parks. It would not serve the residents of these parks to stigmatise them any more than it currently does the residents of Moyross. Rather, we highlight this issue in order to emphasise that the story of the parks plagued by gangland feuds is not the only story that Moyross has to tell. Indeed, for the residents of many parks it is not their story. Moyross is an area which requires investment and public attention as a result of high levels of unemployment and educational disadvantage as well as organised crime. However, our focus group interviews suggest that there are variations, at the level of individual households, but also across the area in terms of tenure, mobility, and indeed the impacts of serious criminality. While small area statistics are enabling us to clarify some of these distinctions in relation to the former (see McCafferty and Hourigan chapters in this volume), as McCullagh notes in Chapter Two, the lack of spatial details in our crime and victimisation data do not facilitate geographical specificity. In any case, we argue that these intra-area variations are not given recognition by a media which, we argue, largely constructs Moyross for an audience of outsiders.

The Importance of Opportunities for Self-reflection

Journalists held their relationships with the community in Moyross to be largely positive, despite the highly critical perspectives of the residents to whom we spoke: 'Hopefully I'm doing a good job. I haven't had too much feedback, which is a good sign.' Complaints are depicted as rare and usually highly specific. Journalists involved in local media in particular feel that they are highly accessible to local residents and as such interpret the low levels of complaints they have received as approval.

In general, however, the community participants who have interacted with journalists as sources or in seeking coverage for events were distrusting of media professionals and organisations and cited examples of their identity not being properly protected, being misquoted, misinterpreted, or inaccurately portrayed: 'You won't be quoted but you know damn well who said what without even mentioning it.' (CP) 'It's just how my words were twisted.' (CP) As a result of such practices one resident will not engage with reporters at all. As a group, our community participants did name a small number of journalists whom they trust, all of whom work for local media, both broadcast and print. One resident stated: 'If you want something positive, I find nine times out of ten it's [name of local journalist] that you'd go to, and then if you want something to hit the headlines it's [name of local journalist].' (CP) It is noteworthy that the journalist whose coverage was found to be the most consistently positive and whose media organisation resident-participants specifically cited as presenting them with a more positive self-image than others is also the journalist-participant who speaks of having had an opportunity for critical self-reflection. He says:

> We've made a conscious decision to do that . . . we are conscious of an imbalance over the years and we, at some point, maybe in the last five years made a decision and said, okay, let's try where possible to give an overall picture on an ongoing basis so that when crime happens – and we must cover it – it is within the context of saying but there's another story here and there are lots of people and events taking place that are worth covering . . . We sat down and thought about it and said, is there an imbalance? Yes. Have we perhaps contributed to that imbalance in large sweep of things? Perhaps we have. So, let's try to make sure that we don't and let's try at least. (JP)

Conclusion

Chapter's One and Three examined the manner in which housing policies have contributed to the creation of segregated and marginalised social spaces. In this chapter, we document the manner in which media constructions also contribute to this process. Moyross faces challenges which merit significant investment and public attention; among these problems is a stigmatised identity. Indeed, Humphreys' research illustrates that 'bad external image' was the only problem (from an extensive list of possible problems presented to her sample) cited by every respondent from Moyross.[18] This image is not merely a (limited) reflection of the challenges that Moyross encounters, it is also one of those challenges.[19] As we have documented in this chapter, the imagined constructions of a social space have very real consequences for those that live there. The social problems that exist in Moyross (and which will take time and investment to redress) deserve media attention. But there is also another story, many other stories, to be told about the twelve parks, about the residents that take pride in them and about their achievements as individuals and communities: 'based on my observations, Moyross is in many respects a fine estate served by a good community centre, and by the activities of the Moyross Development Company.'[20] Our analysis suggests, however, that ensuring these stories achieve sufficient prominence to challenge the stigmatised identity of Moyross will require proactive commitment from the community members, organisations, institutions and media professionals who choose to meet this challenge.

In a media forum on the representation of social exclusion conducted by Devereux and Haynes in 2000, we found that media professionals operating to tight deadlines and in an increasingly insecure occupational environment lack the opportunity for reflection. In such an environment it is all the more difficult to recognise or alter problematic practices and routines. Research such as this can help to bridge this gap, providing media professionals with an opportunity for critical thinking. However, significant change also requires leadership from within media organisations. While broadcast journalists have greater autonomy, it is clearly difficult for newspaper journalists to implement change without the co-operation of the sub-editor or editor. However, in the context of an increasingly competitive commercial environment, it is questionable whether there is a desire for principled reflection or unprofitable decisions. Communities will continue to depend on their own media literacy and the goodwill of individual media professionals ensconced in a culture in which 'if it bleeds it leads' is still the mantra. As audience members we should also be willing to reflect critically on our own media practices and ask whether our purchase decisions are perpetuating or challenging these assumptions about what the audience wants.

12. City, Citizenship, Social Exclusion in Limerick

Cathal O'Connell

In contemporary societies, social exclusion has emerged as a key concept by which to analyse the adverse effects of economic and social processes on different groups in the population. Social exclusion can be understood as the cumulative impact of weak participation or non-participation by individuals or groups in activities, routines and practices taken for granted as normal in a given society. According to the Irish government's Combat Poverty Agency, social exclusion is the process whereby certain groups are pushed to the margins of society and prevented from participating fully by virtue of their poverty, low levels of education or inadequate life-skills. This marginalisation distances them from employment, income, and education opportunities, as well as social and community networks.[1] In addition to material and social disadvantages, socially excluded groups may also experience a lack of power or influence over their lives and over decision-making processes and policies which affect them. Such groups exhibit characteristics such as low income, residency in social housing, long-term reliance on social welfare payments, lone parenthood, early school leaving and risk of unemployment. Demographic characteristics such as age, disability, long-term illness and membership of an ethnic minority can also be cited as factors which compound the risk. In addition to its impact on those who experience it directly, social exclusion also poses serious challenges to policy-makers and service providers as it often signals high levels of social inequality which can result in alienation and social tension in society at large.

On the basis of the definitions used above, social exclusion has clear relevance for another key social policy concept – that of citizenship. Citizenship denotes all that social exclusion is not, since it is 'a status bestowed on those who are full members of a community'.[2] Citizenship encapsulates the cumulative rights, responsibilities and entitlements associated with the democratic revolutions, the modern state and the political movements of the last two centuries. The revolutions of the late eighteenth century established the ideals of liberal democracy and the democratic republic. The modern liberal democratic republic was premised on the principle of the equality of all citizens through political and civil rights. The subsequent development of the nation state through the nineteenth and twentieth centuries entailed the extension of these ideals and the status of citizenship was expanded from the original 'man of property' to include all men and women, rich and poor.

The ideal of equality was elaborated in terms of entitlement to public services in the form of social security, education, health care and housing. These came to be defined as the rights of citizens and the duties of the state. Such rights of citizenship reached their apex in the welfare state of the mid twentieth century. Marshall argued that citizenship ensures that people have entitlements including rights to economic welfare and security, the right to a share in the social heritage of their society, and the right to live the life of a civilised being according to the standards prevailing in society. To attain these rights, the welfare state is understood as the institution which reflects the collective will to protect vulnerable groups from inequality and exclusion through effecting social policies for income maintenance, pensions, health care, education and social services, and the redistribution of wealth through taxation. Where social exclusion occurs to an excessive degree, due to unrestrained inequality and failures of social policies and the welfare state, the citizenship rights of excluded individuals and groups are compromised and undermined. This has profound implications not alone for the excluded themselves but also for society at large, as it results in the erosion of social cohesion and solidarity between groups, and in extreme circumstances can pose challenges to the legitimacy of the state and its institutions.

In the discussion which follows, the evidence relating to the causes, extent and impact of social exclusion will be examined with particular reference to Limerick. The chapter argues that a significant minority of the population now experiences consistent and deepening degrees of social exclusion. It examines how social exclusion has become embedded in the fabric of the city and has given rise to clear distinctions between the 'hollowed-out centre' where poverty and disadvantage are concentrated, and the more affluent suburbs where better-off groups reside. The discussion suggests that one of the consequences of the extreme poverty and social exclusion experienced by a small segment of the population is the potential for a crisis of legitimacy for the state and its agencies.

Deprivation and Disadvantage in Limerick

The analysis of census data presented by McCafferty in Chapter One details the distribution and geography of deprivation in relation to risk of poverty, unemployment and residualisation across Limerick city. It reveals high incidences of poverty and socio-economic marginalisation within areas of social housing and in the city centre wards where private renting is the predominant tenure. The analysis shows that households at risk of social exclusion in Limerick are characterised by long-term reliance on means-tested social welfare or pensions, lone parenthood, residency in social housing or rent-supplemented private rental accommodation, poor educational qualifications and early school-leaving, and weak linkages with the formal labour market. Such households may also contain people who have a long-term illness or disability, and members of ethnic minorities.

The degree of disadvantage being experienced poses a fundamental challenge to the city and the wider Mid-West region in terms of the effects on social inclusion, cohesion and solidarity. It would not be an exaggeration to say that for a minority of the population of the city the idea of citizenship holds little meaning if what that signifies is having their basic needs adequately fulfilled, sharing in the opportunities and possibilities which the city has to offer, and having a degree of influence over the decisions which affect them. Further evidence compiled by the Combat Poverty Agency on educational disadvantage, occupational status, and secondary deprivation relating to quality of housing, living conditions and environmental inequality adds substance to the analysis offered by McCafferty earlier. This evidence also confirms that Limerick is distinctive when compared to other parts of Ireland and in aggregate terms the population of the city is at a higher risk of income poverty and consistent poverty when compared to residents of other Irish cities, the Mid-West region, and the country as a whole.[3] According to the Combat Poverty Agency, at a poverty line of 50 per cent of mean income households in Limerick city are one-and-a-half times more likely than the national average to be poor, and at the sixty per cent line they are 1.3 times more likely to be poor.

The extent of social exclusion in Limerick affirms the authoritative view of the the Institute of Public Health of Ireland (IPH) that socially excluded groups tend to fare badly in relation to a range of social indicators. The IPH has observed that 'they may have lower incomes, poorer education, fewer or more precarious employment opportunities and/or more dangerous working conditions or they may live in poorer housing or less healthy environments with access to poorer services or amenities than those who are better off – all of which are linked to poorer health'. [4]

Inequalities in Limerick are now manifested clearly along spatial lines. They are concentrated in a number of highly disadvantaged districts, creating a 'corridor of disadvantage' which runs from Moyross in the north west, through St Mary's Park in the city centre, to Garryowen, Prospect and Southill on the south-side. Socio-economic deprivation is not confined to local authority housing estates, as these are now connected by large concentrations of low-income rent-supplement households living in apartment complexes in the city centre. As Norris and Coates comment, 'large concentrations of social rented households on the northern and southern peripheries of the city are linked by large concentrations of rent supplement claimants in the city centre.'[5] Many of these households qualify for social housing but have not been allocated dwellings due to shortages in supply. In addition to low-income Irish households, the private rental sector is now heavily populated by immigrant households also in search of affordable rental accommodation. This phenomenon adds an additional dimension to the potential for social exclusion, as many such households come from ethnic minority communities and, though living in the centre of the city, they are vulnerable to high levels of marginalisation and poor integration in social and economic terms.

Compounding disadvantage within the urban core is a serious socio-economic imbalance between the city centre and its suburban and county hinterland. There is a deepening gulf between deprivation in the city and relative affluence in the suburbs. This implies that the city centre is being hollowed out and residualised while the more affluent suburbs become more differentiated from it in demographic, economic and social terms.

The suburban areas, many of which are located outside the city boundary and within the jurisdiction of the Limerick and Clare county councils, are predominantly middle class (Castletroy, Raheen, Cratloe, for example) and have seen extensive residential, economic and commercial development in recent years. Though this is not a phenomenon unique to Limerick, the tightness of its city boundary means the problem is much more acute than in other urban centres. This decline in the city centre, according to the Combat Poverty Agency, 'fits with a model where better off households move to newer and more spacious accommodation in the suburbs, which are often located outside the city boundary or even in neighbouring counties. This leaves poorer households trapped in often older and less attractive accommodation in the cities.'[6]

This process has also been termed 'de-centring' and is a feature of urban development in many western capitalist societies, especially those which have weak urban social policies and have adopted neo-liberal economic policies and lax planning regimes.[7] De-centring is reflected in the trend whereby new office complexes, colleges and universities, science and technology parks, retail malls, residential schemes and leisure facilities are located around the periphery of cities to the extent that some observers have argued that this amounts to a new type of urban form known as the 'edge city'.[8] The migration of economic, cultural, educational, residential and consumer developments to the periphery has reached its most extreme level in the United States and has contributed to severe disinvestment and dereliction in older city centres. The phenomenon is also evident in European cities although the effects have been diluted by the implementation of more effective planning controls and urban social policies. In Ireland, however, where city and regional planning controls have been weak and social policies have been historically accorded lower priority to economic policies, edge city developments have sprung up on a largely uncontrolled and speculative basis, regardless of the effects on established city centres or the consequences for economic marginalisation and sustainable urban development. The growth of edge cities has led to the so-called 'doughnut' effect where the bulk of job creation, commercial investment and consumer spending no longer occurs in the centre but at the edge, and the city literally 'turns inside out'.[9]

In Limerick, the effects of the edge city phenomenon are profound. The proliferation of new investments outside the city has obvious physical effects in terms of the appearance and aesthetics of the built environment as dereliction takes root and development migrates. Households who do not possess cars and rely on poor public transport links may find themselves cut off from the employment opportunities in outlying suburbs, thus compounding their exclusion. It also means that potential benefits and multiplier effects derived from employment and consumer activity are lost to the city, as are income sources from municipal rates, service charges and development contributions. This creates a revenue crisis for the city despite the acute need for an adequate income. With the concentration of disadvantaged households within the city boundary the demands on public services are heightened, as these are the very groups in the population who cannot afford to supplement public provision with the private options availed of by higher-income groups. Furthermore, in the absence of a proper system of local government funding, the city authorities are forced to adopt ever-more-punitive policy measures such as curtailing services, privatisation and imposing additional user charges on an already impoverished population.

The revenue problem of Limerick city has been compounded by the resistance of adjacent local authorities and their political representatives to consider an extension to the borough boundary, which has now become a historical anachronism. Extending the city, or adopting a fiscal arrangement based on financial transfers, would relieve the revenue difficulties and help rebalance the city's demographic and socio-economic profile. Symbolically it would mean that those who live in the county but lead what are essentially urban lifestyles would be formally acknowledged as citizens, taxpayers and consumers of the city proper.

Citizenship and the Welfare State

As stated at the outset of this chapter, one of the defining features of contemporary liberal democratic societies is the concept of citizenship. It denotes full membership of the community through the consolidation of certain rights and entitlements which are afforded to all members of the community without qualification or restriction. Being a citizen signifies a status and brings a constellation of rights, entitlements, duties and obligations underpinned by political, legal and material guarantees. Citizenship acts as a bulwark against social exclusion and provides an inclusive framework based on a common understanding between members of a society.

As noted earlier, in western societies the evolution of citizenship has been an extended and contested process. T.H. Marshall has argued that the modern welfare state is the realisation of this historical process which began with the recognition of civil rights, legal equality and free speech in the eighteenth century, evolved through the struggle for political rights and access to the democratic apparatus in the nineteenth century, and culminated in social rights in the second half of the twentieth century. Social rights embodied guarantees around social security, living conditions, accessible health care, educational opportunity and other basic needs to facilitate engagement in full social participation.[10] As the founding father of the modern welfare state, William Beveridge asserted that the welfare state was designed to eliminate the giant evils of industrial society – want, ignorance, disease, idleness and squalor – through rights-based provision.[11] Thus, Powell has asserted, the welfare state symbolised the realisation of full citizenship for all, which finally put the ghost of the Poor Law and the indignity of charity to rest.[12]

However, not all societies have subscribed to or attained fully rounded citizenship, especially in relation to guarantees of social rights. In this regard, Ireland is an example and many of the social problems occurring in Limerick have their roots in the failure by Irish society and the Irish state to fully commit to the notion of the welfare state and adopt the policy measures it requires, such as progressive taxation and universal social provision. In the absence of an adequate financial underpinning, coupled with a minimalist commitment to social services, social policy in Ireland has remained underdeveloped, narrowly defined and residual. It has failed to evolve towards a rights-based, universalised welfare state. Under universalised arrangements there is an emphasis on using taxation to fund social provision, a commitment to eliminating poverty and tackling income inequalities through redistribution from wealthier to poorer sectors of the population. Universalism also ensures that the stigma of means testing recipients and the substantial administrative costs it incurs are avoided. In its residual form the welfare state is viewed as a drain on the productive economy and those reliant on it are seen as a burden rather than as citizens with rights and entitlements.

In its strongest and most ambitious form, such as the model advanced by Nordic societies, progress towards the elimination of income, health and other inequalities has been achieved through progressive taxation and incomes policies and extensive investment in social infrastructure and universal services which are available to all citizens on an unconditional basis. Thus welfare policies feed directly into reducing inequalities, maintaining social cohesion and contributing to a prosperous and innovative society and economy. In Ireland the welfare state has not developed in either the Nordic universal form or even the less extensive British liberal post-war model, and in comparative terms it can be classed as residual, characterised by means testing and selectivity, and with an emphasis on assisting only those judged to be the deserving poor. The residual character stigmatises recipients as second-class citizens such that dependency on welfare in Ireland has become as much a passport to social exclusion as a protection from it. The rigid adherence to the means test in the Irish social welfare code has had long-term and corrosive effects on the quality of services and ultimately deepens social divisions by marking off recipients from the rest of the population. As Baumann has asserted, once they are reserved for those who need them, services cannot count on the political muscle of those who 'need them not' and so they become a natural target for economies to lower taxes with few voices raised in opposition.[13] This eventually leads to a deterioration in quality, since as Titmuss asserted in cautioning against the creeping expansion of means testing, 'services for the poor are always poor services'.[14]

The culture of means testing has had particularly profound consequences for social policies such as housing provision. Means testing of social housing has resulted in the creation of spatially segregated and socio-economically marginalised areas where poverty is a precondition for access. The concentration of disadvantage without effective interventions to counter it leads to ever-diminishing quality of life for affected households and communities and, as is evident in Limerick, this can often lead to a sense that the only solution is to physically obliterate such areas in the hope that 'Regeneration' will eliminate the root causes of poverty and disadvantage. However, the reality is that problems of poverty and social exclusion are rarely amenable to exclusively spatial interventions.

Similar to other neo-liberal economies, the welfare state in Ireland is assuming a more pronounced disciplinary complexion with a greater emphasis on surveillance, monitoring and micro-management of the behaviour of welfare recipients, rather than tackling the inequalities which are at the root of their vulnerability and exclusion. This trend is typified by recent welfare reforms which prioritise labour market activation and 'job-seeking' initiatives and place a stronger emphasis on 'welfare fraud' than on tackling poverty, and in proposals that social housing applicants should furnish certificates of good character from the authorities in order to get a home. Much commentary on welfare reform is marked by a moral discourse which implies that social exclusion is caused by weaknesses and failings on the part of the poor people themselves rather than being the outcome of structural inequalities and policy failure at a societal level. Such perspectives adopt the language of what Levitas has termed a moral under-class discourse (MUD) which blames the lifestyles, behaviours and attitudes of the poor towards mainstream (i.e. middle-class) society for their own predicament. It asserts that the solution to social exclusion does not necessarily lie in the redistribution of wealth, resources and opportunities but rather through stronger levels of integration and compliance, especially into the labour market, and through the re-instilling of the work ethic and acquisition of 'respectable' cultural attitudes values, and lifestyles on the part of the poor themselves.[15]

In contrast to the hardening welfare regime for the disadvantaged population, for the middle classes a system of generous state subsidies has incentivised them to abandon public services and look increasingly to the marketplace. In Ireland many services such as housing, health care, income maintenance, pensions and education are now delivered via a two-tier system. This means that those with resources can afford to enter the private market with a wide range of implicit and explicit subsidies and supports to reduce the cost, while the poor who lack economic resources are unable to exercise the 'exit option' and are left reliant on residual and means-tested services. The use of welfare to divide between the 'self-reliant' and the 'dependent' segments of the population reinforces mistrust and social distance. In the absence of shared values around welfare and essential social services, disadvantage is recast as danger, and deprivation as a social deviance. The culture of social distance between groups in the population produces a fundamental contradiction in the relationship between the individual and the city. Rather than the welfare state consolidating citizenship by ensuring protection from risk and vulnerability through social policies, in other words social security by society of the individual, the emphasis shifts to an obsession with 'civil security' or concern with society's protection from the 'deviant' individual. This is often used as a justification for adopting draconian measures of policing, surveillance, and social management in poor areas. As Garland has observed, the welfare state has taken on a more overtly disciplinary function and has mutated from its original objective of inclusion to a mission more akin to a penal-welfare state, whereby social policy is increasingly deployed not for the benefit of those who are thought to be conditional citizens with a view to their inclusion but against those who are regarded as non-citizens to punish and in the process further exclude them.[16]

Social Exclusion in Limerick: 'The end of citizenship'?

The question arising from the shift to the post-welfare city is what are the implications for the concept of citizenship? A clue to answering this question can be gained by looking at what has happened elsewhere. In an analysis of recent urban unrest in France, the sociologist Jacques Donzelot has asserted that the 'city falls apart' when the welfare settlement collapses. Social cohesion disintegrates, and social inequality and social exclusion deepen. In Donzelot's analysis, the welfare state traditionally fulfilled a dual function by protecting the individual from the hazards of industrial society on the one hand and protecting society from disaffected individuals on the other by offering social security and sustaining social cohesion. Thus, the protection of society from the individual was achieved through the individual's protection by society.[17]

The architects and planners of the welfare state sought to create a healthy city for all social classes and they attempted to 'monumentalise' this condition of urban equality in the form of full employment, social security, health, education and social housing. However, the equality project faltered with the demise of the industrial economy on which the welfare settlement was founded. Secure employment in manufacturing industries was replaced by large-scale, long-term unemployment, as the transition to the post-industrial economy impacted disproportionately on the poorly educated and low-skilled workforce, poor immigrants and ethnic minorities. They were cut off from the new economy and the opportunities it presented due to lack of skills and educational credentials and became heavily reliant on a retrenched welfare system where the emphasis had shifted from care to control. In French cities this transition to post-welfare city resulted in the suburban high-rise estates known as *banlieues*, originally the foundation stones of the welfare state, becoming the repositories for a surplus and redundant population excluded from the wider city and its economy. Recently these estates have become flashpoints for violent clashes between socially excluded youths and the riot police. This social unrest is symptomatic of the failure of French social policy to vindicate the right to full citizenship. Similarly in Limerick the symptoms are no less acute. Traditional sources of employment for unskilled and semi-skilled workers in food processing, assembly work and manufacturing have evaporated and have been replaced by a labour market which is highly integrated into a competitive globalised economy. The new economy is also post-industrial, highly credentialised, and located in the edge city. Investment and employment opportunities have migrated to the suburbs and the middle classes have followed to avail of them, leaving behind the poor and marginalised. The unskilled and semi-skilled occupational classes are concentrated in the poorer parts of the city and are the subjects of an increasingly disciplinarian welfare system.

Furthermore, Pierre Bourdieu argues that the 'hollowing out' of welfare and of the city leads to the undermining of the public sphere whereby people who are rejected by the state in turn reject the state and its agencies.[18] For a small minority of the population of Limerick, who in media jargon are labelled as inhabiting 'gangland', this has led to a culture of extreme exclusion, apparently lacking in shared values with the wider community. Such is the depth of their exclusion and alienation that they no longer engage in the practice of citizenship or adhere to the civic, political and social norms of the city. Status and recognition are sought, not from shared social codes, for instance through educational attainment and occupational mobility, but through a self-reinforcing subculture based on loyalty to extended family networks and gangs. This view of status is clearly evident in Hourigan's research on fear and crime in this volume.

The extremity of such detachment and exclusion is manifest in serious criminal activity, drug dealing, murder, intimidation and destructive behaviour which damages both these individuals and their own communities. This has led to some parts of the city effectively becoming 'no-go areas', not alone for the police but also for representatives of other state agencies such as local authority staff, health professionals and social workers. Furthermore, residents in some estates who are perceived to be co-operating with the state, or for that matter voluntary and community organisations, though their contact may be of a fleeting and routine nature, are liable to be intimidated or threatened with violence for alleged informing.[19]

In effect, what have emerged in parts of the city are parallel structures of social mobility and status. While these may not amount to a fully fledged threat to the legitimacy of the state, they certainly point to symptoms of motivational crises, signalling, as Habermas has observed, a withdrawal of motivation and legitimation and the unsettling of collective identity.[20] For a younger generation this implies dropping out of school, engagement in delinquency and inducement into drug dealing and drug consumption, which act as an alternative career path to conventional pathways of social and occupational mobility. The state responds with increasingly draconian measures of policing and surveillance, for instance through the deployment of armed police units and helicopter surveillance, that for the most part impact upon the law-abiding members of disadvantaged areas rather than the perpetrators of serious crime. Accordingly, as Harvey has commented, the 'ideals of urban identity, citizenship and belonging become much harder to sustain. Privatized redistribution through criminal activity threatens individual security at every turn, prompting popular demands for police suppression.'[21]

Because of the intergenerational nature of the problem, its resolution can only occur by tackling its root causes. The causes lie not so much within the gang elements themselves, though individual culpability for criminal behaviour cannot be avoided and the rule of law must be robustly applied, but with the cumulative failure of the state and social policy to underpin citizenship rights over an extended period. As Wilkinson observes, extreme inequality promotes life strategies that are less affiliative, more self-interested, antisocial and stressful, and likely to give rise to higher levels of violence and poorer community relations. In contrast, 'less unequal societies tend to be much more affiliative, less violent, more supportive and inclusive'.[22] Extreme inequality in Limerick has given rise to a situation where the overlap between poverty, social exclusion and serious crime signals for some the 'end of citizenship' and raises fundamental questions of what can be done to address the situation. An obvious deduction is that the causes of inequality as well as its symptoms must be addressed if the status of citizenship is to be reasserted for the most excluded of the population of the city.

Limerick's Futures? urban regeneration, regional metropolitanism and national development policy

Limerick is not alone in facing the problems of social deprivation and social exclusion, as poverty and inequality exist across Irish society and their consequences are replicated throughout the state. The profile of poor households in Limerick is mirrored in other Irish cities and towns and their quality of life and citizenship is equally compromised.[23] However, a number of factors distinguish Limerick from other parts of Ireland. Firstly, the depth and scale of social exclusion that occurs within the tight confines of the city itself continue to have troubling social consequences. Secondly, there is a clear spatial aspect to social disadvantage as it is concentrated in the city while the better-off households live in the suburbs. Finally, the rationale of the market means that investment follows the best source of return, which has led to a hollowing-out of the city centre.

Can Limerick overcome the challenges of social exclusion, the 'end of citizenship' and the fiscal problems it faces? The answer to this question is that these challenges can be overcome and it is possible to tackle social disadvantage, renew the city and rejuvenate citizenship, but this can only occur by pursuing social policy as well as economic policy objectives. While the economic system generates profits which are privately appropriated, it is also the source of risks and hazards that are socialised and displaced onto disadvantaged individuals, households and communities. The problems facing the city therefore have their origins in the nature and organisation of the wider economy and its structural transformation over recent decades, and in the absence of a fundamental shift away from capitalism, an accommodation must be sought which places greater emphasis on meeting social objectives around redistribution, equality and social inclusion. There is no necessary contradiction in affording social rights equal standing to economic objectives. In fact, the international evidence suggests that societies which adopt social policies aimed at minimising inequality are frequently the most technologically innovative, socially cohesive and economically prosperous.[24]

Urban Regeneration

To date, much of the response to the problem of deprivation in Limerick has been based on local interventions, targeted initiatives and

Regeneration programmes in disadvantaged areas, without real regard to the exclusionary impact of deeper economic forces which have resulted in the loss of employment and long-term socio-economic marginalisation of the households and communities affected. Exemplary grass-roots community development projects in the city, such as the PAUL (People Against Unemployment in Limerick) Partnership, have engaged in capacity-building and empowerment with disadvantaged communities over several decades and have transformed the lives of many. In recent years, the concept of regeneration has emerged as a further policy development and there are now initiatives to regenerate disadvantaged estates in Moyross, Southill and St Mary's Park which propose social, economic and environmental interventions.[25] Yet such are the structural processes which generate deprivation and inequality that these local strategies are unlikely to be sufficient in themselves to resolve the problem. Within the Regeneration initiatives there is a notable absence of acknowledgement of structural factors and economic inequality as the root causes of the problem of exclusion. Nor is there any evident commitment to the principles of social justice and redistribution of opportunities and resources at a macro level. The underlying discourses of Regeneration in Limerick are derived from an essentially economic paradigm on the one hand and a social integrationist one on the other. The economic discourse emphasises the revalorisation of public spaces and gentrification of housing stock as the primary strategy, while the social integrationist discourse focuses on promoting more effective co-ordination of welfare and social services and housing management practices to better integrate needy households, rather than deal with the root causes of their poverty and disadvantage.

In acknowledging the role local interventions can play, the Combat Poverty Agency has cautioned against undue expectations, especially in terms of the resources available, and that a balance is needed between the view that area-based initiatives serve no purpose until fundamental structural problems are resolved and 'a perspective that encourages unrealistic expectations of the extent to which disadvantaged communities can find solutions to problems many of which can be addressed only by national policies and mobilisation of substantial resources'.[26]

Regional Metropolitanism

Added to the problems of deprivation and disadvantage is the relationship between the city, its hinterland and the wider Mid-West region. Presently this relationship is antagonistic and the city is viewed as a problem rather than a resource. To remedy this tension, a paradigm shift is required which sees the city as the core of the Mid-West region and not the void at its centre. The revenue problem of the city must be addressed seriously if inroads are to be made in alleviating and eventually eliminating the division between city and suburbs. In this respect, a simple extension of the city boundary, though welcome, will not suffice. What is therefore required is a metropolitan approach, which views the city and its environs, and thus the challenges being faced, in a more joined-up regional context. City and county loyalties may persist symbolically but the metropolitan approach must be based on a realisation that the problems of the city are as much the problems of the region and therefore require integrated strategies and political governance structures which erase now out-dated administrative boundaries.

National Development Policy

Through national policy frameworks such as National Spatial Strategy and the development of the Atlantic Corridor, Limerick has a key position.[27] Shannon Airport as the city and the region's most valuable infrastructural link with Europe and the rest of the world must be harnessed as a hub for sustainable development rather than struggling for survival in a cut-throat low-fares environment.

Beyond these there is also the need to revise the relationship between the economic and social domains. The present Irish economic model, underpinned by low-tax neo-liberalism, views social policy and the welfare state as a burden on the productive economy and not as a resource. Clearly, however, this need not be the case and one need only look to the frequently cited 'Finnish model' as an example of how the fruits of economic growth and technological innovation can be harnessed to create a socially inclusive and prosperous society with low levels of inequality and deprivation, strong social cohesion and high-quality public services.[28]

Conclusion

The scale and complexity of the challenges facing Limerick in the first decades of the twenty-first century are deep-rooted and complex and are not amenable to solution either in the short term or by the city acting in isolation. Local, regional and national strategies which recognise the impacts of inequality, the limitations and weaknesses of public policy to date, and the inadequacies of the current welfare model are needed to begin the process of devising an Irish version of the virtuous cycle. Such strategies hold out the possibility of equality, prosperity and social inclusion in equal measure so that Limerick can truly represent itself as a city of shared values, social solidarity and common citizenship for its entire people.

CONCLUSION

Understanding Limerick? Conclusions

Niamh Hourigan

Given the research presented in this text, there can be little doubt about the significance of the problems which have emerged in Limerick city in terms of broader debates about social exclusion and criminality in Irish society. At the heart of Limerick's problems lies a complex interweaving of what could be considered the problems characteristic of a more 'traditional' Ireland such as feuding and inter-family conflict.[1] These problems are intrinsically linked with concerns which lie at the heart of contemporary globalisation, such as unequal economic development in urban areas, social problems within marginalised communities and the growth of the global drugs trade.[2]

Within the Introduction, the model of social exclusion was outlined as the primary framework for examining crime and disadvantage in Limerick city. In Chapter One, Des McCafferty provides a detailed spatial analysis of inequality in the city which demonstrates clearly why this model is so appropriate for understanding Limerick. He highlights not only the sharp divides between disadvantaged and more prosperous areas within the city's conurbation but also the fact that Limerick contains the most disadvantaged electoral districts in the entire Irish state, according to the 2006 census data.[3] Thus, patterns of inequality in Limerick represent an intense microcosm of broader divisions between rich and poor across the Irish state, divisions which have become more pronounced since the early 1990s.[4]

Ciarán McCullagh's analysis of the crime statistics for the city demonstrates how this profound social exclusion has produced a number of distinctive problems in terms of criminality when compared to other regional Irish cities such as Cork and Galway. Limerick is a 'low crime city with a significant crime problem', he concludes. Crime rates in Limerick have declined since 2007,[5] but the criminological profile of the city continues to have its own unique contours.[6] Criminal gangs in the

245

city play an important role in national drugs networks, while collective family identities linked to local feuds remain a persistent source of status in local communities and national criminal networks.[7]

The study of fear and feuding in Limerick city presented in Part Two of the book interrogates how the social exclusion identified by McCafferty and the distinctive crime patterns examined by McCullagh entwine at community level and impact on residents in disadvantaged areas in the city. This study, which I conducted over three years, begins by mapping the sociological diversity of these communities, highlighting the economic and socio-cultural distinctions between the 'advantaged of the disadvantaged', the 'disadvantaged of the disadvantaged', Travellers and core crime families. The relationship between membership of a gang and fear-based status in local communities is traced through the spectrum of local criminal hierarchies. These hierarchies range from children involved in antisocial behaviour to foot-soldiers in their teens and twenties through to 'serious players' from core crime families who have not only local status but notoriety in the national and international media.

In examining the operation of Limerick's 'regimes of fear',[8] the use of intimidation to oppress local residents in areas where gangs operate is described. The parallels between the process of community violence and domestic violence thus become evident. Research on domestic violence demonstrates how this process can begin with small acts of oppression, name-calling, verbal abuse and gradually escalates to physical acts of violence.[9] The cycle of community violence is very similar, as the outrageously violent acts which garner national media attention are often at the apex of a systematic process of intimidation which has been ongoing for a prolonged period of time. In this context, it would be more useful if local government and state agencies began to use the term 'community violence' to describe these forms of intimidation rather than 'antisocial behaviour' which under-represents the serious nature of the problem.[10]

Evidence that criminal gangs utilise the antisocial behaviour of vulnerable minors to support their own activities is one of the most significant findings of the fear and feuding study. Indeed, Chapter Seven provides an overview of how an understanding of the motivations for antisocial behaviour *from the child's perspective* needs to be developed as part of the broader overhaul of child protection services in the Irish state which is required.[11] The study also demonstrates that criminal gangs have adapted themselves effectively to the criminal justice system, re-establishing their feud-related hierarchies within the prison system and using surveillance from prison to monitor communities on the outside. Thus, the solution of imprisoning gang members while providing respite for their neighbours does not necessarily diminish the overall scope of gang activities or reduce their control over pockets of specific communities.

The role of globalisation in contributing to criminality in Limerick is analysed in terms of the city's position as a node in a global drugs commodity chain.[12] Local feuds provided some Limerick families with the skills and experience to successfully exploit the drugs boom of the early '90s in order to initially establish themselves as 'players' in trans-national drugs importation networks.[13] Building on their position in these networks, members of criminal family gangs in Limerick have become skilled trans-national actors using air travel, modern technologies, and the demand for recreational drugs among more affluent citizens to actively subvert their social exclusion.[14] These actors even identify with transnational cultural trends such as rap, a cultural form which reflects their own experience more accurately than much of the output of the Irish national media. Thus, their mode of engaging with national culture has come to embody Manuel Castells' pithy model of 'the exclusion of the excluders by the excluded'.[15]

The key research perspectives presented in Part Three of this volume link the findings of the fear and feuding study to a number of other excellent research studies conducted on social exclusion in Limerick city. These studies focus on the links between those living in socially excluded communities and those who enjoy more wealth, affluence and power in the city. In their study 'Men on the Margins', Kelleher and O'Connor explore the experiences of young men in marginalised communities who have rejected the route of gang participation. They find that these young men struggle to find an alternative position in Limerick society. Their interviewees continued to be deeply excluded, with little chance of marriage or employment. They were fearful of being seen in public spaces in their communities and getting into conflict with members of local criminal gangs. Sport provides one of the few outlets for self-expression and self-affirmation in these difficult circumstances.

Eileen Humphreys' comparative research on social capital and health outcomes across parishes in the city supports much of what Máire Treasa Nic Eochagáin and Frances Minahan have to say about community spirit in Limerick: namely that some of the most disadvantaged areas in the city are also some of the areas with the best community spirit and the most pronounced sense of neighbourliness. However, Humphreys' findings on trust indicate that this community spirit is not sufficient to overcome the social exclusion experienced by residents. In addition, her research on health outcomes shows that neighbourliness and social capital cannot compensate for the physical stresses which poverty and crime can place on marginalised communities.

Eoin Devereux, Amanda Haynes and Martin J. Power's study of media coverage of Moyross in Limerick demonstrates how media analysis which fails to recognise the complex link between social exclusion and violent crime can further contribute to the stigma experienced by residents in disadvantaged communities. They highlight the difficulties experienced by community activists in Moyross in gaining positive coverage for local events as they engage with journalists and sub-editors governed by the diktat 'if it bleeds, it leads'. Their findings are even more worrying in light of the evidence from Part Two that fear-based status is a significant motivating factor for crime. If the media notoriety of Limerick gang leaders is reinforcing their fear-based status, then media coverage which heightens this status is actively contributing to the crime problem in the city.

Finally, Cathal O'Connell's exploration of the link between inequality and citizenship in the Limerick context situates the problems in the city within broader debates about social exclusion in Irish society. He questions whether the profound social exclusion which is evident in Limerick must be the inevitable consequence of integration into the global economy. He contrasts the approach to economic globalisation adopted by successive Irish governments with approaches adopted in other European states such as Finland. In the Finnish context, efforts to redistribute the rewards of economic globalisation more evenly have generated clear dividends in terms of social cohesion. He concludes that one of the most serious consequences of profound social exclusion is the breakdown in the citizenship contract between the state and its most excluded citizens, a breakdown which underpins the rise of organised crime and alternative localised regimes of fear.

In reviewing O'Connell's findings in light of my own research on fear and feuding, I would support his call for a more redistributive approach to economic globalisation. However, even in the more redistributive systems of Scandinavia, some inequality continues to exist. Given that a certain amount of inequality is inevitable, therefore, young men and women also need a moral framework which supports them in resisting the lure of gang participation. Thus, the case of Limerick raises important questions not only about Irish economic models but also the codes of 'civic virtue' which accompanies these models.[16]

The rise of drugs-related organised crime in Limerick occurred during the same period as a deep legitimacy crisis for the Catholic Church and the Irish polity, institutions charged with defining civic virtue in the Irish context. From the early 1990s, members of successive national government administrations were exposed as having been deeply corrupt in carrying out their official responsibilities.[17] Most recently, there has been evidence of widespread mis-dealings between Irish banking institutions and property developers within the construction industry, as well as fraudulent expense claims by politicians.[18] Thus, the culture of civic corruption has not significantly diminished even after the publication of tribunal reports.[19]

Since 2007, the Catholic Church, an institution which had significant moral influence in Limerick's disadvantaged communities evident in Liam Ryan's *Social Dynamite* study,[20] has been exposed as having sheltered paedophiles and protected perpetrators of sexual abuse.[21] Thus, the capacity of members of the Catholic hierarchy to make pronouncements on civic virtue and related moral codes of right and wrong has been widely undermined[22] despite the continuing levels of trust which exist in Limerick communities for local clergy and sisters.[23]

As I conducted my research in Limerick, I made a point of asking interviewees who had been involved in criminal activity at any stage whether they felt their actions were wrong. These respondents were very quick to point out the degree to which the leaders of the above institutions had contravened moral codes. If we accept the findings of O'Connell's research and the fear study which suggests that participation in criminal activity can be a *rational* response to social exclusion, then political and religious elites in Irish society must provide some *moral* challenge to this rational logic. At the moment, it is difficult to identify an institution in Irish society which could convincingly provide this challenge. In responding effectively to poverty-related crime in Limerick city, national stakeholders must consider not only the question 'Why participate in a criminal gang?' but also 'Why not?' What is to be gained from non-participation?' At the moment, given the social exclusion evident from Kelleher and O'Connor's study and the limited value attached to 'being a good citizen/person' evident among Irish elites, very little is to be gained from non-participation.

In 2007, the Irish state launched the Regeneration project in Limerick city as an area-based response to social exclusion in the city.[24] As full funding for Regeneration has only recently been granted,[25] it is too early to fully evaluate the impact that this project will have on social exclusion in the city. However, at this stage it is important to note that Regeneration focuses on four specific areas (Moyross, Southill, St Mary's Park,

Ballinacurra Weston), while McCafferty's research identifies other parts of the city where social exclusion continues to exist.[26] Secondly, although Regeneration has been in existence for three years, there is little evidence of significant improvements in terms of child protection in the city despite a range of projects which do support the children of more advantaged families.[27] However, given that the child protection crisis nationally is so marked, it is difficult to envisage how management in a local intervention such as Limerick Regeneration could ameliorate the current situation. My own research suggests that child protection reform requires resources and legislative change at national level so that projects such as Limerick Regeneration can have a meaningful impact at local level.

The community policing initiatives, the introduction of additional Gardaí and the new powers enacted in the Criminal Justice Act (2009) have had a positive impact on crime rates in Limerick city.[28] However, there is evidence that these initiatives have served in some cases to disperse rather than resolve the problem as members of core crime families migrate to London, the Costa del Sol or rural locations outside the city.[29] This migration has eased the extent of intimidation experienced by some local residents in disadvantaged estates, but it hasn't significantly reduced the extent of the drugs problem in the city.[30] Furthermore, while the dynamic of feuding has reduced in terms of violence, the importance of feud-related identities to families living in these communities does not appear to have diminished at all, suggesting that local feuds could reignite in the future.

The response of gang members to the economic recession and Regeneration has been to introduce significant amounts of heroin on to the streets of Limerick city. The extent of the heroin problem facing the city increased dramatically between 2007 and 2010.[31] The level of heroin addiction now evident in the city has changed the contours of poverty-related crime but has not significantly reduced the extent of the problem.[32] Indeed, it is possible that the heroin addicts who are now participating at the lowest levels of criminal gangs are more vulnerable, more volatile and thus, in some cases, more dangerous than foot-soldier gang members heretofore.

Despite these ongoing problems, the launch of Regeneration has marked a watershed in terms of debates about social exclusion in Limerick city. It represented a critical moment of recognition by the Irish state that there are serious consequences emanating from social exclusion, not only for excluded communities themselves but for Limerick city and Irish society. Evidence from research presented in this volume, however, suggests that the process of Regeneration needs to happen alongside wide-ranging reform of the child protection system in Ireland, if any long-term success is to be achieved.

Finally, it is critical to acknowledge that the economic resources of the criminal gangs which have contributed to making the city so notorious stem from the sales of drugs to consumers. In Chapter Two, McCullagh notes that the majority of the drugs seized in Ireland are cannabis and cocaine, the drugs of choice of middle-class users. Thus, middle-class recreational drug users must bear some responsibility for the severity of drugs-related violent crime which currently exists not only in Limerick but also in west Dublin. As a lecturer at a third-level institution, I am constantly struck by the numbers of students who will buy fair trade coffee or chocolate. These students, who often have low incomes, highlight in lectures the negative ethical consequences which consumer choices can entail in terms of contributing to child exploitation in South America, Africa or South-East Asia. However, the same students do not appear to link this ethic of consumption to recreational drug habits which contribute to the exploitation of children much closer to home. The lack of awareness among middle-class drug users of the ethical consequences of their behaviour for local families and children in disadvantaged communities is a critical issue which must be urgently tackled with public health campaigns.

Scholarly research on social exclusion in Ireland has focused on the degree to which integration into the global economy has generated polarisation between rich and poor and contributed to the emergence of a long-term socially excluded class in Irish society.[33] However, the research presented in this volume suggests that in Limerick, the extended family plays a vital role in shaping the response of this socially excluded class to their marginalisation.

In response to their cultural stigmatisation, residents of disadvantaged estates have retreated into extended family identities to re-imagine their position in society. Across disadvantaged communities in the fear and feuding study, family-based identities constituted the primary source of status and meaning for all groups. Even in cases where individuals were employed in the workforce, their extended family identity was more important to their self-image than their job. This importance of family-based identity among the socially excluded is in marked contrast to the self-image of middle-class Irish citizens who tend to define themselves more in terms of work and career.[34]

In terms of unpicking economic marginalisation, the extended family has also provided the basic framework around which criminal family gangs have organised their drugs distribution operations. There is evidence that for core crime families these activities have yielded monies which have been used to purchase a range of desirable consumer goods which further heighten their family status. By displaying their guns and cars, by identifying themselves at funerals and public events as members of feuding families, these gang members have graduated far beyond the 'scumbag' stigma to becoming figures whose family-based identities provide them with a form of fear-based status which operates successfully in local communities and the national and international media. Thus, as Keohane and Kuhling suggest, recent transformations in Irish society have not diminished the significance of family for some groups but rather changed the ways in which the importance of family is manifested.[35]

Ultimately, it would appear that understanding social exclusion in Limerick city provides a starting point for a range of insights into inequality in Irish society. The current challenge facing the Irish state involves not only unpicking inequality and localised regimes of fear in Limerick but also ensuring that 'lessons are learned' and similar problems are not allowed to emerge in other parts of the Republic of Ireland.

Notes and References

INTRODUCTION: SOCIAL EXCLUSION AND CHANGE IN LIMERICK

1 The motto probably pre-dates the seventeenth century sieges. It is not known exactly when it was chosen but it is a quote from Virgil's *Aeneid*.

2 Although a provincial rugby football team, the Munster team who have won the Heineken Cup are strongly associated with Limerick city and have their home ground, Thomond Park, on the north-side of the city.

3 This is a quote from the Toreador Song, one of the anthems of the Munster team.

4 This figure refers to the numbers of local authority houses within the city boundary at the time of publication. The boundaries of Limerick city are currently under review.

5 L. Finn, 'Limerick tackles suicide rates', *Irish Medical Times*. Available at www.imt.ie; accessed 8 July 2010.

6 Iona Institute, *Marriage Breakdown and Family Structure in Ireland*; available at www.ionainstitute.ie/pdfs/Sept07_marriage_breakdown; accessed 8 July 2010.

7 T. Haase, *Key Profile for Limerick City*; available at www.pobal.ie; accessed 8 July 2010. In the Census 2006, Limerick city had the highest rate of unemployment in the Republic of Ireland at 14.7 per cent. This rate has increased because of the recent economic downturn. In July 2010, 22,275 people were claiming unemployment benefit in the greater Limerick area. N. Rabbits, 'Unemployment still rising in Limerick City', *Limerick Leader*, 5 July 2010.

8 J. Fitzgerald, 'Addressing issues of social exclusion in Moyross and other disadvantaged areas of Limerick city. Report to the Cabinet Committee on Social Inclusion, April 2007; available at www.limerickcorp.ie; accessed 26 July 2010.

9 For a complete overview of the plans and documents published by Limerick Regeneration, see www.limerickregeneration.ie.

10 An Garda Síochána, *Limerick Garda Division Policing Plan 2010*; available at www.garda.ie/Documents/User/Limerick; accessed 10 July 2010.

11 D. Hurley and P. Martin, 'Emergency Response Unit deployed in Limerick', *Limerick Leader*, 8 Apr. 2010.

12 N. Hourigan and M. Campbell, *The TEACH Report: Traveller Education and Adults: crisis, challenge and change* (Athlone: NATC, 2010).

13 N. Rabbits, 'Big boost for Limerick Regeneration as Cabinet approves €300 million', *Limerick Leader*, 16 June 2010.

14 www.cpa.ie; accessed 10 Sept. 2010.

15 R. Lenoir, *Les Exclus: Un Francais sur Dix* [The Excluded: One Frenchman in Ten] (Paris: Le Seuil, 1974).

16 D. Byrne, *Social Exclusion* (Buckingham: Open University Press, 1999).

17 H. Bauder, 'Neighbourhood Effects and Cultural Exclusion', *Urban Studies*, 39, 1 (2002),

pp. 85–93; M. Corcoran, 'Rags to Rags: Poverty and Mobility in the United States', *Annual Sociological Review*, 21 (1995), pp. 237–67; M. Small and K. Newman, 'Urban Poverty after *The Truly Disadvantaged*: the rediscovery of the family, the neighbourhood and culture', *Annual Sociological Review*, 27 (2001), pp. 23–45.

18 W. Bottero, *Stratification: social division and inequality* (London: Routledge, 2005), p. 228.

19 P. Kirby, *The Celtic Tiger in Distress: growth with inequality in Ireland* (London: Palgrave, 2002). See also Combat Poverty Agency, *How Many People are Poor?;* available at www.cpa.ie/povertyinireland; accessed 29 Apr. 2009; C. Whelan and B. Maitre, 'Poverty in Ireland in a Comparative European Perspective' (ESRI Working Paper, No. 265, 2008).

20 L. Sklair, *The Transnational Capitalist Class* (Oxford: Wiley-Blackwell, 2000).

21 J. Beall, 'Globalization and Social Exclusion in Cities: Framing the Debates with Lessons from Africa and Asia', 'Working Papers Series: Development Studies Institute' (London: London School of Economics, 2002).

22 J. Young, *The Exclusive Society: social exclusion, crime and difference in late modernity* (London: Sage, 1999).

23 Beall, op. cit., p. 34.

24 L. Wacquant, 'The New Urban Colour Line: The State and the Fate of the Ghetto in Post-Fordist America', in C. Calhoun (ed.), *Social Theory and the Politics of Identity* (Oxford: Basil Blackwell, 1994).

25 CSO, Census 2006 (Dublin: Stationery Office, 2006–2009).

26 C. Arensberg and S. Kimball, *Family and Community in Ireland* (Cambridge, MA: Harvard University Press, 1940). See C. Curtin and T. Wilson, *Ireland from Below: social change and local communities* (Galway: Galway University Press); H. Tovey and P. Share, *The Sociology of Ireland* (Dublin: Gill & Macmillan, 2000), pp. 202–6.

27 K. Keohane and C. Kuhling, *Collision Culture: transformations in everyday life in Ireland* (Dublin: Liffey Press, 2004).

28 T. Inglis, 'Belonging without Believing? Belief in God among Catholics in Contemporary Ireland', Paper presented at the 'Annual Conference of the Sociological Association of Ireland', Belfast, 9 May 2010.

29 For a contemporary analysis of the more positive aspects of life in Limerick, I refer the reader to the following books: C. O'Flynn, *Beautiful Limerick* (Dublin: Obelisk Books, 2004); D. O'Shaughnessy, *A Spot so Fair: tales from St. Mary's* (Limerick: Margo Press, 2001); D. Lee and D. Jacobs (eds), *Made in Limerick: history of industries, trade and commerce* (Limerick Civic Trust, 2003).

1. Divided City

1 The term Limerick urban area, as used throughout the chapter, refers to Limerick city and its contiguous suburbs, as defined by the Central Statistics Office for purpose of data collection. The term Limerick city (small 'c') is used interchangeably for the same entity. Limerick City (capital 'C') is the legally-defined area administered by Limerick City Council.

2 Central Statistics Office, *County Incomes and Regional GDP 2006* (Dublin: Stationery Office, 2009). Note that income estimates for the City alone are not available.

3 D. Watson, C.T. Whelan, J. Williams and S. Blackwell, *Mapping Poverty: national, regional and county patterns* (Dublin: Institute of Public Administration and the Combat Poverty Agency, 2005). The income poverty rate is for a poverty line set at 50 per cent of the mean equivalent income. The measure of consistent poverty is a modified version of the standard measure.

4 T. Haase and J. Pratschke, *New Measures of Deprivation for the Republic of Ireland* (Dublin: Pobal, 2008).

5 D. McCafferty, 'Aspects of Socio-Economic Development in Limerick City since 1970: A Geographer's Perspective', in L. Irwin, G. Ó Tuathaigh and M. Potter (eds), *Limerick: History and Society* (Dublin: Geography Publications, 1999).

6 The suburbs are here defined as the areas outside the City boundary. The total increase in the population of the urban area over the ten-year period was 12,074, of which 11,574 took place outside the City.

7 To do so is to commit the 'ecological fallacy' of ascribing to individuals the characteristics of the population in the areas that they live in.

8 See, for example, S. Buzar, P. Ogden, R. Hall, A. Haase, S. Kabisch and A. Steinfuhrer, 'Splintering Urban Populations: Emergent Landscapes of Reurbanisation in Four European Cities', *Urban Studies*, 44, 4 (2007), pp. 651–77; R.A. Walks, 'The Social Ecology of the Post-Fordist / Global City. Economic Restructuring and Socio-Spatial Polarisation in the Toronto Urban Region', *Urban Studies*, 38, 3 (2001), pp. 407–47.

9 D. McCafferty, *Limerick: profile of a changing city* (Limerick City Development Board, 2004).

10 It should be noted that the classification of small areas into social area types was not based on their relative location. Hence the emergence of social area types with a high degree of spatial contiguity is testament to the highly structured social geography of the city.

11 The measure of affluence is that developed by T. Haase and J. Pratschke, op. cit.

12 An empty-nest family is defined in the census as one consisting of a couple only (no children) where the female partner is aged between forty-five and sixty-four.

13 O.D. Duncan and B. Duncan, 'A Methodological Analysis of Segregation Indexes', *American Sociological Review*, 20, 2 (1955), pp. 210–17.

14 On average across the four cities, EAs are more than twice as numerous as the EDs and have just under half the population.

15 The values are for the average across all six social classes, weighted by the size of the social class in terms of population.

16 J. Fitzgerald, *Addressing Issues of Social Exclusion in Moyross and Other Disadvantaged Areas of Limerick City, Report to the Cabinet Committee on Social Inclusion*, April 2007. Social housing includes housing provided by voluntary bodies as well as public housing. It should be noted that the number quoted refers to the total constructed, not the number currently being rented. According to the 2006 census, almost 13 per cent of households rent from the local authority.

17 It is likely that a considerable proportion of this consists of private housing acquired and let by the City Council, as opposed to Limerick and Clare County Councils.

18 For a comprehensive account of such policy measures see M. Norris and K. Murray, 'National, Regional and Local Patterns in the Residualisation of the Social Rented Tenure: The Case of Dublin and Ireland', *Housing Studies*, 19, 1 (2004), pp. 85–105.

19 Department of the Environment, *Ireland: Habitat II National Report* (Dublin: Stationery Office, 1996).

20 *Policy Consequences: a study of the £5,000 surrender grant in the Dublin housing area* (Dublin: Threshold, 1987).

21 Usage of the term 'residualisation' here follows that of Norris and Murray, op. cit. who apply it somewhat more broadly than other authors.

22 D. McCafferty and A. Canny, *Public Housing in Limerick: a profile of tenants and estates* (Limerick City Council, 2005).

23 Central Statistics Office, *Survey on Income and Living Conditions, 2007* (Dublin: Stationery Office, 2008).

24 The poverty line in question, and that which is referred to throughout this section, is set at 60 per cent of the median household equivalised income. A person with income below this level is said to be at risk of poverty.

25 An individual is considered deprived if he/she lives in a household that is unable to afford two or more items from a list of eleven basic deprivation indicators.

26 Figures 2 and 3 are based on data for Enumeration Areas (EAs). These are the smallest units for which small area data are available in the 2006 census of population. EA data are not available for previous censuses.

27 D. McCafferty and A. Canny, op. cit.

28 These data were obtained from the City Council's tenant database compiled in conjunction with the 2004 rent assessment.

29 Throughout this section comparative data for Limerick City and suburbs are derived from the 2006 census of population.

30 The analysis of poverty risk is based on household income adjusted for household size and composition, otherwise known as equivalised income.

31 D. McCafferty and A. Canny, op. cit.

32 D. McCafferty, op. cit.

33 D. McCafferty, 'Poor People or Poor Place? Urban Deprivation in Southill East, Limerick City', in D. Pringle, J. Walsh and M. Hennessy (eds), *Poor People, Poor Places: a geography of poverty and deprivation in Ireland* (Dublin: Oak Tree Press, 1999).

34 The number of lone-parent families in the ED of Dock A increased by 75 per cent, albeit from a low base.

35 D. McCafferty and A. Canny, op. cit.

36 A. MacLaren, 'Deconstructing Urban Poverty', in D.G. Pringle, J. Walsh and M. Hennessy, op. cit., pp. 45–76.

37 D. McCafferty and B. O'Keeffe, *Facing the Challenge of Change: a spatial perspective on Limerick* (Limerick City Council, 2010).

2. Getting a Fix on Crime in Limerick

1 D. Hobbs, 'The Firm', *British Journal of Criminology*, 41 (2001), pp. 549–60.

2 E. Dillon, *The Outsiders* (Dublin: Merlin Publishing, 2006); B. Duggan, *Mean Streets: Limerick's gangland* (Dublin: O'Brien Press, 2009).

3 Garda Recorded Crime Statistics 2003–2007 (Dublin: Stationery Office, 2009).

4 C. McCullagh, *Crime in Ireland* (Cork: Cork University Press, 1996), pp. 15–19.

5 Central Statistics Office, 'Crime and Victimization', *Quarterly National Household Survey 2006* (including results for 1998 and 2003) (Dublin: Stationery Office, 2007).

6 Cork City is an exception to this model.

7 The level of detail in the figures is significantly deepened through the use of the new classification system.

8 Other divisions have had higher rates in various years possibly linked to dissident republican activity. Thus the rates in Longford/Westmeath in 2003, Tipperary in 2004 and 2005 and Donegal in 2006 were all higher than the rate in Limerick.

9 The highest rates in each year were in Garda divisions in Dublin and the third-highest rate in 2007 was recorded in Tipperary and probably related to a feud between gangs in two housing estates in Clonmel.

10 *Quarterly National Household Survey 2006*, p. 2.

11 The number was in the mid-thirties for 2002, 2003 and 2005, rising to forty-three and fifty-four in 2006 and 2007 respectively.

12 Within the greater Dublin Metropolitan Region, there is a particular concentration in the Northern DMR.

13 Twenty-three of the thirty-six offences recorded in 2003 were in the Dublin Metropolitan Region. In 2005, the figure was thirty-one out of thirty-six and in 2007, it was forty-five out of fifty-four recorded offences.

14 The crime rate is the number of recorded crimes divided by the size of the population,

expressed by 10,000 or 100,000 of the population. Its purpose is to enable us to make appropriate comparisons of the level of crime, in say, Dublin and Limerick. To do this we need to adjust the figures by the size of each city's population to make the comparisons meaningful. The crime rates used in this chapter are expressed per 100,000 of the population.

15 Somewhat oddly, this is below the rate for Laois/Offaly, a Garda division not conventionally seen as having a significant drug problem.

16 It was only in 2005 that the rate in Limerick moved somewhat in national statistics, with the rate being lower than that of all divisions in Dublin but higher than those in the rest of the country, though only just so by comparison with Louth/Meath and Longford/Westmeath. The rate fell back in 2006 and the number of such crimes fell from a high of seventeen in 2005 to a low of nine in 2007 in Limerick.

17 E. Keogh, *Illicit Drug Use and Related Criminal Activity* (Dublin: An Garda Síochána, 1997).

18 The rate of this crime in Dublin has ranged from a high of 98 per cent of such crime happening in Dublin in 2003 to a low of 91 per cent in 2008.

19 The number of such offences increased quite significantly over the period.

20 J. Lea and J. Young, *What Is To Be Done About Law and Order?* (Harmondsworth: Penguin, 1984).

21 It was also lower than for a number of other regions in the country, such as the South-East and the Mid-East.

22 This figure was overshadowed by the rise in the South-West where the percentage who thought that crime was 'a very serious problem' rose from 33.3 per cent in 1998 to 59.1 per cent in 2006. This was also part of a national pattern where the percentage nationally who thought this way about crime rose from 38.3 per cent in 1998 to 45.9 per cent in 2006.

23 In the Dublin region, the figure fell from 17.2 per cent in 1998 to 10.5 per cent in 2006 and in the South-West from 22.9 per cent in 1998 to 10.4 per cent in 2006.

24 This figure represents an increase from 9.1 per cent in 1998, but the increase is largely accounted for by an increase in the experience of vandalism, up from 3.4 per cent of households in 1998 to 5.1 per cent in 2006.

25 However, the numbers of these crimes reported to the Gardaí increased nationally between 1998 and 2006 but fell in the Mid-West from 100 per cent in 1998 to 85.7 per cent in 2006. For this offence, as for others, the main reason recorded at a national level was that it was 'not serious enough or no loss'. This was down from 55.2 per cent in 1998 to 44.6 per cent in 2006. The most striking change here was the increase from the 13.4 per cent who 'believe that the Gardaí would do nothing' in 1998 to the 22.3 per cent who offered this as a reason in 2006.

26 *The Irish Times*, 24 Jan. 2009. See also Hourigan's study in this volume.

27 The detailed information on gang activities used throughout this chapter is taken from the news section of the website of The National Documentation Centre on Drug Use accessible at www.drugsandalcohol.ie. This is an indispensable resource for researchers in this area.

28 G. Pearson, 'Drug Markets and Dealing: From Street Dealer to Mr. Big', in M. Simpson, T. Shildrick and R. Mcdonald (eds), *Drugs in Britain* (London: Routledge, 2007), pp. 76–92.

29 D. Browne, M. Mason and R. Murphy, 'Drug Supply and Trafficking: An Overview', *The Howard Journal*, 42, 4 (2003), pp. 324–34, quote on p. 326.

30 J. Connolly, *Drugs and Crime in Ireland: Overview 3* (Dublin: Health Research Board, 2006).

31 G. Pearson, op. cit., p. 83.

32 B.D. Johnson, A.L. Golub and E. Dunlap, 'The Rise and Decline of Drugs, Drug Markets, and Violence in New York City', in A. Blumstein and J. Wallman (eds), *The*

Crime Drop in America (New York: Cambridge University Press, 2000), pp. 164–206; quote is from p. 166.

33 P. Reuter, 'On the Need for Dynamic Models of Drug Markets', *Bulletin on Narcotics*, 53, 1/2 (2001); available online at www.unodc.org.

34 G. Pearson and R. Hobbs, 'King Pin? A Case Study of a Middle Market Drug Broker', *The Howard Journal*, 42, 4 (2003), pp. 335–47, quote on p. 341.

35 Ibid., p. 344.

36 US television drama, 'Crime Science Investigation', which focuses on forensic science techniques.

37 D. Hobbs, op. cit., p. 550.

38 Ibid., p. 550.

39 D. Hobbs, 'Going Down the Glocal: The Local Context of Organised Crime', *Howard Journal*, 37, 4 (1998), pp. 407–422; quote is from p. 410.

40 J. McGuigan, 'Towards a Sociology of the Mobile Phone', *Human Technology* 1, 1 (2005), pp. 45–57.

41 J. Hagan, *Crime and Disrepute* (London: Pine Forge Press, 1994), p. 89.

INTRODUCTION: LIVING WITH FEAR AND FEUDING IN LIMERICK

1 L. Ryan, *Social Dynamite* (Cork: Cork University Press, 1966), p. 1.

2 F. Keane, *All of These People: A Memoir* (London and New York: Harper Perennial), pp. 114–15.

3 B. Duggan, 'Gavin and Millie turned into fireballs as they sat in car', *Irish Independent*, 25 Sept. 2007, p. 1.

4 J. Fitzgerald, *Addressing Issues of Social Exclusion in Moyross and other Disadvantaged Areas of Limerick City*, Report to the Cabinet Committee on Social Inclusion, April 2007, pp. 4–5.

5 Ibid., p. 5.

6 J. Young, *The Exclusive Society: social exclusion, crime and differences in late modernity* (London: Sage, 1999); R. MacDonald, *Youth, Underclass and Social Exclusion* (London and New York: Routledge, 1997).

7 M. Norris and C. O'Connell, 'Local Authority Housing Management Reform in the Republic of Ireland: Progress to Date – Impediments to Future Progress', *European Journal of Housing Policy* 2 (2002), pp. 245–67; T. Fahey, *Social Housing in Ireland: a study of success, failure and lessons learned* (Dublin: Oak Tree Press, 1999); C. O'Connell, *The State and Housing in Ireland: ideology, policy and practice* (New York: Nova Science Publishers, 2007).

8 I. O'Donnell and E. O'Sullivan, *Crime Control in Ireland: the politics of intolerance* (Cork: Cork University Press, 2001); C. McCullagh, *Crime in Ireland: a sociological introduction* (Cork: Cork University Press, 1999).

9 Although not an ethnographer, health researcher Johnny Connolly has highlighted a number of the consequences of drugs-related crime and addiction for communities. See J. Connolly, 'Drugs, Crime and the Community in Dublin, Ireland', paper presented to the third meeting of the Pompidou Group Expert Forum on Criminal Justice, Strasbourg, Apr. 2005.

10 R. Merton, 'Social Structure and Anomie', *American Sociological Review* 3, 6 (1938), pp. 672–82; F. Thrasher, *The Gang* (Chicago: University of Chicago Press, 1927); R. Cloward and L. Ohlin, *Delinquency and Opportunity* (Glencoe, IL: Free Press, 1960); J. Short and F. Strodtbeck, *Group Process and Gang Delinquency* (Chicago: University of Chicago Press, 1965); J. Moore, *Homeboys: Gangs, Drugs and Prison in the Barrios of Los Angeles* (Philadelphia: Temple University Press, 1978); J. Hagedon, *People and Folks: gangs, crime and the underclass in a rustbelt city* (Chicago: Lakeview Press, 1988); C. Taylor, *Girls, Gangs, Women and Drugs* (East Lansing MI: Michigan State University Press, 1993).

11 The core interview sample for this research project was 180 persons, approximately 2 per cent of the population of the Regeneration estates (total population 8,981 as per

2006 census). In addition, forty-one interviews were conducted with persons from other parts of Limerick city, Gardaí, social, community and youth workers, psychotherapists and religious working in the communities. Interviews were based on a semi-structured oral narrative interview methodology.

12 Participant observation is a research methodology which was employed to great effect by members of the Chicago school in the 1920s and 1930s, particularly Robert Park, in conducting some of the most important sociological studies on crime, deviance and gang culture. Lofland and Lofland describe it as the process in which an 'investigator establishes a many-sided and relatively long-term relationship with a human association in its natural setting, for the purposes of developing a scientific understanding of that association' (p. 12). In its most simple form, participant observation involves 'hanging out' within a community, chatting to people, getting to know the contours of the local community. The aim of this research approach is to establish not only a description of community life but investigate how members of the community understand their own experience of that community. For further discussion, see J. Lofland and L. Lofland, *Analysing Social Settings: a guide to qualitative observation and analysis* (Belmont, CA: Wadsworth, 1984).

13 Because the information required in this study was highly sensitive and because of the fear itself, interviewees often agreed to be interviewed only on the recommendation of a gate-keeper or key informant within the local community. A snowball sampling approach was used, moving from individual to individual, relying on the recommendation of prior interviewees which would secure further interviews with those who agreed to trust me and discuss this sensitive topic. However, in placing this trust in me as an interviewer, each interviewee was largely depending on their own estimation of the trustworthiness of the individual who had provided the recommendation. For further discussion of the complex ethical and trust issues involved in ethnographic research, see J. Ferrell and M. Hamm (eds), *Ethnography at the Edge: crime, deviance and field research* (Boston: Northeastern University Press, 1998); M. Hammersley and P. Atkinson, *Ethnography: principles and practice* (London: Tavistock, 1983); P. Atkinson et al., *Handbook of Ethnography* (London: Sage, 2001).

14 For each interviewee, a confidentiality agreement was put in place. All interviewees were asked to orient their discussion towards an analysis of general trends in their communities rather than a discussion of specific cases, individuals or families. Each interviewee was warned that confidentiality would be broken if three specific types of information were shared during the interview process. These were evidence of a serious unreported crime, evidence of serious unreported risk of harm to another individual, evidence of serious unreported risk to a child. However, there were no instances where the confidentiality agreement was broken, as informants demonstrated a huge reluctance to name specific families or cases and tended to restrict their discussion of criminality to cases which were either in the public domain already or cases which were known to the Gardaí and child protection services. The reliability and validity of information gathered during interviews on general trends was verified by cross-checking information given with other interviewees across the sample and with the participants in the final focus groups.

15 The entire sample consisted of 102 men and 119 women.

16 This terminology is also used by Sinéad Ní Shúinéar in her study of Traveller feuds in the Midlands. S. Ní Shúinear, *Conflict and Conflict Resolution*, a report for the Navan Travellers Workshop Ltd (Navan, 2005).

3. A History of Social Exclusion in Limerick

1 This refers to the greater Limerick conurbation rather than the population within the boundaries of the city itself (which are under review).

2 F. Prendergast, 'The Decline of Traditional Limerick Industries', in D. Lee and D. Jacobs (eds), *Made in Limerick: history of industries, trade and commerce* (Limerick Civic Trust, 2003).

3 F. McCourt, *Angela's Ashes: A Memoir of a Childhood* (New York: Harper Collins, 1996).

4 Maragaret Mastriani also notes that 'many of the factories in town had their own sports teams and their own bands and choirs and drama clubs which gave the workers great pride and a sense of belonging': M. Mastriani, 'From Crubeens to Computer Chips: Limerick's Industrial Development, 1914–2003', in D. Lee and D. Jacobs (eds), *Made in Limerick: history of industries, trade and commerce* (Limerick Civic Trust, 2003), pp. 13–22.

5 The position of the Redemptorist Fathers within Limerick city culture has been the subject of much debate. Frank McCourt's memoir depicts the Redemptorists as harsh, while the role of the Redemptorist Fr. Creagh in inspiring the Limerick Pogrom in 1904 with his anti-Semitic propaganda has been strongly criticised by modern Irish historians and commentators on racism in Ireland. However, local historians such as former Mayor Frank Prendergast paint a more positive picture of their contribution to Limerick culture and society. The annual novena organised by the Redemptorists in Limerick every June still enjoys capacity congregations for its many ceremonies and contemporary Redemptorists in the city have been actively involved in the pastoral care of asylum seekers, immigrants and other marginalised groups in the city. For further discussion, see F. McCourt, *Angela's Ashes* (New York: Harper Collins, 1996); B. Fanning, *Racism and Social Change in the Republic of Ireland* (Manchester: Manchester University Press, 2002).

6 L. Cahill, *Forgotten Revolution: the Limerick soviet, 1919* (Dublin: O'Brien Press, 1990).

7 T. Johnson,. 'Housing Conditions in 1909', in J. Kemmy (ed.), *The Limerick Anthology* (Dublin: Gill & Macmillan), p. 319.

8 F. Prendergast, *Aspects of Social Conditions in Georgian and Victorian Limerick* (Limerick City Library, 2002), p. 2.

9 Ibid.

10 Personal Communication from Frank Prendergast, local historian and former Mayor of Limerick, 11 Feb. 2009.

11 F. Prendergast, op. cit., p. 2

12 The Ballinacurra Weston scheme was completed in the 1950s, but the lands had originally been selected in 1919, when it was proposed that these sites could be combined with sites at Carey's Road to form a single housing area capable of accommodating at least 5,000 people. The construction of St Mary's Park began in 1935.

13 M. Mastriani, op. cit., p. 14.

14 L. Ryan, *Social Dynamite* (Cork: Cork University Press, 1966), p. 14.

15 Quoted in A. Galvin, *Family Feud: gangland Limerick exposed* (Dublin: Hodder Lir, 2003), pp. 22–3.

16 Ibid., p. 24.

17 L. Ryan, op. cit., p. 41.

18 W. Gleeson, 'Limerick has slums in abundance', *Limerick Leader*, 5 Sept. 1962, p. 1.

19 Ibid.

20 Ibid.

21 Ibid.

22 *Limerick Leader*, 21 November 1962, p. 1; *Limerick Leader*, 21 November 1963, p. 3.

23 *Limerick Leader*, 24 November 1962, p. 1.

24 All otherwise unreferenced quotes are from interviews conducted for the main ethnographic study.

25 L. Ryan, op. cit., p. 9.

26 Ibid.

27 This conflict between the values and lifestyles of advantaged and disadvantaged groups was particularly pronounced in Southill. A survey of press reports on the areas from the *Limerick Leader* and *Limerick Chronicle* in the 1970s reveals considerable press coverage of this conflict which focused very much on the anti-social behaviour of young people from disadvantaged families. For further discussion, see the following press reports: 'Sequel to near riot in Southill', *Limerick Chronicle*, 18 March 1972, p. 1; 'Vandalism rampant in Southilll', *Limerick Leader*, 10 May 1972, p. 1; 'Crime in Southill Region', *Limerick Leader*, 13 June 1972, p. 1; 'Councillors demand Southill Garda Station: Ask Dept to think again', *Limerick Chronicle*, 5 Oct. 1972, p.1; 'Battleground or Playground', *Limerick Leader*, 14 April 1973, p. 1; 'Albert, aged four, collapses after being kicked by horse: deputation from Southill protest', *Limerick Leader*, 19 April 1975, p. 4; 'People in Southill living in fear and terror', *Limerick Leader*, 10 March 1976, p. 1.

28 L. Ryan, op. cit., p. 43.

29 Ibid.

30 *Limerick Chronicle*, 5 Oct. 1972, p.1; *Limerick Leader*, 10 Mar. 1976, p. 1.

31 A. Galvin, op. cit., p. 27.

32 Protest masculinity is a form of masculinity performed by the most socially excluded men who compensate for their powerlessness by behaving in a hyper-masculine fashion, often emphasising their physical toughness and identifying strongly with similar men and boys by participating in gangs. Connell suggests that: 'Through interaction in this milieu, the growing boy puts together a tense freak façade, making a claim to power where there is no real power.' For further discussion see R. Connell, *Masculinities* (Sydney: Allen & Unwin, 1995).

33 A. Galvin, op. cit., p. 26.

34 A. Galvin, op. cit., p. 128.

35 A detailed discussion of the origins of Limerick's core crime families is available in B. Duggan, *Mean Streets* (Dublin: O'Brien Press, 2009).

36 *Limerick Leader*, 10 Mar. 1976, p. 1.

37 *Limerick Leader*, 13 June 1984, p. 1.

38 *Limerick Leader*, 12 Apr. 1986, p. 2.

39 *Limerick Leader*, 4 June 1986, p. 1.

40 *Limerick Leader*, 4 June 1986, p. 1.

41 D. Ferriter, *The Transformation of Ireland 1900–2000* (London: Palgrave, 2005), p. 305.

42 Galvin, op. cit., p. 27.

43 E. Anderson, *Code of the Street: decency, violence and the moral life of the Inner City* (New York: Norton, 1999), p. 34.

44 Peter Squires and Dawn Stephens note a growing preoccupation with increased crime, disorder and antisocial behaviour in social housing in Britain from the 1980s onwards. This concern culminated in the introduction of Anti-Social Behaviour Orders (ASBOs) as part of a range of measures to tackle antisocial behaviour and juvenile crime in the 1998 Crime and Disorder Act. For further discussion see P. Squires and D. Stephens, *Rougher Justice: anti-social behaviour and young people* (Devon: Willan Publishing, 2005).

45 E. Anderson, op. cit., pp. 45–50.

46 B. Duggan, *Mean Streets* (Dublin: O'Brien Press, 2009).

47 Ibid.

48 Galvin, op. cit., p. 128.

49 The rule of thumb indicator of Drug Enforcement Agencies in the United State is that the value of drugs seized by police and customs represents roughly 10 per cent of the total value of the market. Based on this figure, one could estimate the value of the drugs trade in Limerick by 1999 was approximately €30 million. *Irish Independent*, 26 May 2009.

50 Duggan, op. cit.

51 *The Sunday Times*, 31 December 2006, p. 6.
52 The name of this park had been changed to protect the identity of interviewees.
53 Galvin, op. cit., p. 75.
54 Galvin, op. cit., p. 76.
55 Dáil Debates, Vol. 667, Cols 268–88 (13 Nov. 2008); Vol. 651, Cols 212–45 (10 April 2008).
56 *Irish Independent*, 26 May 2009, p. 10.
57 Galvin, op. cit., p. 81.

4. DIVIDED COMMUNITIES

 1 For further information, see McCafferty's chapter in this volume as well as M. Barrett et al., *Community Profile of the Northside and Southside Regeneration Areas of Limerick City*, available at www.hse.ie. See also PAUL Partnership, *GAMMA Statistics*, PAUL Partnership Baseline Data Report (Dublin: Pobal, 2006); J. Saunders, F. Boughton and D. Barry, 'Health Inequalities, Deprivation and Access to Primary Healthcare within the Mid-West Preliminary Findings', Combat Poverty Seminar Series, 23 Sept. 2008, University of Limerick; D. McCafferty and Brendan O'Keefe *Limerick City Profile 2006* (Limerick City Council).
 2 These areas included Garryowen, Watergate, Janesboro and the greater King's Island area.
 3 Because of de-population of certain estates within the Regeneration areas between 2007 and 2010, it is likely that this population has decreased since the 2006 census.
 4 The areas of Limerick City with the highest relative proportions of children are (in order) O'Malley Park, St Mary's Park, Weston, Kileely, Moyross and the area of Garryowen centred on Fairview Cresent. For further discussion, see McCafferty and O'Keefe, *Limerick City Profile 2006* (Limerick City Council).
 5 Ibid.
 6 M. Barrett et al., op. cit.
 7 L. Ryan, *Social Dynamite* (Cork: Cork University Press, 1966), p. 20.
 8 A. Bracken, 'Limerick: Tensions High in City's Flashpoints' *Sunday Tribune*, 13 Apr. 2008.
 9 Newman defines the extended family as 'a family unit including parents and children but also other kin. Extended families are also called consanguine families, meaning they include every one with shared blood.' D. Newman, *Families: a sociological perspective* (New York: McGraw-Hill, 2008). Communities founded on the extended family were more common in pre-industrial societies. Émile Durkheim has written extensively about this form of community within his work on mechanical solidarity. For further discussion, see Durkheim, *The Division of Labour in Society* (London: Macmillan London, 1984 [1893]). Durkheim, *The Elementary Forms of Religious Life* (London: Allen & Unwin: London, 1971 [1912]).
10 The importance of extended family as a marker of identity for people who are participating in the workforce is striking in these communities and is in marked contrast to the importance of work and career in shaping identities for members of Ireland's middle class. For further discussion, see B. Fields, *The Catholic Ethic and Global Capitalism* (Aldershot: Ashgate, 2003).
11 Within the literature on social exclusion and neighbourhoods, a number of other scholars have noted the presence of the same two types of groups. Elijah Anderson highlights the distinction between families with a 'decent' orientation and those with a 'street' orientation. Lupton and Power also note the difference between 'families with problems' and 'problem families'. For further discussion see E. Anderson. *Code of the Street* (New York: Norton, 1999) and R. Lupton and A. Power. 'Social Exclusion and Neighbourhoods' in J. Hills, J. Le Grand and D. Piachaud, *Understanding Social Exclusion* (Oxford: Oxford University Press, 2002).

12 The categories described here are relatively fluid as individuals experience upward and downward mobility linked to broader economic changes. The recent dramatic change in the growth of the Irish economy has had an impact on the socio-economic structure of these communities. For instance, the *Limerick Independent* reported that in May 2009, unemployment in Moyross and Southill had risen to 50 per cent, far above the 11 per cent national average at the time; *Limerick Independent*, 7 May 2009. In addition, this research would suggest that there are greater numbers of more disadvantaged families in some Regeneration areas.

13 In terms of the sample interviewed, the breakdown of the characteristics of the core Regeneration area interview cohort of 180 persons is as follows: advantaged (98 interviewees), disadvantaged (51 interviewees), core crime families (17 – all these respondents were on the fringes rather than at the centre of criminal family gang networks), Travellers (14).

14 L. Ryan, op. cit., p. 44.

15 For discussions of the exclusionary consequences of Ireland's Celtic Tiger boom, see P. Kirby, *The Celtic Tiger in Distress: growth and inequality in Ireland* (London: Palgrave, 2002); P. Kirby, D. Jacobson and D. Ó Broin, *Taming the Tiger: social exclusion in a globalized Ireland* (Dublin: New Island Books, 2006).

16 L. Tolstoy, *Anna Karenina* (London: Penguin, 1995), p. 26.

17 In examining the transition of boys in Philadelphia into criminal gang activity, Elijah Anderson also identified that the absence of fathers and positive male role models was a significant factor in shaping this youth transition. For further discussion, see E. Anderson. *Code of the Street* (New York: Norton, 1999).

18 A range of studies on health and social exclusion demonstrate the greater prevalence of comfort behaviours and addictions among marginalised groups. For further discussion see W. Bottero, 'Hierarchy Makes You Sick', in *Stratification: Social Division and Inequality* (London: Routledge, 2005), p. 186–204.

19 R. Wilkinson, *Unhealthy Societies: the afflictions of inequality* (London: Routlege, 1996), p. 215.

20 Al Absi notes that 'an addict's belief that his or her drug of choice provides relief from stress or control over life's stressors, which is an important component of addiction, actually has some biological basis.' M. Al Absi, *Stress and Addiction: Biological and Psychological Mechanisms* (Boston: John Wiley & Sons, 2007), p. 57.

21 For further discussion on the links between social exclusion and drug use in the Irish context see A. O'Gorman, *Understanding the Social Exclusion–Problem Drug Use Nexus* (Dublin: Health Service Executive, 2006).

22 M. Dunn et al., 'Origins and Consequences of Child Neglect in Substance Abuse Families', *Clinical Psychology Review*, 22, 7 (2002), pp. 1063–90.

23 Ryan, op. cit., p. 20.

24 In August 2009, Combat Poverty and St Vincent de Paul released a statement criticising the lack of regulation being imposed on moneylenders in Ireland. This criticism follows the findings of a number of studies which highlight that Ireland has one of the highest rates of financial exclusion within the EU. J. Hough, 'Regulation of money-lenders failing the most vulnerable'. *Irish Examiner*, 3 August 2009, p. 1.

25 For further discussion see B. Duggan, *Mean Streets*.

26 For discussions of other family feuds in Limerick, see A. Galvin, *Family Feud: gangland Limerick exposed* (Dublin: Hodder Lir, 2003).

27 Duggan, *Mean Streets*, pp. 225–34.

28 See P. Williams, *Gangland* (Dublin: O'Brien Press, 2002); P. Williams, *Crimelords* (Dublin: Merlin Publishing, 2003).

29 Duggan, *Mean Streets*, pp. 225–34.

30 Robert Merton argued that the level of criminality in a society can depend on how

well a society makes cultural goals achievable by institutional means. Conformity involves pursuing conventional goals, such as money, by approved means, such as jobs and educational opportunities. However, children who grow up in poverty may recognise that they will have little chance of success if they play by the rules. Therefore they create an innovative response to their situation by pursing culturally approved goals such as money through unconventional means, such as the drugs trade. Merton argued that gangsters such as Al Capone were really quite conventional in aspiring to the American dream but pursuing it through the only opportunities which were available to them. R. Merton, 'Social Structure and Anomie', *American Sociological Review*, 3, 6 (1938), pp. 672–82; R. Merton, *Social Theory and Social Structure* (New York: The Free Press, 1968).

31 *Irish Independent*, 23 Nov. 2008.

32 *Health Impact Assessment: key recommendations to maximise positive and minimise negative health impacts of physical regeneration* (Limerick Regeneration, 2008).

33 H. McDonald, 'Third gang sets up family rivalries to control drugs', *The Observer*, 2 Feb. 2003.

34 Although the number of Travellers in this study was small, the research on Traveller feuding also drew on the sample of ninety-six interviewed for the TEACH Report which included fifty Travellers. For further discussion see N. Hourigan and M. Campbell, *The TEACH Report. Traveller Education and Adults: crisis, challenge and change* (Athlone: National Association of Travellers Centres, 2010).

35 A good example of this type of journalism is the supplement 'Sin City' produced by *Irish Daily Star Sunday* on the activities of criminal gangs in Limerick. K. Foy, 'Sin City Supplement,' *Irish Daily Star Sunday*, 21 June 2009.

36 J. Helleiner, *Irish Travellers: racism and the plitics of culture* (Toronto: University of Toronto Press, 2000).

37 See M. Corcoran, J. Gray and M. Peillon, *Suburban Affiliations: Social Relations in the Greater Dublin Area* (New York: Syracuse University Press, 2010).

38 J. Young, *The Exclusive Society: social exclusion, crime and difference in late modernity* (London: Sage, 1999).

5. Organised Crime and Community Violence

1 C. Lally, 'Squalid truth of a life of crime', *The Irish Times*, 1 Jan. 2009.

2 Ibid.

3 Garryowen, Watergate, Janesboro and the greater King's Island area.

4 Dept of Social Welfare, *Leaving Fathers Out* (2004). Available at www.welfare.ie/EN/Policy/ResearchSurveyandStatistics. Accessed 14 June 2009.

5 J.W. Messerschmidt, *Masculinities and Crime* (Lanham, MD: Rowman & Littlefield, 1993).

6 R. Sennett and R. Cobb, *The Hidden Injuries of Class* (Cambridge: Cambridge University Press, 1972); R. Sennett, *Respect: the formation of character in an age of inequality* (New York: Penguin, 2003).

7 A range of sociological studies in the US and the UK has demonstrated how hyper-masculine behaviours can become dominant in socially excluded communities. In their study of football hooliganism, Dunning et al. found that aggressive masculinity becomes 'an important source of meaning, status and pleasurable emotional arousal' in deeply disadvantaged communities. Robert Connell describes this process as a performance of protest masculinity where men compensate for social exclusion by supporting each other in engaging in behaviours such as school resistance, substance abuse, vandalism, joyriding and serious violence. See E. Dunning, P. Murphy and J. Williams, *The Roots of Football Hooliganism* (London: Routledge, 1988); R. Connell, *Masculinities* (Sydney: Allen & Unwin, 1995).

8   A. Bracken, 'Gangland killers getting away with murder', *Sunday Tribune*, 31 Aug. 2008.

9   P. Bourgois, *In Search of Respect* (Cambridge: Cambridge University Press, 1995); E. Anderson, *Code of the Street* (New York: Norton, 1999); See also J.W. Messerschmidt, op. cit.

10 E. Anderson, op. cit., p. 10.

11 Community worker Erinma Bell, quoted in A. Hill, 'Gangs want respect, so the innocent die', *The Observer*, 12 Aug 2007.

12 See J. Miller, *One of the Guys: girls, gangs and gender* (Oxford: Oxford University Press, 2000); M. Chesney-Lind and J. Hagedorn, *Female Gangs in America: essays on girls, gangs and gender* (Chicago: Lakeview Press, 1999); D. Burris-Kitchen, *Female Gang Participation: the role of African-American women in the informal drug economy and gang activities* (New York: Edwin Mellen Press, 1997).

13 M. Sheehan, 'Public desparate for crackdown as gangs tear city of Limerick apart', *Sunday Independent*, 23 Aug. 2008.

14 E. Anderson, op. cit., pp. 69–70.

15 Ibid.

16 N. Fyfe and H. McKay, 'Witness Intimidation and Resettlement: A British Case Study', *Transactions of the Institute of British Geographers*, new series, 25, 1 (2000), pp. 77–90.

17 In an open letter published in the *Limerick Leader* which is deeply critical of Limerick City Council's response to these problems, Fr Pat Hogan, parish priest in Southill, describes the experiences of his parishioners in the following terms: 'There came a time when the harassment and violence was such that they abandoned their homes, where all their family memories were embedded in every wall and corner...We have watched the bowed elderly go in the dark of the night, knowing that they will never return. We thought it impossible to lose your home, the place of your family in modern Ireland. They went and some did not survive twelve months . . . Those who left have horrendous stories to tell, to say that they were vulnerable, devastated and deeply upset is an understatement.' *Limerick Leader*, 18 Oct. 2008, p. 6.

18 *Irish Independent*, 13 Oct. 2007, p. 4.

19 See P. Bourgois, op. cit.; E. Anderson, op. cit.

20 For further discussion, see B. Duggan, *Mean Streets* (Dublin: O'Brien Press, 2009), pp. 77–206.

21 See T. Dagleish et al., 'An Experimental Investigation of Hypervigilance for Threat in Children and Adolescents with Post-traumatic Stress Disorder', *Psychological Medicine*, 31 (2001), pp. 5417; M.J. Horowitz, 'Stress Response Syndrome: A Review of Post-Traumatic and Adjustment Disorders', *Hospital and Community Psychiatry*, 37 (1986), pp. 241–9; P. Verhaeghe and S. Jottkadt, *On Being Normal and Other Disorders* (New York: Other Press, 2000).

22 The term foot-soldiers is drawn from US sociological literature on gang cultures. Levitt and Venkatesh define foot-soldiers as gang members in their late teens and early twenties who typically serve as street-level drug dealers. For further discussion, see S. Levitt and S. Venkatesh, 'An Economic Analysis of a Drug-Selling Gang's Finances', *The Quarterly Journal of Economics*, 115, 3 (2000), pp. 755–89.

23 Richard Cloward and Lloyd Ohlin argue that criminality results not only from the very limited legitimate opportunities which are available to young people living in poor neighbourhoods but also from the range of more lucrative illegitimate opportunities available to them. Albert Cohen concurs with this finding, arguing that those who become involved in deviant subcultures 'define as meritorious the characteristics they do possess, the kinds of conduct of which they are capable'. For further discussion, see, R. Cloward and L. Ohlin, *Delinquency and Opportunity: a theory of delinquent gangs* (New York: Free Press, 1966); A. Cohen, *Delinquent Boys: the culture of the gang* (New York: Free Press, 1955).

24 The trend of recruiting children to criminal gangs in Limerick would appear to be mirrored in criminal gangs in other Irish cities. In 2009, an investigation by three journalists at the *Irish Independent* found that criminal gangs were using children as young as twelve to courier guns and drugs, traditionally the work of foot-soldiers in criminal organisations. S. Phelan, 'Gangs' age profile drops significantly', *Irish Independent*, 2 Feb. 2009, p. 19; D. MacDonald, 'Shameful system that leaves children at the mercy of criminal gangs', *Irish Independent*, 3 Feb. 2009, p. 27; S. Phelan, D. MacDonald and T. Tuite, 'Gangs forcing young to be drugs mules', *Irish Independent*, 2 Feb. 2009, p. 18.

25 Padilla's research demonstrates that the earnings of a foot-solider within a gang are considerably more than the socially excluded individual could expect to earn within the legitimate workforce. F. Padilla, *The Gang as an American Enterprise* (New Brunswick, NJ: Rutgers University Press, 1992).

26 In an article in the *Limerick Chronicle*, Superintendent Frank O'Brien of Henry St Garda Station is quoted as saying that the number of heroin addicts has dramatically increased in recent years, up to nearly 600 from 'almost zero' four years ago. A. Sheridan, 'Priest says city is in denial about extent of heroin problem', *Limerick Chronicle*, 17 Aug. 2010.

27 One of the most infamous cases of this type was the shooting of twenty-year-old James Cronin in 2008. He was allegedly told by his fellow gang members to dig a hole to bury guns and then shot on the suspicion that he was about to turn state's witness after participating in a gangland murder. B. Duggan, T. Brady and S. Phelan, 'Bloodbath fears as feud tears gang apart', *Irish Independent*, 9 Apr. 2008; *The Times*, 'Limerick rival clans show no sign of ending conflict', 15 Nov. 2008.

28 The information gathered on children was collected through the participant observation strand of the research. It is the view of this researcher that a detailed and large-scale socio-psychological study is required on child gang participation within Limerick's disadvantaged estates.

29 Despite being neglected, these children are often very attached to their parents, their homes and their primary care-givers and set themselves very clearly against state agents such as social workers who might remove them from the family home. This pattern reflects the findings in a range of studies on child abuse which highlight the intense attachment which may exist between the child and parents in these contexts. For further discussion see D. Celani, *The Illusion of Love* (New York: Columbia University Press, 1994), p. 24.

30 According to Stephen Lyng, the thrill of these activities leaves individuals with 'a magnified sense of self' which is a complete contrast to the 'extremes of boredom and anxiety': S. Lyng, 'Edgework: A Social and Psychological Analysis of Voluntary Risk Taking', *American Journal of Sociology*, 95, 4 (1990), pp. 851–86.

31 The profound impact of praise and positive reinforcement in shaping children's behaviour has been the subject of a range of psychological and sociological studies. For further discussion see W. Hartup, 'Social Behaviour of Children', *Review of Educational Research*, 35, 2 (1965), pp. 122–9; M. Bornstein, *Handbook of Parenting: practical issues of parenting* (New York: Lawrence Erlbaum Associates, 2002). In his study *Code of the Street*, Anderson also found evidence of negative reinforcement of gang participation, i.e. parents criticising children for not being tough enough or participating in this behaviour. The fact that no evidence of negative reinforcement was found during this study, however, does not mean it does not exist. E. Anderson, op. cit.

32 M. Seymour, 'Juvenile Justice in the Republic of Ireland' (Thematic Working Group on Juvenile Justice, European Society of Criminology). Available at www.esc-eurocrim.org/juvenilejusticeinireland. Accessed 9 Sept. 2009.

33 T. Kemper, 'Producing Emotions from Social Relations', *Social Psychology Quarterly*, 54 (1991), pp. 330–42.

34 M. Weber, 'Class, Status and Party', in H.H. Gerth and C. Wright Mills (eds), *From Max Weber: essays in sociology* (London: Routledge & Kegan Paul, 1948), p. 80.

35 Quoted in K. Nash, *Contemporary Political Sociology: globalisation, politics and power* (Oxford: Blackwell, 2000), p. 20.

36 Ibid.

37 M. Foucault, *The History of Sexuality: an introduction*, trans R. Hurley (Harmondsworth: Penguin, 1984), p. 93.

38 M. Foucault, *Discipline and Punish: the birth of the prison*, trans. A. Sheridan (Harmondsworth: Penguin, 1979), p. 25.

39 Until February 2010, Gardaí in Limerick used a relatively antiquated communications system which was regularly scanned by criminal gangs using their more sophisticated technology. Because of a general awareness of this practice in communities, residents were and sometimes still are reluctant to make complaints to Gardaí using phones systems as they believe that they are often subsequently identifiable as informants. D. Hurley, 'New Garda radios for Limerick division can't be monitored by criminals', *Limerick Leader*, 27 Feb. 2010.

40 *Limerick Leader*, 22 Oct. 2008, p. 1.

41 J. Wilson and G. Kelling, 'Broken Windows: The Police and Neighbourhood Safety', *Atlantic Monthly*, March (1982), pp. 29–38; R. Forrest and A. Kearns. 'Social Cohesion, Social Capital and Neighbourhood', *Urban Studies*, 38, 12 (2001), pp. 2125–43.

42 R. Lupton and A. Power, 'Social Exclusion and Neighbourhoods', p. 22.

43 In 2009, MEP Kathy Sinnott described how dumping was being used a 'weapon of terror' in Limerick's deprived estates, insisting 'Waste is a frontline weapon as bad as burning houses out. They don't dump indiscriminately but target specific people and places.' Another local resident added that 'rubbish is often used as a territorial marker', *Limerick Independent*, 22 Apr. 2009.

44 Pete's name has been changed to protect his identity.

45 W. Maynard, *Witness Intimidation: strategies for prevention* (London: Home Office, 1994).

46 C. Mirlees-Black, T. Budd, S. Partridge and P. Mayhew, *The 1998 British Crime Survey: England and Wales statistical bulletin 21/98* (London: Home Office, 1998). MVA, *Main Findings of the Scottish Crime Survey* (Edinburgh: Scottish Office, 1998).

47 C. O'Keefe, 'McAleese signs legislation to allow covert surveillance', *Irish Examiner*, 15 July 2009.

48 L. Campbell, 'The Evidence of Intimidated Witnesses in Criminal Trials', *Irish Law Times*, 24, 16 (2007), p.246.

49 A number of interviewees have also made reference to the problem of jury intimidation. However, as this problem concerns all citizens in the region who participate in juries, it was considered to be beyond the scope of the study.

50 D. Hurley, 'Two men in custody following Roy Collins murder', *Limerick Leader*, 9 Apr. 2009.

51 C. Lally, 'Ireland a more violent place says Garda chief', *The Irish Times*, 12 Jan. 2009; Dáil Debates, Vol. 681, Cols 539–68 (30 Apr. 2009).

52 D. Dutton, *The Abusive Personality: violence and control in intimate relationships* (Guildford: Guildford Press, 2007); L. Harne and J. Radford, *Tackling Domestic Violence: theories, policies and practices* (Milton Keynes: Open University Press, 2008).

53 Both Jock Young and Michael Welch have highlighted the tendency in late modern societies to imprison the socially excluded: J. Young, *The Exclusive Society: Social Exclusion, Crime and Social Difference in Modern Society* (London: Sage, 1999); M. Welch, *Ironies of Imprisonment* (London: Sage, 2005). In 1996, Paul O'Mahony conducted a study of prisoners in Mountjoy and found that their lives closely conformed to 'disadvantaged of the disadvantaged' in this chapter. Prisoners in Ireland also have higher levels of learning disabilities and psychological disorders than the general population. For further

discussion, see. P. O'Mahony (ed.), *Criminal Justice in Ireland* (Dublin: Institute of Public Administration, 2002); Combat Poverty Agency, Submission to the National Crime Council on the Consultation Paper 'Tackling the Underlying Causes of Crime: A Partnership Approach' (Dublin: Combat Poverty Agency, 2002), p. 2.

54 L. Wacquant, *Urban Outcasts: a comparative sociology of advanced marginality* (Cambridge: Polity Press, 2007); L. Wacquant, *Punishing the Poor: the neoliberal government of social insecurity* (Durham, NC: Duke University Press, 2009).

55 P. Kelleher et al., *Voices of Families Affected by Imprisonment* (Limerick: Bedford Row Family Project, 2007), p. 45.

56 Ibid.

57 Ibid., p. 52.

58 Within criminology, there is surprisingly little research on the relationship between criminal hierarchies and the prison system apart from C. Morelli, *Inside Criminal Networks* (New York: Springer, 2009). However, anecdotal evidence suggests that strong relationships between criminal and prison hierarchies are not uncommon and exist in Brazil, Mexico and the Middle East.

59 T. Einat and A. Wall, 'Language, Behaviour and Culture in Prison: The Israeli Case', *Asian Journal of Criminology*, 1, 2 (2006), pp. 173–89; M Kaminski, *Games Prisoners Play: The tragicomic world of polish prison* (Princeton University Press, 2004).

60 Kelleher et al., p. 33.

61 Ibid., p. 40.

62 Ibid., p. 47.

63 Ibid., p. 35.

64 Ibid., p. 36.

65 For further discussion of the monetary needs of prisoners and the difficulties of prison visits see P. Kelleher et a.l,op. cit., p. 15; See also J. Breen, 'The Ripple Effects of Imprisonment on Prisoners' Families', Working Notes, 59 (2008 , pp. 19–24, available at www.jcfj.ie.

66 T. Brady and F. Black, 'Prisoner cell phone cheek sparks jail probe', *Irish Independent*, 2 May 2007.

67 T. Brady, 'Jails to jam calls from prisoners mobiles', *Irish Independent*, 1 Apr. 2008.

68 P. Kelleher et al., op. cit., p. 60.

69 D. Raleigh, 'Minister raps critics of Criminal Justice Bill', *Limerick Independent*, 8 July 2009.

70 D. Held and A. McGrew, 'The Great Globalisation Debate', in Held and McGrew (eds), *The Global Transformations Reader* (Cambridge: Polity Press, 2000), p. 3.

71 Global commodity chain analysis originated in world systems analysis developed by Immanuel Wallerstein (1974). Gereffi and Korzeniewicz argue that these commodity chains consist of 'sets of interorganisational networks clustered around one commodity or product linking households, enterprises and states to one another within the world economy' (1994, p. 2). Nodes are at the points at which specific processes within the commodity chain take place. For further discussion see G. Gereffi and M. Korzeniewicz, *Commodity Chains and Global Capitalism* (Connecticut: Praeger, 1994).

72 J. Holland, *Ecstacy: The Complete Guide: A Comprehensive look at the risks and benefits* (New York: Inner Traditions/Bear Company, 2001).

73 A. Bracken and J. MacCarthy, 'Can anything save Limerick now?' *Sunday Tribune*, 19 Apr. 2009.

74 Europol estimates that there are nine criminal gangs (including Limerick-based gangs) operating drugs smuggling and gun-running activities across Europe. Director of Europol Rob Wainwright has stated that his agency believes that these activities are focused on the 'Northwest European hub', a region that includes Ireland, France, Spain, Holland and some Scandinavian and Baltic states. For further discussion, see

C. Lally, 'Nine criminal gangs active across Europe says Europol', *The Irish Times*, 28 Aug. 2009.

75 In terms of these relationships, there has been speculation about the relationship between Limerick criminal gangs and the Yardies, a UK-based Afro-Carribean gang which has a prominent role in the trade of drugs and guns. J. Woulfe, 'The life and crimes of Mr. Big', *Irish Examiner*. 5 Jan. 2006.

76 A. Papachristos, 'Gang World', *Foreign Policy*, Mar/Apr. 2005, pp. 27–32.

77 Ibid.

78 C. Coulter and S. Coleman (eds), *The End of Irish History: critical reflections on the Celtic Tiger* (Manchester University Press, 2003); R. MacSharry and P. White, *The Making of the Celtic Tiger: the inside story of Ireland's boom economy* (Cork: Mercier Press, 2000); P. Kirby, L. Gibbons and M.Cronin (eds), *Reinventing Ireland: culture, sciety and the global economy* (London: Pluto, 2002). K. Keohane and C. Kuhling, *Collision Culture: transformations of everyday life in Ireland* (Dublin: Liffey Press, 2004).

79 L. Sklair, 'Social Movements for Global Capitalism: The Trans-national Capitalist Class in Action', *Review of International Political Economy*, 4, 5 (2002), pp. 466–526.

80 N. Rabbitts, 'Gangster in Death Threats to Bloggers', *Limerick Chronicle*, 18 Aug. 2009, p. 1.

81 A. Bracken and J. MacCarthy, 'Can anything save Limerick now?' *Sunday Tribune*. 19 Apr. 2009.

82 B. Duggan, 'I know where you are – gang threatens rival on Youtube', *Irish Independent*, 11 June 2009.

83 A. Papachristos, 'op. cit., p. 27

84 J. Hagedorn, *A World of Gangs: armed young men and gangsta culture* (Minneapolis: University of Minnesota Press, 2009), p. 86.

85 U. Mullally, 'Limerick rappers revel in gangster lifestyle as "Stab City Thugs" gain support on Bebo', *Sunday Tribune*. 13 Apr. 2008.

86 M. Kimmel and A. Aronson, *Men and Masculinities: a social, cultural and historical encyclopaedia* (New York: ABC, 2003) p. 660.

87 J.L. Cyr, 'The Folk Devil Reacts: Gangs and Moral Panics', *Criminal Justice Review*, 28, 1 (2002), pp. 26–46.

88 R. MacSharry and P. White, *The Making of the Celtic Tiger* (Cork: Mercier Press, 2001), p. 65.

89 K. Keohane and C. Kuhling, *Collision Culture: transformations of everyday life in Ireland* (Dubln: Liffey Press, 2005), p. 113.

90 J. Lee, *Ireland 1912–1985: politics and society* (Cambridge: Cambridge University Press, 1989).

6. THE SOCIOLOGY OF FEUDING

1 S. McGearty, I. White, H. McGinley, 'Strategy to Reduce the Indicidence of Conflict Involving the Traveller Community in the Midlands', Midlands Travellers Conflict and Mediation Initiative (Birr: Health Service Executive, 2008); S. Ní Shúinear, *Conflict and Conflict Resolution'* Report for the Navan Travellers Workshops Ltd (Navan, 2005).

2 The analysis of Traveller feuds in this chapter draws extensively on primary data gathered for a research on Traveller education and integration written by myself and Maria Campbell. For this study, ninety-six interviews were conducted with Travellers, Traveller educators, Gardaí, local community representatives and health care professionals in four locations: Ennis, Waterford, Dundalk and Mullingar. The research assistant on this project was Deirdre O'Riordan, MA. For further discussion see N. Hourigan and M. Campbell, *The TEACH Report. Traveller Education and Adults: crisis, challenge and change* (Athlone: National Association of Travellers Centres, 2010).

3 J.A. Simpson (ed.), *Oxford English Dictionary* (Oxford: Oxford University Press, 2007), p. 234.

4 C.F. Ansley (ed.), *The Columbia Encyclopaedia* (New York: Columbia University Press, 6th Edition, 2000), p. 255.

5 R. Gould, 'Collective Violence and Group Solidarity, *American Sociological Review*, 64, 3 (1999), pp. 356–80.

6 M. Weber, *Wirtschaft und Gesellschaft* (Tubingen: Mohr, 1980), p. 25. J. Rosenthal, 'Marriage and the Blood Feud in Heroic Europe', *British Journal of Sociology*, 17, 2 (1966), pp. 133–44; É. Durkheim, *Les Formes Élémentaires de la Vie Religeuse. Le Systéme Totémique en Australie* (Paris: Presses Universititaires de France, 1968), R, Gould, 'Collective Violence and Group Solidarity', *American Sociological Review*, 64, 3 (1999), pp. 356–80.

7 J. Grutzpalk, 'Blood Feud and Modernity: Max Weber's and Émile Durkheim's theories', *Journal of Classical Sociology*, 2, 2 (2002), pp. 115–34. Quote from pp. 120–1.

8 É. Durkheim, op. cit.

9 See for example, J. Cusack, 'Revealed: what really happened in Limerick feud', *Sunday Independent*, 2 Feb. 2003; J. Cusack, 'Gang alliances and blood feuds are fuel for violent Ireland', *Sunday Independent*, 27 Apr. 2006.

10 P. O'Donnell, *Irish Faction Fighters of the 19th Century* (Dublin: Anvil Books, 1975;) J. Harrington, *The English Traveller in Ireland: accounts of Ireland and the Irish through fve centuries* (Dublin: Wolfhound Press, 1991).

11 W. Carleton, 'The Battle of the Factions', in *Traits and Stories of the Irish Peasantry*, vol. 1 (Buckinghamshire: Colin Smythe Ltd, 1844); L. Cullen, *Life in Ireland* (London: Batsford, 1968); P. O'Donnell, op. ccit.

12 Statement made by Major Powell to the House of Lords in 1824; Cited in C. Lewis, *Local Disturbances in Ireland* (London, 1836).

13 P. O'Donnell, op. cit., p. 22–3.

14 Personal communication by local Limerick historian and former Mayor of Limerick, Frank Prendergast, 23 Nov. 2008.

15 Ibid.

16 E. Dillon, *The Outsiders* (Dublin: Merlin Publishing, 2006), p. 116.

17 '100 recorded incidents in local feud', *Waterford Today*, 24 Sept. 2008.

18 J., 'Lifestyle of Travellers real enemy', *Sunday Business Post*, 3 August 2008.

19 These interviews were conducted in four sites (Ennis, Dundalk, Waterford and Mullingar) between October 2009 and February 2010. Feuding within the Traveller community has been a significant problem in three of these towns (Ennis, Waterford, Mullingar). The overall sample size for this interview series was ninety-six. Fifty of this sample were Travellers while forty-six were community stakeholders. These stakeholders included members of An Garda Síochána, school principals, local politicians, community activists, and stakeholders in Traveller adult education including managers of Senior Traveller Training Centres and Youthreach programmes.

20 J. MacLaughlin, *Travellers and Ireland: Whose Country, Whose History?* (Cork: Cork University Press, 1995); B. Fanning, *Racism and Social Change in the Republic of Ireland* (Manchester: Manchester University Press, 2002); J. Helleiner, *Irish Travellers: racism and the politics of culture* (Toronto: University of Toronto Press, 2000).

21 See for example M. Donohue, R. McVeigh and M. Ward, 'Misli, Crush, Misli: Irish Travellers and Nomadism', Irish Travellers Movement, www.itmtrav.com/publications/mislicrushmisli.html, accessed 3 March 2010.

22 M. McDonagh, 'Nomadism in Irish Travellers' Identity', in M. McCann, S. O'Siochain and J. Ruane (eds), *Irish Travellers: culture and identity* (Belfast: Institute of Irish Studies, Queens University Belfast, 1994), pp. 46–72.

23 For instance, one of Ní Shúinéar's informants comments, 'see, Travellers don't travel anymore. So you get sick of one another. When Daddy was growing up, they were in a different camp every month, you know what I mean? They'd stay for two or three weeks in the winter, and you'd move off then. But now Sinéad, the result of stopping in

the one place: you don't mix.' Quoted in Sinead Ní Shúinéar. *Conflict and Conflict Resolution* (Navan: A report for the Navan Travellers Workshops Ltd, 2005), p. 10.

24 S. Ní Shúinear, op. cit., p. 10.

25 Ibid., p. 9.

26 Ibid., p. 9.

27 M. Donohue, R. McVeigh and M. Ward, op. cit.

28 All names changed to protect identity of informants.

29 Noreen comments, 'When we have problems with another family, we have one man in our family, the negotiator we call him and he sorts it out but there's a line that we never cross. But he says now that people are crossing that line more and more and the day will come when people don't listen to him no more.'

30 S. McGearty, I. White, H. McGinley, 'Strategy to Reduce the Indicidence of Conflict Involving the Traveller Community in the Midlands', Midlands Travellers Conflict and Mediation Initiative (Birr: Health Service Executive, 2008).

31 The seriousness of the fight is reflected in the demeanour and behaviour of the combatants and the witnesses who 'do not shriek encouragement or insults, as would spectators at a sports boxing match. In fact, they remain silent, impassive, arms folded, well back from the combantants; their solemn demeanour, and role as observers, is like that of the public gallery at court trial.' S. Ní Shúinear, op. cit., p. 8.

32 Ibid.

33 M. Hayes, *Irish Travellers: Representations and Realities* (Dublin: Liffey Press, 2006).

34 F. McGinnity, P. O'Connell, E. Quinn and J. Williams, *Migrants' Experience of Racism in Ireland: survey report* (Dublin: ESRI, 2006), p. 41.

35 Pavee Point, *Garda Diversity Strategy: Submission by Pavee Point Travellers Centre* (Dublin: Pavee Point, 2007), p. 40.

36 N. Joyce, *Traveller: An Autobiography* (Dublin: Gill & Macmillan. 1985); P. Dunne and M. Ó hAodha (eds), *Parley-Poet and Chanter: A Life of Pecker Dunne* (Dublin: A & A Farmer Publishing, 2004).

37 E. Dillon, *The Outsiders: Exposing the Secretive World of Ireland's Travellers* (Dublin: Merlin Publishing, 2006). pp. 118–19.

38 Pavee Point, op. cit., p. 4.

39 H. McDonald, 'Third gang sets up family rivalries to control drugs', *The Observer*, 2 Feb. 2003.

40 J. Guerin, 'Revealed: what really happened in Limerick feud,' *Sunday Independent*, 2 Feb. 2003.

41 See for example R.T. Oakes, 'The Albanian Blood Feud', *Journal of International Law and Practice*, 6 (1997), pp. 177–98; S. Schwandner-Sievers, 'Zur Logik Der Blutrache in Nordalbanien: ehre symbolik und gewaltlegitimation', *Sociologus*, 45, 2 (1995), pp. 109–29.

42 Late Limerick city councillor who was, prior to his political career, involved in some Limerick feuds. For further discussion of his life story, see A. Galvin, op. cit., p. 35.

43 A. Galvin, op. cit., p. 35.

44 For the North American model see J. Hagedorn, *Gangs in the Global City: alternatives to traditional criminology* (Chicago: University of Illnois Press, 2007).

45 In particular, B. Duggan. *Mean Streets, Limerick's Gangland: feuds, lost lives, the future* (Dublin: O'Brien Press, 2009).

46 The attempted murder of Christy Keane and the murder of Eddie Ryan are regarded as being particularly important events in the narrative of the contemporary Limerick feud(s).

47 The most prominent of these families are the McCarthys, Keanes, Ryans, Collopys, Dundons.

48 For further discussion, see B. Duggan, op. cit., pp. 188–206.

49 Ibid., p. 43.

50 Status which dominates all other forms of social prestige. For further discussion, see E. Hughes, 'Dilemmas and Contradictions of Status', *American Journal of Sociology*, 50 (1945), pp. 353–9.

51 Name changed to protect informant. Tommy Red is a senior member of a Limerick feuding family.

52 M. McDonagh, 'Origins of the Travelling People', in E. Sheehan (ed.) *Travellers: citizens of Ireland* (Dublin: Parish of the Travelling People, 2000).

53 K. Allen, 'The Celtic Tiger, inequality and social partnership', *Administration*, 2 (1999), pp. 31–55.

54 N. Hourigan and M. Campbell, *The TEACH Report. Traveller Education and Adults: crisis, challenge and change* (Athlone: NATC, 2010), pp. 30–55.

55 Ní Shúinéar argues that because the Traveller community has no established political hierarchy, no single family can formally claim ascendancy over the other families. If one family member tries to claim superior status for their kinship group over another family, they must be confronted by that other family in order to prevent aspersions being cast on family honour. For further discussion see S. Ní Shúinear 'Irish Travellers: a culture of anti-hierarchy/Viaggiatori irlandesi: una cultura antigerarchica', in P. Giorgio (ed.), *La Dipendenza: Antorpologica della relazioni di domino* (Lecce: Argo, 2005).

56 Ní Shúinear. *Conflict and Conflict Resolution*, p. 40.

57 Historically, the Keane–Collopy and McCarthy–Dundon kinship groups represent the main opposing strands of the Limerick feud, bu, patterns of alliance both within and between these groups are constantly fluctuating. For further discussion, see B. Duggan. op. cit.; A. Galvin, op. cit.

58 P.M. Rodriguez Mosquera, A. Manstead and A. Fischer, 'Honor in Mediteranean and Northern Europe', *Journal of Cross-Culture Psychology*, 33, 16 (2002), pp. 16–36, p. 21.

59 J. Pitt-Rivers, 'Honor and Social Status', in J.G Peristiany (ed.), *Honor and Shame: the values of Mediterranean society* (London: Weidenfeld and Nicolson, 1965), pp. 18–77.

60 J. Hagedorn 'Gangs, Neighbourhoods and Public Policy', *Social Problems*, 38 (1991), pp. 529–42; J. Hagedorn, *Gangs in the Global City: alternatives to traditional criminology* (Chicago: University of Illinois Press, 2007).

61 J. Hagedorn, 'Gang Violence in the Post-industrial Era', *Crime and Justice* 24 (1998), pp. 365–419. Quote, p. 389.

62 B. Duggan, 'Parents in Court over children missing school' *Irish Independent*, 27 Feb. 2009, p.5.

63 J. Lewis Herman, 'Complex PTSD: A Syndrome in Survivors of Prolonged and Repeated Trauma', *Journal of Traumatic Stress*, 5, 3 (1992), p. 378.

64 M. Dwane, 'Self-harm is double the national average', *Limerick Leader*, 31 Mar. 2010, p. 2.

65 M.R. Walker. *Suicide among the Irish Traveller Community 2000–2006* (Wicklow County Council, 2008). Available at www.nosp.ie/book.pdf

66 P. Martyn, 'Trauma of Southill kids as bad as war zone', *Limerick Leader*, 19 Jan. 2009, p. 1.

67 D. Eitle and R.J. Turner, 'Exposure to Community Violence and Young Adult Crime: The Effects of Witnessing Violence, Traumatic Victimisation and other Stressful Life Events', *Journal of Research in Crime and Delinquency*, 39 (2002), pp. 214–37.

68 R.J. Turner and D.A. Lloyd, 'The Stress Process and the Social Distribution of Depression', *Journal of Health and Social Behaviour*, 40 (1999), pp. 374–404.

69 Lorita Purnell, 'Youth Violence and Post-Traumatic Stress Disorder: assessment, implications and promising school-based strategies' in C.W. Branch (ed.) *From Adolescent Gangs: old issues, new approaches* (Philadelphia: Taylor & Francis, 1999), pp. 115–27.

70 Timmy is a composite character of his male clients between the ages of sixteen and eighteen.

71 As above.

72 D. Harney. 'New inter-agency initiative aims to help Travellers stop local feuding', *Offaly Independent*, 2 Oct. 2009.

73 Pavee Point had a mediation service but now they refer clients to a conflict resolution service in Northern Ireland.

74 Since the 1990s, Traveller education initiatives have focused on progression of Travellers into the settled workforce. Not surprisingly, as many Travellers view this progression as a process of assimilation, Traveller education programmes have been relatively unsuccessful in delivering this outcome.

75 M. Dwane, 'Limerick Garda division to get new inspectors and sergeants', *Limerick Leader*, 11 Feb. 2010.

76 One leading member of a feuding family, Wayne Dundon, has suggested in an interview with the *Sunday World* that O'Dea's 2004 intervention 'saved many lives': *Sunday World*, 4 Apr. 2010, pp. 14–15. For further discussion of these conflict resolution attempts, see B. Duggan, op. cit., p. 120. J. Cusack, 'Historic handshake that may end the bloody Limerick feud', *Sunday Independent*, 21 Dec. 2008.

77 Duggan. *Mean Streets*, pp. 278–284.

7. Lessons from Limerick

1 J. Fitzgerald, *Addressing issues of Social Exclusion in Moyross and other disadvantaged areas of Limerick city. Report to the Cabinet Committee on Social Inclusion, April 2007*; available at www.limerickcorp.ie; accessed 26 July 2010.

2 Ibid., p. 9.

3 For further discussion of all these measures, see B. Duggan. *Mean Streets*, pp. 234–260.

4 D. Hurley and P. Martyn, 'Emergency Response Unit to be deployed in Limerick', *Limerick Leader*, 8 Apr. 2010.

5 N. Hourigan, 'Children and the Criminal Justice Bill', *Irish Independent*, 29 June 2009.

6 Limerick Regeneration Agencies, *Phase One Implementation Plan Submission*. Available at www.environ.ie/en/publicationsdocuments/filedownload,23218,en,pdf; accessed 26 July 2010.

7 The crime rate in Limerick was down by 33 per cent in 2010 following a drop of 14 per cent in 2009. See www.rte.ie/news/2010/0301/limerick.html; accessed 26 July 2010.

8 A. de Paor, 'Vandalism of CCTV cameras in Limerick blamed on criminals', *The Irish Times*, 26 Aug. 2009.

9 Blom Hansen and Stepputat highlight the range of informal sovereignties including gangs, vigilante groups, strongmen, insurgents and illegal networks which can emerge in post-colonial societies where power was historically distributed among many forms of local authority. For further discussion see T. Blom Hansen and F. Steppetat, 'Sovereignty Revisited', *Annual Review of Anthropology*, 35 (2006), pp. 295–315.

10 At the outset of the research, a deliberate decision was taken to conduct at least 33 per cent of the participant observation at night. Most of this observation was conducted from inside the homes of local residents in Regeneration estates.

11 Vinnie's name has been changed to protect his identity.

12 The secure Tetra communications system was introduced in Limerick in February 2010. D. Hurley, 'New Garda radios for Limerick Division can't be monitored by criminals', *Limerick Leader*, 27 Feb. 2010.

13 Roxboro Garda Station is open 24/7 and this has contributed to the success of criminal justice measures on the south-side of the city, but the Garda stations on the north-side and King's Island area have more limited opening hours.

14 In 2009, Minister for Justice Dermot Ahern, in a written response to a question tabled by Charlie Flanagan, acknowledged that there was significant overcrowding in Limerick prison. 'Overcrowded prisons not functioning properly', www.breakingnews.ie, 15 Mar.

2009; accessed 16 Sept. 2010. In June 2010, Conor Lally of *The Irish Times* found that the Irish prison service had been forced to free almost one in five prisoners because they simply had no room for them. C. Lally, 'Courts sentencing criminals at quicker rate than State can provide prison spaces', *The Irish Times*, 21 June 2010.

15 See N. Hourigan, 'Children and the Criminal Justice Bill', *Irish Independent*, 29 June 2009.

16 At the time of going to press, two major gang-related trials were ongoing in relation to the activities of criminal gangs in Limerick: K. Hayes, 'Eight men sent for non-jury trial', *The Irish Times*, 24 July 2010.

17 GOI, *Children Act* (Dublin: Government Publications Office, 2001).

18 Leahy and Partners, *Anti-Social Behaviour and the Law* (Limerick: Limerick Regeneration Agencies, 2009).

19 This refers to Section 129 of the *Criminal Justice Act* (2006) which amended Section 52 of *Children Act* (2001). GOI, *Criminal Justice Act* (2006) (Dublin: Government Publications Office, 2006); GOI, *Children Act* (2001) (Dublin: Government Publications Office, 2001).

20 Leahy and Partners, op. cit., p. 37.

21 GOI, *Criminal Justice Act* (Dublin: Government Publications Office, 2006).

22 Ibid.

23 For more information on Garda Diversion Programmes see www.justice.ie/en/JELR/Garda%20Youth%20; accessed 27 July 2010.

24 It is important to note that a range of diversion-type initiatives for the under-twelves has also been piloted and rolled out in Limerick. For a full listing of youth work initiatives see Limerick City Youth Framework at www.youthworkplanlimerickcity.ning.com. See also Limerick Social Inclusion Measures Working Group, www.limericksim.com.

25 Section 162 of the Criminal Justice Act (2006) deals with Behaviour Orders.

26 Leahy and Partners, op. cit., p. 35

27 The poor quality of care for troubled children has been the subject of a number of reports since 2000. Most recently, in July 2010, a study conducted for the now defunct Children's Act Advisory Board found that HSE special care units were failing more than half of the troubled children placed there. N. Baker, 'HSE failing troubled youth in care', *Irish Examiner*, 5 July 2010. However, a number of instances have been highlighted where troubled children in Ireland have been admitted to adult facilities such as prisons and Garda stations or facilities designed to deal with adult mental health issues. For instance, in 2007 *The Irish Times* reported that 165 young people between fifteen and seventeen had been placed in adult detention services. In August 2010, it was reported that the HSE was planning to admit children into a secure unit for troubled children which it had pledged to close down following a damning report by social service inspectors. C. O'Brien, 'HSE to put children in secure unit it promised to close down', *The Irish Times*, 2 Aug. 2010.

28 This Act has subsequently been amended to broaden the definitions of antisocial behaviour: GOI, *Housing (Miscellaneous Provisions) Act* (Dublin: Government Publications Office, 2009).

29 At the time of publication, the greater Limerick conurbation is currently governed by three local authorities: Limerick City Council, Limerick County Council and Clare County Council. This structure is under review.

30 Limerick city has the highest proportion of local authority housing in the country. For further discussion, see chapters by McCafferty and O'Connell.

31 According to an investigation mounted by Barry Duggan of the *Irish Independent*, Limerick City Council had received almost 1,000 complaints about antisocial behaviour since 2006; 1,133 people have been interviewed by four tenancy enforcement officers; 2,079 letters were issued warning about future conduct while 107 verbal warnings were issued to tenants; 37 notices to quit their homes were issued; 12 orders of repossession have come before the courts; 58 tenants voluntarily surrendered their homes after

numerous complaints; 69 homes have been taken back; 4 exclusion orders were made against individuals. For further discussion, see B. Duggan, 'Living on estates of fear', *Irish Independent*, 13 Sept. 2010.

32 A recent report by Community Mediation Works highlighted a number of problems with the reporting structures around antisocial behaviour under current local authority housing guidelines. For further discussion, see Community Mediation Works, *The State of Anti-Social Behaviour in Working Class Communities* (Dun Laoghaire: Community Mediation Works, 2010)

33 This mistrust of local authorities is supported by the findings of Humphreys' research on trust in local communities.

34 There has been a lot of local criticism of the role of the HSE in providing rent subsidy payments to tenants allegedly engaged in antisocial behaviour in this context. See K. Cronin, '24 Hour ASBO Hotline launched in Limerick City', *Limerick Leader*, 3 May 2010.

35 At the time of publication, the report of the Brosnan Review body on local government in Limerick had recommended the launch of a new super authority for the city and county which would also take in parts of Co. Clare in the city. See A. English, 'Limerick: The Third City', *Limerick Leader*, 31 July 2010.

36 GOI, *Children Act* (2001).

37 Probation and Welfare Service, *The Probation and Welfare Service and the Children Act 2001*; available at www.pws.gov.ie; accessed 8 Aug. 2010.

38 U. Kilkelly. 'The Children Act and the ECHR: Matters of Procedure and Substance', Paper presented at the Conference of the Irish Penal Reform Trust, 9 June 2009.

39 These orders include an emergency care order, interim care order, care order, supervision order, interim special order and special care order.

40 The traumatisation of children being taken into care was first noted by Fairbairn in the 1930s. For further discussion, see D. Celani, *The Illusion of Love* (New York: Columbia University Press, 1994).

41 C. O'Brien, 'Monumental failure to protect children in care', *The Irish Times*, 8 June 2010.

42 C. O'Connell, *The State and Housing in Ireland: Ideology, Policy and Practice* (New York: Nova Science Publishers, 2007).

43 For a full overview of these projects see www.limerickregeneration.ie.

44 See www.limerick.ie for a full listing of youth intervention projects in Limerick.

45 In 2009, 951 children were referred to Garda Diversion in the Limerick division, a drop of 300 from the previous year. P. Martyn, 'Gardaí note a drop in youth crime figures', *Limerick Leader*, 25 Aug. 2010, p. 9.

46 C. Coomey, '"Get us the hell out" plead undersiege family', *Limerick Post*, 13 Nov. 2010.

47 J. Katz, *The Seduction of Crime* (New York: Basic Books, 1988).

48 Ibid., p. 9.

49 S. Lyng, 'Edgework: A Social Psychological Analysis of Voluntary Risk Taking', *American Journal of Sociology*, 95 (1990), pp. 851–86, p. 853.

50 Ibid., p. 858.

51 W. Miller, 'Adolescents on the Edge: The Sensual Side of Delinquency', in S. Lyng (ed.) *Edgework: The Sociology of Risk-taking* (New York: Routledge, 2005), pp.161–2.

52 N. Miller, op. cit., p. 162.

53 A. Goodman, 'Addiction: definition and implications', *British Journal of Addiction,* 85 (1990), pp. 1403–8.

54 See R. McCormick, A. Russo, L. Ramirez and J. Taber, 'Affective Disorders Among Pathological Gamblers Seeking Treatment', *American Journal of Psychiatry*, 141 (1984), pp. 215–18.

55 N. Hourigan, 'Community Violence: Fear, Feuding and Related Problems in Limerick City', Workshop Presentation to Health Service Executive, Raheen, Limerick, 21 Apr. 2010.

56 L. Post, Review of 'Changing Addictive Behaviour: Bridging Clinical and Health Strategies', *Journal of Correctional Health Care*, 8 (2001), p. 87; J. Tucker et al. (ed.), *Changing Addictive Behaviour: bridging clinical and public health strategies* (New York: Guilford Press, 1999).

57 This call was made by Anne Marie McMahon, former Chief Superintendent at Roxboro Garda Station, Limerick: M. Hobbins, 'Gardaí call for parents' support', *Limerick Post*, 24 June 2009.

58 It is argued that in 2006 Limerick became a major distribution centre for heroin outside of Dublin. The increasing drug use and particularly heroin addiction became very visible on the streets of these estates during the course of this research. Evidence of a heroin epidemic in Limerick was also highlighted by Kelleher and Associates in their research on prisoners' families for the Bedford Row project. See J. Cusack, 'Gardaí fear epidemic of heroin in rural areas', *Sunday Independent*, 30 Nov. 2008; P. Kelleher et al., *Voices of Families Affected by Imprisonment* (Limerick: Bedford Row Family Project, 2007).

59 S. Brophy, *National Care Planning Project 2005: Independent Evaluation* (Ennis: Health Service Executive).

60 These guidelines have been in place to regulate child protection in Ireland since 1999.

61 *A Report based on an Investigation into the Implementation of Children First: national guidelines for the protection and welfare of children* (Dublin: Ombudsmand for Children's Office, 2010), available at www.oco.ie/childrenfirst; accessed 10 Aug. 2010.

62 Helen Buckley is a senior lecturer in the School of Social Work and Social Policy, Trinity College Dublin.

63 H. Buckley, 'More social workers will not keep children safe', *The Irish Times*, 14 June 2010.

64 The need for the social work system to focus more on frontline interventions was highlighted by the report of the Birmingham Safeguarding Children Board (BSCB) on the death of seven-year-old Khyra Ishaq. See A. Norris, 'Khyra Ishaq: Social services more worried about careers than child's wellbeing', *Daily Telegraph*, 27 July 2010.

65 A report by the Joint Working Group on Mental Health Services and the Police also called for the provision of a 24/7 social worker service in September 2009. In May 2009, a report on the deaths of a family of four including two children in Monageer, Co. Wexford also highlighted the need for an out-of-hours social work service. See A. Healy, 'Call for out-of-hours social worker service', *The Irish Times*, 11 Sept. 2009.

66 The problem of children at risk ending up sleeping in Garda stations at night or at weekends has been highlighted by the Children's Rights Alliance in Ireland and the Association of Garda Sergeants and Inspectors (AGSI). For further discussion, see J. Van Turnhout, '24-Hour Out-of-Hours Social Work service', available at www.childrensrights.ie; accessed 10 Aug. 2010.

67 A. Carey, 'HSE tell court no place for teenager', *Limerick Post*, 31 July 2010.

68 *A Vision for Moyross – Summary* (Limerick: Limerick Regeneration, 2008).

69 In 2010, HIQA found that the HSE were not complying with the requirement for a full assessment of relative carers within sixteen weeks of the child being placed in their care. While there are many benefits to relative and kinship care, Dr Valerie O'Brien writes, 'relative carers are more likely to live in challenging circumstances. Rearing children is resource intensive and the relative carer needs state support if they are to do the job well. For further discussion, see V. O'Brien, 'Family fostering needs its own support system', *The Irish Times*, 1 June 2010.

70 See A. Horvath, 'The Therapeutic Relationship: From Transference to Alliance', *Journal of Clinical Psychology*, 56, 2 (2000), pp. 163–73.

71 H. Ferguson, 'To protect children we must first protect social workers', *The Guardian*, 13 Nov. 2008.

72 In September 2010, Barnardos highlighted that 793 children in care in Ireland had no

assigned social worker. See J. McEnroe, 'No social worker for 800 children in state care', *Irish Examiner*, 15 Sept. 2010.

73 She noted, for instance, that 'Galway had the highest number of reports to the social work department in the State. Dun Laoghaire had the 31st highest. Both had the same number of social work posts. Ombudsman for Children's Office, p. 37.

74 British criminologist Jock Young has highlighted crime as one of the outcomes of social exclusion in a global context. For further discussion, see J. Young, 'Crime and Social Exclusion', in M. Maguire, R. Morgan and R. Reiner (eds), *The Oxford Handbook of Criminology* (Oxford: Oxford University Press, 2007).

75 For a discussion of the histories of a number of young men who have died in Limerick's disadvantaged estates see B. Duggan, op. cit.

76 B. O'Brien, 'What happened to all the missing foreign children?' *The Irish Times*, 27 Feb. 2010.

77 '37 Children die in State care since 2000', 28 May 2010. www.rte.ie/rtenews; accessed 29 May 2010. At the time of publication, investigations were on-going by the Minister for Children concerning the number of children who had actually died in HSE care.

78 *The American Heritage Dictionary of the English Language* (New York: Miffin Company, 2007).

79 The term 'area-based intervention' refers to programmes such as Limerick Regeneration which adopt a spatial approach to targeting social exclusion rather than focusing on specific aspects of policy at national level. Syrett and North describe the difficulties which these programmes have encountered in the UK context in generating long-term economic change in disadvantaged areas:

> Despite an array of approaches that have centred upon varying combinations of interventions related to physical re-development, enterprise promotion and labour market integration, success has been largely elusive. In this regard, a feature of the high profile neighbourhood renewal and NDC initiatives in England has been their relative failure to address the economic dimensions of problems besetting deprived neighbourhoods. These area-based approaches have emphasized an integrated and holistic approach to neighbourhood renewal – including issues of employment and economic development – but the evidence suggests that the economic dimensions of such policy interventions have been weak and governance arrangements have been poorly positioned to deliver effective economic development in deprived areas.

For further discussion, see S. Syrett and D. North, *Renewing Neighbourhoods: Work, Enterprise and Governance* (Cambridge: Policy Press, 2008), p. 45.

80 P. Martyn, 'President to visit on Regeneration launch anniversary', *Limerick Leader*, 31 Dec. 2009.

81 B. Duggan, 'Gavin and Millie turned into fireballs as they sat in car', *Irish Independent*, 25 Sept. 2007.

82 Fitzgerald Report. See Introduction, note 8 for details. John Fitzgerald is a former manager of Dublin City, thus his background is in local government.

83 Fitzgerald lists the first strand of his three-stranded approach as 'dealing with the issue of criminality'. He states, 'This will be fundamental to creating the conditions for other interventions to be successful and for restoring the confidence of local communities.' Fitzgerald Report, p. 3.

84 The other two strands he suggested were initiatives to target economic and infrastructural regeneration and co-ordinated responses to social and educational problems.

85 For a detailed overview of Limerick Regeneration's plans for each of these areas, see www.limerickregeneration.ie

86 K. Hayes, 'Limerick Renewal plan to be unveiled', *The Irish Times*, 10 Sept. 2008.

87 The difference between the Fitzgerald Report and the subsequent Regeneration Master Plan must be highlighted in this context. In terms of housing, Fitzgerald commented, 'Overall then, excluding St Mary's Park, there are approximately 1,000 houses that need serious attention, which is significant for Limerick city but relatively small in national terms . . . Regeneration of O'Malley will almost certainly involve extensive demolition.' This view of the level of physical Regeneration required in Limerick city was considerably different from the picture which emerged in the subsequent Master Plan where it was proposed that all the houses in Regeneration areas be demolished and the estates rebuilt using a public–private partnership model. Fitzgerald Report, p. 14. See also A. Bracken and J. McCarthy, 'Can anything save Limerick now?' *Sunday Tribune* 19 Apr. 2009.

88 M. Cooper, *Who Really Runs Ireland: the Story of the elite who led Ireland from bust to boom and back again* (Dublin: Penguin, 2009); S. Ross, *The Bankers: how the banks brought Ireland to its knees* (Dublin: Penguin, 2010); F. O'Toole, *Ship of Fools: how stupidity and corruption sank the Celtic Tiger* (London: Faber & Faber, 2010).

89 On the discussion forum 'Ireland After Nama', Cian O'Callaghan comments on Limerick Regeneration: 'The project, in keeping with the state's policies for regeneration over the last decade, was to be rolled out through a public–private partnership model. As such, it has always been dependent on the construction and sale of a significant proportion of additional private housing units to fund the replacement of social housing along with a series of environmentally and socially oriented projects. In one of the estates, Moyross, for example, an even 50/50 split between 970 replacement social housing units and 970 additional private units was envisioned. Even during the boom PPP regeneration strategies have frequently led to the sidelining of the interests of existing communities in favour of catering to the interests of private profits for developers. John Bissett's work on regeneration in St Michael's estate, for example, suggests that residents' priorities were consistently marginalized as the PPP sought to build private apartments on the site. With this in mind, it raises serious questions about the future of Limerick Regeneration in the context of the property crash: firstly, whether this private sector funding would be forthcoming at all, and secondly whether it would be desirable if it did, given what must now be an even more conservative property investment climate.' http://irelandafternama.wordpress.com/tag/housing-policy-ireland/. Accessed 1 Sept. 2010.

90 'Budget 2009: €10m for Limerick Regeneration', *Limerick Leader*, 15 Oct. 2008.

91 M. Minihan, 'Limerick Regeneration to begin', *The Irish Times*, 18 June 2010.

92 See the executive summary of the Limerick Regeneration project. Available at www.limerickregeneration.ie/wp-content/uploads/2009/02/Executive_Summary.pdf. Accessed 31 Aug. 2010.

93 P. Martyn, 'Moyross summer camp leaders award night', *Limerick Leader*, 25 Aug. 2010.

94 P. Martyn, 'Moyross garden sowing seeds for positive future', *Limerick Leader*, 9 Aug. 2010.

95 'Law vs the order monks kick habit for charity', *Irish Independent*, 17 May 2010.

96 K. Cronin, 'Youths do justice to elderly groups', *Limerick Leader*, 25 Aug. 2010.

97 See www.limerickregeneration.ie/2008/07/presentation-to-keith-earls/. Accessed 16 Dec. 2010.

98 These programmes included summer camps, the Incredible Years Programme and Amamwele Project Southill. The Regeneration Agencies have also funded a range of sporting and musical activities including 'Sing out with Strings', the refurbishment of the Moyross Outdoor Sports Complex and rugby events with Young Munster RFC and the Shane Geoghegan Trust. For a full listing of these activities visit www.limerickregeneration.ie.

99 Leahy and Partners, *Anti-Social Behaviour and the Law* (Limerick: Limerick Regeneration Agencies, 2009).

100 According to the 'Frequently Asked Questions' section of the Regeneration website, 'The Principal function of the Regeneration Agencies is to get full buy-in and co-operation from other Agencies and Government Departments. This is essential. Also, we need to influence their policies and try and get change in the way that they do their business in the Regeneration Areas for the betterment of the Communities living there. We are satisfied with the progress being made on this issue but further progress is required.' www.limerickregeneration.ie/frequently-asked-questions; accessed 31 Aug. 2010.

101 A. Bracken, 'Clampdown on Limerick crime families', *Sunday Tribune*, 19 Apr. 2009.

102 In an article in the *Limerick Chronicle*, Supt Frank O'Brien of Henry St Garda Station is quoted as saying that the number of heroin addicts has dramatically increased in recent years, up to nearly 600 from 'almost zero' four years ago. See A. Sheridan 'Priest says city is in denial about extent of heroin problem', *Limerick Chronicle*, 17 Aug. 2010.

103 C. Coomey, 'We are losing the war on drugs – Gilligan', *Limerick Post*, 3 July 2010.

104 P. Martyn, 'Methadone clinic for city heroin addicts', *Limerick Leader*, 30 Aug. 2010.

105 In August 2010, Rory Keane of the HSE Mid-West was quoted as saying that there are 175 heroin addicts in the region undergoing methodone treatment, the vast majority in Limerick city. In his view, this suggests that there are more that 500 heroin addicts in the city. He said, 'there are very real concerns about heroin use in Limerick.' J. Woulfe, 'More that 500 heroin addicts in Limerick', *Irish Examiner*, 27 Aug. 2010.

106 At the time of publication, there was considerable press speculation about the location of senior gang members who had left Regeneration estates. It was reported that some individuals had been sighted in London and the Costa del Sol. There were also fears that some gang members would move to parts of counties Limerick, Clare and Tipperary. A series of raids linked to the activities of Limerick gangs during 2010 occurred in Dublin, Tipperary, Offaly and Kerry. See G. Fitzgibbon, 'Limerick Gardaí deny INLA have become active to thwart Dundon move to county', *Limerick Leader*, 11 June 2010. P. Martyn, 'Raids across country target Limerick gang members', *Limerick Leader*, 5 Aug. 2010.

107 Fitzgerald Report, p. 8.

9. MEN ON THE MARGINS

1 R.W. Connell, *Masculinitie* (Cambridge: Polity Press, 1995) or see 2nd edn (Cambridge: Polity Press, 2005).

2 R.W. Connell, 'Growing up Masculine: Rethinking the Significance of Adolescence in the Making of Masculinities', *Irish Journal of Sociology*, 14, 2 (2005), pp. 11–28; quote p. 14.

3 D. Cameron, 'Introduction' to D. Cameron (ed.), *The Feminist Critique of Language*, (London and New York: Routledge, 1998), pp. 1–21.

4 The full report, *Uncertain Futures: An Exploratory Study of Men at the Margins*, on which this article is based can be accessed from www.ul.ie/sociology.docstore/uncertain_futures. We would like to acknowledge the support given to the study by Margaret Griffin, Probation Service, and to the young men who shared their experiences with us. Their names and some personal details have been changed to protect their identity.

5 See Limerick Regeneration, Draft Plan (Limerick, 2008).

6 E. DeCleir, 'Public Housing in Limerick City: A Geographical Perspective', unpublished MA thesis (Limerick: Mary Immaculate College, 2003).

7 John Fitzgerald, *Addressing issues of Social Exclusion in Moyross and other disadvantaged areas of Limerick City: Report to the Cabinet Committee on Social Inclusion* (Dublin, 2007), p. 80.

8 The areas included are: Southill, Ballinacurra Weston, Moyross and St Mary's.

9   The percentage of lone parents with one dependent child less than fifteen years was 63 per cent in Moyross, 63 per cent in Southill and 57 per cent in St Mary's Park.

10 J. Baker, K. Lynch, S. Cantillon and J. Walsh, *Equality: from theory to action* (New York: Palgrave Macmillan, 2004).

11 S.M. Miller, 'Breaking the Credential Barrier' (New York: Ford Foundation, 1967) quoted in S.M. Miller and A.J. Savoie, *Respect and Rights: Class, Race, and Gender Today* (Maryland: Rowman Littlefield, 2002).

12 E. Smyth and D. Hannan, 'Education and Inequality', in B. Nolan, P.J. O'Connell and C.T. Whelan (eds), *Bust to Boom? The Irish Experience of Growth and Inequality* (Dublin: Institute of Public Administration, 2000).

13 C. O'Neill, *Telling It Like It Is* (Dublin: Combat Poverty Agency, 1992).

14 M. O'Donnell and S. Sharpe, *Uncertain Masculinities: youth, ethnicity and class in contemporary Britain* (London: Routledge, 2000).

15 E. Smyth and D. Hannan, op. cit.

16 See P. Willis, *Learning to Labour: how wrking class kids get working class jobs* (London: Saxon House, 1977); M. Mac an Ghiall, *The Making of Men: masculinities, sexualities and schooling* (Buckingham: Open University Press, 1994).

17 R. Sennett and J. Cobb, *The Hidden Injuries of Class* (Cambridge: Cambridge University Press, 1972). See also P. Bourdieu, *Distinction: social critique of the judgement of taste* (London: Routledge, 1984); S.M. Miller and A.J. Savoie, op. cit. (Maryland: Rowman and Littlefield, 2002); R. Sennett, *Respect* (London: Penguin, 2004).

18 E. Liebow, *Tally's Corner* (Boston: Little, Brown, 1967); W.F. Whyte, *Street Corner Society* (Chicago: Chicago University Press, 1943).

19 E. Green and C. Singleton, 'Risky Bodies at Leisure: young women negotiating space and place', *Sociology*, 40, 5 (2006), pp. 853–73.

20 See W.F. Whyte, op. cit.; P. Willmott, *Adolescent Boys of East London* (Middlesex: Penguin Books, 1969).

21 A.W. Connell, op. cit.

22 M.P. Rush, P. Brudell and A. Mulcahy, *The Nature and Impact of Joy Riding in Priorswood* (Dublin: Priorswood Task Force, 2006), p. 14.

23 J. Brannen and A. Nilsen, 'Young People's Time Perspectives: from youth to adulthood', *Sociology*, 36, 3 (2002), pp. 513–38.

24 S. Lyng, 'Edgework: A Social and Psychological Analysis of Voluntary Risk Taking', *American Journal of Sociology*, 95, 4 (1990), pp. 851–86.

25 P. McVerry, *The Meaning is in the Shadows* (Dublin: Veritas, 2003).

26 Committee of Inquiry into the Penal System (Whitaker Report) (Dublin: Government Publications, 1985).

27 See C. Ní Laoire, 'You're Not a Man at All!', *Irish Journal of Sociology*, 14, 2 (2005), pp. 175–94; P. O'Connor, J. Smithson and M. Das Dores Guerreiro, 'Young People's Awareness of Gendered Realities', in J. Brannen, S. Lewis and A. Nilsen (eds), *Young Europeans, Work and Family* (London: Routledge, 2002).

28 R.W. Connell, op. cit.

29 J. Brannen and A. Nilsen, 'From Fatherhood to Fathering: transmission and change among British fathers in four generation families', *Sociology*, 40, 2 (2006), pp. 335–52. Quote p. 340.

30 K. Kiernan, 'Non-Residential Fatherhood and Child Involvement: evidence from the Millennium Cohort Study', *Journal of Social Policy*, 35, 4 (2006), pp. 651–69.

31 F. McGinnity, H. Russell and E. Smyth, 'Gender, Work-Life Balance and Quality of Life', in T. Fahey, H. Russell and C. Whelan (eds), *Best of Times? The Social Impact of the Celtic Tiger* (Dublin: Institute of Public Administration, 2007).

32 The concept of patriarchal dividend is outlined by Connell in 'Growing up Masculine'.

33 J. Brannen and A. Nilsen, 'From Fatherhood to Fathering' .

34 See H. Ferguson, 'Fathers and Home', in K. McKeown, H. Ferguson and D. Rooney (eds), *Changing Fathers: fatherhood and family life in modern Ireland* (Cork: The Collins Press, 1998).

35 P. O'Connor, *Friendships Between Women* (Hertfordshire: Rowe Ltd & Harvester Wheatsheaf, 2002).

36 C.W. Franklin, 'Hey-Home-Yo, Bro', in P.M. Nardi (ed.), *Men's Friendships* (London: Sage Publications, 1992), p. 210.

37 Connell, op. cit.

38 A. Cleary, 'Death Rather than Disclosure: struggling to be a real man', *Irish Journal of Sociology*, 14, 2 (2005), pp. 155–76.

39 M. Begley, D. Chambers, P. Corcoran, and J. Gallagher, *The Male Perspective: young men's outlook on life* (Mid-Western Health Board and National Suicide Research Foundation, 2003).

40 J. Baker Miller, 'The Construction of Anger in Women and Men', in J.V. Jordan, A.G. Kaplan, J. Baker Miller, I.P. Striver and J.L. Surrey. *Women's Growth in Connection: writings from the stone centre* (New York: Guilford Press, 1991).

41 See T. Fahey, L. Delaney and B. Gannon, *School Children and Sport in Ireland* (Dublin: ESRI, 2005); P. O'Connor, *Irish Children and Teenagers in a Changing World* (Manchester: Manchester University Press, 2008).

42 R.W. Connell, op. cit.; Willis, op. cit.; C. Haywood and M. Mac an Ghiall, *Men and Masculinities: theory, research and social practice* (Buckingham: Open University Press, 2003); P. O'Connor, *Irish Children and Teenagers in a Changing World*.

43 R.W. Connell, op. cit., p. 20.

44 M. O'Donnell and S. Sharpe, op. cit.

45 J. Brannen and A. Nilsen, 'From Fatherhood to Fathering'.

46 Limerick Regeneration, Draft Plan (Limerick 2008).

10. Social Capital, Health and Inequality

1 D. McCafferty, *Limerick: Profile of a Changing City* (Limerick City Development Board, 2005); T. Haase and J. Pratschke, *New Measures of Deprivation for the Republic of Ireland* (Dublin: Pobal, 2008).

2 R.G. Wilkinson, *Unhealthy Societies: The Afflictions of Inequality* (London and New York: Routledge, 1996); R.G. Wilkinson, *The Impact of Inequality: how to make sick societies healthier* (London, New York: Routledge, 2005); R.G. Wilkinson and K.E. Pickett, 'Income Inequality and Population Health: a review and explanation of the evidence', *Social Science & Medicine* 62:7 (2006), pp. 1768–84; R.G. Wilkinson and K.E. Pickett, 'The Problems of Relative Deprivation: why some societies do better than others', *Social Science & Medicine*, 65, 9 (2007), pp. 1965–78.

3 See T. Haase and J. Pratschke, *New Measures of Deprivation*..

4 See R.G. Wilkinson, *Unhealthy Societies*.

5 See R.D. Putnam, *Bowling Alone: The Collapse and Revival of American Community* (New York: Simon & Schuster, 2000); R.D. Putnam and R. Leonardi, *Making Democracy Work: Civic Traditions in Modern Italy* (Princeton, NJ: Princeton University Press, 1993); OECD, *The Well-being of Nations: the role of human and social capital* (Paris, OECD, 2001).

6 See R.D. Putnam, *Bowling Alone*.

7 See R.G. Wilkinson, *Unhealthy Societies*; R.G. Wilkinson and K.E. Pickett 'The problems of relative deprivation'.

8 See R.G. Wilkinson, *Unhealthy Societies*.

9 See R.G. Wilkinson, *Unhealthy Societies* and *The Impact of Inequality*; M. Marmot, *Status Syndrome: how your social standing directly affects your health* (London: Bloomsbury Publishing, 2004).

10 See R.D. Putnam and R. Leonardi, *Making Democracy Work*.

11 See T. Haase and J. Pratschke, op. cit.

12 E. Humphreys and D.A. Dineen, *Evaluation of Social Capital in Limerick City and Environs*: *report to the HSE Mid-West area and Limerick City Development Board* (Limerick City Development Board, 2006).

13 E. Humphreys and S. de Burca, *Health Inequalities and Ageing in the Community: Report of the Findings and Conclusions of the Social Study* (Health Systems Research Centre, Dept. of Sociology, UL, 2008). Available at www.ul.ie/hsyrc.

14 R. Groves, A. Middleton, A. Murie and K. Broughton, *Neighbourhoods that Work: A Study of the Bournville Estate, Birmingham* (Bristol: The Policy Press, 2003); E. Humphreys, *The Role of Social Capital in the Economic Development of Disadvantaged Neighbourhoods? A Critical Analysis* (PhD Thesis, University of Limerick, 2005).

15 Putnam, op. cit., p. 167

16 A. Portes and P. Landolt, 'The Downside of Social Capital', *American Prospect*, 26 (1996), pp. 18–22.

17 See M. Woolcock, 'Social Capital and Economic Development: Toward a Theoretical Synthesis and Policy Framework', *Theory and Society*, 27 (1998), pp. 151–208; S. Aldridge and D. Halpern, *Social Capital: A Discussion Paper* (London: Performance and Innovation Unit, UK Cabinet Office, 2002).

18 See R.D. Putnam, *Bowling Alone*; D. Kim and I. Kawachi, 'U.S. State-Level Social Capital and Health-Related Quality of Life: Multilevel Evidence of Main, Mediating, and Modifying Effects', *Annals of Epidemiology*, 17, 4 (2007), pp. 258–69; K. Bolin and B. Lindgren, 'Investments in Social Capital: implications of social interactions for the production of health', *Social Science & Medicine*, 56, 12 (2003)), pp. 2379–90.

19 D.J. Pevalin and D. Rose, *Social Capital for Health: investigating the links between social capital and health using the British Household Panel Survey* (London: Health Development Agency, 2003).

20 L.F. Berkman and T. Glass, 'Social Integration, Social Networks, Social Support and Health', in L.F. Berkman, and I. Kawachi (eds), *Social Epidemiology* (New York: Oxford: Oxford University Press, 2000).

21 B. Kennelly et al., 'Social Capital, Life Expectancy and Mortality: a cross-national examination', *Social Science & Medicine*, 56, 12 (2003), pp. 2367–77.

22 W.J. Wilson, *The Truly Disadvantaged: The Inner City, the underclass and public policy* (University of Chicago Press, 1987).

23 J. Brooks-Gunn, et al., *Neighbourhood Poverty: context and consequences for children* (New York: Russell Sage, 1997); M. Wen et al., 'Poverty, affluence, and income inequality: neighbourhood economic structure and its implications for health', *Social Science & Medicine*, 57, 5 (2003), pp. 843–60; F. Hou and J. Myles, 'Neighbourhood inequality, neighbourhood affluence and population health', *Social Science & Medicine*, 60, 7 (2005), pp. 1557–69.

24 F. Hou, and J. Myles, op. cit., p. 1562.

25 M. Wen et al., op. cit., p. 845.

26 I.G. Ellen and M.A. Turner, 'Does Neighbourhood Matter? Assessing Recent Evidence', *Housing Policy Debate*, 8, 5 (1997), pp. 833–66.

27 W.J. Wilson, op. cit.; F. Hou and J. Myles, op. cit.

28 W.J. Wilson, op cit.

29 See H. Gans, 'Planning and social life: friendship and neighbor relations in suburban communities', *Journal of the American Institute of Planners*, 27, 2 (1961), pp. 134–40; J. Jacobs, *The Death and Life of Great American Cities: the failure of town planning* (New York: Random House, 1961); W. Sarkissian, 'The Idea of Social Mix in Town Planning: an historical review', *Urban Studies*, 13, 3 (1976), pp. 231–46.

30 R. Atkinson, 'Neighbourhoods and the Impacts of Social Mix: Crime, Tenure Diversification and Assisted Mobility,' *CNR Research Paper No. 29* (ESRC Centre for Neighbourhood Research, 2005).

31 See T. Haase, and J. Pratschke, op. cit.

32 See Humphreys, *The Role of Social Capital*; E. Humphreys, 'Social capital in disadvantaged neighbourhoods: a diversion from needs or a real contribution to the debate on area-based regeneration', *Irish Journal of Sociology* 16:2 (2007), pp. 50–76.

33 This scheme offered the possibility for local authority tenants to purchase private sector housing and release the local authority rented housing for occupancy by those on the housing waiting list. See also Chapter Three.

34 I. Docherty et al., 'Civic Culture, Community and Citizen Participation in Contrasting Neighbourhoods', *Urban Studies*, 38, 12 (2001), pp. 2225–50.

35 Generally, while the differences between neighbourhoods are statistically significant, the findings indicate a low to modest association between neighbourhood and trust in the various institutions (i.e. along the range 0 to 1, coefficients of association are between 0.203 and 0.263).

36 In the case of Inner City/Dock area, a significant proportion is neutral (neither trust nor distrust). As such, while the absolute level of trust might seem low, small proportions express distrust in the institutions compared, for instance, with the disadvantaged neighbourhoods where substantial proportions state they distrust the institutions.

37 While differences between the parishes are statistically significant, findings indicate a low to modest association between trust and location with the greatest variation being in relation to trust in the local clergy and sisters and in the social/community and welfare services of the health services.

38 A value of 0 indicates that the proportion showing high and low social capital are equal; any values above 0 indicate that the social capital is positive and values below indicate that the social capital is negative (more people lack it than possess it).

39 This follows the same pattern as that of provincial town neighbourhoods included in a further study, but the levels of social capital in the towns are higher overall and across all dimensions. See Humphreys, *The Role of Social Capital*; 'Social Capital in Disadvantaged Neighbourhoods'.

40 Sixteen issues were included in the neighbourhood study and nine in the study on ageing in the four parishes.

41 K.P. Balanda and J. Wilde. *Inequalities in Perceived Health: a report on the All-Ireland Social Capital and Health Survey* (Dublin: Institute of Public Health in Ireland, 2003); P.A. Hall, 'Social Capital in Britain', *British Journal of Political Science*, 29 (1999), pp. 417–61.

42 The study used the SF36 instrument as a subjective measure of health status. Using this instrument, eight scales of health are developed (e.g. physical functioning, bodily pain, etc.) and two summary components (physical health and mental health). See J.E. Ware et al., *SF-36 Health Survey: manual and interpretation guide* (Lincoln, RI: Quality Metric Incorporated, 1993, 2000).

43 See M. Marmot, op. cit.

44 R.G. Wilkinson, Unhealthy Societies and M. Marmot, op. cit.

45 Based on the Haase Index, 'St. John's A' ED, coinciding with St Mary's Park, has been ranked the most deprived of the 3,409 EDs in the state in the census 1991, 1996, 2002 and 2006. The Index is developed from census variables drawing on the Small Area Population Statistics. See T. Haase and J. Pratschke, op. cit.

46 See McCafferty's chapter in this volume for further discussion.

47 See C. Henning and M. Lieberg, 'Strong Ties or Weak Ties? Neighbourhood Networks in a New Perspective,' *Scandinavian Housing & Planning Research*, 13 (1996), pp. 3–26, quote, p. 8; J. Jacobs, op. cit.

48 P. Hall, 'Regeneration Policies for Peripheral Housing Estates: inward and outward-looking approaches', *Urban Studies*, 31 (1997), pp. 401–24.

11. BEHIND THE HEADLINES

1   METHODOLOGY EMPLOYED

Following the Glasgow University Media Group (see, n. 6 below), the methodology employed in our study adopts a tripartite approach to media analysis, incorporating content, production and reception. Specifically, we have undertaken a qualitative content analysis of print media and broadcast texts, interviews with media professionals and focus groups with residents and community activists in Moyross itself.

PRINT MEDIA CONTENT

Print media content was sampled from four newspapers, which were chosen for their diversity of audiences and styles. Specifically, we selected our sample from a national broadsheet (*Irish Independent*), two national tabloids (*Irish Mirror* and the *Irish News*) and a local imprint (*Limerick Leader*). The time period within which we selected articles was 1 Jan. 2006 to 31 Dec. 2007. We selected this timeframe in order to examine in detail the extensive media coverage of a specific case (an arson attack on two young children – Millie and Gavin Murray) and also to investigate media coverage of the Regeneration project which was subsequently announced in late 2006. Our sampling strategy returned a final total of 420 articles. (*Irish Independent* – 82; *Irish News* – 21; *Limerick Leader* – 179; *Irish Mirror* – 138). Once the articles were accessed they were entered into NVivo software, where they were subjected to qualitative content analysis. Content analysis can be defined as 'a research technique for making valid and replicable inferences from texts . . . to the contexts of their use' (K. Krippendorf, *Content Analysis: An Introduction to its Methodology* (Thousand Oaks: Sage, 2004), p. 18). Content analysis involves identifying themes, concepts, and patterns thereof, within the data. We infer meaning through interpreting these patterns. Themes and concepts may emerge from the data as a result of close reading and constant comparison, a process facilitated by sensitivity to: the relationship between the research question and the text and the relationship between the texts and the context to which meaning will be inferred.

BROADCAST MEDIA CONTENT

Television broadcasts were selected from RTÉ's *Six One News* and *Nine O'Clock News* programmes from 1 Sept. 2006 to 31 Dec. 2006 and using RTÉ's proprietary News Archive. In instances where the same report was broadcast by both programmes, only one was included in our sample. We also included a radio documentary in our analysis made by the local licensed radio station Live 95 FM. The documentary, broadcast in November 2006, was based upon a composite of radio broadcasts concerning the Millie and Gavin Murray story.

LOCAL MEDIA CONTEXT

Limerick's Live 95 FM is owned by the Northern Irish multimedia conglomerate UTV plc. and is the BCI licensed station for Limerick city and county. According to JNLR data, for the period 2007–8 the station had 44.5% of prime-time market share, with 84% of adults tuning in on a weekly basis. Its audience share of younger listeners has come under increasing pressure from the presence of SPIN Southwest owned by the Communicorp Group. The local print media is dominated by the *Limerick Leader* which is owned by the Johnston Group. Previously owned by the Buckley family and for a short while by the Leinster Leader Group, the *Limerick Leader* publishes five titles – the *Limerick Leader* City Edition; the *Limerick Leader* County Edition; the *Limerick Chronicle* and a smaller tabloid version of the *Limerick Leader* on Mondays and Wednesdays. The local print media also includes two free-sheet titles – the *Limerick Independent* and the *Limerick Post*. The national print and broadcast media have a reduced presence in the city. The *Irish Examiner* and the *Irish Independent* both have correspondents based in Limerick. *The Irish Times* and the tabloid media depend upon agency coverage, whileLimerick city is part of a much larger brief for RTE's Mid-West regional correspondent.

RECEPTION ANALYSIS

Two focus groups were conducted in Moyross following preliminary analysis of the print and broadcast media content. Each involved six participants, most of whom were residents of Moyross. In each focus group, one non-resident community activist also participated. Participants were sourced through the Moyross Community Forum, and as such, many of the residents to whom we spoke were active in their community.

PRODUCTION ANALYSIS

Semi-structured interviews were undertaken with five media professionals who work in the print and broadcast media sectors. All but one of the media professionals to whom we spoke have a broad remit with regard to covering events in the Limerick region. One is primarily a crime and court reporter, but also has a secondary, broader remit. A number of key themes emerged.

2   The frustration experienced by local community representatives with the negative image of Moyross and other local authority estates was noted, for example, by Fitzgerald in his report *Addressing Issues of Social Exclusion in Moyross and other disadvantaged Areas of Limerick City* (for full reference see Introduction n. 8). The Fitzgerald Report, which was a precursor to the setting up of the Limerick Regeneration Agency, notes the 'intense negative publicity' (p. 7) received by Moyross in 2006, as well as the wider implications for Limerick city as a whole resulting from its negative (media) image. This theme is repeatedly discussed in the Limerick Regeneration Agency's report *Limerick Regeneration: A Vision for Moyross, Southill/Ballinacurra Weston and St Mary's Park* (Limerick, 2008). It recognises the implications of this negative image for the residents of socially excluded areas and also stresses the wider implications in terms of economic investment in the city.

3   C. Greer and Y. Jewkes, 'Extremes of Otherness: media images of social exclusion', *Social Justice*, 32, 1 (2005), pp. 20–31; A. Hasting, 'Stigma and Social Housing Estates: beyond pathological explanations', *Journal of Housing and Built Environment*, 19 (2004), pp. 233–54; B. Skeggs, 'The Making of Class and Gender Through Visualing Moral Subject Formation', *Sociology*, 39, 5 (2005), pp. 965–82.

4   S. Cottle, 'Ethnography and News Production: new(s) developments in the field', *Sociology Compass*, 1, 1 (2007), pp. 1–16; D. Hesmondhalgh, 'Inside Media Organizations: production, autonomy and power', in D. Hesmondhalgh (ed.), *Media Production* (Maidenhead and Milton Keynes: Open University Press. 2006), pp. 49–90; L. Grossberg et al., *Media Making: Mass Media in a Popular Culture* (London: Sage, 2006); G. Tuchman, 'Qualitative Methods in the Study of News', in K. Bruhn Jensen and N.W. Jankowski (eds), *A Handbook of Qualitative Methodologies for Mass Communication Research* (London: Routledge, 1991).

5   E. Devereux, 'Are You Sitting Comfortably? The Codes and Conventions of Irish Current Affairs Television', *Irish Journal of Sociology*, 1995, pp. 110–34.

6   T. Gitlin, *Inside Prime Time* (London: Routledge, 1994); G. Philo, 'News Content Studies, Media Group Methods and Discourse Analysis: A Comparison of Approaches', in E. Devereux (ed.), *Media Studies: key isues and debates* (London: Sage Publications, 2008), pp. 101–33.

7   S. Hall, 'The Television Discourse: encoding and decoding', *Education and Culture*, 25 (1974), pp. 8–14.

8   E. Devereux, *Understanding The Media*, 2nd edn (London: Sage Publications, 2008); P.J. Shoemaker and S.D. Reese, *Mediating The Message: Theories of Influences on Mass Media Content*, 2nd edn (Boston, MA: Longman, 1996).

9   E. Devereux, *Devils and Angels: Television, Ideology and the Coverage of Poverty* (Luton: University of Luton Press/John Libbey Media, 1998).

10 S. Iyengar, *Is Anyone Responsible? How Television Frames Political Issues* (Chicago: University of Chicago Press, 1991).

11 In September 2006, Millie Murray and her five-year-old brother Gavin were severely burned in an arson attack on their mother's car in Moyross. Three teenagers from Moyross were subsequently convicted of the petrol bomb attack on the children. The arson attack on these two young children was the final catalyst for state intervention in Moyross. The cabinet asked a former Dublin City Manager to carry out an immediate assessment of the issues prevailing in the estate. Fitzgerald reported back on the scale of social exclusion in March 2007 and the Cabinet's Committee on Social Inclusion agreed to the creation of two Regeneration companies to oversee the redevelopment of four estates in Limerick city, including Moyross. While there has been a major focus in the plans (and in their reception) on the moves to physically regenerate these estates through a major demolition and rebuilding programme, there is also a focus on how social regeneration might take place. The estimated cost of Regeneration is in the region of €3.6 Billion Euros. See www.limerickregeneration.ie.

12 There are some notable differences between the local and national media in terms of how Moyross is reported. Stories which had crime as their primary theme account for 52% of the *Limerick Leader* articles, compared to 77% of the *Irish Independent*'s, 88% of the *Irish Mirror*'s, and 90% of *Irish News* articles.

13 J. Kitzinger, 'Media Templates: patterns of association and the reconstruction of meaning over time', *Media, Culture and Society*, 22, 1 (2000), pp. 61–84.

14 V. Lens, 'Public Voices and Public Policy: changing the societal discourse on welfare', *Journal of Sociology and Social Welfare*, 29, 1 (2002), pp. 137–54; M. Edelman, 'Language, Myths and Rhetoric', *Society*, 35, 2 (1998), pp. 131–9.

15 M. Corcoran, 'Social Structure and Quality of Life,' in T. Fahey (ed.) *Social Housing in Ireland: a study of success, failure and lessons learned* (Dublin: Oak Tree Press, 1999,) pp. 125–48.

16 See Chapter Ten.

17 For detailed references on the two large-scale studies on which Humphreys' research is based, see Chapter Ten.

18 See Chapter Ten.

19 See F. Wassenberg, 'Renewing Stigmatised Estates in the Netherlands: a framework for image renewal strategies, *Journal of Housing and the Built Environment*, 19 (2004), pp. 271–92; G. Gourlay, 'It's Got a Bad Name and It Sticks . . . approaching stigma as a distinct focus of neighbourhood regeneration initiatives', paper presented at the EURA Conference, The Vital City, 12–14 Sept. 2007; J. Dean and A. Hastings, *Challenging Images: Housing Estates, Stigma and Regeneration* (Bristol: Policy Press/Joseph Rowntree Foundation, 2000).

20 Fitzgerald Report, p. 4.

12. City, Citizenship, Social Exclusion in Limerick

1 Combat Poverty Agency, *Welfare Policy and Poverty* (Dublin: Combat Poverty Agency, 2007), p. 332.

2 T.H. Marshall, *Citizenship and Social Class* (Cambridge: Cambridge University Press, 1950).

3 D. Watson, C.T. Whelan, J. Williams and S. Blackwell, *Mapping Poverty: National, Regional and County Patterns* (Dublin: Combat Poverty Agency 2005), p. 67.

4 The Institute of Public Health of Ireland, *Tackling Health Inequalities* (Dublin: Combat Poverty Agency, 2008), p. 14.

5 M. Norris and D. Coates, 'The Uneven Geography of Housing Allowance Claims in Ireland: administrative, financial and social implications', *European Journal of Housing Policy*, 7, 4 (2007), p. 455.

6 D. Watson et al., op. cit., p. 73.

7 P. Hubbard, *City* (London: Routledge, 2006).

8 J. Garreau, *Edge City: Life on the New Frontier* (New York: Doubleday, 1991).

9 P. Hubbard, op. cit., p. 47.

10 T.H. Marshall, op. cit.

11 W. Beveridge, *Social Insurance and Allied Services* (Cmd.6404, London: HMSO, 1942).

12 F. Powell, 'Civil Society, Social Policy and Participatory Democracy: past, present and future,' *Social Policy and Society*, 18, 1 (2008), pp. 49–58.

13 Z. Baumann, *Work, Consumerism and the New Poor* (Maidenhead: Open University Press, 2005).

14 R.M. Titmuss, *Commitment to Welfare* (London: Allen Unwin 1968), p. 143.

15 R. Levitas, *The Inclusive Society: Social Exclusion and New Labour* (Basingstoke: Macmillan, 1998).

16 D. Garland, *The Culture of Control: Crime and Social Order in Contemporary Society* (Oxford: Oxford University Press, 2001), pp. 98–102.

17 J. Donzelot, *Quand la Ville se Defait [When the City Falls Apart]* (Paris: Essais, 2006).

18 P. Bourdieu, *Acts of Resistance* (Cambridge: Polity Press, 1998), pp. 4–5.

19 See Fitzgerald Report.

20 J. Habermas, *Legitimation Crisis* (Boston: Beacon Press, 1975) p. 386.

21 D. Harvey, 'The Right to the City,' *The New Left Review*, Sept.–Oct. 2008, pp. 34–42.

22 R.G. Wilkinson, *The Impact of Inequality: How to Make Sick Societies Healthier* (London: Routledge, 2005), p. 23.

23 See D. Linehan and C. Edwards, *City of Difference* (Cork: Cork University Press, 2005).

24 M. Castells and P. Himanen, *The Information Society and the Welfare State: The Finnish Model* (Oxford: Oxford University Press, 2004).

25 See Fitzgerald Report.

26 D. Watson et al., op. cit., p. 149.

27 Government of Ireland, *National Spatial Strategy for Ireland 2002–2020: people, places and potential* (Dublin: Stationery Office, 2002)

28 M. Castells and P. Himanen, op. cit.

CONCLUSION: UNDERSTANDING LIMERICK? CONCLUSIONS

1 For Max Weber, blood feuds emerged in relatively lawless traditional societies where community conflicts were resolved along inter-family lines. Durkheim highlighted the potential for the emergence of feuds in societies characterised by mechanical solidarity, a form of social bonding more characteristic of traditional communal societies. See M. Weber, *Agrarian Sociology of Ancient Civilisation* (London: NLB, 1978 [1908]); E. Durkheim, *The Division of Labour in Society* (London: Macmillan, 1984 [1893]).

2 See P. Bourgois, *In Search of Respect*; E. Anderson, *Code of the Street*; J. Hagedorn, 'Gangs, Neighbourhoods and Public Policy'; J. Hagedorn, *Gangs in the Global City*.

3 Central Statistics Office, *County Incomes and Regional GDP, 2006* (Dublin: Stationery Office, 2009).

4 See P. Kirby, *The Celtic Tiger in Distress: Growth with Inequality in Ireland* (London: Palgrave, 2002); P. Kirby, *Celtic Tiger in Collapse: Explaining the Weaknesses of the Irish Model* (London: Palgrave, 2010).

5 In the first four months of 2010, reported incidents in Limerick were down by 21 per cent: R. Commons, 'Remarkable decrease in crime in 2010', *Limerick Post*, 15 May 2010.

6 For instance, in a recent incident, a man who had turned state's witness was publicly verbally abused and pelted with eggs on his wedding day: A. Sheridan, '"How could they do this" says bride pelted with rocks and eggs at church,' *Limerick Leader*, 21 Aug. 2010.

7 The media interest has now begun to include the partners of well-known criminals and their family activities. For an example, see A. Bracken, 'For better or worse: the gangster's moll', *Sunday Tribune*, 8 Aug. 2010.

8   This term was first used by Judge Carroll Moran following the collapse of a murder trial because two witnesses refused to testify. See 'Keane murder case collapse: community service orders for two locals' 31 July 2006. www.breakingnews.ie/archive/2006/0731/ireland/cwqlaufidql, accessed 22 Aug. 2010.

9   See D. Dutton, *The Abusive Personality: violence and control in intimate relationships* (Guildford: Guildford Press, 2007); L. Harne and J. Radford,. *Tackling Domestic Violence: theories, policies and practices* (Milton Keynes: Open University Press, 2008).

10 The importance of characterising this problem as community violence is highlighted by Garbino et al. in their book on the impact of chronic community violence on children. See J. Garbarino, N. Dubrow, K. Kostelny and C. Pardo, *Children in Danger: coping with the consequences of community violence* (San Francisco: Jossey-Bass Publishers, 1992).

11 Ombudsman for Children's Office, *A Report Based on an Investigation into the Implementation of Children First.*

12 S. Wilson and M. Zambrano, 'Cocaine, Commodity Chains and Drugs Politics: A Transnational Approach', in G. Gereffi and M. Korzeniewicz (eds), *Commodity Chains and Global Capitalism* (Santa Barbara, CA: ABC-CLIO, 1994), pp. 297–313.

13 See B. Duggan, op. cit.; A. Galvin, op. cit..

14 In his review of trans-national actors within globalisation, Willets highlights the role of criminal gang members involved in drugs distribution. P. Willetts, 'Trans-national actors and International Organisations in Global Politics,' in J.B. Bayliss and S. Smith (eds), *The Globalization of World Politics* (Oxford and New York: Oxford University Press, 2001), pp. 356–83.

15 M. Castells, *The Power of Identity: the information age vol. II* (Oxford: Blackwell, 1997), p. 9.

16 The term 'civic virtue' is usually applied to moral codes operating in nations under republican forms of government and refers to the cultivation of habits of personal living that are claimed to be important for the success of the community. For further discussion, see R. Dagger, *Civic Virtues: rights, citizenship and republican liberalism* (New York: Open University Press, 1997). C. Sistane (ed.), *Civility and its Discontents: civic virtue, toleration and cultural fragmentation* (Kansas: University Press of Kansas, 2004).

17 P. Cullen, *With a Little Help from my Friends: planning corruption in Ireland* (Dublin: Gill & Macmillan, 2002); GOI, *Flood Report by Tribunal of Inquiry into Certain Planning Matters and Payment* (Dublin: Government Publication Office, 2002); K. Keohane and C. Kuhling, *Cosmopolitan Ireland: globalization and quality of kife* (London: Pluto, 2007).

18 See M.Cooper. *Who Really Runs Ireland;* S. Ross, *The Bankers;* F. O'Toole. *Ship of Fools;* G. Kennedy. 'Politicians' expenses' *The Irish Times,* 5 May 2009.

19 The major tribunals of inquiry established since the 1990s included the Beef Tribunal established in 1994; The Flood-Mahon Tribunal into planning irregularities which has published four interim reports. The Moriarty Tribunal which focused on payments to politicians and has yet to publish its final report at the time of publication.

20 L. Ryan, *Social Dynamite* (Cork: Cork University Press, 1960).

21 E. Maher and J. Littleton, *The Dublin/Murphy Report: A Watershed for Irish Catholicism* (Dublin: Columba Press, 2010).

22 T. Flannery, *Responding to the Ryan Report* (Dublin: Columba Press, 2009).

23 See Chapter Ten.

24 P. Martyn, 'President to visit on Regeneration launch anniversary', *Limerick Leader,* 31 Dec. 2009.

25 M. Minihan, 'Limerick Regeneration to begin,' *The Irish Times,* 18 June 2010.

26 McCafferty's research highlighted the Dock Road as an area of potential disadvantage. Recent press reports suggest that it is also an area where problems in relation to heroin addiction and drug dealing are developing, causing the Gardaí to launch Operation Waterfront. See C. Coomey, 'Drug den monitored', *Limerick Post,* 28 Aug. 2010.

27 It is important to note that the range of projects and programmes aimed at children

which have been established by the Limerick Regeneration Agencies have been significant. For a full listing of these activities visit www.limerickregeneration.ie.

28 The crime rate in Limerick was down by 33 per cent in 2010 following a drop of 14 per cent in 2009. See RTÉ news; www.rte.ie/news/2010/0301/limerick.html; accessed 26 July 2010.

29 A. Bracken. 'For Better or Worse'.

30 S. Bardon, 'Heroin addicts aged 10', *Irish Daily Mirror*, 20 Aug. 2010; C. Coomey, 'Outrage that Limerick to lose 11 drug workers', *Limerick Post*, 5 June 2010.

31 Supt. Frank O'Brien of Henry St. Garda Station is quoted as saying that the number of heroin addicts has dramatically increased in recent years, up to nearly 600 from 'almost zero' four years ago. A. Sheridan, 'Priest says city is in denial about extent of heroin problem', *Limerick Chronicle*, 17 Aug. 2010.

32 Supt Frank O'Brien is also quoted as saying, 'the use of heroin has had a major impact on other crimes, with heroin addicts frequently appearing before the courts on charges of thefts and burglaries, which have been carried out to feed their habits.' A. Sheridan 'Priest says city is in denial about extent of heroin problem', *Limerick Chronicle*, 17 Aug. 2010.

33 P. Kirby, *The Celtic Tiger in Distress*; P. Kirby. *Celtic Tiger in Collapse*.

34 See B. Fields, op. cit.

35 K. Keohane and C, Kuhling, *Collision Culture*.

Index

abuse 66, 69, 81, 134, 141
addiction 45, 49, 53, 67–8, 81–2, 136–9, 141, 174, 250
adult education 122, 159, 161, 163, 184
advocacy 151–2
affluence levels 7, 8, 9
age profiles 8, 16–17, 60, 205, 206
ageing 189
alcohol 45, 46, 67–8, 175, 181, 183
Allen, Tommy 49
Anderson, Elijah 55, 56, 76, 77–8
Angela's Ashes (McCourt) 44
antisocial behaviour 50–51, 53–6, 78, 82–3, 131–40, 197–8, 207, 239–40
Anti-Social Behaviour and the Law (Leahy et al.) 1132
arms dealing 31, 32, 54, 97–8; *see also* firearms offences
arson 27, 30, 53–4, 88, 175, 215, 225, 226
assault 69, 82, 88, 92, 174–5; *see also* fighting
asylum seekers 4
Atkinson, R. 190

balanced reporting 217, 228
Ballinacurra Weston 9, 15, 16, 18, 19, 45, 52, 56, 60–61, 150, 211
Ballynanty 9, 12, 19, 71, 157, 200
Barrett, M. 60
Baumann, Z. 236
Bedford Row Project 90–97
Begley, M. 181
belonging 193
Beveridge, William 235
Blaney, Neil 47
bonding social capital 188, 195–6, 201–2, 205, 207

Border region 29
bouncers 33
Bourdieu, Pierre 239
Bourgois, Phillippe 76
Brannen, J. 178, 180
bridging social capital 188, 201–2, 205, 207, 210
broken window syndrome 86
Brophy, Sinéad 141–2
Buckley, Helen 142
bureaucracy 142–3
burglaries 26, 30, 51
buzz 136–9

Campbell, Anthony 33, 34
cannabis 26, 56, 175
car ownership 7, 8, 234
Carew Park 17
Carney, Justice Paul 74
Carlow 26
Castells, Manuel 247
Castletroy 7, 190, 191, 193–207, 226
Catholic Church 44, 101, 104, 159–60, 200, 248–9
CCTV 59, 127, 160
Celtic Tiger 13, 98, 100–101
Central Criminal Court 122, 127
Central Statistics Office (CSO) 15, 24, 25, 27
Child Care Act 134–5
children
    abuse of 66, 69, 81, 134, 141
    achievements of 158
    activities for 49, 52–3, 155–6
    antisocial behaviour by 50–51, 53–6, 78, 82–3, 131–40, 176–8, 183, 197–8, 207

Behaviour Orders 133
detention system for 133, 143–4
effects of feuding upon 117–18
facilities for 135–6
foster care 144
in gangs 69–70, 81, 82–3, 131–2, 147–9
Garda Diversion Programmes 132–3, 136
neglect of 68, 69, 81, 141, 149
Ombudsman for 142, 147
parental control of 50, 53, 66–7, 83, 134, 136, 139–40
prosecution of 83, 132
protection of 68, 134–5, 140–49, 152–3
taking into care 134–5, 143–4, 149
Children Act 132, 134
Christ the King parish 190, 192, 193–207
citizenship 230–31, 235–41
city centre 8, 19, 190, 191, 193–207, 233
Clare County Council 12, 233
Cleary, A. 180–81
clergy, confidence in 198–200
clubs *see* nightclubs
Coates, D. 233
Cobb, J. 173
cocaine 26, 32, 56
Collins, Roy 33, 34, 89
Collopy gang 56
Combat Poverty Agency 230, 232, 233, 242
Commission on Itinerancy 106
Community Councils 49, 53
community groups 49, 52–3, 159–60, 162
community leaders 49, 163–4
community services 5, 8, 14, 19–20, 64, 151; *see also* social services
community spirit 155–66, 185, 193–6; *see also* neighbourliness
confiding 180–81, 184
conflict resolution 107–8, 122–4
Connell, Robert 169, 171, 176, 178
Connolly, John 32
consistent poverty 3, 15, 232
consumer goods 100–101, 174
consumption levels 8, 9
contested sovereignty 129
Corcoran, M. 226
Cork 10, 11, 24, 25–7, 220
Corpus Christi parish 190, 192, 193–207
counselling 181, 184

courts, confidence in 198–200
crime
antisocial behaviour 50–51, 53–6, 78, 82–3, 131–40, 176–8, 183, 239–40
arms dealing 31, 32, 54, 97–8
arson 27, 30, 53–4, 88, 175, 215, 225, 226
assault 69, 82, 88, 92, 174–5
burglaries 26, 30, 51
and children *see* children
community responses 33
connection with social exclusion 42, 46–59, 68–9, 71, 72–3, 148
drug dealing 23, 25–6, 31–7, 54, 56–9, 70, 79, 81–2, 97–8, 114–15, 174–6, 182, 239, 250–51
drug use 26, 35–6, 37, 56, 67–8, 81–2, 99–100, 153, 174, 250–51
explosives offences 25, 32, 174
fear of 27, 28, 29–30
firearms offences 25, 26, 30, 57, 82
joyriding 53, 98–9, 176–7, 183
media focus upon 213, 215, 216–17, 220
murder 24–5, 30, 31–2, 33, 94, 161–2, 174, 239
offensive weapons offences 25
official statistics 24–7, 42, 56–7
public perceptions of 29–30, 36, 42
receiving stolen goods 51, 54
reporting of 27, 28–9, 30, 53, 54, 57, 87–9, 160
robberies and muggings 26–7, 29, 51
shootings 82, 89
small-scale crime 46–7, 49–50
theft 46–7
victim survey statistics 27–31
see also criminal families; criminal gangs
Criminal Assets Bureau 34, 59, 122, 126–7
criminal families 51, 54–9, 70–71, 78–83, 84–5, 109–12; *see also* criminal gangs; feuding
criminal gangs
arms dealing 31, 32, 54, 97–8
conviction of 74, 88–9, 130–31
core members of 70–71
drug dealing 31–7, 54, 56–7, 70, 79, 81–2, 97–8, 114–15, 174–6, 182, 239, 250–51
and extended families 62

feuding 42, 51, 56, 62, 66, 70, 79–81,
    90–93, 95, 109–12, 113–15, 116–20,
    122–5, 182
and globalisation 97–102
and 'hard man' culture 75–8, 98–9
intimidation by 31, 32, 43, 57–8, 74, 81–
    3, 87–90, 92, 98–9, 113–14, 124,
    131, 239
murders 30, 31–3, 174
and prison 90–97
power hierarchies 78–83
production of fear 84–90
recruitment to 70, 80–82
relations with Gardaí 129–31
reprisals by
surveillance by 81, 84–5, 87, 95–6
territorial strongholds 31–2, 55, 57–8,
    79, 85
see also criminal families; feuding; teenage
    gangs
Criminal Justice Act 127, 131, 132, 250
criminal justice system 74, 88–9, 122, 123–
    4, 126–31
cultural tensions 48–50

Daly, John 94
de-centring 233–5
DeCleir, E. 170
demographic data 5–9, 60–61, 191–2
depression 86
deprivation see poverty
dereliction 85–7, 203, 225, 226, 234
Devereux, Eoin 213, 229, 248
Dillon, E. 106, 109
differential rents scheme 13
disability 232
Discipline and Punish (Foucault) 84
disguised compliance 144
Dissimilarity Index 10–11
domestic violence 45, 53, 67, 89–90, 96,
    122, 161
Donzelot, Jacques 238
Dooradoyle 7
dress codes 63, 99
drinking see alcohol
drug dealing 23, 25–6, 31–7, 54, 56–9, 70,
    79, 81–2, 97–8, 114–15, 174–6, 182,
    239, 250–51
drug use 26, 35–6, 37, 56, 67–8, 81–2, 99–
    100, 153, 174, 250–51

Dublin
    crime 24–7, 28, 29, 30, 31, 33
    criminal gangs 33, 131
    drug dealing 25–6, 33, 56–9
    media representations 220
    tenancy surrender scheme 13–14
Dundon, Dessie 31
Dundon/McCarthy gang 31–2, 34, 56
Durkheim, É. 104

Earls, Keith 151
economic growth 3
economic recession 13, 150, 250
ecstasy 56
edge city phenomenon 234–5
edgework 137–8, 176–7
editors 217–19
education 49, 58–9, 61, 64–5, 75, 122,
    171–3, 182, 184
educational attainment levels 8, 9, 205, 206,
    232
Einat, T. 92
emigration 46
employment 3, 7, 8, 9, 12–13, 17, 45–6, 64–
    5, 158, 178–9, 182, 232, 238–9; see
    also unemployment
empty nest families 8
episodic frameworks 213, 214
equality 231, 238–9
ethnic minorities 55, 232, 233, 238
Exclusion Orders 133
explosives 25, 32, 174
extended families 62–3, 64, 66, 80–81, 89,
    112–15, 144, 251–2

factorial ecology 5–6
factory closures 12–13, 52, 239
Fahey, Tony 42
fair fights 108
families
    importance of 61–3, 72
    instability of 66–7
    and status 62, 78–9, 112–15
    see also criminal families; extended families
family honour 112–15
family households 7
fatherhood 75, 170, 180
fear
    of antisocial behaviour 51
    of child protection services 68

of crime 27, 28, 29–30
and criminal gangs 57–8, 70–71, 75–83,
   95–6
and globalisation 97–102
and prison 90–97
production of 83–90
of reporting and testifying 74, 85, 87–9,
   113–14, 124
of reprisals 28, 30, 32, 87–9, 113–14
and respect 50, 75–8
see also intimidation
Ferguson, Harry 144
Ferriter, D. 54
feuding
criminal gangs 42, 51, 56, 62, 66, 70,
   79–81, 90–93, 95, 109–12, 113–15,
   116–20, 122–5, 174–6, 182
definition 103–5
and family 112–15
history of 105
and stress 115–20
in the Traveller community 106–9, 112–
   13, 115–16, 120–22
ways of addressing 120–5
see also criminal families; criminal gangs
fighting 50, 51, 62–3, 108; see also assault
firearms offences 25, 26, 30, 57, 82; see also
   shootings
Fitzgerald, Brian 33
Fitzgerald Report 12, 42, 126–7, 150, 153–
   4, 170
foreign nationals 4, 8
forensics 34
foster carers 144
Foucault, Michel 83–4, 85
France 239
Franklin, C.W. 180

Gaisce awards 158
Galvin, A. 46, 50, 59
Galway 10–11, 24, 220
gambling 67–8
gang culture 63, 99–100
gangs see child gangs; criminal gangs;
   teenage gangs
Gardaí
accessibility of 130
activity of 32, 126–31
calls for Garda sub-station 50, 53
community Gardaí 126–31, 160

complaints of harassment 108, 177
confidence in 28–9, 30, 89, 127–8, 198–
   200
conviction rates 89
dealing with children 132–3
dissatisfaction with 54, 177
distrust of 45, 177
Diversion Programmes 132–3, 136
effectiveness of 51, 54
Emergency Response Unit 59, 122, 127
crime statistics 24–7, 42, 56–7
Operation Anvil 31, 127
persons known to 36
policing policy 126–31, 240
reporting of crimes to 27, 28–9, 30, 53,
   54, 57, 87–9, 160
and Traveller community 108–9, 120–21
visibility of 126, 127–8
Garland, D. 238
Garryowen 8, 233
gender profiles 16–17
gender roles 179–80
Gilligan gang 34
girl guides 49
Gleeson, Willie 47
Glenagross Park 48, 57
globalisation 4, 97–102
Goodman, Aviel 138, 139
Gould, Roger 104
graffiti 62, 82, 85, 136
Grutzpalk, J. 104
Guerin, Veronica 34
gun crime see arms dealing; firearms offences;
   shootings

Haase Index 190
Habermas, J. 240
Hagan, J. 37
Hagedorn, John 99, 115
Halpin's 52
'hard man' culture 51, 62–3, 75–8, 98–9,
   176–8
Harte, Patrick 33
Harvey, D. 240
Haynes, Amanda 229, 248
health 185–7, 188–9, 193, 198–200, 205–7,
   208–9
Health Service Executive 133–5, 141–3,
   146–7, 149, 152–3
Held, D. 97

Herman, Judith 116–17
heroin 35, 141, 175, 250
Hill, A. 76–7
Hobbs, R. 33
hope 165
horses 56, 72, 85, 177, 225, 226
Hourigan, Niamh 31, 32, 226, 227
Household Budget Survey (CSO) 24, 27–31
household types 7, 8, 11–12, 15–17
Housing Act 133
housing policy 13–14, 19–20, 42, 47–8,
    133–4, 237
housing types
    local authority rented 8–9, 11, 12, 13–
        14, 232, 233
    owner-occupied 7, 11
    privately rented 8, 9, 52, 232, 233
    and segregation 10–14, 42
    slums 44–5, 47
    tenure-mixing 20, 48–9, 209–10
housework 178, 179–80
Humphreys, Eileen 72, 128, 144, 148–9,
    226, 229, 247–8
Hyland, Martin 33
Hyland gang 33, 34
hyper-vigilance 79–80, 82, 96, 117, 118–19

images 225
immigration 4, 8, 196, 233, 239
inclusiveness 196, 197–8
income poverty 3, 18, 232
industry 3, 12–13, 52, 238–9
informing 45, 57, 87–9, 240
infrastructure 47–8, 150, 236, 243
in-migration 8
Institute of Public Health of Ireland 232–3
institutions, confidence in 198–200, 207–8
interdependence 45, 61–2, 155–66
internet 98–9
intimacy 45, 61–2, 63, 78, 155–66, 193–4
intimidation 28, 31, 32, 42–3, 50, 53–4,
    57–8, 81–3, 87–90, 92, 98–9, 239
    of witnesses 74, 88–9, 113–14, 124, 131
Irish Independent 116, 214
Irish Times 135, 142, 213
Irish Travellers Movement 121
Iyengar, S. 213

Janesboro 8, 12
Johnson, Thomas 45

journalists 212, 214–15, 217–19, 221–5,
    227–8
joyriding 53, 98–9, 176–7, 183

Kaminski, M. 92
Katz, Jack 137
Keane, Christy 31, 34, 110
Keane, Feargal 41
Keane, Kieran 31
Keane, Liam 34
Keane gang 56
Kelleher, Patricia 92–3, 148, 247
Kelly, Aidan 31
Kelly, Mikey 46, 50, 51, 109
Kemmy, Jim 57
Kennedy Park 12
Kenny, Brendan 152
Keohane, K. 100–101
key money 57, 88, 134
Keyes Park 17, 19, 162
Kildare 26
Kileely 9, 12, 157, 200
Kilkenny 26
King's Island 191, 193–207
knife crime *see* offensive weapons offences
Kuhling, C. 100–101

labelling 63, 92–3, 211, 221–2, 226–7; *see
    also* stereotyping; stigmatisation
land use planning 9, 20, 47–8, 186, 210
Laois 26
Leddin, Frank 51–2
Lee, Joe 101
Levitas, R. 237
Liebow, E. 173
Limerick
    affluence levels 7, 8, 9
    age profiles 8, 16–17, 60, 205, 206
    car ownership 8, 234
    city centre 8, 19, 190, 191, 193–207, 233
    crime *see* crime
    criminal families 51, 54–9, 70–71, 78–83,
        84–5, 109–12
    criminal gangs *see* criminal gangs
    demographic data 5–9, 60–61, 191–2
    disadvantaged communities *see* local
        authority estates
    drug dealing 23, 25–6, 31–7, 54, 56–9,
        70, 79, 81–2, 97–8, 114–15, 174–6,
        182, 239, 250–51

drug use   26, 35–6, 37, 56, 67–8, 81–2, 99–100, 153, 174, 250–51
education   49, 58–9, 61, 64–5, 75, 171–3, 182, 184
educational attainment levels   8, 9, 205, 206, 232
employment   3, 7, 8, 9, 12–13, 17, 45–6, 64–5, 158, 178–9, 182, 232, 239
feuding see feuding
gender profiles   16–17
health   185–7, 193, 198–200, 205–7, 208–9, 232–3
history of   44–50
household types   7, 8, 11–12, 15–17
housing policy   13–14, 19–20, 47–8, 133–4
housing types   7, 8–9, 11, 13–14
immigrant population   4, 8, 196, 233, 239
industry   3, 12–13, 44, 52, 239
infrastructure   47–8, 150, 234
land use planning   9, 20, 47–8, 186, 210
local authority estates   8–9, 12, 14–22, 42, 46–59, 60–73, 133–4, 150–54, 155–66, 170, 211–29, 233, 242; see also individual estates
local government   22
media coverage of   23, 42, 72, 100, 109, 151, 211–29
migration within   8, 18–19, 207–8
murders   24–5, 30, 31–2, 33, 161–2, 174, 239
neighbourhood effects   14, 56
policing   126–31, 240; see also Gardaí
population growth   3, 4, 8
population trends   18–19
poverty   3, 11, 14–18, 45–7, 52–3, 58, 68–9, 148, 156–7, 208, 231–5, 237
quality of life   185–6, 193, 202–3, 207, 209, 237
Regeneration programme   18–22, 41–2, 136, 150–54, 162, 163, 170, 183, 213–14, 215, 237, 241–2, 249–50
slums   44–5, 47
social area types   7–9
social capital   185–7, 190–210
social classes   7, 8, 9, 11, 44, 186, 205–7
social exclusion see social exclusion
social inequalities   185–6, 208–9, 232–3, 238–41

social segregation   10–14, 42, 185, 237
social services   5, 8, 14, 19–20, 64, 68, 134–5, 141–9, 152
socio-spatial variation   5–9
student population   9
suburbanisation   4, 12
suburbs   7, 12, 44, 190, 193–207, 233–4
Traveller community   71–2
unemployment   9, 11, 13, 15–16, 20, 48, 49, 52–3, 58, 170, 182, 232
welfare system   17, 64, 65, 67, 170, 198–200, 232, 235–9
see also individual areas of Limerick
Limerick Assessment of Needs System (LANS)   152
Limerick Chronicle   98
Limerick City Council   8, 13, 47, 58, 122, 133
Limerick Clothing Company   52
Limerick County Council   12, 233
Limerick Foróige   153
Limerick Independent   219
Limerick Leader   47, 214, 219
Limerick Local Government Committee   22
Limerick Post   219
Limerick Youth Service   153
linking social capital   188, 198–200, 201–2, 205, 207
literacy   171
litter   78, 85, 86, 136
Little Sisters of the Assumption   159, 161
Live 95 FM   215, 219
Liveline radio show   94
Lloyd, D.A.   118
local authority, confidence in   198–200
local authority estates   8–9, 12, 14–22, 42, 46–59, 60–73, 133–4, 150–54, 155–66, 170, 211–29, 233, 242; see also individual estates
local authority housing   8–9, 11, 12, 13–14, 232, 233
local government   22
local media   218–19, 223–4, 228; see also media coverage
Logan, Emily   142
lone-parent families   8, 11, 15–16, 19, 53, 58, 60–61, 64, 66–7, 170, 232
Lupton, R.   86
Lyng, Stephen   137, 176–7

Mac an Ghiall, M. 172
McAleese, Mary 158
McAnaspie, Daniel 149
McCafferty, Des 36, 60, 227, 232, 245, 250
McCarthy/Dundon gang 31-2, 34, 56
McCourt, Frank 44
McCullagh, Ciarán 42, 227, 245-6
McDonagh, Michael 106, 112
McGearty, S. 108
McGrew, A. 97
McVerry, P. 177
managerial social class 7, 8
marginalisation 10-14, 37, 58-9, 75-6, 100-101, 169-84, 214; see also social exclusion
marriage 46, 62, 170, 179
Marshall, T.H. 231, 235
masculinity 51, 62-3, 66, 75-8, 98-100, 151, 169-84
Mastriani, Margaret 46
Matterson's 52
Maynard, W. 87-8
means testing 236-7
media coverage 23, 42, 72, 100, 109, 151, 211-29
men, marginalisation of 75-6, 169-84; see also masculinity
Merton, Robert 42
middle classes 44, 157, 237-8
Midlands region 29, 30, 120-21
Midlands Traveller Conflict and Mediation Initiative 120
Mid-West region 27-31, 154, 242-3
migrants, returning 55-6
Miller, S.M. 171
Miller, William 137-8
mobile phones 94-5
Monaleen 190, 191, 193-207, 226
money-lending 53, 68-9
moral under-class discourse 237
Moran, Justice Carroll 74
Moyross 9, 12, 14, 15, 17, 19, 47-9, 50, 52, 53, 56, 57, 60-61, 71, 150, 155-61, 175, 190, 191, 193-207, 211-29, 233, 242
Moyross Partners 159
muggings 26-7, 29f
murder 24-5, 30, 31-2, 33, 34, 94, 161-2, 174, 239
Murray, Gavin 78, 159, 213, 215, 225

Murray, Michael 124
Murray, Millie 78, 159, 213, 215, 225
music 99-100

National Care Planning Project 141-2
national media 218-19; see also media coverage
National Spatial Strategy 243
Nationwide (RTÉ) 225
negativity 164-5, 213-14, 216, 217-18, 219
neglect 68, 69, 81, 141, 149
negotiators 108
neighbourhood effects 14, 56, 188-9
neighbourliness 45, 48, 61-2, 155-66, 188, 193-5, 209
newcomers 196, 197-8
Ní Shúinéar, S. 107, 108, 113
nightclubs 33, 56
Nilsen, A. 178, 180
Nordic countries, welfare system 236
Norris, Michelle 42, 233
North-West region 28

O'Brien, Carl 135
O'Connell, Cathal 36, 42, 135, 248-9
O'Connor, Pat 148, 247
O'Dea, Willie 122
O'Donnell, Ian 42
O'Donnell, M. 172, 182
O'Donnell, P. 105
Offaly 26
offensive weapons offences 25
O'Malley Park 16, 18-19, 20, 162
Ombudsman for Children 142, 147
O'Neill, C. 171
Operation Anvil 31, 127
organised crime 31-5, 42-3, 51; see also criminal families; criminal gangs; drug dealing
O'Sullivan, Eoin 42
Our Lady of the Rosary parish 190, 192, 193-207
out-migration 18-19, 207-8
owner-occupied housing 7, 11

Papachristos, Andrew 98, 99
parachuting journalism 224
paramilitaries 54-5, 57
parental control 50, 53, 66-7, 83, 134, 136, 139-40

part-time working 9
Pavee Point 108–9, 121
Pearson, G. 33
People Against Unemployment in Limerick
   (PAUL) 201, 242
Pitt-Rivers, J. 114
planning 9, 20, 47–8, 186
policing policy 126–31, 240; *see also* Gardaí
population growth 3, 4, 8
population trends 18–19
post-traumatic stress syndrome 116–18
poverty 3, 11, 14–18, 45–7, 52–3, 58, 68–9,
   148, 156–7, 208, 213, 231–5, 237
Powell, E. 235
power 83–7, 129
Power, A. 86
Power, Martin J. 248
power hierarchies 51, 62–3, 75–8, 78–83,
   91–4
prejudice 220–21; *see also* stigmatisation
prison 42, 76, 90–97, 130–31, 177–8, 183
privacy, lack of 61–2
privately rented housing 8, 9, 52, 232, 233
production research 212–13
professional social class 7, 8, 11
Prospect 233
protest masculinity 51, 176–8
psychotherapy 139
public spaces 173–8, 183–4
pubs 33, 175, 181, 183
punishment violence 33, 62, 70, 82, 89; *see
   also* reprisals
Purnell, Lorita 118
Putnam, R.D. 187, 189

quality of life 185–6, 193, 202–3, 207, 209,
   237

rap culture 99–100
Reay, Paul 33
reciprocity 189, 193–5; *see also* neighbourliness
redistribution of wealth 236, 237
refugees *see* asylum seekers
Regeneration programme 18–22, 41–2,
   136, 150–54, 162, 163, 170, 183,
   213–14, 215, 237, 241–2, 249–50
regional metropolitanism 242–3
rehabilitation 91, 149
remote journalism 224

Rent Supplement Scheme 19, 133–4, 233,
   234
Rental Accommodation Scheme 19
rented housing
   differential rents scheme 13
   local authority 8–9, 11, 12, 13–14, 232
   private 8, 9, 52, 232, 233
   Rent Supplement Scheme 19, 133–4,
      233, 234
   Rental Accommodation Scheme 19
   tenancy surrender scheme 13–14, 52–3,
      198
   tenant purchase scheme 8, 13–14
reporting of crime 27, 28–9, 30, 53, 54, 57,
   87–9, 160
reprisals 28, 30, 32, 87–9, 113–14; *see also*
   punishment violence
republicanism 55
reputation 50, 51, 62–3, 75–8, 93, 148,
   176–8, 239–40
Residents' Forums 127, 159, 162
residualisation 14, 18–20, 232
respect 50, 51, 62–3, 75–8, 176–8, 239–40
Reuter, P. 33
risk-taking 136–8, 176–7
robberies 26–7, 29, 51
role models 66, 151, 163, 180
RTÉ 213, 225
Ryan, Eddie 31, 110
Ryan, Frank 31
Ryan, Liam 41, 46, 48, 49, 61–2, 66, 68,
   101, 249
Ryan gang 56

St Mary's Park 9, 15, 16, 19, 20, 45, 52,
   56, 60–61, 150, 185, 190, 211, 233,
   242
St Munchin's parish 190, 192, 193–207
St Patrick's Institution 143–4
St Vincent de Paul society 160
scouts 49
The Seduction of Crime (Katz) 137
self-esteem 85–7, 161, 163, 179, 215, 221
self-harm 117   (one earlier)
semi-skilled social class 8, 9, 19
Sennett, Richard 75, 173
Shanker, Stuart 117
Shannon Airport 243
Shannon Banks 7
Sharpe, S. 172, 182

shootings 82, 89; *see also* firearms offences
single-parent families *see* lone-parent families
slums 44–5, 47
social capital 185–210
social class 7, 8, 9, 11, 36–7, 44, 186, 189, 205–7
social cohesion 185–6, 195–6, 197, 238
social diversity 189–90, 209–10
   (also tenure mix refs??)
Social Dynamite (Ryan) 41, 101, 249
social exclusion
   and citizenship 230–31, 235–41
   connection with crime 42, 46–59, 68–9, 71, 72–3, 148
   and disadvantage 230, 232–5
   history of 44–59
   media representations of 214, 229
   and men 75–6, 169–84
   overcoming 241–3
   and prison 90–97
   statistics on 60–61
   see also marginalisation
social inequalities 185–6, 206, 208–9, 232–3, 238–41
social mobility 64–6, 188, 198, 207, 209, 240
social networking websites 98–9
social segregation 10–14, 42, 185, 237
social services 5, 8, 14, 19–20, 64, 68, 134–5, 141–9, 152
social workers 141–9
socio-spatial variation 5–9
South-West region 28, 29
Southill 9 ,12, 13, 14, 15, 17, 18, 47–9, 50, 52–3, 56, 60–61, 71, 141, 150, 161–6, 211, 233, 242
spatial inequality 10–14, 48–9
speed 56
sport 151, 163, 181–2, 184
sub-editors 217–19
suburbanisation 4, 12
suburbs 7, 12, 44, 190, 193–207, 233–4
status 50, 51, 62–3, 75–8, 93, 100–101, 148, 176–8, 239–40
stereotyping 72, 219–20, 224, 225, 226–7
stigmatisation 49, 58–9, 63, 64–6, 75, 93, 148, 151, 158, 203–4, 210, 213–14, 215, 219–22, 226–7, 229
stolen goods 51, 54

street credibility 63, 77–8, 132, 176–7
stress 67–8, 79–80, 86, 115–20, 137, 172, 181
student population 9
suicide 117, 181
sulky racing 56, 177
surveillance 59, 81, 84–5, 87, 95–6
Survey on Incomes and Living Conditions (CSO) 15

taxation 236
teenage gangs 50–51, 53–6, 69–70, 81, 82–3
tenancy surrender scheme 13–14, 52–3, 198
tenant purchase scheme 8, 13–14
tenure-mixing 20, 48–9, 209–10
territorial strongholds 31–2, 55, 57–8, 79, 85
testimony 74, 88–9, 114–15, 124
theft 46–7
thematic frameworks 213, 214
Thomondgate 8, 200
Titmuss, R.H. 236
trauma 116–20, 181
Traveller community 71–2, 106–9, 112–13, 115–16, 117, 120–22
Turner, R.J. 118
two-tier systems 237–8

unemployment 9, 11, 13, 15–16, 20, 48, 49, 52–3, 58, 170, 182, 213, 232; *see also* employment
United Kingdom 34, 55–6, 76–7, 87–8, 236
United States 33, 42, 55, 76, 90, 98, 118, 234
universalism 236
unskilled manual social class 8, 9, 11, 19
upward mobility 64–6, 188, 198, 207, 209, 240
urban regeneration 241–2; *see also* Regeneration programme

vandalism 85–7
victim survey statistics 27–31
victimisation 27
vigilantism 55, 130
violence
   connection with social exclusion 42, 46–59, 68–9, 71, 72–3
   and masculinity 51, 62–3, 75–8

as punishment 33, 62, 70, 82, 89; *see also* reprisals
see also crime; criminal gangs; feuding
voluntary associations 188, 208

Wacquant, Loic 90
Walker, Mary Rose 117
warzone metaphors 214
Waterford 10, 11, 26, 106
weapons *see* arms dealing; firearms offences; offensive weapons offences
Weber, Max 83

welfare dependency 65, 170, 232
welfare system 17, 64, 65, 67, 170, 198–200, 232, 235–9
Westbury 7
Whyte, W.F. 173
Wilkinson, R.G. 240
Williams, Paul 94
Willis, P. 172
witness intimidation 74, 88–9, 113–14, 124, 131
working classes 44, 52